The Gift
of Grace

THE GIFT OF GRACE

The Future of Lutheran Theology

Edited by
Niels Henrik Gregersen
Bo Holm
Ted Peters
Peter Widmann

FORTRESS PRESS
Minneapolis

THE GIFT OF GRACE
The Future of Lutheran Theology

Scripture quotations are from the New Revised Standard Version Bible, copyright ©1989 by the Division of Christian Education of the National Council of the Churches of Christ in the USA and used by permission.

Cover Design: Marti Naughton
Cover image: © Brand X Pictures
Book Design: James Korsmo

Library of Congress Cataloging-in-Publication Data

The gift of grace : the future of Lutheran theology / edited by Niels Henrik Gregersen ... [et al.].
   p. cm.
  Based on a conference held Jan. 16–19, 2003 at Aarhus University, Denmark.
  Includes bibliographical references and index.
  ISBN 0-8006-3686-4 (alk. paper)
  1. Lutheran Church—Doctrines—Congresses. 2. Lutheran Church—History—Congresses. 3. Grace (Theology)—Congresses. I. Gregersen, Niels Henrik, 1956–
  BX8065.3.G54 2005
  230'.41'09051101—dc22

2004024821

The paper used in this publication meets the minimum requirements of American National Standard for Information Sciences - Permanence of Paper for Printed Library Materials, ANSI Z329.48-1984.

Manufactured in the U.S.A.

Contents

Why do we believe what we believe?

Part IV. Justice
145

Part V. Comparisons
179

Part VI. Ecumenics
213

Part VII. World
251

Part VIII. Science
305

In memory of
Timothy F. Lull

Contributors

OSWALD BAYER, Professor of Systematic Theology, Eberhard-Karls-Universität, Tübingen, Germany

RICHARD BLIESE, Academic Dean, Professor of Missions, Luther Seminary, St. Paul, Minnesota, USA

PAUL S. CHUNG, Lecturer, Pacific Lutheran Theological Seminary, Berkeley, California, USA.

HERMANN DEUSER, Professor of Systematic Theology, Johann-Wolfgang-Goethe Universität, Frankfurt am Main, Germany

DIRK EVERS, Institut für Hermeneutik, Eberhard-Karls-Universität, Tübingen, Germany

NIELS HENRIK GREGERSEN, Professor of Systematic Theology, Copenhagen University, Denmark

CRISTINA GRENHOLM, Associate Professor, Karlstad University, Sweden

ERIC GRITSCH, Emeritus Professor of Church History, Lutheran Theological Seminary at Gettysburg, Pennsylvania, USA

GUILLERMO HANSEN, Professor of Systematic Theology, ISEDET University, Buenos Aires, Argentina

JAN-OLAV HENRIKSEN, Professor, Lutheran School of Theology, Oslo, Norway

BO HOLM, Assistant Professor, Aarhus University, Denmark

GEORGE HUNSINGER, Hazel Thompson McCord Professor of Systematic Theology, Princeton Theological Seminary, Princeton, New Jersey, USA

ANTJE JACKELÉN, Associate Professor of Systematic Theology, Lutheran School of Theology at Chicago, Illinois, USA

ROBERT W. JENSON, Senior Scholar for Research, Center of Theological Inquiry, Princeton, New Jersey, USA

THEODOR JØRGENSEN, Professor of Systematic Theology, Copenhagen University, Denmark

LOIS E. MALCOLM, Associate Professor of Systematic Theology, Luther Seminary, St. Paul, Minnesota, USA

MICKEY L. MATTOX, Researcher, Historical Section, Marquette University, Wisconsin, USA

MONICA MELANCHTHON, Head of the Old Testament Department and Professor of Women's Studies, Gurukul Lutheran Theological College and Research Institute, Chennai, India

AMBROSE MOYO, Bishop, Executive Director, Lutheran Communion in Southern Africa

FIDON MWOMBEKI, Deputy General for the Northwest Diocese of the Evangelical Lutheran Church, Tanzania

CHOONG CHEE PANG, Professor of New Testament Studies at Trinity Theological College, Singapore

TED PETERS, Professor of Systematic Theology, Pacific Lutheran Theological Seminary, Berkeley, California, USA

SIMO PEURA, Docent, Institute for Advanced Training, Evangelical Lutheran Church of Finland

RISTO SAARINEN, Professor of Ecumenical Theology, University of Helsinki, Finland

CHRISTOPH SCHWÖBEL, Professor of Dogmatics and Ecumenical Theology, Ruprecht-Karls Universität, Heidelberg, Germany

DAVID G. TRUEMPER, Professor, Valparaiso University, Valparaiso, Indiana, USA

VÍTOR WESTHELLE, Professor of Systematic Theology, Lutheran School of Theology at Chicago, Illinois, USA

PETER WIDMANN, Professor of Systematic Theology, Aarhus University, Denmark

Preface

Niels Henrik Gregersen and Ted Peters

IN PREPARING THIS BOOK, we set before ourselves two questions. One asks about the status quo of contemporary Lutheran theology. The other asks the question, *Quo vadis?* (Where are you going?). What is the state of Lutheran theology at the beginning of the twenty-first century, and where do we go from here?

We thus attempt to offer a fairly representative collection of live options within current Lutheran systematic theology, topically centered on classical issues of Lutheran concern. The reader will thus find sections on grace, cross, justification, and comparisons, but also sections on justice, world, ecumenics, and science.

We thereby wish to acknowledge that the Lutheran tradition, after all, is not only a theological movement following in the wake of Martin Luther and his sixteenth-century disciples. Almost immediately, Lutheranism also developed into a cultural vision for the common people. As recently argued by John Witte Jr. in *Law and Protestantism*, Lutheranism left for the future both a theological and a cultural legacy: "A good deal of our modern western law of marriage, education, and social welfare, for example, still bears the unmistakable marks of Lutheran Reformation theology."[1] For example, most people today regard marriage as both a civil and a spiritual institution; education is today regarded as a fundamental right of a citizen and as a duty of the state to provide; and care for the poor and needy is in most Christian societies seen as an indispensable office of the state and as a calling for its citizens. Lutherans, alongside others, care for the common good in society; justice as well as justification mark the Lutheran legacy. The Lutheran affirmation and even celebration of ordinary life, of the created life in calling, may be well worth pursuing today, even if it also might involve conflicts with an excessive individualism and consumerism found in today's Western and Eastern societies.

This volume nonetheless gives special emphasis to the doctrinal dimensions of current Lutheranism. The reader of the book will find substantive contributions from scholars in both northern and southern hemispheres. And the spectrum of positions spreads from the liberationist on the left to more classic shapes of doctrine on the right, and from the "low church" angle of Lutheran theology to the "high church" angle of evangelical catholicity. In terms of ecumenical positions, the volume includes supporters and opponents of the *Joint Declaration on the Doctrine of Justification*

---

1. John Witte Jr., *Law and Protestantism: The Legal Teachings of the Lutheran Reformation* (Cambridge: Cambridge Univ. Press 2002), 295.

between the Roman Catholic Church and the Lutheran World Federation, signed October 31, 1999. We are fortunate also to have received substantive contributions from friends of grace outside of Lutheran theology.

We see our task as different from those pursuing a "Lutheran identity," if one thereby understands a self-sufficient body of theology or a self-enclosed cultural identity. Our task, rather, is to lift up the charisms of Lutheran theology ("charism" in the sense of entrusted gifts that continue to inspire). What are the contributions that Lutheran theology may bring to the ecumenical church and to the world as a whole? What have Lutherans to learn from other shapes of Christian faith and theology? And how can we in this generation be the faithful stewards of the gifts of Reformation theology, so that the worldwide family of Christian churches can benefit?

We should not speak about the charisms of Lutheran theology without also being aware of the challenges that face any confessional theology today, especially the challenges posed by cultural pluralism. The seeds of Lutheran insight were sown in a distinctively European garden, where they sprouted and grew in Germanic and Nordic soil. But, over centuries, they have been borne on the winds of global change so that now they grow on every continent and blossom in countless languages and cultures. With each soil comes a different cultural climate, a different context of interpretation. Making it still more complicated, globalized citizens are on the move, shifting from context to context, from location to location, from cultural soil to cultural soil. The fruits of Lutheran theology require many differing methods of harvest, not a single standardized one. We see Southern and Eastern contexts as opportunities for developing an array of Lutheran-inspired theologies bearing unpredictable fruits.

In addition to geographical pluralism, we are aware of academic challenges to Lutheran theology as well. It is probably fair to say that with a few notable exceptions, Lutheran theology no longer can claim intellectual hegemony in international discussions of theology. Fifty years ago, we experienced the preeminence of Rudolf Bultmann and Paul Tillich, and just twenty-five years ago, theologians of the caliber of Gerhard Ebeling, Eberhard Jüngel, and Wolfhart Pannenberg were in the middle of their extraordinary careers. It was the Lutheran theologians of the once overpowering tradition of German scholarship who dominated, whereas in the present generation, Germany is but one among other centers of theological inquiry. The academic center has moved somewhat from central Europe toward the Anglo-Saxon world, from the German and Scandinavian languages toward English. In the United States in particular, self-conscious confessional theology has combined academic theology with personal spirituality, abstract concepts with ethical mandates, the erudite with the vernacular. It is here sensed with urgency that theology has to be communicated not only to colleagues and theological students but also to more general audiences. This constitutes some of the gifts of American theology to the wider academic theology. Many interdisciplinary initiatives, such as those between science and theology and between Christianity and the other religions, have developed in this new climate.

The question is now: in which direction should Lutheran theologians move? Certainly we are living in a postconfessionalist, global setting. Therefore we need to rethink many of the theological concepts that so far have served as identifying marks of what it means to be a Lutheran: *sola gratia, sola fide, sola scriptura* (grace alone, faith alone, scripture alone), to mention a few. But even if we live in a postconfessionalist age, we are not necessarily living in a postconfessional age. Maybe the search for the clarity of the gospel is today needed more than ever—and so also the will to speak about God and God's world in the vernacular. Neither has the prophetic motivation for influencing our society at large withered away. On the contrary, it may be a suitable time for reflecting again on the possibilities for articulating the gifts of Lutheran theology to the wider *oikumene* and to the different cultures that we inhabit, some of them quite hostile to Christian faith commitments.

Nevertheless, in the world of cultural interchange, the old Roman principle applies: *Do ut des!* (I give so that you can give). There is, and there should be, an unashamed giving and taking. In relation to the gospel of grace, however, the Roman principle term needs a slight, but all-important twist: *Do quia des!* (I give, because you have given). There is here an unashamed sense of having received all that we can and are so that we may be empowered to pass it on.

In being a human, and in being a Christian, there is the gift of receiving, but there is also the gift of passing on.

Acknowledgments

THIS BOOK HAS GROWN out of a global convocation called "The Future of Lutheran Theology: Charisms and Contexts" held at Aarhus University, Denmark, January 16–19, 2003.

The editors were the main organizers of this conference, and we have many to thank. The editorial council of *Dialog: A Journal of Theology* has provided an all-important impetus for the conference in the first place and has subsequently offered invaluable space for prepublishing and postpublishing a series of papers in two special issues, *Charism and Context: Global Lutheran Theology for the Future* (Winter 2002) and *The Legacy of Reformation Theology* (Spring 2003). We wish to thank the council for all its advice in the process of planning the conference, and the publisher, Blackwell, for permission to reprint the articles.

The conference was generously supported financially by the Aarhus University Research Foundation, in celebration of the seventy-fifth anniversary of Aarhus University; the Danish Ministry of Ecclesiastical Affairs; and the Center for Theology and the Natural Sciences (CTNS), Berkeley. Additional support came from The Lutheran World Federation (LWF), the Vereinigte Evangelisch-Lutherische Kirche Deutschlands (VELKD), and the dioceses of Haderslev, Viborg, Aalborg, and Lolland-Falster in Denmark. We are deeply grateful for the willingness of these sponsors to support the conference.

We further wish to thank student of theology Helle Rosenkvist for her excellent job as conference secretary, Ph.D. student Marie Vejrup Nielsen for carefully organizing the papers for this publication, and the Danish-Canadian Linda Kristensen Bolet, M.Div., for revising the papers of the non-native English contributors. We are grateful for their engagement and accuracy.

Professor Timothy Lull, the fifth organizer of the conference and former president of the Pacific Lutheran Theological School (PLTS), has been present in our minds while completing this project. We have missed him and his voice since his untimely death during the spring of 2003. This book is dedicated to the memory of Tim Lull.

—January 15, 2004
The Editors

Abbreviations

AP	Apology of the Augsburg Confession.
BC	*Book of Concord: The Confessions of the Evangelical Lutheran Church*, eds. Robert Kolb and Timothy J. Wengert (Minneapolis: Fortress Press, 2000).
BSLK	*Die Bekenntnisschriften der evangelisch-lutherischen Kirche*, 11th ed. (Göttingen: Vandenhoeck & Ruprecht, 1992).
CA	The Augsburg Confession (*Confessio Augustana*).
CD	Karl Barth, *Church Dogmatics*.
FC	Formula of Concord, in *Book of Concord*, 481–660.
JD	The Lutheran World Federation and The Roman Catholic Church, *Joint Declaration on the Doctrine of Justification* (Grand Rapids, Mich., and Cambridge, U.K.: Eerdmans, 2000).
JD (1995)	The 1995 draft of *Joint Declaration on the Doctrine of Justification*.
LW	Luther's Works, American edition. 55 vols. (Philadelphia: Fortress Press; St. Louis: Concordia, 1955–86).
LWF	Lutheran World Federation.
NRSV	*New Revised Standard Version* of the Bible.
PG	Migne, *Patrologia cursus completus, Series graeca*, 161 vols. (Paris: 1857–1866).
PL	Migne, *Patrologia cursus completeus, Series latina*, 121 vols. (Paris: 1844–1855).
SL	*The Sermons of Martin Luther* (Grand Rapids, Mich.: Baker, 1983).
StA	*Martin Luther Studien Ausgabe*, 6 vols. (Berlin: Evangelischer Verlagsanstalt Berlin, 1979–99).
STh	Thomas Aquinas, *Summa Theologiæ*.
WA	Martin Luther, *Luthers Werke: Kritische Gesamtausgabe*, 67 vols. (Weimar: H. Böhlau und Nachfolger 1883ff.).
WADB	Martin Luther, *Luthers Werke: Kritische Gesamtausgabe: Die Deutsche Bibel*, 12 vols. (Weimar: H. Böhlau und Nachfolger, 1912–1961).
WATR	Martin Luther, *Luthers Werke: Kritische Gesamtausgabe: Tischreden*, 6 vols. (Weimar: H. Böhlau und Nachfolger, 1912–1921).

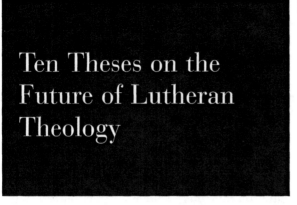

Ten Theses on the Future of Lutheran Theology

Niels Henrik Gregersen

I t is difficult to predict, especially about the future, as a proverb has it. But fortunately the task of theology is not so much about prognostication and accommodation as it is about making decisions regarding where to go. In this introduction, my aim is both to restate and reconstruct central doctrinal tenets of Lutheran theology.[1]

I do so in the light of ecumenical experiences of the twentieth century. I hereby assume that the formative Christian traditions will not be postconfessional, but postconfessionalist. That is, the task of articulating the basic contours of Christian faith will be as important as ever, but the distinction between Lutheran and other Christian confessions is not in general a difference of being right and being wrong (or vice versa) but a difference of doctrinal concerns within the one Christian church. The Nicene Creed of 381 is here *the* central Christian dogma that continues to carry the ecumenical consensus.

In the following theses, I argue that many of the well-known Lutheran doctrines, such as the distinction between hidden and revealed God or between law and gospel, should not be treated as Lutheran "principles" that only await a proper systematization. Rather, these distinctions emerge out of a liturgical practice of scriptural listening, which is keenly aware of the limitations of human knowledge about God in the concrete context of being addressed by a Word of God, which calls for a response. In short, the identity of a Lutheran theology should not be found in a system of "Lutheran theology," but in a commitment to develop theologies in attentiveness to first-order Christian practices of divine-human communication. Here, further common grounds with the other families of Christian faith are likely to emerge.

I further argue that a classical Lutheran theology needs to be reconstructed in response to the new challenges that face the churches in a global, multireligious world. A fundamental hiatus between "us" and "them,"

---

1. This article is a revised version of "Ten Theses on the Future of Lutheran Theology: Charisms, Contexts, and Challenges," *Dialog* 41/4 (Winter 2002): 264–72.

Christians and non-Christians, was taken for granted by Luther and the other magisterial Reformers. Accordingly, Luther did not question the logic of terror concerning eternal salvation, a logic that he inherited from his nominalistically poised Augustinianism. Already the fathers of the Formula of Concord (1577) corrected Luther's views concerning predestination, but further theological work is yet to be done. I am convinced that a Lutheran theology addressing these issues will benefit from a continuous dialogue both with the Reformed theologian Karl Barth and with post-Vatican II Roman Catholic theology.

---

1. Lutheran theology is gifted by the work of Martin Luther, at once a charismatic and a catholic reformer of the medieval church. But no theologian should expect Luther's sixteenth-century work to include solutions to all theological problems of the twenty-first century. Neither should Lutheran theology treat Luther as infallible; he was not.

Realizing the contextual distance between Luther and ourselves is an imperative starting point for a future Lutheran theology. It is, however, a difficult one. Luther was a uniquely charismatic person who rearticulated biblical faith in a self-involving way that also involved his disciples and readers. Luther combined existential bite with doctrinal precision and thus reformed the Catholic church from within. No wonder Lutherans from the beginning regarded Luther as an icon of faith. Much against Luther's own intention, his followers have even named a church after him. All this, however, should not disguise the distance in worldview and mentality between sixteenth-century and twenty-first-century theology.

Luther's theology needs to be seen in a historical perspective, as evidenced in contemporary Luther scholarship. The medieval church, however, has often been used as a mere foil against which the radical newness of Luther's theological decisions was supposed to shine forth. More recent scholarship shows us that this is a historical myth produced by evangelical historians, driven by hidden dogmatic agendas. Luther's theology emerged in a climate of monastic Augustinianism and of Ockhamism, flavored by elements of Renaissance thought. His thought models continued to be saturated by the intellectual movements of his day. Moreover, where earlier historiography saw modernity as beginning from the age of the Renaissance and Reformation, today's historiography identifies the shift from Old European to Modern European thinking in the period between 1650 and 1750. This means that Luther and the Reformation era are now seen as a variety of late medieval thinking, placed far away from us. For better or worse, Luther was not a forerunner of modernity nor of postmodernity.

In contrast to historical scholarship, systematic theology comes into being by making the distinction between *quaestio facti* and *quaestio juris*.

The first issue is concerned about historical correctness, the second about the meaning and validity of truth-claims.[2] In my view, the future of Lutheran theology should accept the rule that quoting Luther for a view does not automatically establish theological legitimacy, not even in a "Lutheran" theology. A few examples may suffice. What Luther said about Jews and Muslims and about Copernicus and natural philosophy is in actuality not helpful in understanding Judaism, Islam, and modern science. Even worse, New Testament scholarship suggests that Luther also misinterpreted St. Paul, because he read Paul with the lenses of Augustine's doctrine of original sin. Although Luther's interpretation of Paul is indeed highly illuminating, the incongruence between Luther and Paul constitutes a difficult problem for a Lutheran theology, not least of all in light of the principle of *sola scriptura*.

For better or worse, Luther was not infallible in his own time. And no one should expect that Luther's works entail the keys to solving all issues pertinent to twenty-first-century theology. Rather, Luther's theology constitutes one charism among others within the wider catholic heritage.

> **2. Luther's awareness of the catholicity of his theology is ubiquitous in all his writings but particularly emphasized in his later work. With hindsight, Luther can be said to have overused Augustinian tradition by further radicalizing it. A future Lutheran theology will have to counterbalance the Augustinian track of Luther's thought by giving further emphasis to Luther's inspiration from the Greek patristic tradition.**

The myth of Luther as the lonely individual who stood up against the entire tradition is no longer tenable. Luther's theology was nurtured by the tradition he reformed. Alongside his provocative sharpness and exclusiveness, Luther understood his theology as a gateway to the universal Christian faith (*fides catholica*).[3]

Historically, Luther belongs first and foremost to the Augustinian monastic tradition of "practical" theology, highly critical of scholasticism, a tradition from which there is much to be learned. But Luther also inherited Augustinian views that made him blind to other options within Christian orthodoxy. An example is Luther's unqualified adoption of the doctrine of double predestination in *The Bondage of the Will*. For example, Luther read the story of Jacob and Esau in the framework of Augustinian thought.

---

2. This problem has been shown and exemplified by Theo Dieter, *Der junge Luther und Aristoteles: Eine historisch-systematische Untersuchung zum Verhältnis von Theologie und Philosophie* (Berlin: Walter de Gruyter, 2001), 8–11, 635–42.

3. In his later disputations, Luther repeatedly refers to *fides catholica* as normative teaching; see, e.g., "Disputatio de divinitate et humanitate Christi" (1540), WA 39/2, 92–121, 119 (not translated in LW).

Luther could not see what the story was about: the difference between a great blessing from Abraham to Jacob, and a fatherly blessing, that was not quite as good, to Esau. Instead, Luther found a story of God's eternal love to Jacob and of eternal hatred of Esau, "prior to the creation of the world."[4] This view is hardly biblical, and it was correctly revised by the fathers of the *Book of Concord*.[5] However, the theological favoritism went unaltered, and consequently the Lutheran doctrine of unconditional grace was always expressed against the background of a *massa perditionis*. This assumes that the vast majority of the human race will suffer infinite and endless pain in hell (cf. CA 17).

Already Erlangen theologians like Werner Elert and Paul Althaus pointed to the fact that Luther learned more from the Eastern fathers than did most of his contemporaries. More recently, the Finnish Luther research has done much to retrieve the persistent presence of Greek Orthodox ideas in Luther's work, especially the motif of the real participation of the believer in the being of God. This brings back into the doctrine of justification a new emphasis of the activity of the living Christ in the union between him and the believer. Also, the links between the soteriology of deification and the Trinitarian conception of God have been clarified.[6] Contemporary Lutheran theology owes much to this new interpretation of Luther. However, the Finnish Luther research has so far confined itself to historical and semantic interpretations of Luther's texts. What is needed to supplement this approach is an open discussion of the limits to Luther's thought, limits that may not be retrievable by mere interpretation. A future Lutheran theology needs to see Luther's theology as part of a bigger package, one that involves alternatives to the Augustinian logic of terror (see theses 7 and 8, below).

---

3. Important for the future of Lutheran theology is Luther's practical theology. The liturgical, pastoral, and catechetical dimensions of Luther's theology contain untapped resources for theological reflection. Luther did not only distinguish between essentials and *adiaphora*, but also valued the traditions that contribute to the well-being (the *bene esse*) of the church without being prescribed by God.

---

4. LW 33:199; WA 18:725.

5. As is well known, Article XI of the Formula of Concord (1577) had the courage to clarify and correct Luther's thinking on this point; see Bengt Hägglund, "Die Rezeption Luthers in der Konkordienformel," *Luther und die Bekenntnisschriften*, ed. Luther Akademie Ratzeburg (Ratzeburg: Martin Luther Verlag, 1981), 107–20; and Rune Söderlund, *Ex Praevisa fide: Zum Verständnis der Prädestinationslehre in der lutherischen Orthodoxie* (Hannover: Lutherisches Verlagshaus, 1983).

6. The main points are easily accessible in *Union with Christ: The New Finnish Interpretation of Luther*, ed. Carl E. Braaten and Robert W. Jenson (Grand Rapids: Eerdmans, 1998).

Luther's embeddedness in catholic tradition can be seen in different ways. Some emphasize Luther as exegete and see Luther's theology as always developing in response to particular polemical situations.[7] However, one can also see Luther's theology as growing out of reflections on the typical or reiterative situations that constitute what it means to become and remain a Christian person: listening to the Bible, confessing one's sins, taking refuge in the word of absolution, confessing the creed, rejoicing in God in psalms, praying to God in need, and seeking a deeper understanding of faith, hope, and love. In this interpretation, the liturgical, the pastoral, and the catechetical aspects of Luther's thinking demand renewed attention. Luther's polemical writings are important but even more so are his reflections on first-order utterances of Christian faith.[8]

If one looks into *The German Mass* and other practical writings on the order of the liturgy, one immediately discerns Luther's insistence on the right to ask about the usefulness of tradition. However, Luther did not simply divide up things into evangelical essentials and the adiaphora of catholic tradition. Luther knew that penultimate questions need to be handled with utmost theological sensitivity. The usual dichotomy between fundamentals and variables does not encompass Luther's approach to tradition. The practical church reforms of the Lutheran Reformation exhibit at least four different approaches to the Christian tradition. (1) What is essential for the church (its *esse*) is not only an abstract minimum of liturgy or doctrine but all the seven marks of the church: Word, Baptism, Eucharist, absolution, ordination, prayer and praise, and the bearing of the cross. (2) What is good for the *esse* of the church, though not prescribed by God (the *bene esse* of the church) should be retained as long as it is useful. (3) The adiaphora of the church (its *non ad esse*), such as garments and incenses. And finally (4) practices that definitely need to be removed from the church (the *contra essentiam ecclesiae*), such as the penance system. As is evident from his practical reforms of the mass, Luther's insistence on the clarity of the gospel is always accompanied by and mediated by his instruction to ordinary believers about first-order practices. For these define what it means to be and remain a Christian.[9]

what
about
charity
??

7. So Leif Grane, "Luther's Cause," *Lutherjahrbuch 1985* (Göttingen: Vandenhoeck & Ruprecht, 1985), 46–63; here 62: "A 'Luther's theology,' meaning a survey of his 'doctrine,' or an exposition of Luther's doctrine of this or that, can, therefore, never be in accordance with Luther unless it interprets everything in connection with the precise historical conditions. To say it bluntly: the contents of Luther's theology is inseparable from the way and the form. One could be tempted to use Søren Kierkegaard's expression: the way is all."

8. There is, of course, nothing new in this interpretation. These aspects have been highlighted in mid-twentieth-century theology, e.g., in the work of Peter Brunner and Regin Prenter. In Prenter's case (as well as in my own), this appropriation of Luther is mediated by the profound Danish theologian, historian, and educator, N. F. S. Grundtvig (1783–1872).

9. See George Lindbeck, "Martin Luther and the Rabbinic Mind," in *Understanding the Rabbinic Mind: Essays on the Hermeneutic of Max Kadushin*, ed. Peter Ochs (Atlanta: Scholars Press, 1990), 141–64. Lindbeck points to the interrelation between narrative

> **4. The "core" of Luther's theology should not be sought in a specific system of "Lutheran theology" nor in the doctrine of justification taken in isolation. Luther's great discovery that the word of forgiveness is unconditional on the part of God and unconditioned by specific human activities took place in the context of first-order Christian practices that precede doctrinal formulation.**

Lutheran thinking has often been caught up in a theological essentialism, searching for the "kerygma" (Rudolf Bultmann), "the eternal message" (Paul Tillich), "the Word in the words," and so on. This essentialism goes hand in hand with a theological minimalism that is characterized by a combination of strong general assertions with a correspondingly thin bone of content.

Not even the doctrine of justification with all its exclusives (*sola gratia, sola fide*) should be treated as a core of Lutheran theology. For the meaning of "justification" can only be determined within a wider network of propositions and ontological commitments. For example, the semantic meaning of *Confessio Augustana* 4, on justification, can only be understood in light of the doctrine of God and the anthropology that precedes the article (CA 1–3) and with reference to the reflection on the church and the sacraments that follows it (CA 5–15). Neither can the kerygma be understood apart from the parables of Jesus, the stories of his life, death, and resurrection, and the promise that we shall participate in his life-story with God. Philosophically speaking, the meaning of the word "justification" cannot be determined apart from the sentences specifying its contents and meanings, and those sentences cannot be understood apart from their *Sitz im Leben* in which they are uttered. The theological implications of this insight are many. The gospel is not a gospel without somebody "for whom" it can be heard as a gospel. Justification is thus the article on which the church stands and falls in the precise sense that without God's justification of the sinner everything else is in vain. For all that God has done is in vain, if it does not liberate the sinner today. With this understanding, the article of justification is indeed a second-order criterion for all theology, but not a doctrine that is itself an object of belief. *The saving power of Christ, and not a doctrine of justification, is what must be believed.* Both for the sake of the clarity of the gospel (which is not a doctrine) and for the sake of the explanation of faith (which is a matter of doctrine), a distinction must be made between a first-order address of the biblical message and the second-order theological reflection on this message.

The doctrine of justification thus only makes sense as a guide that directs the troubled sinner to seek God's Word of promise. In the word of

---

dogma (*haggadah*) and law (*halacha*) in Luther's catechisms. See further the parallel analysis of Martha Ellen Stortz, "Prayer as Formation," in *The Promise of Lutheran Ethics*, ed. Karen L. Bloomquist and John R. Stumme (Minneapolis: Fortress Press, 1998), 55–74.

absolution, the sign and its meaning coincide. The meaning of absolution happens while being spoken. Luther does not point behind the Word to a hidden God behind the Word, but directs the believer to find God, peace, and blessings in the *verbum externum* (external word).[10] It should be added to this observation, though, that the meaning of the Word of promise is only unambiguous when it is also *used* appropriately for this particular purpose (see thesis 5, below). A sign means something for somebody in a specific context, as Charles Sanders Pierce said. Without its *Sitz im Leben* in first-order Christian practices, the doctrine of justification cannot be specified. Luther's great discovery was not a new theology of justification but a rediscovery of the simple address of the Word of God. In this context, one can talk about the unconditionality of the gospel. The gifts of the Word of God are not dependent on a specific human preparation of one's mind-set; not dependent on a certain character formation; not dependent on a specific cultivation of church practices; and not dependent on allegiance to a specific theology of justification. And yet there are practices involved in the process of approaching the gospel as gospel. These practices cannot be disclaimed as quasi-meritorious; rather, they are part of what it means to be justified by God.

> **5. The distinction between law and gospel belongs properly to the first-order level of divine address and human response. The law-gospel dialectic should not be abstracted from this concrete situation and should not be used as a theological principle that necessarily structures all doctrinal expositions of Christian faith.**

The distinction between law and gospel has its objective basis in the fact that the Word of God in scripture uses different forms of address to human beings: the conditional address of requirement (law), and the unconditional utterances of divine promise (gospel). In the case of the law, the logical form is: "*If* you remember me, *then* I'll remember you." In the case of the gospel, there are no such conditions: "I promise to be your God," "Come to me, all you who are burdened. . . ." However, the distinction between law and gospel cannot be abstracted from these concrete divine-human communications. Luther was keenly aware of the fact that even though God speaks a gospel, we often make God's gospel into a law.[11] In his sense, the very distinction between law and gospel depends on the human reception (without assuming that this is an autonomous act). Or to

10. Cf. the important study by Oswald Bayer, *Promissio: Geschichte der reformatorischen Wende in Luther's Theologie* [1971] (Darmstadt: Wissenschaftliche Buchgesellschaft, 1989), which in detail elaborates how Luther's theology of the Word overcame the traditional Platonic "hermeneutics of signification" that the early Luther had inherited from Augustine.

11. See, e.g., Luther, "A Brief Instruction on What to Look for and Expect in the Gospels" (1521), LW 35:117–24.

put it otherwise, the distinction between law and gospel can only be made from the perspective of the gospel as received by faith. Apart from the relation between the gospel and its hearer, there exists no distinction between law and gospel; all will be perceived as law, as part of an ongoing negotiation between God and humanity.

The distinction between law and gospel is necessary to safeguard the unconditional character of the gospel itself. However, Luther's dialectic of law and gospel should not be elevated into a principle that necessarily rules all "Lutheran theology." The law-gospel distinction belongs to a first-order theology of divine-human speech acts, not to the second order reflection of the God-world relation in general. As soon as Luther's notion of the law is doctrinalized and divided into the two classic functions (the *usus civilis* [civil function], which addresses what should be done in the earthly realm, and the *usus theologicus* [theological function], which terrifies the consciousness to seek refuge in the gospel), a Lutheran theology faces at least three problems. First, the *usus civilis* tends to reduce the manifold contents of divine commandment into a generalized principle; what is lost is the sense in which God's law entails concrete advice about what should be done to let life flourish. Second, the *usus theologicus* is conceived within the aforementioned logic of terror. What is lost is the sense of wrestling with the law; an incentive to discern what actually lies in one's hands to do, and what ultimately lies in God's hands. Third, a doctrinalized version of the functions of the law cannot express the extent to which the New Testament consistently instructs the believer to act according to his or her belief: "Let the same mind be in you as was in Jesus Christ" (Philippians 2).

---

6. Luther's rediscovery of the external word of law and gospel presupposes an ontology of divine reality prior to, simultaneous with, and subsequent to the proclamation of the Word. Today it is particularly important to recover a notion of God's presence in the world at large. Luther's doctrine of the hidden God is a necessary placeholder for an awareness of God's majestic being; but the identification of the reality of God can only be offered via the doctrine of the Trinity.

Luther's theology is sometimes treated as a theology of the Word. And rightly so, as we have seen. But Luther's theology could also be called a theology of the elements. Luther's Eucharistic theology entails a theology of God's presence in the elements of bread and wine. But Christ, the incarnate divine Logos, also inhabits every corner of the universe—as a *Chryst-all*, as Luther is saying in a wordplay between "crystal" and "Christ-in-all."[12]

---

12. Cf. Niels Henrik Gregersen, "Natural Events as Crystals of God: Luther's Eucharistic Theology and the Question of Nature's Sacramentality," in *Concern for Creation: Voices on the Theology of Creation*, ed. Viggo Mortensen (*Tro & Tanke* 1995:5) (Uppsala: Svenska Kyrkans Forskningsråd 1995), 143–58.

Similarly, Luther's Eucharistic writings entail what may be termed a social ontology, a conception of the qualified divine presence in actions of loving and sharing between brothers and sisters.[13]

The particular Lutheran doctrine of the being of Christ "in, with, and under" the elements was highlighted already in the Formula of Concord Article X. Luther's sacramental theology of creation, however, shows the shortcomings of some of the most influential paradigms of Luther research of the last century. Interpretations of Luther in terms of a personalistic ontology (W. Joest) or of a relational word-event (G. Ebeling) are not sufficient. What is needed is a reflection on the relation between Christ and creation. After all, Luther's sacramental theology seems to suggest that Christ and Spirit share the life of all creatures, whether or not they share in the life of God. Here is a domain to be explored by the future of Lutheran theology.

Luther's notion of the hidden God in *The Bondage of Will* should be seen as a placeholder for an ontology of divine presence in the world. Luther never developed any such ontology, but he nonetheless both presupposes and affirms a strong view of the ubiquity of Jesus Christ. Against some of Luther's own formulations, however, the hidden God should not be seen as a second (or fourth) divinity lurking somewhere behind the curtains of the revealed Triune God, nor as a mere symbol for the limits of human understanding. The point is exactly that God *is* and remains the same God— Father, Son, and Holy Spirit—prior to the revelation, simultaneous with revelation, and after it.[14] The sense in which God remains God also apart from God's relation to humanity is a presupposition of classical Christian theism that needs to be reformulated within a Trinitarian ontology of the divine self-giving persons.

---

7. Luther's doctrine of the Trinity is an explication of Luther's Christology and serves as the unifying center of Luther's theology; The doctrine of the Trinity (a) entails Luther's ontology of Godself in so far as God's being is revealed, (b) encapsulates Luther's ontology of the gift that is common both to God's creative and redemptive work, and (c) articulates the unifying intention between the contrasting speech acts of law and gospel.

Luther did not present any "doctrine" of the hidden God, since the infinite God cannot be circumscribed by finite categories (*Le Dieu défini est le Dieu fini!*). However, the hidden God serves as a placeholder for the Trinity, the eternal and infinite community of Father, Son, and Holy Spirit. While

---

13. Cf. Niels Henrik Gregersen, "The Chalcedonian Structure of Luther's Sacramental Realism," in *Kirche zwishen Heilsbotschaft und Lebenswirklichkeit: Festschrift für Theodor Jørgensen*, ed. Dietz Lange and Peter Widmann (Frankfurt: Peter Lang Verlag, 1996), 177–96.
14. Cf. Regin Prenter, "Luther als Theologe," in *Luther und die Theologie der Gegenwart: Referate und Berichte des Fünften Internationalen Kongresses für Lutherforschung*, ed. Leif Grane and Bernhard Lohse (Göttingen: Vandenhoeck & Ruprecht, 1977), 112–29; 120: "Die

the hidden God can only be adored because God is beyond communication, the Trinitarian God can be praised because Christ is God's own communication to human creatures.

Luther's theology of the Trinity is modeled after the pattern of the self-giving love of Jesus Christ. Not only the Son, but also "the Father has given himself to us, with all his creatures" (Large Catechism, explanation of the First Article of the creed). All this has been given me "without any merit or worthiness on my part" (Small Catechism, explanation of the First Article). In a similar way, the Holy Spirit is conceived as the one who gives by letting all members of the church share in the community of God and saints. "Of this community I also am a part and member, a participant and co-partner in all the blessings it possesses" (Large Catechism, explanation of the Third Article). Alongside this outward-directed love, however, God is from eternity to eternity involved in the self-giving mutual love between Father, Son, and Spirit. The self-identity of God as love precedes and structures God's self-giving love toward creation. Luther's theology of the Trinity thus entails what might be called Luther's theology of glory.[15]

In light of Luther's theology of the Trinity, it is possible to see why the dialectic between law and gospel should not be accorded a fundamental status in a Lutheran theology. The relation between the hidden God and the Trinity is similar to the relation of the law to the gospel. Only in the light of the doctrine of the Trinity can the role of the hidden God be acknowledged as the temporary placeholder for the appearance of the real God. Thus there exists no other hidden God than the Triune God, who takes off the masks of the hidden God, even if only in the mode of faith. Accordingly, the hiddenness of God is a veil that describes our epistemic limitations, not the ontology of God.

Dare we say in the same manner that there never was a divine law that was disconnected from the gospel? Or that the Torah ultimately derives from Logos, the Wisdom of God? Could it be that just as there is one loving Triune God behind the hidden God, so there is one Word of grace beyond the differentiated speech acts of divine law and gospel? To my knowledge, no text of Luther actually says this. However, if one dares to say so (as Karl Barth did in the twentieth century), one would have to claim that there is no part of creation that has been created without the divine intention of redemption. Again, Luther does not say this. On the contrary, he says, "Outside this Christian community, however, where there is no gospel, there is also no forgiveness, and there also can be no holiness."[16] The reason is

---

beliebte Formel, dass sich Gott *in* seiner Offenbarung verbirgt, entspricht den Gedanken Luthers nicht. Luther war kein dialektischer Theologe. . . . Aber der Gott, der sich offenbart, bleibt, wenn er sich offenbart, *Gott.*"

15. See Christine Helmer, "Luther's Theology of Glory," *Neue Zeitschrift für systematische Theologie* 42/3 (2000): 237–245.

16. Luther, Large Catechism, *BC* 438.

again that Luther, no less than Calvin, worked on the Augustinian assumption of the horrible decree of double predestination (see thesis 2, above).

The question for a future of Lutheran theology is whether we should continue Luther's Augustinianism, or whether we should return to the greater orthodoxy of, say, Gregory of Nyssa? (As for myself, I have answered the question by posing it).

> **8. A Trinitarian theology of the Holy Spirit has not been adequately articulated within classical Lutheran tradition. Usually the work of the Spirit is divided up as life-giving Creator and as sanctifying Redeemer. What is needed, however, is a theology of the Holy Spirit that is able to articulate that the vivifying and transforming works of the Spirit are always coordinated for the one and whole-hearted purpose of the fulfillment of creation.**

According to classical Lutheran tradition, the *Spiritus Creator* is everywhere in the universe. This universality of the vivifying Spirit, however, is not sufficiently correlated with the sanctifying work of the Holy Spirit. Even though there are exceptions from this picture in the writings of Luther, the disconnection between the general order of creation and the specific order of salvation dominates Luther's Augustinian worldview.

This received view has made it difficult for Lutheran theology to develop a theology of religions and to relate to cultures outside of Christendom. Certainly, the pagans and other non-Christians would all know about the law of God, but they would not have a clue about the gospel. Accordingly, those who happen to live outside the Jewish-Christian civilization will allegedly all be lost forever. In the history of Lutheranism, there have been two resolutions to this impasse. One resolution is to enlarge the idea of the divine law into a notion of an "original revelation," that is, by expanding the notion of creation so as to embody not only the sense of divine law but also of divine grace (e.g., Emil Brunner). The other solution is to relegate this question to holy silence, to the inscrutable ways of God that will forever be beyond our reach (e.g., Paul Althaus).

I believe that both these proposals, respectable as they are, evade the real issue. Both solutions elaborate on the idea of the hidden God, the first by minimizing the epistemic hiddenness and the second by maximizing it. I believe that the only way out will be to rethink Luther's doctrine of the Triune God. The crucial point will be that the Triune activities are always taking place in peace and mutual agreement (cf. the German term *Drei-Einigkeit*). Accordingly, the work of the Spirit will always integrate the work of creation (by Luther appropriated to the Father) and the work of redemption (by Luther appropriated to the Son). The works of the Spirit are always attuned to both the mind of the Father, from which the Spirit was sent (*ex patre*), and to the Wisdom of the Son through whom the Spirit is flowing (*per filium*). Thus the Spirit does nothing that is not in accord with the redemptive will of the eternal Word of God; yet the Spirit is not bound to the sermonic Word of God. If this were the case, salvation would be locked into the walls of the Christian churches; there would not be much salvific light for the world outside the old Christendom. To avoid this absurdity, a theology of the Holy Spirit is required that will enlarge the horizons of a traditional Lutheran theology by coordinating the works of the Spirit as creator and as the fulfiller of creation.

> **9. Luther's theology of creation is characterized by an unusual freshness and breadth. Luther's doctrine of creation is conceived after the model of justification: life is an unmerited gift, and yet a gift that opens up for divine-human interaction. In both cases, the received dichotomy between a purely active God and a purely passive creature will need to be transcended. Contrary to what has often been said, Luther developed an orthodox doctrine of synergism.**

Luther's doctrine of creation is multifaceted. In a temporal dimension, not only the beginning of the world is important but also its preservation from death and evil. Likewise, it is not only important that creation continues but also that the divine blessing continues to effect a blossoming of creation. In the spatial horizon, Luther's doctrine of creation in the Small Catechism refers to the fruitful interpenetration between the spheres of nature (sun, moon), of social conviviality (house, spouse, children, work), and of individual existence (body, senses, and mind). A strong affirmation of ordinary life is everywhere expressed. The world of creation is rich in phenomena in which God speaks to us—even in a pit of a peach or in the noise of the working place. Accordingly, God's creation is not something that we need to have a theory about; it speaks to us through the ways in which the spheres of the cosmos, of social life, and of personal life are woven together and in conjunction generate the earthly blessings of ordinary life: cooked meals and social company, sex and love, houses of physical shelter, artistic beauty, and social conviviality.

The First Article of faith is permeated by insights coming from the Second and Third Articles of faith. We find in both cases the same structure of divine creation: first, moving all so that it moves, and second, handing over divine powers to the creatures to facilitate an array of interactions between God and creatures.[17] What Luther in all cases denies is the free will's "own powers" and staying "capacities." Yet what he affirms is that in this cooperation with God, human beings are brought to do things beyond their own capacities. Paul cooperates with God when he instructs the Corinthians and builds up their community. Also, the ungodly cooperate

---

17. See the still classic treatment of Gustaf Wingren, *Luther on Vocation* [1942] (Philadelphia: Muhlenberg Press, 1957), 123–42 (on cooperation). But see Kenneth Hagen, "A Critique of

with God, but without their knowledge and "without the grace of the Spirit."[18] The interesting point is that Luther cannot be described adequately as a simple monergist who claims that God does all and human beings do nothing. According to Luther, human beings are not entirely passive when they are used by God as his instruments. Paradoxically, the more we are united with God, the more we are enabled to do. Thus, both regarding creation and regarding justification, Luther can, without any hint of fear of self-righteousness, refer to our "own will" and our "own justice."[19] Luther thus elaborated an orthodox doctrine of synergism that avoids both a puppet monergism and a modern separation between God and human beings. The more intimate the relation is to God, the more the human person is empowered.

It seems obvious that the same model that Luther developed in the context of justification also has potential for rethinking a theology of nature. Nature should never be perceived as devoid of God. Rather, the powers of nature are empowered by the presence of the God who finds delight in creating creativity rather than repeating structures.[20]

---

10. The future of Lutheran theology should transcend the unhealthy dichotomy between "conservative" and "liberal" theology. Lutheran theology has particular reasons for developing a public Christian theology and unique resources for doing so.

Much of current theology has been partitioned according to schema of liberal versus conservative or evangelical, culture-oriented versus church-oriented, modern versus postmodern, and so on. With many of my European colleagues, I find these schemata stultifying. For example, in the 1950s the Niebuhr brothers were termed neo-orthodox, but now, postmortem, they have been recategorized by many as liberals. Name tags are, of course, open for discussion, but the church suffers from theological sputtering when speaking about Christian faith in the public square. What is needed is the ability to distinguish between internal self-descriptions of faith and external descriptions. For theologians to be able to communicate matters of faith, it is imperative that one can speak both the fluid, fast,

---

Wingren on Luther on Vocation," *Lutheran Quarterly* 16/3 (2002): 249–74. Hagen argues that Wingren one-sidedly concentrates on the role of law and death in vocation while neglecting the importance of the joys of vocation. If Hagen is correct, Wingren's later work has certainly overcome such a gloomy view of creation.

18. "De servo arbitrio," LW 33:241–43; WA 18:753f.

19. See "Two Kinds of Righteousness" (1519), LW 31:297–306 and Regin Prenter's concise interpretation in "Luther's Synergismus?" in *Theologie und Gottesdienst* (Aarhus: Aros, and Göttingen: Vandenhoeck & Ruprecht, 1977), where he argues that Luther teaches an orthodox doctrine of synergism, also *in loco iustificationis* (with respect to the topic of justification).

20 Cf. Niels Henrik Gregersen, "The Idea of Creation and the Theory of Autopoetic Processes," *Zygon: Journal of Religion & Science* 33/3 (1998): 333–67.

generalized and superficial language of newspapers and TV, and the ritualized, slow, content-specific and deep language of first-order Christian language.

It seems to me that Lutheran theology is particularly motivated for developing a public theology. Lutherans believe that God's Word speaks in the vernacular. If God is able to speak in plain American English or Danish, theologians should try the same. A theology that speaks in a sectarian self-confident tone should be met with a great deal of suspicion. For the message of the church is finally not about traditions (new or old) but about the *viva vox evangelii* (the living voice of the gospel); not about identity formation (old or new) but about living out of the external Word of God. Accordingly, Lutheran tradition is strongly disinclined to believe that a specific type of philosophy or theological system is essential for the expression of the gospel. Neither Aristotle and Thomas nor Hegel and Pannenberg are prerequisites for understanding what Christianity is about—but they may indeed prove very helpful!

It seems that Lutheran traditions are also well equipped for developing public theologies. Lutherans are geared for enduring tensions between internal and external descriptions of the world and of their own faith. In Luther's early theology of the cross, we find a principle of contrariety, stating that where people usually only experience humiliation, the theologian of the cross finds the presence of the redemptive power of Christ. But also Luther's more mature theology of the Word handles the difference between the pedestrian observation that it is "just a human being" who speaks the word of absolution and the realization that she or he does so on behalf of God. In this sense, the much-criticized two-kingdoms doctrine allows the Christian to live in several worlds at the same time and to endure the differences between them.

The capacity for living with contradiction rather than in neat uniform schemata may be an important stress test of a Lutheran spirituality. Lutheran tradition engages with the world on the assumption that Christians are not in possession of ultimate solutions to complex problems in the world. One has to listen. One has to try out solutions, step by step. In this world, Christians have to develop models of ethics and conviviality that also are workable "in a world where the Christians live far apart from one another."

As Martin Luther once said . . .

GRACE

Part

I

IN TRADITIONAL LUTHERAN TERMS, grace means the favor of God or acceptance by God that we receive without any work or merit on our part. In Luther's own work, however, grace is not solely external to the believer; grace exists not only "in the eyes of God." The grace of God is also a charism in an emphatic theological sense: a gift in which God's own self is present. Christ is thus present in faith as the righteousness that justifies the sinner, and the Holy Spirit is present as the divine love inhabiting the believer and restlessly active in renewing the believer's heart and mind.

It should be noted from the outset, however, that the emphasis on divine grace is not a Lutheran prerogative. Rather, grace is a divine charism given to the Christian church, where and when it pleases God. According to Christians everywhere and at all times, God certainly finds pleasure in giving grace (some would say: also outside the walls of the church). The principle of *sola gratia*, "by grace alone," was and is shared by both Roman Catholic and Reformation theology. The sixteenth-century debates concerned the extent to which one could also speak of a "created grace." Luther abandoned this concept and did not want to speak of grace apart from the living and incarnate God present in "uncreated grace" (as it was expressed in the tradition from Augustine and Peter Lombard). The real divisive issue, however, was about the manner in which the human being may cooperate with the gift of grace. In his controversial principle of *sola fide*, "by faith alone," Luther famously argued that the human being can neither prepare for grace nor collaborate with grace as an independent free subject. Rather, it is divine grace that assumes, changes, and cooperates with the sinner. So "it is no longer I who live, but it is Christ who lives in me" (Gal 2:20). In the act of grace, the believer is absorbed in Christ, and the very division between created and uncreated grace becomes obsolete. Divine grace is self-communicative by sharing itself with the graced creatures.

The question, then, is how to conceptualize grace. How can God be both external to us, *extra nos*, and internal to us, *in nobis*? Robert W. Jenson proposes an original Trinitarian exposition of the theology of grace. The Father is the ungifted giver, the Son the act of grace in whom God and humanity are one, and the Holy Spirit the internal liberating gift of grace. Christoph Schwöbel follows up on Jenson's interpretation by arguing that a genuine

Trinitarian understanding of grace implies that there can exist no ungraced nature. The important distinction, rather, is between grace and sin, not between grace and nature. Monica Melanchthon points to the Old and New Testament backgrounds for the theology of grace, and she argues that grace means that all that exists has to be attributed an intrinsic value. As such, the message of grace has special significance for the victims of exclusion, exemplified by Dalits, women, and indigenous peoples. Cristina Grenholm points to the temptation of taking theological abbreviations such as "grace" as harmonious concepts rather than being aware of the tensions in the biblical traditions and exploring how the various views relate to present-day situations. Risto Saarinen focuses on the notion of gift and communication. He argues that social theory conceives of two paradigms of communication, one emphasizing the gift or *munus* to be passed on, the other highlighting counseling and dialogue. The understanding of grace as a free unconditional gift is thus defensible in light of current communication theory. Still, however, "a free lunch has to be eaten." Bo Holm, by contrast, argues that there can exist no such thing as a pure gift. More precisely, divine grace as gift should be construed as a gift initiated by divine generosity but given in the expectation that the recipient passes the gift on to others. A theology of grace should thus be developed as a theology of the divine surplus rather than as a theology that understands divine grace as a mere reaction to human deficits.

—NIELS HENRIK GREGERSEN

Triune Grace

Robert W. Jenson

The assignment of this chapter[1] imposes two mandates. I am to seek a more adequate doctrine of grace, presumably because present doctrines are deficient, an assumption with which I concur. And I am to envision a future for "Lutheran theology," which for me is more problematic.

Perhaps I have sinned in accepting this assignment. For, if "Lutheran theology" describes anything like a self-bounded complex of theologoumena, generated from or organized around a particular insight or conceptual move of Luther or the Confessions—perhaps *ein reformatorischer Durchbruch* (a Reformation breakthrough)[2]—then I am unable and indeed unwilling to envisage any future for it. I am ever more convinced that theology must be done for and in the name of the ecumene if it is to be theology and not ideology and, moreover, that the notion of a theological complex that one must accept or reject more or less entire[3] is for the pilgrim church a snare and a delusion—God and his perfected saints know such a theology, but we do not. So I will interpret that part of my assignment to mean that the theological legacy of Luther and of theologians who have called themselves Lutheran may contribute to a more adequate ecumenical doctrine of grace, and that I am to undertake a construction that along the way mediates contributions of that sort.

The Usage of Scripture

We do need some place to begin, and I will indeed use a Lutheran near-dogma. Melanchthon decreed: *"Sed nos . . . nomenclaturam hanc facimus*

---

1. Originally published as "Triune Grace," *Dialog* 41/4 (Winter 2002): 285–93.
2. Which in my—here admittedly somewhat amateur—judgment never occurred.
3. Two noteworthy constructions of such a putative "Lutheranism" are Werner Elert's *Morphologie des Lutherthums*, whose considerable individual contributions I do not mean to denigrate, and the entity supposed by recent German-Protestant protesters against the *Joint Declaration* with Roman Catholicism. The book Eric Gritsch and I wrote and called *Lutheranism* makes only a very weak version of the claim—but even that is too much.

gratiae, secuti phrasin scripturae, ut sit gratia favor . . . dei erga nos" (But we . . . lay down this nomenclature for grace, following the usage of Scripture, that grace is the favor of God . . . toward us). Then he tidied the rest of the semantic field: *"Donum ipse spiritus sanctus. . . . Fructus spiritus sancti fides, spes, caritas et reliquae virtutes"* (The gift is the Holy Spirit himself. . . . The fruits of the Holy Spirit are faith, hope, charity, and the rest of the virtues).[4]

Melanchthon accompanies his definitions with quite remarkable denunciations[5] of any who might dissent from them. He names Thomas Aquinas as a special sinner; therefore in some of the following I will take Thomas as a counter to Melanchthon. It is already a sign of complexities not perhaps fully recognized by Melanchthon that Thomas in fact starts his nomenclature of grace with the same specification as does Melanchthon: the first meaning of saying that someone is graced is that he *a Deo diligitur*[6] *in vitam aeternam* (is chosen by God for life eternal).[7] This is surely other language precisely for what Melanchthon calls *"favor dei"*[8] and indeed, by speaking of choosing for ultimate blessing rather than of favoring, is if anything sharper than Melanchthon's formula. Thomas does, to be sure, signal secondary meanings, the very notion of which is rejected by Melanchthon; we will shortly come to that matter.

It is indeed easy to find passages in the New Testament, and especially in Paul, where the Vulgate's *gratia*, from which comes the English "grace,"[9] denotes what Melanchthon calls *favor dei*. There are many places where the Vulgate rightly translates χάρις with *gratia* and where one can paraphrase with *favor dei*—so many that listing would be bootless. But it is also easy to find other places in Paul—and the rest of the New Testament—where χάρις is used as a near synonym for its derivative χάρισμα, charisma, or for δωρεά, gift, is nevertheless plausibly translated in the Vulgate with *gratia*, and cannot be replaced with *favor dei*.

This observation does not yet pose a major problem for the Melanchthonian nomenclature. The New Testament semantic field here in question is rhetorically rather than conceptually structured; and such a semantic field need not therefore lack underlying conceptual distinctions, which a later sorting-out of vocabulary may serve to disclose. In the present case, however, the stretch between Melanchthon's claimed *phrasis*

---

4. 1521 *Loci communes*, "De Gratia" (On Grace).
5. Particularly for one who was supposed to be such a *Leisetreter*.
6. There may be an association here with other of the shifting formations of the same root and prefixes, such that we are to hear that this choice is a loving choice.
7. *Quaestiones de veritate*, 27.1.
8. That choosing and showing favor come to the same thing, will be more obvious if we remember the premodern sense of "favor," as in "grace and favor" for a monarch's choice of someone to a status or post.
9. German *Gnade* carries a different inheritance. Does this make any difference?

Scripturae and the actual scriptural usage is so severe as to suggest a genuine mismatch. In some places where χάρις is used with every appearance of heavy-duty theological reference, and where one really must translate with *gratia*, one would paraphrase with *favor dei* only if determined in advance to do so and willing to adopt Procrustes' methods.

Choosing from the concordance listing at near random, we may consider Rom 1:5, ". . . through whom we have received grace and apostleship to bring about the obedience of faith . . . among all the nations. . . ." If we are sufficiently determined, we can decree that since we know what χάρις *must* mean, we shall say that here it stipulates a precondition of the next mentioned gift of apostleship, in that God's favor is a precondition of his giving such a mission. But the text as it stands certainly seems to parallel "grace" with the apostolic mission given Paul and so to conceive grace as something like the mission that is transmitted to Paul, perhaps as the moral and spiritual endowment coordinate to the task. Or there is 2 Cor 1:15, "I wanted to come to you first," ἵνα δευτέραν χάριν σχῆτε, which surely begs to be translated, "so that you might receive a second helping of grace"—though not perhaps in a version for liturgical use. Paul scarcely refers to a reiteration of God's becoming favorable to the Corinthians, to be triggered by his visit. Or for a non-Pauline instance, John 1:16: ὅτι ἐκ τοῦ πληρώματος αὐτοῦ ἡμεῖς πάντες ἐλάβομεν καὶ χάριν ἀντὶ χάριτος, "Of his fullness we have all together received, grace added to grace." To *receive* ever *more* out of a "fullness" certainly sounds like something is being transferred.

One very simple text can give us much to think about and perhaps can be a first pointer on our way. First Corinthians 1:4 reads, "I give thanks to God always for you because of the grace of God which was given you in Christ Jesus." Can "grace" here mean the favor of God? Plainly it can, and it probably does. But must it not nevertheless also point to something about the Corinthians that Paul can observe? As he elsewhere observes and gives thanks for such things as congregations' steadfastness or generosity? It seems to do this also. Thus the most straightforward reading of the passage is that Paul does not here distinguish between God's attitudinal act and the act's observable correlate in us. Indeed, may not such a passage be a clue that the distinction is in general inappropriate in reading Paul?

Pondering such phenomena, one may well think that Thomas, with his analogical spreading out of plural uses of *gratia*, was closer to the *phrasis Scripturae* than was Melanchthon. Thomas makes what Melanchthon calls *favor dei* the first sense of *gratia* and then moves to a second, analogously related sense or set of senses. The passage already cited continues: one is graced *non solum* (not only) in that he enjoys God's favor but also *ex hoc quod datur ei aliquid donum* (from this, that a certain gift is given to him). Here of course appears "created" grace, grace that is predicated of the creature, and that in the notorious phrase is *gratia gratum faciens* (grace that makes [the creature] grateful [in God's eye])—all abhorred by right-think-ing Lutherans.

And indeed, I have myself indulged in some polemics against late-medieval and Tridentine doctrines of grace, particularly deriding "salami-slicing" distinctions of "graces." Should I now repent thereof? Not, I think, altogether—though indeed I regret a stray sentence or two denouncing the notion of created grace *tout court*. For if the hypothesis about Pauline usage just stated is correct, then of course also the scholastic distinction between uncreated and created grace divides what Paul does not; moreover the ever-finer distinctions that have followed in its train are indeed close to absurd, and their variously construed mutual relations have indeed been the occa-sion of much practical Pelagianism.

Trinitarian Deficiency

If, as seems plausible, Paul must in this matter be our primary mentor, our task is to conceive as one that χάρις with which Paul was acquainted as one. Grace, I suggest, is indeed *favor dei* and just so an endowment of the believer. Luther sets the same task: "Gratia Dei et donum idem sunt . . ." (God's grace and his gift are the same thing . . .)—or, as it turns out, the "same one."[10] But how is such an identity possible? It would seem possible only if God's grace-given-as-endowment is the gracious God himself.

I suggest that the way is shown by an obvious, but often unconsidered point: what *favor* in *favor dei* means must depend on which God *deus* denotes. "The grace of which God do you have in mind?" is the kind of ques-tion whose neglect often, in philosophy or theology, is a flaw common to both sides of a controversy and the source of the controversy's difficulty. All branches of at least the Western theological tradition have, I suggest, sub-liminally conceived God, when speaking directly of his grace, in too unitar-ian a fashion. The subject of grace is regularly simply "God" or, if God is identified as the Son or the Spirit, then the Son or the Spirit, for all the dic-tion shows, is evoked as if he acted by himself. Nor is this remedied merely by saying that it is for Christ's sake that God regards us favorably and that the Spirit is given to those in God's favor; these familiar propositions are, of course, true, but they do not make a Trinitarian notion of grace itself.

When the God of grace is thought of with respect to his grace as if he were a monotheos, the relation between grace as *favor dei* and the difference grace makes with us will necessarily be conceived in one or both of two ways. Most likely it will be conceived as a causal relation: God's act of being favorable to us effects good things in us.[11] Or, if one sees this will not do,

---

10. WA 56:318, 28. Cited from Simo Peura, "Christ as Favor and Gift: The Challenge of Luther's Understanding of Justification," in *Union with Christ: The New Finnish Interpretation of Luther*, ed. Carl E. Braaten and Robert W. Jenson (Grand Rapids: Eerdmans, 1998), 43.
11. I am not, of course, using the word here in its full medieval range, which covers also for-mal and final causation.

since the God-creature relation is not in fact causal, the alternative is to conceive the relation as a more or less Platonic participation.

If, on the other hand, the triunity of the God of grace is kept firmly in mind, we are able to conceive God's grace as the gift of himself, for this God has the sort of self that can be given. You and I do not; no matter how sacrificially and deeply I love, I cannot quite "give myself" but only strive to do so, because as finite I am not in myself a community and so have no hypostatic self to give. If I did fully succeed in giving myself, this would be death, which undoes the gift.[12] The Triune God does not suffer this deficiency.

When the *favor dei* is—again, no doubt subliminally—thought of as a cause, it will have to be accommodated to actual New Testament usage—insofar as that is possible—by pairing it with some *effects*, by a doctrine of "created grace," or by something distinguished from such doctrine only by insistence that it is different. When the *favor dei* is thought of as a participable quality, it will be accommodated to New Testament usage—insofar, again, as possible—by a paired doctrine of "theological" virtues, particular *participations* in God's goodness, or again by something only terminologically distinguishable.

Neither move can be fully satisfactory. It will at this point be useful to look again at Melanchthon's and Thomas's teachings with a more critical eye. Melanchthon first.

Melanchthon's teaching has one great virtue: following Luther,[13] he identifies the *donum*, that which the favor of God effects in us, as the Holy Spirit himself. Thus his doctrine is that much Trinitarian. Here Melanchthon maintains Augustine's position on a question about which medieval theology mostly—and exceptionally—disagreed with Augustine. Or rather, Melanchthon starts out to do this but will not quite carry through. Peter Lombard posed the question for subsequent theology: Is the love that unites believers with God and among themselves the same love that unites the Father and the Son, that is, the Spirit himself, as Augustine taught, or is this love a reality *created* in us, and so other than the Spirit?[14] Peter took Augustine's side, but he was in this matter not generally followed. Augustine, Peter, Luther, and Melanchthon were surely right and the majority wrong. If the Spirit is indeed a personal lover, he has nothing to give as the gift of love but himself; the gift *in* genuine gifts *of* love is always the giver. Thus Luther says about love, "It is not enough to have the gift, if the giver is not there."[15] There doubtless also is advantage in Melanchthon's use of the biblical word "fruits": it directs our minds back to the biblical texts and counters the tendency to conceive the relation of Spirit and endowment as effective causation.

---

12. Sundry postmodernists have sufficiently explored this dialectic. Apart from them, there is here, of course, the heart of an entire doctrine of atonement.
13. Peura, "Christ as Favor and Gift," 48.
14. *Sententiarum libri quatuor*, I.d.xvii.2.
15. WA 56:308–9, 2.

But within a causal or participatory grasp of the relation between favor and gift, these advantages exact a price. Melanchthon—here unlike Luther—has to make an additional distinction, to obtain effects of and/or participations in grace. The love, which is *actual* in the life of believers and which is a "virtue," is by that distinction understood *not* as the Spirit himself but rather as a consequence of his being given; the Spirit, after all, is not himself the love that binds us. And so it further eventuates that faith and hope are consequences of the Spirit's being given and, for good measure whatever other virtues one might think suitable to Christian life. Which leaves the gift, which the Spirit himself is, experientially empty. I think it hard to deny that Lutheran church life and piety have for the most part known the Spirit not as himself the shaping energizer and energy of believing existence but as the by itself unexperienced explanation of certain phenomena; pietistic movements within Lutheranism have in any case regularly made that diagnosis.

Turning to Thomas, the advantages of his way of dividing are, one may think, two. One is a sort of straightforward simplicity: grace is, first, God's utterly unmerited act of choice and, second, the analogous gifts that accrue to those chosen. The other is the suitability of the notion of created grace to make the—thoroughly scriptural!—claim that these gifts actually belong to us, who are creatures.[16] I think also that we need not worry overmuch about any inherent works-righteousness in the notion of created grace; the worry afflicts Protestants who disregard Thomas's analogy-logic. What is produced in us that is *gratum* to God is precisely and only the analogue of his own act of *favor*.

Nevertheless, here too there is the disadvantage of the advantages. Once the language about created grace is in place, the proliferation of graces does seem inevitable. And of course the Augustinian invocation of the Spirit himself is not even verbally honored; the disappearance of the Spirit so often charged against "the Latins" by Orthodox theology is actually formalized terminologically.

A Trinitarian and Lutheran Proposal

So how might we do it better, that is, with more attention to the fact that the gracious God is specifically the Triune God? We must of course honor the maxim that the externally directed works of the Trinity are not divided among the three, *opera trinitatis ad extra indivisa*, lest we portray three gods. But first, grace, insofar as it is an *opus*, is not all that obviously only *ad extra*, for God surely is in some sense gracious in himself and, as triune,

---

16. And we may note that the Lutheran scholastics, who were always more under pressure of Scripture than most theologians, ended up by making lists of graces distinguishable from medieval lists only in detail.

would be gracious also without creatures. If the Trinitarian "missions" are even analogically one with the "processions,"[17] and if the missions of the Son and the Spirit are grace, then the begetting of the Son and the breathing of the Spirit are the primary analogical referents of "grace." This observation leads to another question about grace, to which I will come at the end. And, second, the maxim fits the specifically biblical God only if not construed to mean that Father, Son, and Spirit do the same thing but rather that each external work of the Trinity is indivisibly the *mutual* work of Father, Son, and Spirit, in which work each person has his differentiated role.[18]

We may begin with the Father. The absolute contingency, which the Father simply *is*, constitutes the contingency of divine favor, without which it would not be grace. As the μόναρχος, the determining beginning anterior to which there is not even nothingness, the Father answers, and indeed *can* answer, to no instance but himself. So, in this context, he shows favor *if* he shows favor and *to whom* he shows favor and is moreover the sole determinant of what constitutes favor and of whether there is anyone to show it to; and not even he can alter this utter contingency without *per impossibile* ceasing to be the Father.

Yet the favor of God is not therefore arbitrary. For the Son *is* the favor of God, and Jesus of Nazareth is the Son. Thus the favor of God is determinate even for the Father, who looks to Jesus in his life and death to know of whom and of what he is the Father, and so what is his own favor and to whom he shows it—something on the lines of[19] the *Solida Declaratio*'s[20] or Karl Barth's christological specifications of election must be true. But having said that, we must return to say again that it lies in the absolute contingency that is the Father, that this also is true.

If we speak of gift, the Father is thus the ungifted giver. The Son and the Spirit are in different ways the gift. We will consider the Son first. Here we will invoke some specifically Lutheran insights at the decisive points.

The existence of Jesus as the Son, the existence of the θεάνθρωπος, the "God-man," is the *act* of grace, it is what God *does* as *favor ipsius Dei*. Favor is not in God's case a sheer decision in a moment or—what with God is not really different—a sort of settled disposition, as may be suggested by both Melanchthon's and Thomas's language; it is an event, indeed a history.[21] The existence of Jesus the Christ, constituted as this person and not

---

17. That they are at least analogically one is a chief burden of the recent flood of Trinitarian essays.

18. This point obviously marks a bone of contention among interpreters of the tradition. Here I hope to avoid these broils and to stick simply with the—I hope—uncontested proposition itself.

19. Not necessarily Barth's exact version.

20. See esp. *Solida Declaratio*, 11.65–67.

21. At our time in history, this sounds Barthian, because we have relearned it from him. But in concept if not in terminology, the point is ancient.

another by his particular life and death, is the event that God is there for us and that this is favor and not disaster. For this to be true, two conditions must obtain, both innovatively taught by Luther and more or less maintained by the Lutheran scholastics.

The first such condition of the posited identity (θεάνθρωπος = act of grace) is the notorious *communicationis idiomatum genus maiestaticum* (communication of the attributes of majesty) and indeed of *genus tapeinoticon* (of humility). Luther's vehemence in the eucharistic controversy with Oecolampadius and Zwingli did not derive simply from allegiance to the words of institution; indeed, when Luther jumped in so passionately on the side of his radical young Swabian followers, the targets of his polemic had some grounds for surprise. Luther's attention had been called to a threat to the actuality of grace, and it is this that truly sparked his passion.

"Beware! Beware, I tell you, of the 'alleosis!'"[22] It is the devil's mask. In the end, it construes such a Christ, that were Christ indeed so, I would not want to be a Christian."[23] As for the God who appears in this Christ, Luther can only cry, "Don't give me any of *that* God!"[24] The object of Luther's horror is any presence of God that is not a presence of the human Jesus, of an appearing θέος who is not θεάνθρωπος. What appalled Luther was the thought of encountering a "sheer separated God and divine person, without humanity."[25] To someone whose teaching proposes such a possibility, Luther has to say, "No, buddy! Anywhere you confront me with God, there you must just so confront me with his humanity."[26] It is *the chief condition* of God's turning to us being an act of *grace*: "Anywhere you can say 'Here is God,' you must also say 'Here is Christ the man.'"[27]

So Luther teaches the communion of attributes without reservations. Not only must one "attribute to the whole person whatever happens with either of the natures,"[28] but one must go on, "because deity and humanity in Christ are one person," to attribute "also to the deity everything that happens with the humanity, and vice versa."[29]

Luther saw clearly that if there were a God like the one who appears in Scripture, except for being the man Jesus, or even not always being the man

---

22. Zwingli's word for his weak, but in fact fairly traditional version of the communion of attributes.

23. WA 26:319: "Hüt dich. Hüt dich—sage ich—fur der Alleosi. Sie ist des Teuffels Larven. Denn sie richtet zu letzt ein solchen Christum zu, nach dem ich nicht gern wollt ein Christen sein" (LW 37:218: "Beware, beware, I say, of this alloeosis, for it is the devil's mask since it will finally construct a kind of Christ after whom I would not want to be a Christian . . .").

24. Ibid., 332: "Mir aber des Gottes nicht!" (LW 37:218: "But no God like that for me!")

25. Ibid., 333.

26. Ibid.: "Nein Geselle! Wo du mir Gott himsetztest, da mustu mir die Menscheit mit hinsetzen" (LW 27:219: "No, comrade, wherever you place God for me, you must also place the humanity for me").

27. Ibid., 332.

28. Ibid., 322.

29. Ibid., 320.

Jesus, this God would be named Death. No one can see the biblical God and live, except as God has the face of the Son. What was finally at issue in the eucharistic controversy was whether God's turning to us is *favor* or *ira*.

The second condition of the identity (θεάνθρωπος = act of grace) is this God-man's transcendence of the difference between being external to us and being internal to us. Christ can be the *act* of grace just and only in that precisely as someone other than I, he is God's own love and righteousness. He himself becomes—and here we can indeed use the scholastic language—the *forma* of my moral and spiritual existence before God, my *gratia gratum faciens* (the grace that makes me gracious). Luther can simply substitute Christ for love in the famous scholastic formula *fides caritate formata* (faith formed by love) to derive the formula *fides Christo formata* (faith formed by Christ) as the maxim of his doctrine of sanctifying life.[30]

It is fatal to separate Christ as the external act of grace from the Spirit as the internal gift of grace; *both* are imparted, even "infused." That anyway is Luther's teaching: the Father's *favor* is his will "to pour Christ and the Spirit with his gifts into us."[31]

Luther's theology can posit this simultaneity of Christ's external and internal presence, in that he understands the presence of the risen Christ as primally *Word*.[32] That the externality of Christ as the word addressed to us is vital for Luther is of course a Lutheran platitude and need not itself be argued here. When I am *addressed*, the externality of the one addressing me is ineluctable: I do not direct my attention, as when I turn to see something, but am directed. By seeing I make objects, which—as two centuries of philosophical reflection have made clear—means that what I only see is not truly other than me. Hearing, I am uncontrollably called to, by someone's address, who just so maintains his or her place as other than me. For Luther, that I cannot overcome the externality of Christ's presence is what makes it grace for me; could I do so I would, and then I would control righteousness, perhaps as "my faith," and so possess righteousness unrighteously.

What is now being rediscovered about Luther is that the converse also obtains: the one who as his word is other than us is *grace* for us just and only in that he rules from *within* us.[33] Precisely the Word takes over the soul in a way in which objects of sight do not. Faith notoriously—and especially for Luther—comes by hearing and, to cite the proposition from Luther's 1535 *Galatians* that has become the watchword of "the Finnish school," "*in*

30. WA 40/1:229.

31. ". . .Christus und den Geist mit seinen Gaben in uns zu giessen. . . ." Cited from Peura, "Christ as Favor and Gift," 43.

32. Whether he practically eliminates seeing from the apprehension of the present Christ, as some self-described Lutherans now do, is a question for another time. If he does, he is wrong.

33. This is, of course, the great contention of the "Finnish school." See Tuomo Manermaa, *Der im Glauben gegenwärtige Christus* (Hannover: Lutherisches Verlagshaus, 1989); Simo Peura, *Mehr als ein Mensch?* (Mainz: Philipp von Zabern, 1994).

ipsa fide Christus adest" (in faith itself, Christ is there).[34] Which together is to say: *by hearing, Christ enters.* "Everything [Christ] is and does is present in us and there works with power, so that we are utterly deified, so that we do not have some part or aspect of God, but his entire fullness."[35] Here we must spend a few paragraphs.

"Believe in Christ," Luther admonishes in "The Freedom of a Christian," "in whom are promised all grace, righteousness, peace and freedom. If you believe, you have it; if you do not believe, you do not have it."[36] But *why* does the one who believes the word of promise merely thereby "have" the goods it speaks about? The reason, according to Luther, is an ontological mutuality of the soul and the word: the moral content of that to which someone hearkens determines his or her moral and spiritual quality. The one who believes the gospel is righteous, etc., because the word of the gospel "has all good things for its content" and because "the soul of the one who clings to the word in true faith is so entirely united with it that all the virtues of the word become virtues of the soul also."[37]

At the very beginning of his theological reflection, Luther made a momentous switch on a central piece of Aristotle's phenomenology. Aristotle had noticed that there is nothing *to* the apprehending soul—νοῦς—but on the one hand a sheer potentiality of apprehending something, and on the other hand whatever is apprehended. In Luther's own formulation of the Aristotelian maxim: "So the objects [of minds] are the being and act of minds, without which they would be nothing, just as matter without forms would be nothing."[38]

Luther adopted Aristotle's principle but changed its context and import. For Aristotle, the paradigm mode of apperception was *seeing*, so that in Aristotle's doctrine we are what we stare at. Since, according to Luther, God is present to us first as word, for Luther the paradigm of apperception is hearing,[39] so that we are what is addressed to us: "Do not be surprised when I say we become the Word. The philosophers too say that the intellect, through the act of knowing, *is* the known object, and that sensuality, through the act of sensual perception, is the sensed object. How much more must this hold of the spirit of the Word?"[40]

We *are* the "good things" we hear in the gospel just in that we hear them; they enter us with the message addressed to us. Luther's actual doctrine of justification by faith is nearly the opposite of the doctrine popularly

---

34. WA 40/1:229.
35. WA 17/1:438.
36. WA 7:24.
37. Ibid.
38. WA 20:26–27.
39. If used with skepticism about the notion of Luther's "discovery," Ernst Bizer, *Fides ex auditu* (Neukirchen: Neukirchner Verlag, 1958).
40. WA 1:29.

attributed to him: we are justified by faith because faith is listening to the gospel, because the gospel communicates God's "good things," and because in hearkening we are actually shaped to what we hear.

It is "for Christ's sake" that believers are righteous, in that the gospel word to which faith hearkens is both about him and spoken by him. This enables Luther's other and better known statement of why faith makes righteous—itself taken straight from the fathers: "Faith . . . unites the soul with Christ, as a bride with her bridegroom. From this marriage it follows . . . that Christ and the soul have everything together."[41] As the soul is united with the gospel it hears, it is united with Christ whose word this is, so that the two become one personal subject, of the believer's sin and of Christ's divine righteousness. Then the second "swallows up" the first.

Thus Christ as *Word* is both *extra nos* (outside us) and *qua fide in nobis* (as faith in us), and just and only in this simultaneity he is the act of grace. Nor are these simply two aspects of his reality; it is precisely the character of Christ's externality, as Word, that sets him within us; and vice versa, it is precisely the character of his internality as Word that maintains him without us. He is external to us as a word always calls to us from outside us; he is internal to us as a word always preempts our inwardness.

If the Son is as *donum* the act of God's giving, the Spirit is *donum* as the freedom of any true gift and as the love that is Christ's character within us, and so the Spirit is the interior moral quality of the gift.[42] Within a properly triune framework of doctrine, we do not need to mitigate this proposition. Where the relation of the graceful God to graced creatures is conceived either as causal or as participatory, teaching that the Spirit himself is the love and freedom that animates our lives seems to make the Spirit an effect or analogue of God the giver, and so less than God. But where the relation is conceived as involvement of the believer with the tri-personality of God, these threats do not obtain.

The Spirit, we may in this context say, is God's freedom as person and so, as freedom, able to free others to love one another. In the life of the Triune God, the Spirit frees the Father for the Son and the Son for the Father, to be himself the love between them. In the same way he liberates us also.

In such scenes as Luke's Pentecost, Christ pours out the Spirit from heaven. But if indeed Christ rules from within the believer's heart, then heaven and believing hearts are not in this connection separate locations; then we may equally say that Christ pours out the Spirit from within us. If we ponder this paragraph and the previous together, we come to the Spirit's specific role in God's grace. The Spirit is a liberator who, because he is given from

41. Ibid., 25.
42. The impossibility of a true gift has been a preoccupation of the French and their American epigones for some years now.

within us, does not suffer the dialectics of other would-be liberators, who just in that their liberating activity is *directed* to us end up by binding us to themselves. "I will write my Torah on their hearts . . . and they shall no longer."

The question has been unanswerable whenever it has been asked: Is the Holy Spirit/grace resistible? When both answers to a yes-or-no question are unsatisfactory, this is often a sign that the question itself misdescribes the situation. Here the intractable question supposes that the Spirit or grace comes from outside and can/cannot be kept out. In a lapse, even the great Augustine sometimes envisioned the situation that way: grace, he said, "cannot be repelled by however hard a heart."[43] But this is indeed a misdescription; grace is neither resistible nor irresistible, since we are never in a position to resist or want to resist, successfully or unsuccessfully. The one who pours out on us the liberating Spirit does so from his heavenly throne hidden within us. The Spirit indeed opens the gate of our hearts, to the Father and to one another—from inside.

Nature and Grace

We must now, more briefly, consider that other problematic earlier announced—though whether it is indeed finally other than the one just considered is not clear to me. In the tradition, "grace" generally appears as the contrast to something else, and its import is in part shaped by the contrast. The phenomenon appears already in the New Testament; a non-Pauline instance is John 1:17, "The Law indeed was given through Moses; grace and truth came through Jesus Christ."

In the tradition from the high Middle Ages on, the pole to grace is most often marked by the notion of "nature." The spiritual and moral meaning of "grace" is thus partly determined by an answer to the question, How are nature and grace related? The issue is perhaps most clearly displayed by a dispute within twentieth-century Roman Catholic theology.[44]

Tridentine theology, including standard "Thomism," proposed to meet the Reformation critique of alleged improper teaching of human works by safeguarding the "gratuity" of grace, which in turn was to be done by a strict separation of nature and "supernature." Nature, established by creation, is one sphere, in which we are called and enabled to do good by our created powers; the reality opened by grace is another, in which God's act is dispositive, and in which all good is the "supernatural" fruit of grace.[45] The good that is the end of the natural realm is not salvation, though it is truly good; thus we are not saved by works. Traditional Calvinism taught much

---

43. Augustine, *De praedestinatione Sanctorum*, viii.13: "a nullo duro corde respuitur."

44. For this, with the citations, see Robert W. Jenson, *Systematic Theology* (New York: Oxford University Press, 1997–1999), 2:65–68.

45. And, of course, the shadow hanging over any attempt to found creation in grace is indeed cast by Pelagius.

the same thing, in the language of "covenants." In both cases grace acquires something of the character of a bolt[46] *senkrecht von oben* (from above).

The theology that in part triumphed at the Second Vatican Council, the so-called *nouvelle theologie* of Henri de Lubac and others, proposes a different view—also in its interpretation of Thomas. In this theology, nature itself is said to be founded in grace by the act of creation, which is a graceful act. Thus, while it is possible within human life to distinguish natural from "supernatural" aspects, our natural morality and religiosity have no other *telos*, nothing else that can satisfy their constituting aspiration, and so no other *forma*, than the salvation that is by grace. Were there no grace, there would be no nature. Karl Barth's mature position is remarkably similar.[47]

The classical Lutheran dogmaticians were, so far as I can tell, inattentive to this question and simply adhered to the most general tradition. Thus Johann Gerhard, whom I always consult as typical, specifies a double goal of creation:[48] "The ultimate goal of creation is the glory of God,"[49] which "includes another and secondary goal, i.e., that all things are created for the use and benefit of humankind." The link, of course, is that man is God's image.[50] One might think that an act with these two characters would be an act of *favor dei*, but—again, as far as I can see—this connection is not made.[51]

There is an opening here that ought to be exploited. We have seen reason to think that de Lubac and his colleagues had the right of it over against the old-line Thomists, and at least this Lutheran regards those reasons as admirably "Lutheran." And yet the old-line Thomists' objections to the "new theology" were not without foundation. For creation and redemption, nature and grace in the language here in use, are not in Scripture simply the same thing. The Catholic "new theologians" and those like myself who take their side are therefore bound to give some answer to the question, What distinguishes them? Following lines deeply laid in the tradition, de Lubac said that there are two different "initiatives" of grace; the one "brings into being," the other "calls."[52] But if we accept this solution, so that a nature itself uncalled, founded in a divine act different in kind from the word of grace, is nevertheless an aptitude for that call, the hemi-demi-semi-Pelagian dialectics lie instantly in wait.

46. Perhaps not with the "superlapsarian" Calvinists.
47. Robert W. Jenson, *Alpha and Omega: A Study in the Theology of Karl Barth* (New York: Nelson, 1963), 112–40.
48. "De Fine Creationis."
49. *Loci theologici*, iv.v.85.
50. Ibid., 86: *"propter usum et utilitatem hominum."*
51. Among likely readers of this essay are many who know the history much better than I; I would be glad to be informed of error here.
52. On this whole discussion, with the citations, see Robert W. Jenson, *Systematic Theology*, 2:66–69.

Here again it can be Luther to the rescue. In his *Ennaratio in Genesin*, commenting on the creation-story's recurring "and God said,"[53] he consciously rejects the exegetical tradition and teaches that the Word by which God in Genesis creates, and the Word which is incarnate as the gospel-call, are *both* "an uttered word by which something is ordered and enjoined."[54] God's act to create us and his act of what the tradition calls "grace" are but two addresses of one word, two utterances in a single conversation of God with his creature. And if that is the case, nature as what the first utterance calls forth and graced life as what the second calls forth are related as events in a narrative; and the Pelagian problematic does not arise.

Whether we name the call that summons us into being "grace" or not is perhaps partly a matter of linguistic decision. Yet it would seem to be a possible Lutheran contribution, here precisely in ecumenical context, to point to creation's foundation in that word which is not another word when it is the word of grace.

A Last Word

What is grace? Grace is God favoring us with himself.

And what about the future of Lutheran theology? If it wishes to maintain itself *as* Lutheran theology, it has no future—or anyway should not. On the other hand, if we who are in one way or another labeled or self-labeled "Lutheran" are willing to ask: What true, good, and useful theologoumena and insights have emerged in our history, and how might we now incorporate them into theological construction? then we will find much to present within the church's continuing theological enterprise. It is the ambition of this chapter to be a sample of how that might work.

53. WA 42:13.
54. Ibid., 15.

CHAPTER 2

The Quest for an Adequate Theology of Grace and the Future of Lutheran Theology: *A Response to Robert W. Jenson*

Christoph
Schwöbel

It has often been said that the crucial insight of the Reformation is a modification of the medieval doctrine of grace.[1] However, this modification concerns the very center of the Christian faith. In the biblical traditions and in the history of Christian teaching, the concept of grace serves to denote the distinctive characteristic of the relationship of the Triune God to his creation, which thereby defines the way in which creation is called to respond to God. If the Christian understanding of grace, summarized from a Lutheran perspective in the message of justification, is that which functions as the "diacritical principle" (C. H. Ratschow),[2] distinguishing Christianity from other religions and defining the identity of what it means to be Christian, the modification concerns the heart of Christian identity. It can be seen as the specific Reformation interpretation of what makes Christian faith Christian and, I might add, what makes faith the fundamental human act of relating to God. The Reformation insight into the interpretation of grace is therefore that which Lutheran churches have to contribute to the ecumenical dialogue, and it defines the perspective from which they perceive the character and structure of the Christian ecumene. The ecumenical perspectives of Lutheran theology are based in the Reformation insight into the character of God's grace. This is why the task cannot consist in asking how the Reformation insight into the character of divine grace can be made to fit preconceived notions of the Christian ecumene and of the task of ecumenism. Rather, the task consists in understanding the character of the Christian ecumene and the task of ecumenism from the perspective of the insight of the Reformation.

Robert Jenson concentrates on five related questions. His argument that grace must be conceived as triune grace shows how these questions can be

---

1. Originally published as "A Quest for an Adequate Theology of Grace and the Future of Lutheran Theology: A Response to Robert Jenson," *Dialog* 42/1 (Spring 2003), 24–31.
2. Cf. Carl Heinz Ratschow, "Rechtfertigung. Diakritisches Prinzip des Christentums im Verhältnis zu den anderen Religionen," in Carl Heinz Ratschow, *Von den Wandlungen Gottes* (Berlin: De Gruyter, 1986), 336–75.

answered in a Trinitarian framework. The main thesis, with which I whole-
heartedly agree, can be formulated in the following way: An adequate theology of grace can only be conceived as a theology of triune self-giving; and
conversely, an adequate theology of the Trinity must be conceived as a theology of grace. The understanding of grace and the understanding of God
as Trinity are mutually dependent. Let us briefly concentrate on the five
questions and their answers, because they supply the groundwork of theological argument for the main thesis. Jenson notes that in Paul, the chief
witness from Scripture, grace can be understood both as the favor of God
and as the gifts God bestows.

The first question therefore is, What is the relationship between the favor
of God and the gifts of grace? Jenson answers this with Luther's thesis *Gratia
Dei et donum idem sunt* (God's grace and his gift are the same thing). This,
however, requires understanding the gift that God gives as endowment to his
creatures as nothing other, or rather, nobody else but God.

The second question is, Who is God who can give himself in his grace
in such a way that this giving does not result in death but in the promise of
eternal life? The answer: Only if the God of grace is the Triune God can
God's grace be perceived as God's self-giving.

The third question can be phrased in this way: If God's grace is the self-
giving of the Father, the Son, and the Spirit, how is God's presence in grace
to be characterized? Jenson answers, "If we speak of gift, the Father is the
ungifted giver; Christ and the Spirit are in different ways the gifts." Christ
has to be understood in such a way that in his person deity and humanity
are one so that everything that belongs to God is in Christ and everything
that happens with Christ's humanity because of the unity of his person also
concerns the deity. As such the self-gift of God in Christ transcends the difference between being external to us and being internal to us.

The fourth question is this: How can this transcendence of the difference between externality and internality be understood? Jenson's answer:
Christ as Word encounters us *extra nos* (outside of us) as the Word that we
cannot say to ourselves; but once we are addressed by this Word, the soul is
united in faith with the word it hears, and so Christ's being in us through
faith redefines our inwardness. "Thus Christ as word is both *extra nos* (outside us) and *qua fide in nobis* (as faith in us), and just and only in this
simultaneity he is the act of grace." Similarly, the Spirit is God's freedom in
person who thus is able to liberate us—from the inside—to love one another.
For Jenson the mode of God's self-giving in Christ and the Spirit eliminates
the possibility and the necessity of distinguishing between created and
uncreated grace and solves the problem of the irresistibility of God's grace:
"grace is neither resistible nor irresistible, since we are never in a position
to resist or want to resist, successfully or unsuccessfully."

The fifth question is, How are nature and grace related? Jenson's
answer: Understanding God's grace as triune grace enables us to see the act

of creation and the act of grace as two intrinsically related utterances of the same word. The juxtaposition of "nature" and "grace" is overcome by the identity of God who creates by his word and gives himself in grace through the same word. The final thesis: "Grace is God favoring us with himself" shows Lutheran theology to be "an ecumenical theology of grace."

A response is most interesting and the discussion most lively if there is violent disagreement between the author of the essay and the respondent. If this is what you expect, I must disappoint you. I completely agree with Jenson's thesis that the Lutheran understanding of grace must be construed in Trinitarian terms. Indeed, this is, in my view, the only reconstruction that makes sense of Luther's conception.[3] Therefore I emphatically agree with what I take to be the overall thesis of Jenson's chapter, which I have phrased in the following way: An adequate theology of grace can only be conceived as a theology of triune self-giving; and conversely, an adequate theology of the Trinity must be conceived as a theology of grace. The understanding of grace and the understanding of God as Trinity are mutually dependent. We differ, as I perceive it, in a number of emphases and nuances that lead to a different view of the character of the Christian ecumene and therefore of the task of ecumenical theology. Let me try to explain that in a number of points.

Distinction between God's Work and Our Work

The central issue of Luther's protest against what he saw as problematical deviations from the truth of the gospel in the late medieval church, rooted in theological errors of its leading theologians, concerns the question of the relationship between what God has done, does, and promises to do for the salvation of his estranged creatures and what humans are called to do and can do in relationship to God. In his debate with Erasmus 1525, Luther expresses this issue as the question of the relationship between God's power and human power (*virtus Dei et nostra*) and between God's work and our work (*opus Dei et nostrum*). "It therefore behooves us to be very certain about the distinction between God's power and our own, God's work and our own, if we want to lead a godly life."[4] For Luther this relationship contains the "whole sum of things Christian" (*summa Christianarum rerum*) the key to godly living (*si volumus pie vivere*). Luther's general criticism of the medieval doctrines of grace and of the way in which the question of grace is dealt with in the practice of the church is that the distinction between God's work and human work has become blurred and that therefore their relationship cannot be adequately perceived. Because it ignores the distinction between *opus Dei* and *opus hominum*, the medieval church

---

3. Cf. not just for the similarities of title: Christoph Schwöbel, "The Triune God of Grace: The Doctrine of the Trinity in the Theology of the Reformers," in *The Christian Understanding of God Today*, ed. J. M. Byrne (Dublin: The Columba Press, 1993), 49–64.
4. LW 33:35.

does not have an adequate theology of grace, and therefore the Reformation is concerned with finding such an adequate theology. In his debate with Erasmus, this issue is focused in the question whether there is such a thing as a *liberum arbitrium* (free will) in human beings. This, however, is not only an anthropological question; it is at its core a theological question, the question whether God is the triune God of grace: "For if I am ignorant of what, how far, and how much I can and may do in relation to God, it will be equally uncertain and unknown to me, what, how far, and how much God can and may do in me, although it is God who works everything in everyone [1 Cor 12:6]. But when the works and power of God are unknown, I do not know God himself, and when God is unknown, I cannot worship, praise, thank, and serve God, since I do not know how much I ought to attribute to myself and how much to God."[5]

Grace Fulfills Human Destiny

The question of grace is by no means a purely theoretical issue. It concerns the practice of the Christian life. The abuses Luther saw in the ecclesial situation of his day—from the indulgence teaching to the confusion of spiritual and worldly power, from the mass as sacrifice to misplaced claims about papal authority—all point to decisive theological mistakes that are mirrored in distortions of the Christian life. The task of theology is therefore to redirect Christian practice to the truth of the gospel as it is witnessed in Scripture and Christian proclamation and authenticated by God the Spirit. The theology of grace must be reflected in a life enabled and restored by the promise of God's grace. It is therefore not surprising that Luther always places the question of grace in a personal experiential context. The question "How do I get a gracious God?" is often depicted as the stimulus that led to the formative insight of the Reformation. The question may not be understood in terms of an individualistic quest for grace. In the context of Luther's day, it referred to the ultimate eschatological judgment of God about each human person. The question of grace is therefore the question of the fulfillment of the human destiny: How can humans become what they are meant to be?[6] It is in this context that the distinction between God's work and the human work must be seen. Entirely in accordance with the nominalist traditions of the doctrine of grace, the question was for Luther what humans can and must contribute to the achievement of their destiny. What can we contribute, no doubt empowered by God's grace but nevertheless by actively pursuing the goal that grace has set before us, so that God will receive it graciously? The measure of God's grace is thereby

5. Ibid.
6. If we see the connection between the question of God's grace and the fulfillment of the human destiny, the connections between the doctrine of justification and the Eastern understanding of *theosis* should not come as a surprise.

defined by the quality of the human contribution toward the realization of the human destiny. The question of grace becomes the question of justice, following the logic of deed and consequence.

In the preface to volume one of his Latin works, Luther gives a vivid description of how the question of divine justice drove him to despair, even into the hatred of God, as long as he perceived it as the question of the right human work.[7] The gates of paradise, however, opened when Luther discovered in the constant engagement with Paul's understanding of *diakaiosyne* that justice is not the justice by which humans actively fulfill the divine commandment, i.e., actively contribute to the achievement of their destiny. It is the justice that is actively brought about by God in Christ through the Spirit and can only be passively received by humans. God's grace is not about God's gracefully receiving human works and acknowledging them as merits; it is about God's giving. And it is not about relative and conditional giving, relative to the worthiness and the merit of the recipient, but its character is absolute and unconditional giving. For Luther, this discovery is borne out by the witness of Scripture: the work of God means what God effects in us; the power of God means how God empowers us; wisdom of God means how God makes us wise.[8] The notion of justice suddenly makes sense if it is interpreted from the discovery that God's grace is communicative grace. It is through the gift of God's grace that the human destiny is fulfilled.

The Triune God's Self-Giving

But what does God give? As long as God gives *something*, this something could then be interpreted as an endowment that humans receive and then employ as a support for their own work. Luther discovered step by step that the notion of grace must be understood in terms of God's triune self-giving and apply to all God's acts from creation to redemption or reconciliation to sanctification.[9] In the "Confession concerning Christ's Supper" of 1528, Luther gives a description of this divine self-giving, which later forms the backbone of the exposition of the creed in the Large Catechism. After the exposition of the Apostles' Creed we read:

> These are the three persons and one God, who has given himself to us wholly and completely, with all that he is and has. The Father gives himself to us, with heaven and earth and all the creatures, in order that they may serve us and benefit us. But this gift has become obscured and useless through Adam's fall. Therefore the Son subsequently gave himself and

7. WA 54:179–87.
8. ". . . ut opus Dei, id est, quod operatur in nobis Deus, virtus Dei, qua nos potentes facit, sapientia Dei, qua nos sapientes facit, fortitudo Dei, salus Dei, gloria Dei," WA 54:186, 11–13.
9. Cf. Simo Peura, "Das Sich-Geben Gottes," in *Luther und die trinitarische Tradition*, ed. J. Heubach (Erlangen: Martin Luther Verlag, 1994), 131–46.

bestowed all his works, sufferings, wisdom, and righteousness, and has reconciled us to the Father, in order that restored to life and righteousness, we
might also know and have the Father and his gifts.

But because this grace would benefit no one if it remained so profoundly hidden and could not come to us, the Holy Spirit comes and gives
himself to us also, wholly and completely. He teaches us to understand this
deed of Christ, which has been manifested to us, helps us receive and preserve it, use it to our advantage and impart it to others, increase and extend
it. He does this both inwardly and outwardly—inwardly by means of faith
and other spiritual gifts, outwardly through the gospel, baptism and
through the sacrament of the altar, through which as through three means
or methods he comes to us and inculcates the sufferings of Christ for the
benefit of our salvation.[10]

There are a number of points to note here:
1. If grace is to be understood as God's self-giving, it cannot be
restricted to one particular stage of the story of the relationship between
God and his creation. Grace defines the structure of the whole history of salvation. This structure is Trinitarian in character. All God's works *ad extra*,
are indivisible, but they nevertheless show a Trinitarian differentiation
whereby each person contributes personally and specifically to every divine
work in indivisible communion with the others. Grace characterizes in this
way both each chapter of the divine-human drama and the whole story.

God's creation, the self-giving of the Father, is characterized by its gratuity, which is motivated only by the kind of being that God is in the community of the three persons. Therefore, creation is not a given but a gift.[11]
The Fall of Adam and Eve consists in not accepting the gift as gift but in
treating it as a given that is somehow at their disposal. Treating creation and
most importantly our own createdness as a given that is at our disposal
obscures the giver in the gifts of creation.

By healing the broken relationship between the Triune Creator and his
sinful creatures, the grace of redemption restores the grace of creation for
God's redeemed creatures. In Christ we can recognize God as the loving and
gracious Father. Reconciliation with God is the gift of Christ's gracious self-
giving. Wherever Luther explains this point, he follows the two axioms of
patristic soteriology. The first axiom, hammered out in the debates with the
Arians, is this: Only God can save. Therefore Christ must be fully God in
order to save us. The second axiom, hotly debated with Appollinarius,
Eutyches, and others of that ilk, is expressed in Gregory Nazianzen's phrase,
"The unassumed is the unhealed."[12] In order to save us, Christ must be truly

10. LW 37:366.
11. On this particular aspect, see Christoph Schwöbel, "God, Creation and the Christian
Community: The Dogmatic Bases of a Christian Ethic of Createdness," in *The Doctrine of
Creation*, ed. Colin E. Gunton (Edinburgh: T & T Clark, 1997), 149–76.

human. In Christ the unity of deity and humanity in the unity of his person is such that he can truly take our place and suffer our fate and through this communicate his grace not from without as *Deus ex machina* but from within human history. The self-giving of Christ is developed in Luther in such a way that he asks, What kind of person is the incarnate Son so that the miraculous exchange can become real? The answer is the doctrine of the *communicatio idiomatum* (communication of attributes).

The grace of sanctification is the way God's self-giving in the Spirit transforms the human heart by illumining it with the truth of the gospel so that the Spirit in giving himself gives God's grace as the truth of the message of grace. In this process the transcendence of the Spirit is preserved. The Spirit encounters us contingently in the freedom of his person from without, but in such a way that he transforms us from within. In our passage from the Confession of 1528, Luther explains that by referring to what the Spirit does externally as the gospel, Baptism, and the Lord's Supper. God's grace as the truth of the message of the gospel in which Christ gives himself to us encounters us in the word of the gospel and in the signs of the sacraments. What we encounter externally is "interiorized" by the Spirit and becomes the innermost reality in our hearts. If we consider this carefully, the distinction between created and uncreated grace becomes redundant. If grace is truly God's self-giving, it is always uncreated, God's creative grace; but the way in which God engages creation in the self-giving of the Son and the Spirit takes the very materiality of created existence into the act of divine self-giving. Furthermore, the whole system of stages, steps, or grades in the process of the application of grace becomes redundant. If the Father, the Son, and the Spirit give truly themselves, they cannot give more or less; they give themselves completely and totally. The system of the stages of graces is replaced by the Trinitarian logic of divine self-giving.

2. God's self-giving has a particular direction. For he has created us so that he might redeem and sanctify us, says the Large Catechism. This direction is inherent in God's triune action from the beginning. The creation is already an expression of God's will to be in communion with his creation. This original will, which is anchored in God's triune being, the will to be in communion with his creation is actualized in the self-giving of the Son and the Spirit. The dynamic of God's Trinitarian work is completed in the Spirit. The self-giving of the Spirit is the eschatological fulfillment of the protological decision of God to be in communion with his creation, which is actualized through the reconciling self-giving of the Son. And so, in achieving its goal, God's will corresponds to his being. We can recognize this unity of God's Trinitarian self-giving only in the Spirit through the Son. The Large Catechism carefully explains that in the order of knowing, following the *ratio cognoscendi* (manner of knowing), we always start with the work of

---

12. Gregory of Nazianzen, *Epistulae*, CI.

the Spirit, who enables us to see Christ, the Son, as the mirror of God's heart in whom we recognize God not as a terrible judge but as a loving Father. This discloses the *ratio essendi* (manner of being), or rather, the *ratio agendi* (manner of proceding) to us. We can see that God's Trinitarian action is graceful in that from the beginning it aims at establishing communion between the Creator and his creatures.

If we understand this logic of God's Trinitarian self-giving, it becomes clear that we do not need to explain it in terms of the relationship of nature and grace. The term *nature* distracts from the insight that creation is from the start a gracious act of God. There is no ungraced nature. What the distinction between nature and grace attempts to conceptualize is the relationship between the triune work of creation and the triune work of reconciliation and sanctification. God's reconciling and sanctifying grace restores the insight into God's creative grace. The real difference is not between grace and nature, but between grace and sin where sin is understood as denying that everything that is, is because of God's grace.

3. God's gracious self-giving is directed toward establishing, restoring, and fulfilling communion with creation. God gives himself in order to bring us to himself.[13] The aim of giving is the communion between the triune giver and those who are by his giving brought into communion with him. Luther can in this way combine the question of how the individual person can receive God's grace (the question that is answered in the penitential system of the medieval church) with the overall question of how God achieves his will of grace for the whole creation. It is precisely through bringing persons by his triune self-giving into communion with their creator that the economy of salvation reaches its goal. There is only one process of salvation; the personal and the economic aspects are identical in that the objective of the whole divine economy is achieved through bringing persons into communion with the Triune God. Therefore, accepting God's grace through the triune self-giving of God and becoming a member of the communion of faith, the church, is one and the same act.

Sola Gratia and *Sola Fide*

What is the result of God's triune self-giving? It is the constitution of Christian faith. We can see here how the *sola gratia* and the *sola fide* are intrinsically linked together. The *sola gratia* is intended to express that we are saved through God's Trinitarian self-giving alone. The grace of the Triune God has no other presupposition than the being and will of God himself. In this sense, it is truly unconditional. Its only condition is God's triune life

---

13. The aim of the divine self-giving is that God brings us to himself. In the German text of the Large Catechism, there is a strict correspondence between God's *Sich-Geben* (giving of himself) and *Zu-sich-Bringen* (bringing to himself).

itself. The exclusive character of God's grace is at the same time the ground for its inclusive character. Precisely because grace is grounded in God's self-giving alone, it can include all those who as sinners can contribute nothing to their salvation. The self-giving of the Triune God is the ground and subject matter of faith. In Luther's understanding, faith is a total description of human existence. Luther's famous definition that human being means being justified by faith in the *Disputatio de homine* makes precisely this point.[14] We are what we believe in, or, rather, who we are is determined by whom we believe in. The faith that is constituted by being justified by God through Christ in the Spirit is the unconditional trust in God the Father, the Son, and the Spirit as God gives himself in creation, reconciliation, and sanctification. Therefore faith cannot be and need not be supplemented by works. And therefore faith is not a stage, which must be transcended in order to receive its final form in love. According to Luther it is not *fides caritate formata* (faith formed by love). Quite the contrary, love must be understood as the fruit of faith: it is *caritas fide formata* (love formed by faith). The constitution of faith is completely passive; it is the process of being illumined by the truth of the gospel of Christ as the way in which God himself brings us into communion with himself. But this passive constitution of faith is at the same time the reconstitution of the human capacity to act in accordance with the will of God. This is why for Luther in the exposition of the Catechism the Ten Commandments demonstrate what we are called to do but cannot do by our own means. The law demonstrates the soteriological powerlessness of human beings. It is faith interpreted in the logic of God's Trinitarian logic of self-giving that reconstitutes the human capacity to act, to do freely and spontaneously what God wills.

The Church's Witness to Grace

To create such faith as the unconditional trust in God's self-giving grace, God employs the human acts of witnessing to the truth of the gospel of Christ in the preaching of the gospel and in the celebration of the sacraments. These human acts are employed by the Triune God as instruments of bringing sinners into communion with God by authenticating the message of Christian witness for them and thus create faith. As Luther said in the "Confessions concerning the Lord's Supper," the gospel, Baptism, and the Sacrament of the Altar are the "means or methods [through which] he comes to us and inculcates the sufferings of Christ for the benefit of our salvation." However, God's self-giving, although it employs human means or methods, remains God's act. Because grace is God's self-giving, it cannot be somehow transferred to a human tradition or institution that is empowered

---

14. *"Disputatio de homine"* 1536, WA 39/1:176, 33–35: "Paulus . . . breviter hominis definitionem colligit, dicens hominem iustificari fide."

to administer or dispense the grace of God. The Trinitarian understanding of God's grace as triune self-giving underlines the distinction and relationship between God's work and the work of humans. All the church can do and must do is witness to and proclaim the gospel of God's self-giving grace, trusting in the promise that the Triune God will employ these human acts as methods and means of his self-giving in the sovereign freedom of his grace—*ubi et quando visum est Deo* (where and when it pleases God).

The Reformation Contribution

If this view of grace as God's Trinitarian self-giving is the decisive insight of Reformation theology, then it is this message that the churches of the Reformation have to offer in ecumenical conversations as their particular gift. The future of Lutheran theology will depend—so it seems—on its faithfulness to the liberating insight of the gospel of God's grace.

In conclusion, I point to some of the issues of the life of the church in society where the original insight of the Reformation seems to have special relevance.

First, if faith is grounded in God's Trinitarian self-presentation in which God the Spirit authenticates the gospel of Christ as the truth about the relationship of God the Father to his creation, then the authority in the church is, strictly speaking, the authority of God's grace and truth. It is an authority—an authority *in* the church as long it is an authority *for* the church, even over against the church in the freedom of God's grace. God's grace constitutes faith and can only be received in faith. Therefore faith, the faith that is constituted in God's Trinitarian self-giving, is the seat of authority in the church, "because," as Luther say in *On the Bondage of the Will*, "it is in the nature of faith not to be deceived."[15] This infallibility of faith is the certainty that is granted when God the Spirit authenticates the truth of the gospel of Christ. It is infallible in that it is grounded in God's self-giving, in the self-giving of the God who *is* grace and truth, and who alone can bind the human conscience. The authority of God's grace and truth is absolutely binding, and it completely relativizes the claims of any other authority to be infallible. The famous scene of Luther at the Diet of Worms in 1521 is thus viewed from a theological perspective as not an extraordinary heroic scene but the ordinary situation of all Christians who are free because they are captives to the Word of God.

Second, if God's grace—God's triune self-giving that employs human acts of proclaiming the gospel in Word and sacrament—is the foundation of the church, which believes itself to be a creature of the divine Word, it is not surprising that this is expressed in the structures of church life. According to the Lutheran Reformation the church is at the same time *eccentric*,

15. LW 33:88. WA 18:652, 7: ". . . fidei est, non falli."

because it's one foundation is God's triune self-giving, and *polycentric*, because God's triune self-giving creates communities of worship, witness, and service that are the church. With regard to its empirical organization, the church does not have to be monocentric, because the principle of its unity is God's self-giving, which is witness in Word and sacrament.

This has, third, striking consequences for how we perceive the task of ecumenism. According to the Lutheran Reformation, the constitution of faith, the constitution of the church, and the constitution of communion between the churches are all rooted in God's triune grace, all three—faith, the church and communion between the churches—owe their existence to one and the same triune act. The ecumene has its foundation in God's work; it is to be seen as *opus sanctae Trinitatis* (work of the holy Trinity). Ecumenism, as a calling of Christian churches, as *opus hominum fidelium* (work of human faithfulness), is therefore the process in which the churches grant one another communion by acknowledging that the grace of the Triune God is the foundation of their being.[16]

Fourth, the implications of the Reformation view of grace as God's self-giving go far beyond the confines of ecclesial concerns like authority, church structure, and ecumenism. Perhaps the most striking implication is the redefinition of what it means to be human. The widespread creed that humans are what they are and who they are in virtue of what they do is decisively challenged in the Reformation. Luther's thesis *hominem iustificari fidem* (man is justified by faith), in his view nothing more than a reformulation of Paul's interpretation of the gospel, maintains that human beings are not defined by their capacities or incapacities. They are not defined by what they do and can do, but by what God gives to them. Therefore the dignity of human persons is not dependent on their possession of certain qualities that specify their capacities. Because of that, the dignity of the human extends to the very first moments and to the last moments of our life on earth, when our capacities may not yet or no longer be in evidence, and for all moments in between. What makes humans human is their absolute dependence on God's gift of grace, on God giving himself. Because human dignity is grounded in God's grace, it is inviolable. Violating human dignity means denying God's grace. Human rights are inalienable because they are essentially divine gifts of grace. Denying human rights means denying that God is a God of grace.

Fifth, the Reformation understanding of God's grace will only be plau-

---

16. For two different theological interpretations of ecumenism, its bases and tasks, cf. R. W. Jenson, *Unbaptized God: The Basic Flaw in Ecumenical Theology* (Minneapolis: Fortress, 1992), and Christoph Schwöbel, "Gottes Ökumene: Über das Verhältnis von Kirchengemeinschaft und Gottesverständnis," in *Befreiende Wahrheit: Festschrift für Eilert Herms zum 60. Geburtstag*, ed. W. Härle, M. Heesch, and R. Preul (Marburg: Universitätsbuchhandlung und Verlag Braun-Elwert, 2000), 449–66.

sible if the churches and theologies of the Lutheran tradition can avoid the fateful alternative between a freedom without grace and a grace without freedom. If God's grace is understood as God's Trinitarian self-giving, which God freely gives so that we may be liberated for freedom through Christ (Gal 5:1), we might be able to retain and regain the insight that the freedom of God's grace is, for humans, the grace of freedom. If Lutheran theology can remain faithful to the promise of the gospel, it should not have to worry about its future.

CHAPTER 3

The Grace of God and the Equality of Human Persons

Monica Melanchthon

G race" expresses the human being's all-pervading conviction that he or she is the object of a divine benevolence that no philosophy can easily define, and this conviction itself has led to diverse theologies of union with God.[1] For all its beauty and potential for being a source of strength, the teaching on grace and the manner of its operation could become alienating if not properly handled.

My point of departure for this chapter is the context of poverty and exclusion, particularly poverty and exclusion caused by caste and gender. It has often been acknowledged that all of us are victims and perpetrators— sometimes simultaneously—in the culture of our present-day society, which produces persons who are excluded and barred from various arenas of life: economic, political, social, cultural, and religious. The excluded include those who are poor, women, Dalits, indigenous peoples, people suffering from HIV/AIDS, and all those whose human worth is negated and annulled by society's logic of separation and alienation. The law of exclusion and seg- regation that governs our world does not provide for the functioning of grace. Those who are excluded—the outcasts—are considered expendable and even disposable.[2]

In this context, the justice of God and the equality of human persons realized by the doctrine of divine grace is a sign of hope. This message speaks to us of the viability of a reasoning that is guided by the power of faith and grace, in opposition to the law that oppresses, excludes, and seg- regates. Tamez very astutely asks:

> Is it possible to adopt a logic of grace and not of merits? If we believe that
> God raised from the dead the innocent crucified one—the excluded person
> par excellence—we might be able to trust in a new logic of life in which the

1. A previous version of this essay was published in *Dialog* 42/1 (Spring 2003), 8–19.
2. Elza Tamez, in her preface to the North American edition of *The Amnesty of Grace: Justification by Faith from a Latin American Perspective*, trans. Sharon H. Ringe (Nashville: Abingdon, 1993).

law is not imposed from above, in opposition to the worthy life of human beings. Instead, by this new logic we recognize them as persons who have been renewed and rendered worthy through the justice and grace of God, so that they can choose their own history, guided by the power of the Spirit.[3]

The context therefore demands rather urgently the need for a new interpretation of themes or doctrines such as divine grace that respond to this reality of oppression and inequality caused by structural sin. Grace is the core concept of Reformation theology. Grace is also partially visible in the fabric of India's culture. The former can make the latter even more visible.

The theme of divine grace appeared on the Indian theological agenda when efforts were being made to articulate a comprehensive theology relevant to the Indian context.[4] Many have recognized and acknowledged that this idea is actually found under various forms in many religious traditions, even in those deriving from such apparently anti-grace standpoints as Yoga, Vedanta, or Theravada Buddhism (with their emphasis on human effort in religious experience). The attempts to articulate an Indian theology of grace have only just begun, and the following problems have been identified.[5] Hermeneutical problems are the tension between the affirmation of difference, the awareness of convergence, and the need for a cross-cultural interpretation. There is also a dialectical problem, the tension between grace as a quality of life and grace as an event of judgment. The former is often foremost in any discussions on grace, and there is a need for a more serious consideration of the latter, particularly in the context of the Indian festivals, which are mostly celebrations of God's victories over evil. It is perhaps in these terms and context that the dimension of hope in the concept of grace is generally perceived in our culture; a greater awareness of this dimension is needed to interpret more authentically the present-day stirrings among the poor and the oppressed of our villages.

Grace and determinism, grace and *karma*, grace and freedom, are classical problems of the theology of grace. We are aware of the area of mystery in which grace moves and of the limitations of all theological formulations and starting points. There is the problem of the relation of the cosmic order to the freedom of God affirmed by the theology of grace. In the light of the Christian understanding of creation, we might at times be tempted to minimize the tension between the two concepts. But then we must stress also a

3. Ibid.
4. Kulandran Sabapathy, *Grace: A Comparative Study of the Doctrine in Christianity and Hinduism* (London: Lutterworth, 1964); C. M. Vadakkekara, O.S.B., ed., *Divine Grace and Human Response* (Bangalore: Asirvatham Benedictine Monastery, 1981); Joseph Jaswant Raj, *Grace in the Saiva Siddhantham and in St. Paul* (Madras: South Indian Salesian Society, 1989).
5. C. M. Vadakkekara, O.S.B. ed., "Introduction," *Divine Grace and Human Response*, 3–4.

certain continuity between creation and grace and a certain immanence of one in the other. Only then can the cosmic order be seen not as a negation but rather as a symbol of grace. This calls for a more wholistic approach to the relation of God and the world and to a change in our modern "innate" tendency to think of the world and the "natural order" as a mechanical, automatic giant machine, almost unrelated to the ineffable mystery that is at the heart of all existence.

For the Christian, grace is anchored in the person of Jesus Christ, the Word of God, "full of grace and truth," in whom the grace of God has appeared, allowing us a "taste" of the salvation that has been the longing of humankind. This Christocentricity of grace finds itself in tension with its universality, also stressed both by the Christian and the Indian conscious-ness. This is indeed the crucial question of all Asian theology.

A particular question governs my inquiry into the doctrine: What are the implications of God's grace for the equality of humanity in every realm of truth and life? Or, rather, how does the experience of the oppressed impact upon current understandings of divine grace?

The Grace of God

Any attempt to define grace is obviously difficult and would probably call for an account of the entire Christian religion, because all other doctrines of Christianity also directly or otherwise attest to the gracious activity of God.

The Hebrew Concept of Grace

For the Hebrew, God's graciousness toward humanity was not an abstract concept nor even a quality inherent in God but was understood more con-cretely as the manifestation in history of God's condescending goodness and God's gracious love for humanity. The two attributes of the breath of life and the image of God guarantee human beings a privileged place among living things and call them to the grace of full communion with God. In the calling to co-creatorship lies the gracious act of God and the definitive prophecy about the nature and vocation of human beings.[6] It confers on all people a worth or dignity that no person or system—whether political, economic, or social—can take away. This calling extends to all of humanity. This generous conferring of dignity and calling has its origin and basis in the free and unmerited love of God, which is at the root of all creative activity.[7]

The grace of God is more apparent in that God did not inflict death (in all its totality) on humankind as punishment for their disobedience, as was previously warned, but granted them to live on and have progeny. While the

---

6. Kenith A. David, *Sacrament and Struggle: Signs and Instruments of Grace from the Downtrodden*, WCC Mission Series (Geneva: World Council of Churches, 1994), 49.
7. John Macquarrie, *The Faith of the People of God* (London: SCM, 1972), 49.

creation account is a record of the struggle between the power of light and the power of darkness in the universe, it is no less a record of the struggle between the power of good and the power of evil in human society.

The biblical record portrays some of these struggles, beginning with the story of Adam and Eve and the forbidden fruit in the garden and Cain killing his brother Abel. In this way, the Yahwist writer sketches the gradual deterioration of humankind. There is an increase of sin parallel to the increase of human knowledge and skill. The more clever and adaptive the human being becomes, the more he or she turns against the Creator. The human being was set in the garden to live under the divine will in contented productivity, but by exceeding his/her productive limits, all of the human being's inventiveness is now corrupted.[8] This process of the "deterioration of the human situation," as Norman K. Gottwald puts it, continues in the books of the Old Testament, resulting in an ever-widening separation between the Creator God and human beings.[9]

In spite of this separation, the Creator God does not give up on God's people or on God's creation. The deterioration and separation are accompanied by the magnanimous rescue of God's people, as revealed particularly in the Exodus story, the election of the people of Israel, and the making of the covenant. Against Israel's deteriorating fidelity toward Yahweh, the prophets hold up God's faithful love that proposed new and gracious interventions in history to realize God's promise for Israel and humankind (cf. Isa 9:1-6; 11:1-9; 42:1-9; 65:17; Ezek 34; et al.).

The Concept of Grace in the New Testament

The reality of grace in the New Testament is permeated through and through by the reality of Christ, who was born in human flesh, who died a sacrificial death, and who lives on as the risen, glorious Lord. It has its source in God's infinitely gracious love for humankind (John 3:16-17). And the gift that God through God's self-giving has graciously intended and realized through Christ for humankind is that, in him and through him, human beings may become partakers of the divine nature (2 Pet 1:3-4).

For Paul this grace is the content of the central Christian experience. In Paul's own self-understanding, the revelation of Christ that was given him was a grace inasmuch as it was a gracious gesture of God's love when he least deserved it. Paul did feel himself to be a new creation of God's grace after his encounter with Jesus Christ (2 Cor 5:17). Having thus experienced his new state of being justified and reconciled with God through Christ, Paul came to realize that God was in Christ reconciling the world to Godself, not counting their trespasses against them. He would, moreover, get the inner

---

8. Norman K. Gottwald, *The Hebrew Bible: A Socio-Literary Introduction* (Philadelphia: Fortress, 1985), 332. Cf. also Gerhard von Rad, *Genesis: A Commentary*, Old Testament Library (Philadelphia: Westminster, 1961).

9. Norman K. Gottwald, *A Light to the Nations* (New York: Harper, 1959), 457.

conviction that God had entrusted him with the ministry of reconciliation (2 Cor 5:18-20), that he had been set apart to preach Christ to the Gentiles, and that he had been called by God through God's grace (Gal 1:15). His apostleship was a free gift of God and a grace that he in no way merited: "By the grace of God I am who I am" (1 Cor 15:10a).

Luther and Grace

Grace is the central doctrinal concern of the Lutheran Reformation. According to Martin Luther, grace "is never present in such a way that it is inactive, but it is a living, active, and operative Spirit."[10] Grace is God's continuing action upon us—"the continuous and perpetual operation or action through which we are grasped and moved by the Spirit of God."[11] Grace is not a "momentary operation" but "the continuation of a work that has been begun."[12] More specifically, grace is a divine work of "perpetual duration" all through our life on earth, whereby "we live continually under the remission of sins."[13] Therefore, although we are and continue to be sinners, not just partially but completely, and although nothing less than perfect righteousness is pleasing before God,[14] grace is effective within us. Although sin clings to us closely, wrote Luther,

> yet grace is sufficient to enable us to be counted entirely and completely righteous in God's sight because God's grace does not come in portions and pieces, separately, like so many gifts; rather it takes us up completely into its embrace for the sake of Christ our mediator and intercessor, and in order that the gifts may take root in us.[15]

Christ's perfect righteousness, fully ours by faith, is always "the basis, the cause, the source," of all righteousness instilled in us slowly but surely.[16] For Luther this doctrine had meant that grace came to faith in three basic modes: once for all, again and again, and more and more—in that order of significance, through Word and Sacrament.[17]

The image of "continuation and perpetual operation" espoused by Luther is important, because it implies that grace does not stand at the beginning of Christian faith alone but that it accompanies Christian faith in every moment of its career, giving it substance, nerve, and shape. From the

10. Martin Luther, LW 31:13.
11. LW 12: 377–78.
12. LW 12:377.
13. LW 34:164.
14. LW 27:86; 34:127.
15. LW 35:370, rev.
16. LW 31:298.
17. George Hunsinger, *Disruptive Grace: Studies in the Theology of Karl Barth* (Grand Rapids and Cambridge, U.K.: Eerdmans, 2000), 299.

above one can identify four aspects of grace: (1) Grace is the gratuitous favor shown by God the Creator through the Lord Jesus Christ. (2) Grace is the gift of a new and redeemed existence. (3) Grace is the favored relationship of humanity, which is adorned by God's gift of redeemed existence. (4) Grace is the response of humanity given to God in freedom and love and thanksgiving. The first three aspects are seen as constitutive of the Christian's transformation and as explicative of one's experience of possessing a divinized existence in Christ. The fourth aspect refers us to the way the Christian gives expression to the newness of existence. It is this fourth aspect that I would like us to pay special attention to, especially as it concerns the Reformation charism in the context of India.

I cannot emphasize enough the fact that while divine grace is something that can be heard, thought about, and contemplated on, its inner meaning can only be derived through experience. This is the case not only in terms of how grace operates in the divine but also how it empowers individuals and communities. Life and participation in Jesus Christ brings about social awareness, and this can mean real anguish. This new awareness brings about a sense of urgency that may seem "fanatic" to others who would confine social awareness to community assemblies. The greatest anguish is the yawning gap between one's insight into the world and sin gained and one's crucial generosity in response. For such insight brings with it imperatives to action that may involve crucial decisions. Graced with the Spirit of Christ and the spirit of the poor, one is empowered to transform anger and frustration into a never-fading struggle for action. The driving force for such action is the knowledge that one is not alone but with Christ and others in struggle. This is the grace that enables and calls upon people and bestows upon them the power to identify rampant forces of evil, sin, and tyranny and to denounce them. A theology of grace must therefore emphasize this liberating function of God in us, for grace makes us more capable of love: love of God *and* love of neighbor.

An Ancient Question: Is Grace for All?

In nontechnical language, the answer is this: The experience of divine grace is not intended for a few but for all. Despite temperament and environment, despite sin or disposition, the benefits of Christ, both for our world's sake and for our own, are meant to be everybody's. But we are free, as every person loved by another is still free personally to resist and finally even to refuse to respond actively to the love that is offered. If our experience of the grace of Christ is not strong, continuous, and rich, the fault is not in Christ but in us. Christian awareness begins with the conviction that divine grace and the human person have already been connected meaningfully and constructively by God's own action. There is something incongruous, therefore, about Christian theological discourse that questions the possibility of meaningfully relating grace and the equality of humanity. Whether human persons are equal because of the grace of God is not a question for the Christian, for he or she should know that all human persons are equal by the grace of God, which forms the milieu from which his or her own existence has emerged. The assertion that Christian discourse presupposes the equality of human persons made possible by the grace of God rests upon a certain understanding of what is constitutive for Christian life and belief, namely, that for the Christian one of the first facts of life and belief is the equality of human persons and the realization of that equality. There are several forms in which this primary datum of existence can be Christianly stated. One statement of it has been the affirmation that God made human life in the image of God (Gen 1:26-27).

Grace for All in Creation

The affirmation that God is Creator of heaven and earth establishes a rationale for acknowledging the intrinsic value of all things and for urging that every creation and the whole creation be treated with respect. It is the distinctive character of humanity, however, to be created in the image of God—although the mark of God's image in our humanity is a long-standing theological argument.[18]

The declaration is a polemic against idols,[19] but it is also against limiting the privilege of the image of God to certain people or individuals or to a certain gender, class, caste, or race. It is all humanity, and every individual—not just the king or the upper castes or men—whom God has made in God's image. The verse is a reaction against the ideology of the king or the Pharaoh as "the image of God." It is against the arrogation by a few of the privilege of humanity as such.[20] The whole of humanity is created in the image of God.

The biblical text uses to the plural in order to leave no doubt about this: "God created them." The duality of the sexes implies the plurality of the

18. Although *image* is the more important word here, we also need to understand that the word *likeness* is also used in the verse. What is God like? Or should the question be, What is the human like? The text is not saying that God is like a human being but rather that the human being is in a relation of likeness to God. Though the word *image* is more important and ambiguous, its meaning is defined and limited by the word *likeness*. The meaning of *image* therefore lies in the word *likeness*. Humanity is to be a created representation of the Creator here on earth, to be the image of divine glory.

19. H. Blocher, *In the Beginning: The Opening Chapters of Genesis*, trans. D. G. Preston (Leicester, England and Downers Grove, Ill.: InterVarsity, 1984), 86; Cf. also James Barr, "The Image of God in the Book of Genesis: A Study of Terminology," *The John Rylands Library* 5 (1968), 11–26.

20. Phyllis Bird, "'Male and Female He Created Them': Gen. 1:2b in the Context of the Priestly Account of Creation," *Harvard Theological Review* 74/2 (1981): 159. Contra Walter Brueggemann, *Genesis*, Interpretation (Atlanta: John Knox, 1982).

persons. Being immediately associated with the proclamation of creation as the image of God, the phrase undoubtedly intends to teach also that both man and woman participate equally in the privilege.[21] The Hebrew word *'adam* therefore refers to the human species as a whole: "So God created humankind in God's image." The image refers to the undifferentiated collectivity of humankind: "In the image of God, God created them." Gender, on the other hand, is referred to individuals of the species: "male and female God created them." The carefully guarded language of Gen 1:26-27 does not allow the masculine to define the image. If the divine image characterizes and defines the whole of the species of humanity, it cannot be denied to any individual of the species. To be human is to be made in the image of God. Both female and male are therefore made equally in the image of God. There is therefore no basis for discrimination or differentiation. This declaration in Genesis is indisputable and permanent. It is essential to human identity. Distinction on the basis of gender, professions, caste, language, race, etc., is excluded in this declaration. Where such distinctions are used to deny individuals or groups the full essence and nature and status of humanity created in the image of God, they contradict the word of creation.[22] The feminist insistence that the woman images the divine as much as the man and that she is equally important to the understanding of humanity as representative of God on earth and in the world is biblically right and sound.

The doctrine of creation has given rise to the affirmation of our common humanity and, eventually, also to the notion of essential and universal human rights. Within the doctrine of creation, one can discern the contours of basic human rights. The doctrine of creation provides grounds for respect for life and justice and the right for all human beings to claim them. This means the right of equality of access to basic life needs as well as political, economic, and cultural goods for all people. This view of creation wrought by a gracious God, with its emphasis on the sociality of human nature, provides the basis on which to formulate relationships between human persons.[23]

As Walter Altmann writes, it is not difficult to make linkages between grace and the indisputable value of every human being:

> Grace radicalizes respect for human dignity, in that it attributes this dignity to the free will of God and not to nature. Over against the multiplicity of ideological and social claims such as production and property, culture

21. H. Eilberg-Scwartz, "The Problem of the Body for the People of the Book," in *Reading the Bibles, Writing Bodies: Identity and the Book*, ed. T. K. Beal and D. M. Gunn (London and New York: Routledge, 1997), 34–55.

22. Bird, "'Male and Female He Created Them,'" 159.

23. Lois Gehr Livezey, "A Christian Vision for Sexual Justice: Theological and Ethical Reflections on Violence against Women," *In God's Image* 10 (1991): 27.

and property, culture and power, the valuing of the human being for what he or she is, even and especially in deficiency, weakness, impotence, and marginality, returns us to the path that leads to Jesus of Nazareth, born in a stable and killed on a cross.[24]

The liberation and grace wrought in the saving presence, death, and resurrection of Jesus Christ is therefore available to all, for in Christ there is neither Greek nor Jew, slave nor free, male nor female.

The Victims of Inequality and Oppression: The Case of India

Broadly defined, *oppression* "refers to the dynamic forces, both personal and social, that diminish or deny the flourishing"[25] of people. The reality of mass poverty, oppression, marginalization, exploitation, powerlessness, and discrimination of certain sections of society reveals the structural and systemic nature of injustice in India. The collective and cumulative nature of their oppression enables us to see that oppression and injustice experienced by these groups is not solely the product of individuals' malicious intent to "oppress." Instead, it is the product of larger institutional and social forces. Dalits and backward castes, women, indigenous people, children, minorities, victims of HIV/AIDS—all continue to be the permanent victims of these unjust structures.

Dalits

The Indian constitution abolished untouchability. And yet entire villages in several states remain segregated by caste, while in urban areas Dalits still suffer discrimination, harassment, and victimization. In the rural areas, Dalits are denied entrance into the higher-caste sections of villages and temples, and even water or tea from cups and glasses used by the upper castes. In urban centers, caste operates in more subtle ways in recruitment for jobs, promotions, and career advancements. The Dalits, discriminated against by and from birth, are the poorest of the poor and remain so. They are comprised mainly of the unorganized working classes, bonded laborers, sanitation workers, unemployed or underemployed, slum and pavement dwellers, the homeless, etc. They are the most malnourished, illiterate or less educated, and sick. They are brutalized and killed when they demand fair treatment. They are denied justice, even legal justice, protection, assistance, education, health care, and the possibility of mobility. For centuries they have been victims of aggression, rape, assault, scorn, and rejection. Threats to survival, a stigmatized identity, and utter powerlessness are the main features of Dalit

24. Walter Altmann, *Luther and Liberation: A Latin American Perspective*, trans. Mary M. Solberg (Minneapolis: Fortress Press, 1992), 41.
25. Serene Jones, *Feminist Theory and Christian Theology: Cartographies of Grace* (Minneapolis: Fortress, 2000), 71.

predicament.[26] The backward castes too share the same, but in varying degrees. This reveals that caste is one of the key social mechanisms through which this sort of social and economic injustice is maintained and sustained in India. The present market economy under the pretext of economic growth works to the advantage of the custodians of these unjust structures, namely, the affluent upper castes—those who have power and wealth. Furthermore, we are today witnessing the steady rise of defenders of the status quo and of fundamentalist forces in the form of Hindu majoritarianism equipped with the ideology of Hindutva, who are working against the upward mobility of Dalits and their attempts to reclaim and regain identity and dignity. These forces are working toward arresting the growing solidarity among the marginalized sections of the Indian society by stoking communal passions.[27] The predicament of the Christian Dalits isn't any better. Their experience of rejection, discrimination, and marginalization exposes the shallow commitment of the church to their struggle for justice.

Women

The experience of women across the world—irrespective of race, caste, or class—is one of oppression, subjugation, marginalization, powerlessness, and exploitation. Despite efforts and attempts toward better participation, violence against women and other blatant forms of discrimination and exploitation go unquestioned.[28] The denial of equal wages, ownership of resources, and participation in political life—to mention only a few examples—continue to victimize women economically. This is made possible by support from traditional patriarchal cultures. Of these, the Dalit women are the worst victims because of the interaction of caste, class, and gender.[29] In the effort to maintain order and cultural identity, patriarchy deprives women of their humanhood and dignity both within society and the church. Patriarchy is a mechanism that derives its strength through the enforcement of exclusion while nurturing a culture of domination.[30]

Indigenous People

The pre-invasion and pre-colonial societies that developed in their territories consider themselves as distinct from other sections of the societies now prevailing in those territories, or parts of them. They today form the present

26. Ambrose Pinto, ed., *Dalits Assertion for Identity* (New Delhi: Indian Social Institute, 1999).
27. Monica J. Melanchthon, "Persecution of Christians," *Dialog* 41/2 (Summer 2002): 103–13.
28. Yayori Matsui, "Violence against Women in Development, Militarism and Culture," *In God's Image* 10 (1991): 22–28.
29. Annie Namala "Dalit Women: The Conflict and the Dilemma," unpublished paper presented at a workshop on Dalit Women at the Anveshi Research Center for Women's Studies (1995).
30. Arlene D'Mello, "Image, Status and Reality of Asian Women in Asia and in Australia: An Insight into Their Personhood," *In God's Image* 8 (1989): 19–22.

nondominant sections of society and are determined to preserve, develop and transmit to future generations their ancestral territories and their ethnic identity as the basis of their continued existence in accordance with their own cultural patterns, social institutions and legal systems.[31] Identified also as tribal communities or *Adivasis (adi* = original, *vasi* = inhabitant), about 427 of these groups have been listed in the scheduled tribes list of the Indian constitution. The Mundas, the Oraons, the Bhils, the Todas, and the many tribes in the northeast of India (the Nagas, Mizos, and others), are a few. These indigenous groups have enjoyed a deeply spiritual relationship with their lands, which is basic to their beliefs, customs, culture and very existence. But the ruthless appropriation and exploitation of their territories and renewable and nonrenewable resources have not only forcibly displaced and compelled them to migrate, rendering them homeless in the cities, but have also placed some of these groups on the brink of extinction. They vary in socioeconomic conditions but share problems such as poverty, inadequate education, socioeconomic isolation and the continuing exploitation by nontribal groups.

The monopoly of the socially dominant groups over the political and economic power structures and mechanisms has resulted in the turning of democratic institutions into instruments for self-aggrandizement for the socially and economically privileged. More than fifty years of planned development has resulted in the affluence of only a few sections of Indian society. The models of development adopted have proved to be unsustainable, with disastrous consequences for the environment and the many poor and indigenous people whose lives depend on it. The destruction of the environment, particularly the land, which traditionally belonged to the indigenous people, has resulted in impoverishment, misery, displacement, exploitation, and erosion of their culture and identity, and it threatens their very survival as a people. Treated as liabilities, they experience further fragmentation, exclusion, and possible extinction.[32]

Are These People Graced?

When reality is perceived as a division of people into different kinds of dominant and subordinate, superior and inferior groups, one form of oppression cannot be overcome unless all forms of oppression are overcome. Such a reality also gives one the impression that some are probably more graced than others. The oppressed and those rendered unequal sometimes feel that the dominant have taken even their share of divine grace. In the context of

---

31. Albert Minz, "Dalits and Tribals: A Search for Solidarity," in *Frontiers of Dalit Theology*, ed. V. Devasahayam (Chennai: Gurukul, 1997),133.
32. Deenabandhu Manchala, "Mission as Struggle for Justice: From the Perspective of Those who are Denied Justice," in *Quest for Justice: Perspectives on Mission and Unity*, ed. George Matthew Nalunnakkal and Abraham P. Athyal (New Delhi/Nagpur/Chennai: ISPCK/NCCI/Gurukul, 2000), 45.

their experience of oppression, what does the grace of God mean? What are the implications of divine grace for those who have been rendered unequal and dispensable, unclean and polluting, marginalized, subjugated, exploited, and dehumanized by the dominant? If grace is for the salvation of all, if grace, after all, is given to the lowly, the poor, and the weak, if the gospel of grace is an inclusive one, why are they excluded? Grace seems to be channeled through social and ecclesiastical laws, through the institutions of society and an all-male church. Power is therefore the issue. The proximity of power dilutes the thrust of the gospel. Power diminishes the clarity of an ideology of equality. Who can change the oppressive situation of these communities mentioned above? Dominant groups and privileged groups are notoriously bad at justice making, because justice requires a right reading of the social reality, of social power, and of social goods. Everyone's interests are served by the special privileges he or she holds.[33]

Hence, it seems that, in the final analysis, it is they themselves—the Dalits, the women, and the indigenous peoples who need to work out their liberation.[34] The poor are beginning to realize that there is no place for them in the system, and they have arrived at two simultaneous judgments. First, there is no justice in the system, and there is little point in continuing to hope that something will be delivered by the dominant, the rich, and the powerful. Second, this does not mean the end of the world, and they should work out their path to salvation; they know how to, and they are convinced that the rich and the powerful do not. While the poor do feel exploited and excluded, they are in the process of seeking their own ethical domains, which are providing them with their own "models" for moving along.[35] It is timely and essential to affirm the agency and personal responsibility of the victims of oppression as well as the perpetrators. Affirming such responsibility on the part of the oppressed becomes a way of breaking a cycle of oppression from one generation to another.

Sin: Grace Rejected and Ignored

Discussions on sin have often focused on theodicy and the relationship between our responsibility for sin and the larger reality of oppression and evil in the world.[36] How do we define sin? How do we discern it? Sin is collusion with evil, defined as the systemic structures or patterns of oppression in economic, political, and social life, and where sin is defined as "those free, discrete acts of responsible individuals that create or reinforce these structures of oppression."[37] Sin is, above all, sin against the Spirit and the

---

33. Reinhold Niebuhr, *Moral Man and Immoral Society* (London: SCM, 1963), 117.

34. Manchala, "Mission as Struggle for Justice, 45.

35. Monica J. Melanchthon, "Poverty and Plenty: Bridging the Gap: Some Insights from the Perspective of the Poor in India," *NCCI Review* 121/9 (October 2001): 763–81.

36. Serene Jones, *Feminist Theory and Christian Theology*, 95.

37. Mary Potter Engel, "Evil, Sin and the Violation of the Vulnerable," in *Lift Every Voice:*

structural sin embedded in a corrupt society and church. The unforgivable sin is the use of coercive power exercised through ecclesiastical and societal institutions to repress and to quench the Spirit—and the worst affected are the women, Dalits, and other oppressed minorities.

In Dalit theological discussions of sin, we are often reminded that it is a sin to oppress others, but it also a sin to allow oneself to be oppressed. Hence the oppressed contend that it is not only the oppressor who is sinful but the victim too. While the sin of the oppressor is the oppression of the poor, the sin of the oppressed is identified as "the failure to take responsibility for self-actualization."[38] The experience of the oppressed is the interrelation between cultural expectations and their internalization. It is an experience that in the course of history has never been free from cultural role definitions. Mary Daly lists some of the characteristics of "women's sin": psychological paralysis, feminine anti-feminism, false humility, emotional dependency, lack of creativity[39]—many of which are often applied to the oppressed in general. Where the root of sin is understood to be sexism itself, it is an easy and logical step to come to the understanding that the fruit of sin for women is self-denial and submissiveness, with the concomitant tailorings according to race and class.[40] Where the root of sin is casteism, the fruit of sin is also understood as self-denial, submissiveness, and a passive and resigned acceptance of their sad plight. Sin is therefore the lack of self-definition and assertion.

In this regard, Kathryn Green McCreight reminds us that a surprising, unqualified understanding of women's sin (one that has not taken into consideration the factors of culture, race, and class on the effects of sin on women, which might nuance and qualify the discussion) has held sway in the fields of feminist theology.[41] We have derived "totalizing assumptions about woman and woman's submissiveness" that rest on the assumption of a totalizing anthropology of the feminine.[42] Such claims, she says, only "reinscribe rather than overcoming and subverting" them and this "totalizing is similar to the logic of colonialist discourse."[43]

Constructing Theologies from the Underside, ed. Susan Brooks Thistlethwaite and Mary Potter Engel (San Francisco: Harper, 1990), 155.

38. Valerie Saiving Goldstein, "The Human Situation: A Feminine View," *Journal of Religion* 40 (1960): 100–112. Cf. also Judith Plaskow, *Sex, Sin and Grace: Women's Experience and the Theologies of Reinhold Niebuhr and Paul Tillich* (Washington, D.C.: University Press of America, 1980), vii.

39. Mary Daly, *Beyond God the Father: Toward a Philosophy of Women's Liberation* (Boston: Beacon Press, 1973).

40. Ann E. Carr, *Transforming Grace: Christian Tradition in Women's Experience* (San Francisco: Harper, 1988).

41. Kathryn Greene McCreight, "Gender, Sin and Grace: Feminist Theologies Meet Karl Barth's Hamartiology," *Scottish Journal of Theology* 50/4 (1997): 419–20.

42. Ibid., 421

43. Ibid.

The question is whether the sin of all the oppressed is the same—lack of self-actualization. What might be the differences between the oppressed person who believes in Jesus Christ and the one who does not? Should we look for any? When viewed from the perspective of the secular activist, the sin of the oppressed is the lack of self-assertion. In fact, the activist would claim that it is the right of the oppressed to rebel against injustice.

According to this line of argumentation, the oppressed do not necessarily need to be humbled or to deny the self, because more often than not they have little of their own self to be humbled or to deny. Instead, they need to come to know themselves so as to acknowledge that they are a "self" and to define and assert that self.[44]

I am reminded here of the lament tradition within the Hebrew Bible, which contains many instances of the sufferer questioning and accusing Yahweh for the intensity or length of the suffering, sometimes even expressing doubt in the trustworthiness of God. To give voice to one's suffering, doubts, and anxieties and to seek retribution is an assertion of one's identity. The laments seem to sometimes express a faith that puts Yahweh in the wrong. What kind of a faith is that? Where does it get its power? The answer is much simpler than some people may think. It is the faith of an individual fighting against suffering even if it is warranted (brought about by sin) at times. It is a faith that gives one the right to question and contradict the highest social and theological authorities—the Scriptures, even Yahweh. It is a faith that finally satisfies one's thirst for justice that one's prayer for retribution and healing has been heard. And so the lesson we learn is that wherever we know that theological convictions and Christian traditions result in suffering, we have the right and duty to contradict them. This is self-assertion, individual and communal.

But a word of caution here: there are limitations on the extent to which one can assert oneself. Our understanding of sin or self-assertion should contribute to bringing about reconciliation between the oppressor and the oppressed within the body of Christ. But then does not an emphasis on self-assertion contradict the New Testament and Christian expectation of self-denial?

I here call upon one of the key theological descriptions of Luther, which is that in Christ we are simultaneously righteous and sinners. According to Luther's doctrine of *simul iustus et peccator*, believers are totally righteous in Christ while yet remaining totally sinners in and of themselves. We are righteous in that we believe in Jesus Christ, and we are sinners because we do not live the kind of life that reflects a life of discipleship in Christ.[45] The only way we know what sin is in and of itself is by knowing first who Jesus

---

44. Ibid., 417.

45. Cf. Karl Barth's understanding of discipleship in Jesus Christ. "To go beyond oneself in a specific action and attitude, and therefore to turn one's back upon oneself, to leave oneself behind. . . . Inevitably, the individual who is called by Jesus renounces and turns away from

is.[46] "Where there is genuine knowledge of sin, it is a matter of the Christian knowledge of God, of revelation and of faith and therefore of the knowledge of Jesus Christ.[47] If knowledge of sin is gained through life in Christ, then sin is everything that works against the creation, the will, and the order of God. Only God can overcome sin.[48] Following Jesus calls for a denial of the self, which the oppressed cannot afford to do.

Self-denial in the context of faith and life in Jesus Christ is not the denial of one's self and identity and humanity but the denial of one's complicity in systems and acts of sin, the rejection of our obedience to God and Jesus Christ. Similarly, self-assertion in the context of Christian faith is the affirmation of the self, one's faith and freedom.

The sinner is therefore not just the oppressor but also the oppressed who is slow to act. The former is in need of humiliation, and the latter is in need of exaltation. And in both cases, the need is in relation to the totality of life and action. If we are all simultaneously sinners and righteous beings, then both the oppressor and the oppressed are made equal by sin. This equality wrought by sin is not between humanity and humanity but between God and humanity. "Indeed sin in all its manifestations is absolutely equalizing. Such an understanding of sin breaks down some of the distinctions between the sin of the oppressed as self-denial and the pride of the oppressor,"[49] the male or the Brahmin. This equalizing aspect of sin is not necessarily a matter of celebration. For centuries, women have been told that

---

himself [sic] as he was yesterday. To use the important New Testament expression, he denies himself." Karl Barth, CD 4/2 (Edinburgh: T & T Clark, 1958), 538.

46. It has been asked if those unaware of their oppression are also sinful. From a faith perspective, my response would be that if they are living lives in God (have an understanding of God as the gracious Creator who created them in the image of God) or in Christ, then they would be aware of their complicity in their oppression.

47. CD 4/2:381.

48. "The death of Christ," stated Luther, "shows that our wills are impotent by nature" (LW 33:142). Without grace no one can will what is good (LW 33:112). In the absence of grace, "free choice cannot will anything good, but necessarily serves sin" (LW 33:147). This bondage of the will means that "salvation is beyond our powers and devices, and depends on the work of God alone. . . . It is not we, but only God, who works salvation in us" (LW 33:64). "All the good in us is to be ascribed to God," for "the mercy of God alone does everything" with respect to our salvation, and "our will does nothing, but rather is passive; otherwise, all is not ascribed to God (LW 33: 35). To say that the will is passive means "the will is not a cause, but a means through which grace is accepted" (LW 34:196). Just as God creates us "without our help" so that we contribute nothing to our being created, so also God regenerates us by faith "without our help" so that we contribute nothing to our being re-created (LW 33:243). We become children of God "by a power divinely bestowed upon us, not by a power of free choice inherent in us" (LW 33:157). However, although there is thus no such thing as a "neutral" free will (LW 33:237), nevertheless "[God] does not work in us without us" but actually grants us by grace again and again the freedom we would not otherwise enjoy (LW 33:243). Human beings who are by nature at war with grace are thus transformed into its friends (LW 33: 250)." See: George Hunsinger, Disruptive Grace, 301–2.

49. McCreight, "Gender, Sin and Grace," 427.

they are by their very being prone to sin and are sinful and lesser human beings—an afterthought of the Creator God. Dalits have been told that they are in the state of poverty and suffering by virtue of their sin; they are unclean and polluting and do not originate from God. This leveling of humanity in the sight of God by sin is helpful for the oppressed to gain some self-respect and courage. Such a leveling calls for humility on the part of the oppressor.

The action called for on the part of the Dalits and women and the poor is to overcome their sin of complicity in systems and structures of oppression. They could be empowered to do so by the grace of God. What is also needed is to recognize the strength of God through the witness of the Word of God, exemplified in stories such as those of Hagar, Rahab, Judith, the wise woman of Abel Macaah, the wise woman of Tekoa, and others who knew Yahweh and knew of Yahweh's covenant and the promise inherent in the acts of the God of Israel. They fulfilled their roles and identity in the wisdom of God despite the odds against them.

A Community of Equals: A Graced Community

In the context of exploitation and oppression, grace has to be seen and understood as the saving presence of Yahweh, who has a special concern for the oppressed and who works wonders to free them from the land of bondage and sin. The same saving presence of Yahweh is available also to the oppressors, to free them from the sin of pride.

Graced by God's saving presence, the human becomes like God, for it is in order to make the human divine that God becomes human and the human is healed through grace. Such a person is marked by joy, peace, contentment, and compassion for others. So also, the person transformed by grace is filled with the gifts of the Spirit: love, joy, peace, self-control, gentleness, and so on (cf. Gal 5:22-23). If we have really understood the meaning of becoming human, we will realize that only when we are really accepted in love—and that is grace—can we become human. This is then the humanizing aspect of grace. We come to exist as human beings by grace. Consequently, only through grace can we attain the fullness of our humanity and build a community of equals.

We are a caste-, race-, and gender-driven people. We can see the disastrous consequences of such an attitude in some of the recent events in the world. No religious community has been able to free itself from this deep-rooted malaise. Against this tragic situation, grace must be seen as that divine wisdom that enables the human being to recognize and acknowledge God and transcend these petty differences. It involves a serious effort to change dominant systems and structures, to undertake modes of social relations most beneficial to the people. The risks involve a confrontation with the social, economic, and political powers that create injustice and prevent peace. This involves the mobilization of the gifts of the Spirit bestowed on us by the grace of God in the service of the community. In other words, it involves the tapping of the internal resources that lie within us. Our faith teaches us that to tolerate and accommodate oppression is the path of the weak, of those who have given up on themselves. Self-abnegation without an understanding of one's dignity and self-respect as a person leads to humiliating servility. It is faith in Christ, in the Word, and in the example of Christ that give us a sense of self-worth and dignity.

Hence, any theology of grace must clearly affirm not only that grace frees the human being from all sorts of ghetto attitudes but must also present grace as a community-building force.[50]

---

50. Subhash Anand, "Towards an Indian Theology of Grace," in Vadakkekars, *Divine Grace and Human Response*, 448.

CHAPTER 4

Grace, Transcendence, and Patience: *A Response to Monica Melanchthon*

Cristina Grenholm

The problem Monica Melanchthon addresses is the following: If God's grace is the basis for the equality of human beings, why do we not promote it but rather find ourselves involved in oppression?[1] Her thesis is not that it is because we are still living in this world and not in heaven. Neither is it because we do not have the resources, being sinners who neither know nor have the ability to do good things. According to Melanchthon, it is because we are cast-, race-, and gender-driven cowards. This is true of both oppressors and oppressed.

Theologians interpret experiences in terms of theological concepts. In this case, the concept of grace is an interpretation of life that means that, in a profound sense, life is a gift. The theological reflection presented by Monica Melanchthon relates this beautiful theological concept to the ugly experience of oppression. There are, of course, other ways of defining the role of theologians and theology, and there are other definitions of grace. However, given this point of departure, we can reflect further on the role of theological concepts. How can we explicate the process of relating theological concepts to experience? Something I find worth pondering is the character of theological conceptualizations. In my theological work, I have come to regard theological conceptualizations as abbreviations.[2] Abbreviations are of different kinds: (1) summaries of complex theological presentations, (2) looser clusters of thoughts, and (3) phenomena consisting not only of theories but also of various practices. These three kinds of abbreviations share two characteristics. First, they are easily reiterated. Second, they provide shortcuts in theological reflection. In other words,

1. The present article is a slightly revised version of "Grace and the Equality of Persons: A Response to Monica Melanchthon," *Dialog* 42/1 (Spring 2003), 20–23.
2. This view has been presented in Swedish in "Genderisering och livsåskådningsreflexion: Könsanalytiska perspektiv på teologisk forskning" [Genderization and Reflection on Views of Life: Gender Perspectives on Theological Research], in *Var skall jag finna en nådig Gud?* [Where Can I Find a Gracious God?], ed. Anne-Louise Eriksson (Uppsala: Teologiska Institutionen, 2002), 83–95.

they simplify communication. However, they are also deceptive. It is easily forgotten or overlooked that they are abbreviations.

Grace is an important abbreviation in Lutheran theology. A theological conceptualization like "grace alone" can be taken as an abbreviation in all three respects mentioned above. (1) It is a summary of, for example, Luther's commentary on Galatians. (2) It is connected with a cluster of thoughts: a view of sin, double predestination, and the understanding of faith. (3) It is an abbreviation of what it means to be a Lutheran, singing Lutheran hymns, going to work and seeing it as a vocation, etc. As with other abbreviations, it is more often reiterated and used as a shortcut than thoroughly reflected upon, as I have the opportunity to do here.

Several contributors to this volume highlight problems that are implied in Lutheran abbreviations, e.g., the view of other religions. Melanchthon takes her point of departure in some solutions to these problems, the view of other religions included. Her contribution is not only critical but also creative.

Monica Melanchthon has a broad concept of grace. Grace for her is almost equivalent to life. Consequently, grace is primarily related to creation and not to salvation. Grace is also almost equivalent to love. Thus, there is no absolute distinction between grace as something we receive passively and grace as an impetus for action.

Melanchthon also has a corresponding broad concept of sin. Sin is the structural explanation for the fact that grace is not allowed to guide our lives toward equality. Sin is also individual and, in the words of Mary Potter Engel, defined as "free, discrete acts of responsible individuals that create or reinforce these structures of oppression."[3]

However, theological reflection not only concerns theological concepts as such. There are also contextual and analytical dimensions involved in the process.[4] Contextually, Monica Melanchthon wants us to take into account the urgency for action caused by her understanding of the concept of grace. Grace promotes equality and stands against the many forms of oppression she sees all around. Theologically, grace is for all—but in reality it is not. The contrast is serious. This is what threatens human existence individually, nationally, regionally, and globally. This is what calls for theological reflection.

---

3. Mary Potter Engel, "Evil, Sin and the Violation of the Vulnerable," in *Lift Every Voice: Constructing Theologies from the Underside*, ed. Susan Brooks Thistlethwaite and Mary Potter Engel (San Francisco: Harper, 1990), 155. Also quoted by Monica Melanchthon.
4. My response is based on a development of a model of the process of biblical interpretation originally presented in Cristina Grenholm and Daniel Patte, "Overture: Receptions, Critical Interpretations and Scriptural Criticism," in *Reading Israel in Romans*, ed. Cristina Grenholm and Daniel Patte (Harrisburg, Pa.: Trinity Press International, 2000), 1–54. Its further application on broader theological issues will be published in Cristina Grenholm, *Moderskap, asymmetri, kärlek* [Motherhood, Asymmetry, Love], forthcoming.

Analytically, Melanchthon approaches biblical texts thematically, seeing them as a cumulative story. The knowledge of human beings increases simultaneously with sin. Still God remains faithful to human beings. God does not give up. God continues to be gracious. Luther's writings are used in a similar way. Melanchthon refers to texts that fit into the same theme of God not giving up on humanity.

Harmonious, Disharmonious, and Inclusive

I will now further characterize the three dimensions involved in theological reflection as used by Monica Melanchthon—the analytical, the contextual, and the conceptual. Melanchthon's essay is analytically harmonious. The New Testament is not understood to add anything concerning the grace of God as compared with the Old Testament. Neither does Luther fall outside the pattern. The sources provide a univocal basis for reflection. By contrast, the article is contextually disharmonious. Melanchthon takes her starting point in life. She focuses on human oppression and suffering and underlines how human equality, based on the fact that life is a gift given equally to all human beings, is violated and offended. It is important to note that those addressed are not just the oppressors but also the oppressed, who are urged to reclaim their own dignity. All have to assume responsibility. Also the oppressed have to lift their voices. Melanchthon does not make the oppressed share the responsibility for causing oppression, but the oppressed have a role in dealing with and overcoming oppression. This is understood contextually, as a factual matter. The oppressors are not interested in reducing their own power. Women's issues are part of this. Women have had to speak up for themselves, and they have been able to contribute to their own emancipation. The oppressed need to raise their voices against the oppressors, since those in power are not willing to assume responsibility for liberating the oppressed. Taking responsibility for something that was imposed on you is, of course, unfair. However, in many situations it is the only alternative to remaining within the status quo.

Finally, the article is conceptually inclusive. Grace is widely understood as, and not interpreted as being opposed to, a call for action. The distinction between creation and salvation is by and large taken to be irrelevant. Furthermore, sin is defined not only in terms of self-affirmation, but also in terms of not taking on the responsibility of self-actualization.

With this short characterization of Monica Melanchthon's contribution as a background, I would like to raise some questions to promote further dialogue. I will point to an analytical alternative compatible with, but different from her contribution; I will agree with her contextual point of departure, and I will move in another direction concerning the understanding of the theological concept of grace.

Dialogue with the Bible and with Luther?

I find the harmonious analytical approach helpful. We do need harmonious views of the Old and New Testaments. We have too many unwarranted disharmonious views. However, I do not see any reason why Melanchthon's proposal could not also be combined with acknowledging the tensions within biblical and theological texts. Our biblical sources may actually be interpreted as mirroring the urgent tensions of our contexts.

Similarly, Luther could be approached in a different way concerning tensions within Luther's own works and conflicts between Luther and other ways of thinking. This is also a critique that needs to be directed to many others who quote Luther as part of their work when doing Lutheran theology. It is frustrating that there seems to be support for most critical corrections of Luther in Luther's own works. Luther is not always as Lutheran as we think. One explanation is that we often use his abbreviations, but of course he provides more than that. His valuable shorthand insights are balanced but also partly contradicted by longer presentations, wider clusters of thought, and the combination of theory and practice. What is often interpreted as the richness of Luther's work needs also to be treated as tensions and contradictions that call for further reflection, according to my view.

I also think that it is obvious that there is a need for corrections of Luther. This is what I find in Melanchthon's paper, although it is not presented in that way. The abbreviation of double predestination should be confronted and more universalistic perspectives developed. The narrower understanding of sin and grace needs to be broadened so as to also include the sin of not affirming oneself. Furthermore, a theology of growth and flourishing needs to be developed and not just rejected by shortcut references to "grace alone."

Perhaps Monica Melanchthon disagrees with me on this point and has a more generous interpretation of Luther. However, much of what she is saying could be said in a dialogue with Luther that goes beyond looking for his support. To pursue the theme of the paper, Monica Melanchthon could treat Luther more like an equal partner in theological discussion. She does not have to be a systematic theologian to do that. Luther was also a biblical scholar.

Theological Temptations

The disharmonious context is something of which we need to be constantly reminded. With philosopher of religion Grace Jantzen, I can say that theologians have probably been too much preoccupied with questions like "Does God exist," while most people have been worrying about how to exist or survive—and there is a connection. Had they (and we) dealt more with physical than metaphysical issues, theologians throughout history could have contributed to the struggle against all forms of oppression in a more forthright and effective way.[5]

There is a theological temptation for us to interrelate various theological abbreviations rather than explore how they relate to life. Dogmatic conflicts concerning who should be included in the people of God have overshadowed real life problems of exclusion. Urgent problems of existence have had to give way to wearying disputes concerning doctrines of predestination. Both theological reflection and contextual awareness are needed, and they should be interrelated. I agree with Monica Melanchthon concerning this point. I oppose those stating that context is secondary in relation to theological reflection. It needs to be part of the process in any theological endeavor.

Transcendence and Patience

Finally, I want to make a proposal to move in another direction at the conceptual level. Inclusive concepts are indeed necessary to balance our tendency toward simple divisions and distinctions. I think that Monica Melanchthon provides helpful corrections and reminders in this respect. Locating the foundation of human equality in creation is one possibility. Nobody created his or her own life. This is a universal truth that makes us equal. However, the problem is that we seldom experience this as a truth. We are more often treated as unequal than not. An alternative close at hand is to say that we are equal in failing to attend that goal, i.e., in weakness or sin. Although scholars disagree, Lutheran faith has been associated with the view that what we primarily have in common is sin. We are all sinners. One problem with this kind of conceptual emphasis is that such equality cannot be celebrated.[6] And that which cannot be celebrated cannot empower us.

Equality based on creation, almost equivalent to life, can be celebrated in a way sin cannot. Or does it have to be experienced to be celebrated? Melanchthon risks getting trapped in the very problem she is addressing. She poses the question: Why do we not promote grace? We could ask another question in return: How could we? If grace is given with creation, we ought to be able to experience it, but we do not. The equality of persons is an ideal that is constantly betrayed. This is at least as much a source of disappointment as a source of empowerment. However, there is more in theology than what can be said with reference to creation.

---

5. Grace M. Jantzen, *Becoming Divine: Towards a Feminist Philosophy of Religion* (Bloomington: Indiana Univ. Press, 1999); see esp. 6–26.

6. For a development of whether universalism should be based in views of sin or faith, see my article "A Theologian and Feminist Responds," in *Reading Israel in Romans*, 105–23. There I also reflect on the possibility of celebration. However, in that article the alternative I see to universal sin is universal faith or hope.

The French philosopher Alain Badiou is not a believer, but he can help us see a point at the core of Christianity, namely, in the resurrection. Badiou puts forth a nonreligious interpretation of Paul's letter to the Romans, arguing that the basis for universalism, that is, for the view that human beings are equal, cannot be empirical but has in some sense to be transcendent, founded beyond our control.[7] His fascination with Paul is precisely that the apostle confesses that the basis of universalism is beyond our control. Paul does this in terms of the resurrection, which Badiou understands is to be interpreted mythologically. As human beings, we constantly establish divisions and hierarchies. The equality of persons is a matter of faith according to Badiou.

I think it is important to note that we need not make an exclusively Christian interpretation of universalism as proclaimed by Paul, that is, with a clear reference to Christ. To Christians and non-Christians alike, equality is not primarily experienced but transcendent, something beyond our control. We need to be able to interpret the universal significance of the resurrection of Christ in terms that can be shared and recognized by all, that is, universally.

The advantage of such a transcendent view of equality as compared to an immanent view is that it serves as a critical corrective against any categorization. We are indeed caste-, race-, and gender-driven, as Monica Melanchthon points out. We look for categories by which we can make distinctions between people and evaluate them. The distinctions provide standards we measure up to or do not measure up to. Our equality is something that has to be believed but that cannot always be experienced. Such a view, based in the abbreviation of the Second Article of faith but not understood in an exclusively Christian sense (and thereby excluding some people from the start), could be an alternative to locating the foundation of equality in creation. We have all received grace beyond our control and daily experience.

The crucial issue, then, is whether we can somehow acknowledge grace as real even though equality is not, i.e., whether we can believe that there is a power that keeps moving us in the direction of equality or not. That issue can be settled both in religious and nonreligious ways, as Badiou shows. It can be seen as an issue of optimism or pessimism for Christians and others alike. Or, to use more traditional Christian terminology, it is a matter of trust.

Grace need not be mystically or moralistically understood. As Melanchthon points out, we have the resources for a better life, which have been given us for free. Again I agree with Monica Melanchthon. Grace challenges our willingness to receive the free gift of life. Grace understood in this direction, more in line with the abbreviations of the Second (and Third)

---

7. Alain Badiou, *Saint Paul: La Fondation de l'universalisme*, 3rd ed. (Paris: PUF 1999).

Articles of faith than with the first, can be celebrated and thus empowering. However, is it not a risk that grace expressed primarily in transcendent terms loses the connection with real life? Yes, there is a risk. Still, I believe we have improved the situation. While Monica Melanchthon's position leaves us with the question of how we could promote grace, a transcendent view has an answer: We believe in grace.

However, such a belief calls for a special attitude. Also believers in transcendent equality have to face the ugly experience of oppression. What is needed is patience. We have to take into account that we are caste-, race-, and gender-driven cowards who resist the gift of life.[8] But we should also take into account that we are created in the image of God. A final connection to Monica Melanchthon's article can thus be made: We may try to be Godlike in not giving up on humanity.

---

8. For the role of patience in belief, see Carter Heyward, *Saving Jesus from Those Who Are Right: Rethinking What It Means to Be Christian* (Minneapolis: Fortress Press, 1999); e.g., "Christians who believe that God is beyond all such longing, vulnerability, and incompleteness are bound to reject the *sacredness* of this deeply human yearning and may even see it as a sign of spiritual weakness, confusion, or bad faith" (p. 25).

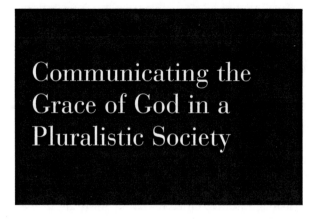

Communicating the Grace of God in a Pluralistic Society

Risto Saarinen

Communication

The notion of communication originates from two historical root meanings. The one dealing with communion or *koinonia* (Greek) should be obvious to all theologians. Communication takes place in a community; at least some togetherness and relationship must be presupposed in order that one can communicate. The other root meaning deals with the Latin word *munus*, which can mean a gift, a task, or both. A communicating person has or knows the *munus*, the gift and task. The gift is disseminated through communication.

The dual or dialectic meaning of the English word "communication" is likewise related to these two roots. In many old-fashioned contexts, for instance, when someone is said to present a scientific communication, the aspect of disseminating the *munus* is emphasized. But in many modern or modernistic contexts people like to emphasize the *process* of communication, its interactive and relational nature. The modern view of communication stresses the reciprocity and dialogue inherent in the community; the message should be relevant so that it can be understood and nurtured. For the sake of contextual relevance and dialogical interaction, the sender is called to modify, reformulate, and thus to manipulate the message.

On the other hand, if we lay our emphasis on the *munus*, on the gift and task, we highlight the authenticity of the message independently of its target group. The sender is called on to take care of the authenticity of the message and, furthermore, to disseminate it as effectively as he or she can. The sender should not modify or manipulate the message, and the sender can be rather careless with regard to how the message is received. The receiver is not dependent on the interactive process of communication. The receiver is left free to do whatever he or she likes to with the message. In the *munus* model, the sender thus loses the control over the message and the message remains receiver-centered after its dissemination.

These two models of communication reflect the two old, well-known paradigms for transmitting the gospel. The model of preaching and proclamation

often stresses the authenticity of our gift and task. The model of counseling and dialogue stresses the communal aspect of Christian discourse. At
the same time, we are facing the two twentieth-century paradigms of communication science. It has often been claimed that much of the twentieth-
century mass media was characterized by broadcasting and dissemination,
that is, by one-way communication in which no dialogue was possible. But
luckily, so goes the prevailing opinion, the shortcomings of this paradigm
were to some extent compensated by dialogical models of group work,
democratic grassroots movements, and also by the new media, which aims
at interactive two-way communication.[1]

In the world of secular communication, many scholars have believed
that, whereas the broadcasting and dissemination paradigm is authoritarian, the dialogical or communicative paradigm is inherently democratic and
can therefore avoid the shortcomings of the dissemination model. This belief
has been accompanied with the idea of authority-free communication: if the
group or community can freely discuss a topic, it can achieve a rational consensus that approaches the truth.[2]

More recently, however, media researchers have become aware that the
dialogical model is not as innocent as it might seem. The advantage of controlling and modifying the message with the help of interactive possibilities
has its price. This price can consist of several factors, and it can become
very high. First, the message may lose something of its integrity or authenticity when it becomes modified in the process of communication. An
extreme form of this problem becomes visible in the kind of group work
where the group believes that the message emerges out of nowhere as a
result of mere discussion. Second, the sender's possibility of controlling the
message may be a disadvantage. If the sender is wrong in the first place, the
sender nevertheless has the possibility of conjectures and new pretexts when
the group reacts. Thus a wrong opinion does not die out but continues its
existence in a modified fashion. Third, it can be argued that an interactive
model cannot disseminate messages truly effectively. Advertising, for
instance, is only rarely done in an interactive fashion. Advertisers are convinced that one-way announcement or broadcasting simply works better.

Because of such reasons, some media scholars have turned toward the
rehabilitation of the old paradigm of broadcasting. John Durham Peters, for
instance, claims that both paradigms of communication are in fact classical.
He labels the dialogical paradigm as the model of Socrates, who always
approached the truth by means of dialogue and interactive counseling. The
dissemination or *munus* paradigm is for Peters the model of Jesus, since in

1. See John Durham Peters, *Speaking into the Air: A History of the Idea of Communication*
(Chicago: Univ. of Chicago Press, 1999).
2. See, e.g., N. Rescher, *Pluralism: Against the Demand for Consensus* (Oxford: Clarendon
Press, 1999). Rescher writes against Jürgen Habermas.

the parable of the sower the seed was distributed effectively everywhere without interaction or even regard to whether the soil was fertile.

Whereas the Socratic model is private and esoteric, since the addressed person or people are carefully chosen insiders or group members, the dissemination model of Jesus is exoteric and public. In the parable of the sower, diverse responses to a uniform event are portrayed. Peters employs the example of gift giving as an illustration in which a one-way dissemination is valuable. Gift giving can become something more than an economic exchange. Although one probably has to presuppose some reciprocity in the final analysis of gift giving, it is essential that one can distinguish a unilateral action of giving from the bilateral economic exchange and that the one-way giving sometimes displays an added value in comparison with the two-way exchange.

Peters does not aim at a neoconservative rehabilitation of one-way authority. He wants to show that both dissemination and dialogue are needed for good and wholesome communication. In the final rounds of the game of communication, it is the interplay of self and other that is at stake. The dissemination paradigm has an inherent tendency to emphasize the others, that is, the message and the receivers. The dialogue paradigm may, if it forgets the freedom of the others in their otherness, become a constrained and unfruitful occupation with the self or with the few insiders. It is the balance between self and others that must be kept in mind in good communication.[3]

Grace as Gift

After these preliminary remarks on communication theory, I now turn to my actual topic. In view of the limitations of this chapter, I concentrate on only one aspect of grace, namely, grace as gift.[4] Calling grace an unmerited gift of God that is not achieved by our own works is a distinctively, although not exclusively Lutheran way of speaking. Since the notion of gift is inherent in the concept of communication as well, it offers an adequate, although far from exhaustive, perspective on our theme.

Lutheran theology of grace and justification has often been explained, and rightly, I think, in terms of God's free gift of forgiveness and new life. Our relationship to God does not consist of buying and selling but of receiving the gift. The reciprocal economy of accomplishments and performances

---

3. Peters, *Speaking into the Air*, esp. 57–58.

4. For some other aspects, see Risto Saarinen, "Gnade: Systematisch-theologisch," in *Religion in Geschichte und Gegenwart*, 4th ed., 3:1032–35. For the following reflections, which are entirely of my own responsibility, I am nevertheless indebted to various scholars: Prof. Miroslav Volf and his doctoral students, who invited me to participate in their seminar on "Grace and Gift" at Yale on October 28, 2002; Dr. Sammeli Juntunen of Helsinki, who also lectured in that seminar; Dr. Bo Holm of Aarhus, whose works we Finns have discussed on many occasions.

is replaced by the somewhat one-sided economy of gift giving. In this giving, God must remain the sovereign giver in order that the gift language does not change into a language of payments and achievements. The so-called new Finnish Luther interpretation emphasizes this by saying with Luther that God's being is in giving.[5] In this sense, Lutheran theology presupposes the priority and uniqueness of God, the idea of letting God be God. God is not a partner in dialogue but the sovereign giver.

In April 2002, the Lutheran World Federation organized a meeting, "Justification Today," in which the problem of communicating the grace of God in today's world was extensively elaborated. Prompted by the tragic events of September 11, 2001, the group reports of this meeting emphasize the otherness of God:

> In Martin Luther's theology justification is related to the salvation event, but not in an individualistic manner. Lutheran theology rejects the charges of excessive preoccupation with the self. The message of justification speaks of a God who is not there primarily to satisfy our egoistic wishes and needs. "Let God be God" is Luther's message which challenges the egoism of the human individual and the humankind as a whole. God, who is true love, gives us everything as a gift. This love calls for a wider scope of experience and understanding of God's engagement than our egoism allows. The almighty God cares for the world in a manner which transcends all egoism.[6]

The group report sets out to overcome the so-called salvation egoism by focusing on God as the great Other who transcends our small wishes. When the group report addresses Lutheran social ethics, the same principle is applied to the neighbor. The neighbor must not be seen as one's competitor and rival, but as the other who has his or her genuine freedom and otherness:

> Justified sinners are called to care for justice in their families, communities, societies, and in the world as a whole. The message of grace and justification teaches us that the laws of competition, rivalry, achievement, and efficacy do not ultimately determine who human beings are. We must cease to see our fellow humans as rivals in order to recognize their true humanity. In this sense justification by faith is a counter-cultural principle in the societies determined by today's exclusively profit-oriented market economy

5. Luther, WA 4:269, 25: "Hoc est esse deum: non accipere bona, sed dare" (This is how it is to be God: not to receive goods, but to give). See Simo Peura, "Christ as Favor and Gift," in *Union with Christ: The New Finnish Interpretation of Luther*, ed. C. Braaten and R. Jenson (Grand Rapids: Eerdmans, 1998), 42–69.

6. Risto Saarinen, "Ethics in Luther's Theology: The Three Orders," Seminary Ridge Review (Lutheran Theological Seminary at Gettysburg), 5/2 (Spring 2003): 37–53.

based on competition. Justification can thus bring forth the fruits of care and friendship, but also disinterested freedom and respect of the others in their genuine freedom and otherness.[7]

In these passages, the transcendence of God and the otherness of divine gift are emphasized. This emphasis is not merely introduced as an abstract theological principle, but it becomes applied to concrete circumstances and can thus make a criticism of the value systems of today's societies, especially of neoliberalist market economy. We can see from this example that a message does not need to be adapted to the prevailing circumstances in order to become relevant. The picture of divine gift giving is a relevant idea precisely because of its otherness. If we first seek relevance, we may remain bound to the limits of our egoistic needs. Turning away from these allows us to see relevance elsewhere.

In the early history of Lutheranism, many social reforms, like education and poor relief, were coherently seen as applications of the core theological doctrine.[8] Theological concentration and social relevance were partners; the theology of grace as gift did not lead to social quietism.

The Gift of Forms of Life

There is one particular dimension in Martin Luther's theology in which the connection between the divine giving and the social dimension is especially important, namely, Luther's view of the three estates or orders, in German *Dreiständelehre*. Luther scholars have repeatedly pointed out the great historical importance of this theory for Lutheranism.[9]

I have argued elsewhere[10] that the theory of the three orders in fact comes from late medieval nominalism, in which various kinds of divine ordinances were treated as divine promises, divine gifts or donations, or as the two testaments or covenants of God with humankind. Various misrepresentations of the three orders have occurred because scholars have not been aware of this medieval background. In terms of nominalist theology, it is adequate to treat the three orders as gifts that involve a promise and a covenant.

Luther's three orders are the family, the state, and the church. God's gift of Eve to Adam—and of Adam to Eve—established the family as the

---

7. Ibid.

8. This has been convincingly argued, e.g., in John Witte Jr., *Law and Protestantism: The Legal Teachings of the Lutheran Reformation* (Cambridge: Cambridge Univ. Press, 2002).

9. See Wilhelm Maurer, *Historical Commentary on the Augsburg Confession* (Philadelphia: Fortress Press, 1986); O. Bayer, "Natur und Institution: Luthers Dreiständelehre," in *Freiheit als Antwort* (Tübingen: Mohr, 1995), 116–46, and Witte, *Law and Protestantism*.

10. Saarinen, "Ethics in Luther's Theology." The following paragraphs draw on material from this paper.

nuclear society. God's gift of moral order, and later the gift of salvation in Jesus Christ, that is, the two testaments, established the ecclesial order. The state was an emergency order established after the Fall. In principle the state or society can be reduced to families and is therefore not really an independent order.

The orders are established by God. They are no contracts of the usual kind, but they follow the structure of gift and promise. In this sense they are not dialogical or reciprocal in their basic outlook but reflect the being of God as the giver. Of course everything is created by God and is thus in a sense a gift, but the family and the church are gifts of special order. They are permanent structures in which God's goodness and grace are apparent in a particular manner. One may note that the term "estate" (*Stand*) is misleading, since for Luther every human person belongs to all three orders at the same time. Each of the orders is a form of life (*genus vitae*)[11] in which the Christians exercise their duties. Luther repeatedly stresses how the Christian should understand that the form of life is a gift, which is not to be won through competition, merit, or achievement, but which is at hand here and now to be received.

Luther often points out in what sense the three orders involve cooperation between God and humans. With regard to the family and the state, human beings cooperate as secondary and instrumental causes. A parent nursing a child is the instrument of caretaking, which is ultimately done by God. In terms of late medieval theology, this was far more than a minimal degree of causality. It was thought of as a rather significant causality of cooperation, since it represents a mode of physical and natural causality. In the church, human cooperation is significantly less for Luther—it is almost nothing. I will not discuss here the tricky question of what ecclesial cooperation finally is. I will only mention that Luther affirms a greater degree of human cooperation in the form of life of the family, while at the same time both forms of life presuppose that the divine action is basically a gift.

Sociology of Gifts

Lutheran theology confronts us with the conceptual issues related to gifts. In what sense do gifts involve cooperation between the giver and the receiver? In the twentieth century, this question was asked by anthropologists and sociologists. Today it is asked by many philosophers and communication scholars as well. This question has always been asked by Western theologians, among them also Luther. I have already remarked that some communication scholars want to rehabilitate the old idea of communication as transmitting a *munus*, a gift, from sender to receiver. In philosophical sociology, the rehabilitation of a traditional idea of gift has recently been

11. For this notion, see, e.g., WA 40/1:544, 24; WA 43:21, 3; 43:198, 30.

undertaken by some anti-utilitarian scholars, perhaps most notably by Jacques T. Godbout.[12] It is important to realize that the concept that Lutherans have analyzed so extensively for centuries has now become prominent in other fields of human inquiry as well—and to some extent with accents similar to Lutheranism. I will briefly present Godbout's results before returning to the issue of grace and cooperation in the theology of gift.

Godbout follows Marcel Mauss's classical study *Essai sur le don* (*The Gift*)[13] in claiming that we cannot simply reduce the reality of gift giving to the simple utilitarian models of economic exchange. But in a manner that differs from Mauss's, and against many other anthropologists, Godbout argues that there are something like free gifts, that is, disinterested giving. Gifts are not simply extended or delayed reciprocity but a rather autonomous cultural and semantic category that should be carefully distinguished from the two other basic forms of exchange, that is, from the economic relationships of buying and selling, and from the public sector, which includes taxes and other duties to the state and society. In addition to the *homo oeconomicus*, we should acknowledge the *homo donator*, the rather altruistic agent who voluntarily serves other people, buys Christmas presents for children, and exercises charity.

We see that both John Durham Peters in communication theory and Jacques Godbout in sociology rehabilitate the commonsense idea that people give gifts, disseminate messages, and fulfill tasks unilaterally and that this is quite ordinary behavior. This does not mean, however, that the receiver does not do anything or remains passive. Even a free lunch is eaten by its receiver. Like many other theorists of the gift, Godbout thinks that some activity from the part of the receiver is conceptually necessary, or almost conceptually necessary in order that we can speak of gifts. Freedom from both the part of the giver and from the part of the receiver is almost necessarily presupposed in the act of gift giving. Emphasizing the character of gift and downplaying the idea of payment do not decrease this freedom but probably increase it.[14]

Godbout illustrates this state of affairs with Escher's drawing "Day and Night." Giving implies receiving, as the white birds and the landscape in this drawing, when seen together, constitute the black birds flying in the opposite direction, or vice versa. Causation is not implied but a conceptual picture drawn through the idea of giving a gift. A gift does not consist of putting something mechanically somewhere, but the very idea of gift takes

12. Jacques T. Godbout, *L'Esprit du don* (Paris: La Découverte, 2000). Caillé's postface printed in this edition is important since it discusses the reception of Godbout's work between 1992 and 2000.

13. Marcel Mauss, "Essai sur le don. Forme et raison de l'échange dans les sociétés archaiques," in *L'Année Sociologique, seconde series 1923–1924*. English translation: *The Gift: The form and reason for exchange in archaic societies*, trans. W. D. Halls (London: Routledge, 1990).

14. Godbout, *L'Esprit du don*, 296–98. For the sake of brevity, I here ignore the relevant but complicated work of Jean-Luc Marion and John Milbank. See, e.g., J. Milbank, "Can a Gift Be Given?" *Modern Theology* 11/1 (1995): 119–61.

it for granted that something is received as well. At the same time, however, the idea of gift remains distinct from buying and selling. The counteract of receiving is different from the counteract of buying, just as the act of giving is genuinely different from the act of selling. In both cases, there is some kind of reciprocity, but they remain different cases.

Responsive Reception

For Luther, the parent who nurses a child is receiving God's gift in the natural ordinance of the family. The child is receiving care from both God, the primary cause, and from the parent, the secondary cause. The parent is both giving and receiving at the same time. In fact, the very same act of nursing is both giving and receiving for the parent. The paradigm of gift giving is for Luther nothing like idleness. In the orders of household and society, there is enough active work for all human powers, at the same time that these orders are to be seen in terms of gift.[15]

At this point, someone might think that my presentation is not fully coherent. First, I highlighted the importance of one-way communication and gift giving, saying that instead of all quasi-democratic and quasi-interactive models of reciprocity, we should again see the advantages and the relative fairness of one-way models. Second, I pointed out that Lutheran theology in its understanding of grace as gift is compatible with one-way communication theory and anti-utilitarian sociology. But now, as a third point, from this theoretical construction the human person as a relatively free subject unexpectedly appears, a subject who is capable of cooperation or at least responsivity.

Let me try to make the third point coherent as well. I stressed that in modernist communication theory, in utilitarian sociology, and in the theology of self-righteousness, the two-way dialogical principle was a prerequisite or a precondition of the contract between giver/sender and receiver. The two-way traffic constitutes these phenomena. But in Peters's gift model of communication, in Godbout's anti-utilitarian theory of *homo donator*, and in Luther's view of grace as gift, the receiver's freedom is not constitutive of the process described, even though it is maintained as a part of the end result. The gift-like process or phenomenon was described without presupposing the receiver's interaction with it. So, at least one can conceptualize the paradigm of gift in this one-way manner. My third point is only the contention that in this conceptualization the receiver's freedom can be and is in fact maintained.

There is one sense, I admit and even claim, in which a responsive receiver is not only an appendage in the process of giving but must be presupposed in any theory of giving and gift. The very concepts of giving and gift in ordinary language normally presuppose that the object is a responsive

---

15. Luther; cf. WA 50:652 and Saarinen, "Ethics in Luther's Theology."

and animated being. I can give a book to you, but I do not give the book to the bookshelf but simply put it there. I never give gifts to bookshelves or other inanimate objects. Animals are an interesting borderline case: I can give something to a dog, e.g., food or a ball. But normally we do not give gifts to animals. In this sense the vocabulary of giving presupposes some responsibility and openness in the receiver. To use Escher's drawing as an illustration, the white birds of giving have the black birds of receiving as their shadow. This sense does not, however, diminish the point that gift giving highlights the one-way traffic, which distinguishes it from dialogue and exchange.

Sacrifice

There is yet another feature of gift giving that is prominent both in contemporary philosophy and in Luther. I mean the concept of sacrifice, which is normally understood as a special way of effective giving. In offering a sacrifice the giver is trying to prompt the expected response in an almost magical or mechanistic manner. A sacrifice is often expected to work *ex opere operato*, by the mere performance of an act. We are all familiar with the Lutheran criticism of the sacrifice of the mass. In the context of this criticism, Luther developed a general view of the human person as a being who is everywhere tempted to please God through offering good works as sacrifices. This sacrificial behavior is for Luther a sophisticated kind of self-righteousness, which he vehemently opposes.[16]

Perhaps also here it does not harm Lutheran theologians to be aware of some parallel philosophical discussions. Some Christian philosophers, like René Girard, have claimed that we should become aware of our sacrificial behavior and, in the final analysis, give up sacrificial models of thought because they are inevitably connected with violence. I have great sympathy for Girard and think that Luther's criticism of sacrifice resembles his ideas.[17]

Giving up all sacrificial behavior sounds very Lutheran. Generally speaking, it also communicates well with today's world. But on a closer look, the claim to abandon all sacrifices creates a problem, which has been spelled out by Jacques Derrida and many others.[18] If the enlightened and generous person gives up all sacrifices, what is this person actually doing?

---

16. V. Vajta, *Theologie des Gottesdienstes bei Luther* (Göttingen: Vandenhoeck & Ruprecht, 1952), shows this in an exemplary manner.

17. Risto Saarinen, "René Girard and Lutheran Theology," in *Theophilos: A Journal of Theology and Philosophy* (University Luterana do Brasil) 1/2 (2001): 317–38.

18. See, e.g., H. de Vries, *Religion and Violence: Philosophical Perspectives from Kant to Derrida* (Baltimore: Johns Hopkins Univ. Press, 2002), 200–207 (discussion among Girard, Jean-Luc Nancy and Derrida), and Godbout, *L'Esprit du don*, 292–98 (Girard and Godbout).

He or she is "sacrificing the sacrifices" at the altar of one's own enlightened generosity. But through performing this final sacrifice, the person becomes even more bound to the archaic idea of sacrifice. The final sacrifice or the last self-centered gift does not bring about the expected result, because it merely repeats the mode of sacrificial behavior. Instead of getting rid of the last problem, you have two problems. This philosophical criticism of Derrida has a certain theological counterpart in Protestant discussions relating to the liturgical forms of the Eucharist: if you aim at sacrificing everything that is sacrificial, you will end up with more problems than you had in the beginning.[19]

The Lutheran view of the grace of God as a gift and a promise, which "can admit of no sacrifice," as Luther says,[20] does communicate well. There is, however, a limit to this communication. Divine giving and human receiving and giving can be understood in a rather profound manner, but they cannot be fully understood. Up to a point, it is advisable to stress the passivity of the receiver. But beyond this point, it is more advisable to mention the personal involvement and responsiveness of the receiver. Likewise, up to a point, one should stress that mercy cannot admit any sacrifices. But beyond this point, one's enlightened generosity again becomes sacrificial. This is, I think, what we can communicate about God's grace as gift with the distinctive understanding of Lutheran theology.

Plurality, Trinity, and the Other

My last point concerns the alleged "pluralistic" character of today's society. Jesus' parable of the sower highlights that there was plurality in his time as well. The parable both realizes and ignores the problem of plurality. The message must be disseminated, and the one who has ears will hear. The event of dissemination is uniform and the responses are diverse. But there remains in the parable a final indifference with regard to this diversity. The observation of this indifference does not make it easy to address pluralism.

There is one direction that I do not find particularly helpful. The Lutheran theology of gift outlined here is not easily connected with some versions of today's Trinitarian theology. I mean those Trinitarian theologies that stress the reciprocity and the dialogical character of Trinity and employ this theological resource for drawing analogies between human communities and the inner-Trinitarian communion.[21] I have serious doubts whether

---

19. Cf., e.g., R. Jenson, *Systematic Theology 2: The Works of God* (New York: Oxford Univ. Press 1999), 218, 266–67.
20. Luther, WA 8:518.
21. I have addressed this issue in more detail in "The Concept of Communion in Ecumenical Dialogues," in *The Church as Communion*, ed. H. Holze (Geneva: LWF, 1997), 287–316, see 290–99; and in "East-West Dialogues and the Theology of Communion," in ibid., 317–38,

the dialogical life among the three divine persons can serve as a helpful example in debates concerning the diverse or even pluralistic nature of human societies. The otherness of God as giver and the particular character of grace as gift are easily forgotten if our theology of communion is primarily based on the idea of reciprocal dialogue. To put the point very bluntly: grace should be communicated in terms of free gift rather than as mutual sharing. In the model of sharing, we get too close to ourselves and ignore the other.

Of course any reflection on grace and gift should nevertheless be coherent with Trinitarian theology. We do identify the Christian God as Father, Son, and Holy Spirit. There are many historical reasons to stress the importance of inner-Trinitarian life and the distinct characters of the three persons. But there is also a risk of projecting our own wishes and diversities into God, thus seeing ourselves where we should see the other. "For between Creator and a creature there can be noted no similarity so great that a greater dissimilarity cannot be seen between them." This famous definition of *analogia entis* was given by the Fourth Lateran Council in 1215 explicitly to downplay the view that the unity between Father and the Son would be comparable to the unity among the disciples of Christ, as expressed in John 17. Ecumenists and theologians of communion have a tendency to forget the dissimilarity between divine unity and human fellowship.

Instead of dialogical Trinitarianism, I would start an elaboration of plurality with the quote from the Lutheran World Federation group report: "Justification can thus bring forth the fruits of care and friendship, but also disinterested freedom and respect of the others in their genuine freedom and otherness."[22] I will not elaborate on this but will only point in a certain direction. It may be that the authentic seed disseminated or the true gift given contains such wisdom and such depth of the divine riches that it will surprise both myself in my limited self-understanding and the others in their otherness. The apostle Paul reminds us of this element of uncontrolled surprise when he says in Rom 11:33-35: "O the depth of the riches and wisdom and knowledge of God. . . . For who has known the mind of the Lord? Or who has been his counselor? Or who has given a gift to God to receive a gift in return?"

---

see 329–30. The issue is complex: I find, e.g., L. Boff, *Trinity and Society* (Maryknoll: Orbis, 1988) problematic; but M. Heim, *The Depth of the Riches* (Grand Rapids, Eerdmans, 2001), 123–65, treats the analogy in an insightful manner. For the contemporary Trinitarian misuse of Gregory of Nyssa, see the thematic issue of *Modern Theology*, October 2002.

22. See n. 6, above.

CHAPTER 5

Luther's Theology
of the Gift

Bo
Holm

T
he concept of the gift is of a special kind. It has its place very near
the center of any theological articulation. Not without reason, the
article "Gabe" in *Religion in Geschichte und Gegenwart* claims that
"gift" is an "Urwort der Theologie," a primordial theological word.[1] The
truth of this claim is hard to contest. It is, however, more difficult to handle
the idea of the "economy of the gift" in theology, particularly in a Lutheran
context. This difficulty arises because the common definition of gift and giving includes a certain reciprocity that appears to be in conflict with the
understanding of grace as a pure gift in Lutheran theology.

The following survey explores how applying some modern sociological
investigations in the nature of gift and giving to Luther's writings could
resolve this apparent conflict. Contemporary theologians like Jean-Luc
Marion, Wolfhart Pannenberg, and John Milbank have applied a socio-
anthropological concept of reciprocity to theology in very different ways.[2]

1. Oswald Bayer, "Gabe II. Systematisch-theologisch," *Religion in Geschichte und Gegenwart*,
4th ed. (Tübingen: Siebeck Mohr, 1998–2003), 3:445: "Als Urwort der Theol. erschließt sich
G. konkret im Bezug zur religionswiss. Erkenntnis der kulturanthropologisch fundamentalen
Bedeutung der G. Charakterisiert die mit diesem Wort gemeinte vielgestaltige materielle wie
symbolische Reziprozität bis hin zum Opfer eine allg. zugängliche und allen einleuchtende
menschliche Erfahrung, so steht Gottes Kommen in die Welt und sein Dasein in ihr gegen diese
Erfahrung und die ihr entsprechende Erwartung: Es ist im genauen Sinn des Wortes paradox;
es zerbricht jedes berechnende 'do ut des.'" (As a primordial word in theology, the G. [Gift]
opens up its meaning in a more concrete sense when it is viewed in its relationship with the
knowledge in the science of religion of the fundamental meaning of G. from a cultural-
anthropological point of view. When this word, and the abundant material and symbolic reciprocity including also sacrifice captured by this word, characterises a common accessible and
obvious human experience, then the coming of God into the world and his presence in the
world stand against this experience and the corresponding expectation. It is paradoxical in a
direct sense of the word. It ruins every calculating "do ut des.")
2. Cf. John D. Caputo and Michael D. Scanlon, eds., *God, the Gift, and Postmodernism*
(Bloomington and Indianapolis: Indiana Univ. Press, 1999); this includes a discussion between
Jacques Derrida and Jean-Luc Marion; Wolfhart Pannenberg, *Systematische Theologie III*
(Göttingen: Vandenhoeck & Ruprecht, 1993), 71–114; John Milbank, "Can Morality Be

Indeed, the latter two brought this concept into a direct discussion with the Lutheran tradition. In addition, there has been an intense interest in the concept of the gift (*donum*) by Luther, in general, in recent Luther research. However, although we do have investigations into the centrality of the gift by Luther,[3] a proper investigation into the function of the gift exchange and reciprocal structures and models in Luther's writings is nevertheless hard to find.[4]

Justification as a Pure Gift: A Lutheran Misunderstanding?

It has been quite common to introduce the Lutheran concept of justification by claiming its nature as a pure gift.[5] God gives—the human being receives. God gives for free, expecting nothing in return. The more than problematic distinction between *agape* and *eros* within the Lutheran tradition has helped to stress this point. This very point is emphasized in the Lutheran tradition as well as in a considerable number of Luther quotations. Justification is far removed from the calculating interest that presumably lies within any concept of reciprocity.

The understanding of justification as a pure gift may seem to exclude any economy from the center of Lutheran theology. On the other hand, if justification means a renewed fellowship with God and if mutuality is an irreplaceable part of any kind of social interaction, then a form of reciprocity has to be found even in Luther's understanding of grace as a free gift.

It is also possible to find a great number of formulations that obviously imply a kind of reciprocal structure, such as the "happy exchange" and the metaphorical use of the matrimony in Luther's writings. If the concept of reciprocity could be used to elucidate Luther's doctrine of justification, it would be possible to reintegrate under a new perspective the social dimensions of the doctrine. Furthermore, it could contribute to a fuller picture of what an understanding of Luther's theology as a theology of self-giving love could contain. The introduction of a more social "gift terminology" shows how the strict definition of a "free gift" blurs the relation between one-sidedness and mutual interaction in the relation between God and human beings.

Christian?" John Milbank, *The Word Made Strange* (Oxford: Blackwell, 1997), 219–32; John Milbank, "Can a Gift Be Given? Prolegomena to a Future Trinitarian Metaphysic," *Modern Theology* 11 (1995): 119–61.

3. See, e.g., Simo Peura, "What God Gives Man Receives: Luther on Salvation," in *Union with Christ*, ed. Robert W. Jenson and Carl E. Braaten (Grand Rapids: Eerdmans, 1998); Antti Rainio, *Summe des christlichen Lebens* (Helsinki: Univ. of Helsinki, 1993).

4. Antti Raunio, *Summe des christlichen Lebens*, 360: "Auf Grund dieser Ergebnisse ist die Analyse von Luthers Verständnis der communio sanctorum als Liebesgemeinschaft eine Aufgabe der weiteren Forschung. Dazu gehört eine eingehende Untersuchung dessen, wie Luther das Geben bzw. das Schenken versteht."

5. See, e.g., Leif Grane, *The Augsburg Confession: A Commentary* (Minneapolis: Augsburg, 1987), 59.

Furthermore, a reading of Luther's writings in light of its fundamental social dimensions could sharpen the understanding of such crucial problems as sanctification and ethics in the Lutheran tradition.

The Concept of Reciprocity: Some Basic Distinctions

To introduce the economy of the gift into a seemingly economy-hostile domain demands some necessary distinctions. A brief introduction to the most basic of these differentiations is sufficient for the following considerations.

According to sociologist Marshall Sahlins, different types of reciprocity can be defined along a continuum whereby balanced reciprocity is the midpoint with negative reciprocity at one end and generalized reciprocity at the other.[6] The midpoint of balanced reciprocity contains the most obvious kind of reciprocity: the direct exchange. However, with regard to sociality, the balanced reciprocity is neutral. It contains a balance of distinctly calculated economic and social interests and therefore encompasses the common use of the word *reciprocity*.

The unsociable extremity, the negative reciprocity, described as "the attempt to get something for nothing with impunity," is the most impersonal sort of exchange, aiming at maximizing utility at the other's expense and including such actions as gambling, chicanery, and theft. Its polar opposite is generalized reciprocity, which incorporates Malinowski's term "pure gift." Yet, pure gift is also based upon a concept of reciprocity. "This is not to say that handing over things in such form, even to 'loved ones,' generates no counter-obligation, but the counter is not stipulated by time, quantity, or quality: the expectation of reciprocity is indefinite."[7]

In this scheme, it is important to notice that the differences between the various forms are not based on different degrees of reciprocity but rather on different degrees of sociability. What makes generalized reciprocity difficult to describe, especially for those involved, is that in focusing on the reciprocal aspects, there is a tendency to change toward a more balanced type of reciprocity and thus a less social one. This last factor, which has been thoroughly investigated by Pierre Bourdieu, is one of the main reasons there are difficulties connected with an investigation of the function of reciprocal structures in Luther's theology.[8] In his work, Bourdieu has shown how an internal participating description of a social praxis could be entirely opposite to an external observing description, and that while both views are adequate, neither is able to describe the actual logic of practice. This basic difference between practice and objectified practice, between "experienced" truth and "objective" truth, is exemplified in Jacques Godbout's *The World of the Gift*, wherein he describes the difference between the happy marriage,

6. Marshall Sahlins, *Stone Age Economics* (Chicago: Aldine, 1972), 185–205.
7. Ibid., 194.
8. See Pierre Bourdieu, *The Logic of Practice* (Stanford: Stanford University Press, 1990).

in which the couple do each other favors, and the marriage in fundamental crisis, in which every deed and favor is counted and measured. This difference is, however, not meant by Godbout to be a defense for the free, unilateral, and one-sided gift, and he can therefore quote Mary Douglas when she says: "The free gift does not exist—except insofar as it is a sign of asocial behavior—for the gift serves above all to establish relations, and a relationship with no hope of return, a one-way relationship, disinterested and motiveless, would be no relationship at all."[9] Godbout, and with him also the critique of Bourdieu by Alain Caillé, is, by his positive use of the idea of an "un-economic" gift exchange, trying to solve the more misanthropic consequences of Bourdieu's theory, whereby even the most social, disinterested giving in the end is based on an objective, economic "truth," although hidden or "misrecognized."

Luther and the Gift: The Economy of Justification

Sahlins's scheme becomes interesting for Luther research when it is possible to find the same main types of reciprocity in the center of Luther's understanding of justification. Luther's sermon on Matt 11:2-10 from the "Wartburg-postil" (1522) is an illustrative example.

The sermon opens with a discussion of earlier interpretations, and Luther criticizes the tendency to place doubt in the heart of John the Baptist. He knew exactly who Jesus was. John the Baptist is then placed in a certain role in relation to his own disciples and to the reader of Luther's sermon: "Christ must increase while he must decrease."[10] This was the hidden agenda when John sent his disciples to Jesus, and it is an expression of his twofold office. This is one of two main themes throughout the whole sermon. The other is the one that gives Luther occasion to end his sermon quoting 1 Cor 4:20, and in a translation differing from the one he normally prefers: "The kingdom of God is not in word but in deeds" (German: Das reych gottis stehet nit yn worten, ßonden ynn thatten"; SL follows the normal translation, "but in power"). In the middle of the sermon, Luther gives an elaborate explanation of the difference between law and gospel, caused by the rhetorical question, "But what does it mean when Christ says: 'The poor have good tidings preached to them'?"[11] An explanation of the utility of the gospel is provided at the end of the sermon.

The "works" of Jesus appear for the first time at the end of the introduction, where Luther consciously uses them to underline his point. The works play a significant role as the clearest evidence for Jesus' status as Son of God. When the disciples confront the reality of Jesus' works with the

---

9. Jacques Godbout in collaboration with Alain Caillé, *The World of the Gift*; trans. Donald Winkler (Quebec: McGill-Queen's Univ. Press, 1998), 7.
10. *SL* 1:89; WA 10/1:2, 149.
11. *SL* 1:98; WA 10/1:2, 155.

scripture, a certain answer becomes evident. The exposition of the relationship between word and works follows the themes from the introductory sermon "Eyn kleyn unterricht": that Christ refers to his deeds is set forth as a
true example to be followed. That not all have the power to make the blind
see is not an acceptable objection, since Jesus has done enough other works
that can be imitated.[12]

The greatest of these works is preaching the gospel to the poor. This
argument is not only meant to counter a possible objection, but is also rea-
sonable from an "economic" point of view. The objection would point out
the immediate conflict between Jesus' reference to his works and the saying,
"Not the life, but the doctrine should be judged." The contradiction, however, disappears in Luther's view when teaching also is considered to be a
work. The economic side of this argument will be explored after the following turn toward Luther's interpretation of the sentence, "and the poor have
good tidings preached unto them."

The only way Luther can explain these words is by referring to the two
primeval words of God: law and gospel. This duality can, among other
places, also be found in Luther's understanding of the function of John the
Baptist. John is simultaneously a messenger of the glory of Christ as well as
a messenger of the necessary repentance of humankind. Facing the law
leads human beings to two different kinds of behavior: presumptuous self-
confidence or despair.

The "economic" structure behind self-confidence consists of the idea
that the relationship with God is based on a "balanced reciprocity." It contains the expectation that it is possible to earn eternal goods with temporal
gifts. But the "presumptuous" self-confident human being has not yet realized that to control or bribe God with goods and pious works is impossible.
One has to deny one's self-will and to give oneself up. While that is the only
adequate gift to give, it is also impossible. It is the gift that no human being
can give, because he or she lacks the desire to give it. By only looking at outward deeds, one misses the face of Moses. Only where there is no interest in
reward or punishment can the law be fulfilled. One has to abandon oneself
to the will of God.[13]

Luther's argumentation can be understood in one of two ways, either as
an anti-eudemonistic self-offering, as is the case in the theology of Karl
Holl, or as an emphasis of the fact that the law can only be fulfilled when
punishment and reward have lost their meaning or logic.[14]

---

12. *SL* 1:93f.; WA 10/1:2, 153.

13. *SL* 1:97; WA 10/1:2, 156: "Not for the sake of heaven or hell, honor or disgrace, but for
the sole reason that he considers it honorable, and that it pleases him exceedingly, even if it
were not commanded."

14. WA 10/1:1, 158: "Wer nu dran glewbt, der empfehet die gnade und den heyligen geyst,
davon wirt denn das hertz frolich und lustig ynn gott, und thutt alsdenn das gesetz freywillig
umbsonst, on furcht der straff unnd on gesuch des lohnß; denn es hatt an der gnade gottis satt

The word *despair* (*Verzweiflung*) is used by Luther to characterize the consequence of a correct understanding of the underlying structure of "works-righteousness." Behind the "presumptuous" self-confidence lies not a "balanced reciprocity" but a "negative reciprocity." Already the understanding of the relationship with God as a matter of balanced reciprocity is an example of theft and robbery, an attempt to take without giving. Despair is then the necessary consequence when it is realized that giving is impossible, and it becomes clear that the impossibility of giving is the impossibility of fellowship. And because death is the ultimate individualization (cf. the introduction to the *Invocavit* sermons), the law is "a law unto death" and the letter "a letter that killeth."[15] The law is a law unto death, because it only demands and never gives. Examined from an external view, things look rather different. From this perspective, the law nearly gives back the possibility of an adequate relationship to God, but only nearly.

The logic in the exchange seems to show this. That is why humility for Luther never can be a human work but has to be a work of God, a humiliation. From the internal logic, this attitude toward God cannot be thought of as a gift but has to be considered as a total denial of the possibility of giving.[16] But from an external point of view, the denial of the possibility of giving could serve as an adequate "counter-gift." From an internal perspective, however, within the realm of the law, it is impossible to understand this counter-gift to God positively—or as a gift at all. The missing positive articulation follows under the realm of the gospel, as explained below.

The structure of despair is repeated in the gospel, although now positively displayed. God now gives everything that was lacking before, as justice and life. Here faith functions as an organ for reception. Faith receives everything from God and honors God at the same time. For this reason, faith is a work, the only work acceptable for God. Here lies the difference to the law's "nearly." In the gospel, the impossibility of giving turns into a possibility of giving.

One can now give oneself to God without any concern for reward or punishment, because the giving no longer happens on the basis of deficiency and absolute poverty but instead out of abundance and richness. The structure has three steps that can readily be found in Luther's "The Freedom of

---

und gnug, dadurch dem gesetz ist gnug geschehen." *SL* 1:99: "Whosoever now believes the Gospel will receive grace and Holy Spirit. This will cause the heart to rejoice and find delight in God, and will enable the believer to keep the law cheerfully, without expecting reward, without fear of punishment, without seeking compensation, as the heart is perfectly satisfied with God's grace, by which the law has been fulfilled."

15. *SL* 1:98; WA 10/1:2, 157.

16. Pierre Bourdieu has inspired this point. See Pierre Bourdieu, *Outline of a Theory of Practice* (Cambridge: Cambridge Univ. Press, 1977), 3–10: "Because the operation of gift exchange presupposes (individual and collective) misrecognition (*méconnaissance*) of the reality of the objective 'mechanism' of the exchange."

a Christian," although the elaboration there does not have the same coherence. First, there is God's promise, then faith, and, last, the reception of grace and the Holy Spirit as an expression of the now reestablished fellowship with God.

There are, however, also certain passages by Luther that seem to express a very conscious denial of any kind of reciprocity.[17] When Luther says that the kingdom of Christ is "sufficient of itself" and "needs no one's help," it sounds like an exclusion of human giving, and thereby as an exclusion of human beings from the divine fellowship. The self-sufficiency of the kingdom of God has to mean something different, and the following sentence gives this different answer. Christ is compared to a worldly king, and while Christ already is rich, it is futile to give him anything. Instead, Christ is looking for people to whom he can spread his richness, in order that they can distribute this richness further on. Luther's argumentation follows here the scheme of *donum-exemplum*. The denial of reciprocity is here not a total denial but an underlining of the necessary asymmetry in the divine exchange.

At the end, Luther explains the utility of the gospel.[18] Two things should be learned: faith and love. That means to receive and do good deeds. The faith should be praised, and the love should be done. Marcel Mauss's old insight is here reflected in the adage: a gift not passed on becomes loot. The gifts of God have to be distributed to the neighbors in order to remain gifts.

From the mutual relationship between God and the human being in faith follows now a distribution that at first seems unilateral. However, the distribution or passing on can actually be interpreted as part of a larger exchange—first, because the service for the neighbor is also a service for God, and second, because mutuality is realized between fellow Christians when they serve as "Christs" for each other, as Luther formulates it in "The Freedom of a Christian."

Accordingly, if the neighbor remains only a recipient, he or she never has the possibility of participating in the fellowship. To avoid the isolation of the neighbor, it is necessary for him or her to partake in the source of giving. There is then also a social reason behind Luther's calling the preaching for the poor the greatest work. The social extremity of generalized reciprocity begins its realization here: in the mutual giving and carrying in the church. In such deeds is the Kingdom of God. And so, the kingdom of God is not in words but in further giving.

---

17. See, e.g., *SL* 1:103; WA 10/1:2, 161: "But my kingdom, because it seeks not its own advantage, but rather bestows benefits upon others, is sufficient of itself and needs no one's help; therefore, I can not bear to be surrounded by such as are already sufficient of themselves, such as are healthy, rich, strong, pure, active, pious, and able in every respect. To such I am of no benefit."

18. Cf. WA 10/1:1, 167: "Jtzt ists tzeyt, diß Euangelion auch uns nutz machen." Eng. trans. *SL* 1:109: "Now is the opportunity for us to receive a blessing from this Gospel lesson."

A Theology of Deficit or a Theology of Surplus?

To claim that Lutheran theology has been focused on uncovering the fundamental sinfulness, not only of human nature in general, but also of the Christian in particular is quite evident. The Christian is the bankrupt sinner whose only possible rescue is to grasp God's grace. This kind of economic reasoning, according to which all human righteousness is to be destroyed,[19] is present throughout Luther's writings but is strongest in his earliest work. Human beings have nothing at all to give. Reciprocity is denied. But besides this theology of deficit, it is also possible to find another kind of economic reasoning in Luther's writing, a theology of surplus or plenitude. This theology of surplus is no less important, considering that the theology of deficit itself only serves to isolate the individual. The only way a Christian could live according to the will of God is to give God the only thing God wants, the faith Godself has given, and give the rest to his or her neighbors without destroying the potential for further giving. The last point is critical and illustrates how the basis of a Lutheran ethic is a theology of surplus. This theology of surplus involves a positive integration of the concept of reciprocity. Only by describing the renewed mutual fellowship between God and humanity is it possible to articulate the necessary positive condition behind any further giving.[20] Luther's late critique of the mendicant friars in the *Disputation on Matt 19:21*,[21] in which his main point is that it is necessary to have in order to give, underscores the importance of retaining the ability to give while giving.[22] And, by the help of the previous sermon, true giving could be formulated as a giving that enables the recipient to participate in the giving. Justification is the opening of reciprocity, making realized reciprocity itself the gift of grace.[23]

The only reason Luther was able to integrate so strongly a concept of reciprocity in his theology was his strong emphasis upon God's self-giving as the precondition for any further giving. From this point of view, the interest in economy is not necessarily always that of self-interest; from the perspective of divine infinite plenitude, all questions of self-interest are basically

---

19. See, e.g., the introduction to the early lecture on Paul's letter to the Romans.

20. Making giving possible becomes for Luther also a criterion for doctrine. Only the doctrine, which itself is able to give what it describes, is pure and true. See Bo Holm, "Zur Funktion der Lehre bei Luther," *Kerygma und Dogma* (forthcoming).

21. WA 39/2:39–91.

22. See further Rudolf Hermann, "Luthers Zirkulardisputation über Mt 19,21," in *Gesammelte Studien zur Theologie Luthers und der Reformation* (Göttingen: Vandenhoeck & Ruprecht, 1960), 222: "Bemerkenswert scheint es mir sodann zu sein, wie Luther zwar selbst von Opfern, Aufgeben usw. redet, aber dabei immer die positive Voraussetzung hinter allem, was nach Negation klingen können, hervorhebt. Man muß erwerben und haben, um geben zu können. Gilt das gewiß von geistlichen Dingen, so hier auch von sehr irdisch realen."

23. So Dietrich Korsch, "Freiheit als Summe: Über die Gestalt christlichen Lebens nach Martin Luther," *Neue Zeitscrift für systematische Theologie und Religionsphilosophie* 40 (1998). See also in the same volume, Bo Holm, "Wechsel ohnegleichen."

irrelevant, and the objectified economy no longer needs to be hidden but has to be revealed. Only when social interaction is seen apart from a previous gift of surplus is the human being doomed to try to avoid his own inevitable bankruptcy. And, since the conditioning divine plenitude is not of this world, it must be preached ever anew to remain an earthly reality.

There is one contemporary extrapolation of this argumentation that has not been my focal point but is worth noting here. It has become impossible to maintain the view that the major Lutheran objection is the total rejection of any *"do ut des"* (I give that you may give) structure—although this has been a very conventional way to look at it—a rejection that also lies behind the traditional dichotomization of *eros* and *agape*, of self-interest and des-interest. Instead, the major objection should concern a self-centered, calculating *do ut des*, because the main focus in Christian life should be that of giving one's neighbor the possibility of giving. The Christian gives to make the neighbor give. Without the integration of the human gift, which is understood not as primarily self-destruction but parallel with the divine self-giving, there is no justification at all. And because justification is the opening of reciprocity, justification is the transformation of a self-centered *do ut des* to an opening social *do ut des*. Consequently, it is possible to concentrate the economic structure of Luther's doctrine of justification in the twofold sentence "Deus dat ut dem, et do ut des" (God gives that I may give, and I give that you may give).

CROSS

Part

II

THE THEOLOGY OF THE CROSS (*theologia crucis*) is often seen as specific to Lutheran theology. The stress on Christ's suffering and death implies not only a radical understanding of the necessity of Christ's sacrifice for the salvation of the sinner but affects the whole character of theology. According to Luther in his famous *Heidelberg Disputation* (1518), the cross denies all attempts of a *theologia gloriae*, that is, human speculative efforts to attain knowledge of God. Instead, human beings should follow God's own way of humiliation and find God in the flesh, that is, in suffering, shame, and death. Since Walther von Loewenich's *Luther's Theologia Crucis* (1929), twentieth-century Lutheran theology has often interpreted itself as a *theologia crucis* while emphasizing the passivity of faith and separating theology from speculative metaphysics. The following two contributions develop the theology of the cross in new directions.

Lois Malcolm regards Luther's understanding of the cross as a profound way of thinking about a central problem that faces theologians in the twenty-first century, namely, the right use of spiritual power. The centrality of Christ's death on the cross implies a new understanding of power, both divine and human. The issue at stake, though, is not the satisfaction required by God, but rather the interchange between God and humankind. In Paul and Luther, there are fruitful ways of discriminating between violent distortions and life-giving uses of that notion.

Fidon R. Mwombeki challenges the traditional understanding of Luther's theology of the cross while criticizing the implication that both God's revelation and human responses can be articulated only through a passive human suffering and not by actively changing the social world. This traditional view is not in accordance with important concerns of Luther and also is unable to address the present situation in Africa. Christ's suffering certainly has redemptive power, but at the same time, it is meant to liberate human beings from suffering, namely, when suffering is inflicted by fellow human beings. In the African experience of being victims of violence, neglect, and injustice, the theology of the cross is unacceptable if it implies compliance with that situation. The theology of the cross has to be reinterpreted and corrected by a "theology of the blood," which expresses a paradoxical unity of life and death, suffering and liberating activity.

The two contributions thus move away from the last century's main line of interpreting Luther; they open up new contexts, but at the same time they go back to neglected insights in Luther's work.

—PETER WIDMANN

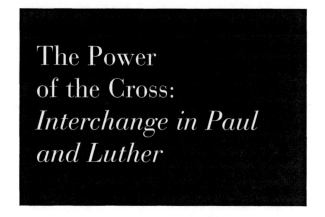

CHAPTER 7

The Power of the Cross: *Interchange in Paul and Luther*

Lois Malcolm

The widespread secularization sociologists and theologians had predicted for this century has not occurred.[1] In many parts of the world, interest in religion and spirituality persists. Indeed, Christianity and Islam continue to spread—and especially in forms that seek to retrieve or conserve traditional beliefs and practices. There may be a decline among "mainline" Christian denominations in North America and Europe,[2] but this decline coincides with the growth of global Christianity and, in particular, evangelical and Pentecostal expressions of Christian faith.[3] There also has emerged a strong interest in spirituality[4]—both within and outside Christianity—that stresses the immediate experience of God's presence and activity. The argument can be made that the central problem facing theologians in the twenty-first century will not primarily be that of the "crisis of cognitive claims," the validation of Christian beliefs in view of intellectual criticism of them, but that of discriminating among or discerning appropriate uses of spiritual power.[5]

Martin Luther's "theology of the cross" offers a profound way of thinking about such discernment. According to Luther, a "theologian of the

1. Peter Berger, *The Desecularization of the World: Resurgent Religion and World Politics* (Grand Rapids: Eerdmans, 1999), and Harvey Cox, *Fire from Heaven: the Rise of Pentecostal Spirituality and the Reshaping of Religion in the Twenty-first Century* (Reading, Mass.: Addison-Wesley, 1995).

2. "Mainline" churches include Lutherans, Presbyterians, Anglicans (including Episcopalians), and Methodists, among others.

3. Philip Jenkins, *The Next Christendom: The Coming of Global Christianity* (Oxford: Oxford Univ. Press, 2002), and Samuel P. Huntington, *Clash of Civilizations and the Remaking of World Order* (New York: Touchstone, 1997).

4. Wade Clark Roof, *The Spiritual Marketplace: Baby Boomers and the Remaking of American Religion* (Princeton: Princeton Univ. Press, 1999).

5. Compare David Tracy's early work *Blessed Rage for Order: The New Pluralism in Theology* (New York: Seabury, 1975) with his more recent work as described in my interview with him: "The Impossible God: An Interview with David Tracy," *Christian Century* 119/4 (February 13–20, 2002): 24–31.

cross" calls a thing "what it is" in contrast to a "theologian of glory," who calls "evil good and good evil."[6] And this theology of the cross is not a mere epistemological tool; it lies at the heart of Luther's soteriology, Christology, and doctrine of God.

Yet the meaning of Jesus' death not only in Luther's theology but also in Christian theology in general—at least since Anselm wrote *Cur Deus Homo?*—has been a matter of dispute. Anselm argued that Jesus had to die to satisfy God's "honor"—to pay the "debt" human beings owed God. In turn, his contemporary Abelard charged that Anselm's argument did not do justice to God's love. How could a good God sacrifice Jesus for his own "honor"? This criticism emerged again in Socinian and Enlightenment criticism of Christianity and since Kant has been the standard polemic of liberal theologians against the use of sacrificial themes in Christian theology. Most recently, feminist theologians have been the most trenchant critics of the theological focus on Jesus' death.[7]

Three issues lie at the heart of this polemic. (1) Why is the cross so theologically significant to Christian theology? (2) What does it imply for who God is—and the kind of power this God wields? (3) What does it imply for human beings—and the kind of power they are to wield?[8]

In this chapter I address these questions by examining some of Paul's and Luther's most influential references to the theological significance of Jesus' death. First, I argue that "interchange" or "exchange"—rather than "satisfaction"—lies at the heart of their theologies of the cross and conceptions of divine and human power. I then suggest that Luther introduces "tragic" and "theogonic" themes into Paul's more positive "Adamic" account of redemption. I conclude by discussing the implications of these two conceptions of "interchange" for contemporary theology and practice.

"Interchange" in Paul

My use of the term "interchange" draws from Morna Hooker, who uses it in her analysis of Paul to describe what Irenaeus described a century after Paul: "Christ became like us in order that we might become like him."

---

6. See Gerhard Forde's translation of thesis 28 of the *Heidelberg Disputation* (1518) in *On Being a Theologian of the Cross: Reflections on Luther's Heidelberg Disputation (1518)* (Grand Rapids: Eerdmans, 1997), 112. See also Mary Solberg, *Compelling Knowledge: A Feminist Proposal for an Epistemology of the Cross* (Albany: SUNY Press, 1997).

7. See, most recently, Rita Nakashima Brock and Rebecca Ann Parker, *Proverbs of Ashes: Violence, Redemptive Suffering, and the Search for What Saves Us* (Boston: Beacon Press, 2001).

8. In *Proverbs of Ashes*, Brock and Parker reiterate criticisms against Jürgen Moltmann's *The Crucified God* that were initially raised by Dorothee Soelle in *Suffering* (Philadelphia: Fortress Press, 1975). For Moltmann's position, see chapter 6 of *The Crucified God: The Cross of Christ as the Foundation and Criticism of Christian Theology* (Minneapolis: Fortress Press, 1993). For his response to feminist criticisms, see his *Experiences in Theology: Ways and Forms of*

Christ fully entered the human condition precisely so that men and women might be able to share in his condition by becoming "in Christ" or "with Christ."[9] Three influential texts demonstrate that Paul interprets the event of Jesus' death not as a satisfaction of God's honor but as an "interchange" that presents God's justice or righteousness in a very different light.

First, in Rom 3:25, Paul speaks of Jesus Christ as the one whom God put forth as a "sacrifice of atonement by his blood" (*hilasterion*). Paul alludes here to Lev 17:13-15, where the blood of animal sacrifices was sprinkled on the Day of Atonement for the community's sin. But this "sacrifice of atonement" displays the "righteousness" (*dikaiosyne*) of God in a distinctive way. It demonstrates God's "righteousness" by showing how God in "divine forbearance . . . passed over the sins previously committed" and "justifies the one who has faith in Jesus" (Rom 3:25, 26).

Second, in Gal 3:13, Paul describes how Christ becomes a "curse" (*katara*) for us. Paul quotes Deut 21:23 in its LXX version—"cursed is everyone who hangs on a tree"—which declares that the body of a hanged criminal is to be buried immediately rather than left to contaminate the community. The Hebrew version of this verse is even more explicit about the fact that this body is the "curse of God." But, as with Rom 3:25, an interesting logic is at work. According to Paul, Christ's becoming "curse" ushers in a new age of the Spirit: "Christ redeemed us from the curse of the law by becoming a curse for us . . . in order that . . . the blessing of Abraham might come to the Gentiles, so that we might receive the promise of the Spirit through faith" (Gal 3:13-14).

Third, in Rom 5:12-21, Paul compares Adam with Christ as individuals whose acts have very different consequences for humanity; they stand as "types" that exemplify two ages—the old and new creation. This passage contrasts how Adam's "trespass" led to "condemnation for all" and Christ's "act of righteousness" leads to "justification and life for all" (Rom 5:18). Nonetheless, this contrast is an asymmetrical one. In 5:15-17, Adam's "trespass" (*paraptoma*) is contrasted not with Christ's obedience but with the "free gift" (*charisma*) that "exercises dominion" in Christ and therefore in the rest of humanity.[10]

In these three examples, the satisfaction of God's "honor" is not what is at stake in Jesus' death. Rather, a different kind of righteousness is depicted,

---

Christian Theology, trans. Margaret Kohl (Minneapolis: Fortress Press, 2000), 375–76, n.134.

9. See Morna Hooker, *From Adam to Christ: Essays on Paul* (Cambridge: Cambridge Univ. Press, 1990). Hooker quotes Irenaeus: *"factus est quod sumus nos, uti nos perficeret esse quod est ipse"* ([The Word of God] did become what we are, that He might bring us to be even what He is Himself) (*Adv. Haer. V praef.*).

10. Ibid. See also Gustav Wingren's treatment of Romans 5, Philippians 2, and Genesis 3 in *Gospel and Church*; trans. Ross MacKenzie (Edinburgh and London: Oliver and Boyd, 1964).

a righteousness linked with the "passing over of sins" and "free gift" (in Romans 3 and 5) and a new age of the Spirit (in Galatians 3).

The contrast in Rom 5:12-21 suggests something else as well, especially if we relate it to the "Christ hymn" in Phil 2:5-11 and the story of Adam and Eve's sin in Genesis 3. Adam's "trespass" was that he disobeyed God's injunction not to eat the fruit of the tree of the knowledge of good and evil. He and Eve ate this fruit because they wanted to be "like God" (Gen 3:4)— even though as the earlier creation story maintains, they were created in the "image of God" (Gen 3:27). By contrast, Christ's "free gift," if we interpret Romans 5 in light of Philippians 2, is identified not with Christ's grasping to be like God but with his emptying himself (*kenosis*), being born in "human likeness," humbling himself to death—"even death on a cross" (Phil 2:7, 8)—even though he already "was in the form of God" and thus had "equality with God" (Phil 2:6). This contrast between Adam and Christ suggests a contrast between two kinds of power, (1) a power that grasps over against (2) a power that empties itself for another.

Moreover, if what human beings are given in Christ's "emptying" is Christ's life, then they too share in the distinct kind of power that—to use the language of Rom 5:17—"exercises dominion" in his life. Thus, in Philippians 2, Paul appeals: "Let the same mind be in you that was in Christ Jesus" (v. 5); "be of the same mind" (v. 2), have the "same love," do nothing from "selfish ambition," but "in humility regard others as better than yourself" (v. 3), looking "to the interests of others" (v. 4).

We can trace similar themes in Galatians. What is entailed in the "new age of the Spirit" that this "curse" ushers in (3:14)? In Galatians, Paul argues that the promise given to Abraham is now given to the Gentiles who believe (3:6-18). The "law"—and its distinction between "circumcision" and "uncircumcision"—has been replaced by a "new creation" in Christ (6:15). A new age has been ushered in; in Christ there is no distinction between "Jew or Greek," "slave or free," and "male and female" (3:28). All who "belong to Christ" are now "Abraham's offspring" and "heirs according to the promise" (3:29). What they share, as echoed in Romans, is a real adoption, having in their hearts "the Spirit" of God's "Son" who enables them again to cry, "Abba! Father" (4:6, 7; see also Rom 8:15-17). But this "adoption" and the inheritance it entails are Christ's identity. Thus the power and freedom involved is not to be used "as an opportunity for self-indulgence." Christians are called to love, indeed, to be "slaves to one another" (5:13). As those who "belong to Christ" and "live by the Spirit," they are not to "become conceited, competing against one another, and envying one another" (5:24-26).

That a different kind of power is enacted in Christ's death is especially exemplified in Paul's meditation on the "wisdom and the power of the cross" in 1 Cor 1:18—2:5. In what may be an allusion to Philippians 2, Paul asserts that he did not proclaim the gospel to the Corinthians with "eloquent wisdom, so that the cross might not be emptied (*kenothe*) of its power" (1 Cor 1:17). It is the "foolishness" (*to moron*) and "weakness" (*to asthenes*) of the cross that enacts the power and wisdom of God. This foolishness and weakness are not simply a negation of human wisdom and power. They enact a distinct kind of power and wisdom—"Christ" as the "power of God and the wisdom of God" (v. 24).[11] God's foolishness, Paul notes, is wiser than human wisdom; God's weakness is stronger than human strength (v. 25). Not only has this power created a new humanity out of old divisions between Jew and Greek (v. 24); it uses what is "foolish," "weak," and "low and despised" to shame the "wise" and "strong," and "reduce to nothing things that are" (vv. 27, 28).

Like the adoption described in Galatians 4 (and Romans 8), this wisdom is given by the Spirit, who "searches everything, even the depths of God" (v. 10). And what this Spirit endows is the capacity to "discern all things" and, indeed, "be subject to no one else's scrutiny" (v. 15). Paul infers that those who have the "mind of Christ" can "know the mind of the Lord" and indeed "instruct him" (v. 16).[12]

But this power is not to be identified with "boasting" or "jealousy" and "quarreling" (3:3). Paul appeals to the Corinthians to be of the "same mind" and the "same purpose"; they are not to be aligned with different theological factions (e.g., of Paul, Apollos, or Cephas) (1:10-17). Paul returns to this appeal in chapter 3. "Do not boast of human leaders," he tells his readers, "all things are yours"—"whether Paul or Apollos or Cephas or the world or life or death or the present or the future—all belong to you, and you belong to Christ, and Christ belongs to God" (3:21-23).

Two Senses of "Interchange" in Luther

Interchange and the "Joyous Exchange"

Luther depicts "the joyous exchange" (*frölichen Wechsel* or *admirabile commercium*) of a marriage union[13] in his treatise on "The Freedom of a Christian."[14] In this exchange, Christ is a husband who himself has not

11. See Michel Corbin's analysis of "redoubling negation" in "Négation et transcendance dans l'oeuvre de Denys," *Revue des sciences philosophiques et théologiques* 69 (1985): 41–76. See also Bernard McGinn's discussion of Dionysius in *The Foundations of Mysticism*, vol. 1 (New York: Crossroad, 1991), 157–82 and an analysis of this pattern in Anselm, Søren Kierkegaard, Emmanuel Levinas, Jacques Derrida, among others, in Mark C. Taylor, *Nots* (Chicago: Univ. of Chicago Press, 1993).

12. Paul quotes "For who . . . has instructed him?" (Isa 40:13), cited also in Wis 9:13; see also Rom 8:9; Gal 4:6; and Phil 1:19.

13. Compare Bernard of Clairvaux's *Commentary on the Song of Songs*. See also Eph. 5:26-27 and Hos 2:19-20.

14. "The Freedom of a Christian" (1520) has a Latin version (WA 7:49–73) and a German version (WA 7:20–38). English translations can be found in *Martin Luther's Basic Theological*

sinned or died—and is not condemned—yet by the "wedding ring of faith" shares in the "sin, death, and pains of hell," which are the "soul's," his bride's,[15] making them his own, as if he himself had sinned, suffered, and descended into hell.

Drawing on Paul's theme of adoption, Luther asserts that what Christ imparts in this exchange is his inheritance, his "birthright"—his "liberty" and "spiritual power," which makes him a "king" or a "lord." By faith, the Christian is like Christ a "lord of all things without exception." All things are subject to him in the sense that they are "compelled" to serve him in "obtaining salvation." Luther quotes Paul in Rom 8:28—"all things work together for good"—and 1 Cor 3:21-23—"all is yours," the world, life, death, past, present, and future. But "the Christian is not placed over all things to have and control them with physical power." Indeed, the more Christian a person is, the more sufferings he or she will endure. Rather, this power is a spiritual power—a power "made perfect in weakness" (2 Cor 12:9), a power that compels the "cross and death" to work for one's salvation (referring to Rom 8:28 again).

Moreover, Luther contends, one can only "serve the neighbor," that is, truly seek the other person's advantage, if one is "free" and a "lord." Drawing on Phil 2:5-11, Luther depicts how—though in the form of God and "rich in all good things that he needed no work or suffering to justify and save him"—Christ was not "puffed up by them" and thus did not use them to "assume power over us" but instead became a human being like us, taking on the form of a "servant," so that he might "become ours." Likewise, a person who is "justified" by God (and thus a "lord") will, like Christ, serve the neighbor spontaneously out of an "abundance of riches," not out of need or duty but "satisfied with the fullness and wealth" of her faith.

Interchange and the "Wrath of God"

Luther also describes this exchange in his commentary on Gal 3:13. In this context, however, he describes how Christ became "curse" for us, taking on God's wrath—God's "curse" or punishment against sin—in order to free us from it.[16] Although he draws again on Phil 2:5-11, his focus here is on how Christ became "the greatest thief, murderer, adulterer, robber, desecrator, etc., there has ever been in the world." Christ became "Peter the denier, Paul the persecutor, blasphemer, and assaulter, David the adulterer," even "the sinner who ate the apple in Paradise," and "the thief on the cross." He "wrapped himself up in our sins"—our "curse, death, and every evil." Evils

Writings, ed. Timothy Lull (Minneapolis: Fortress Press, 1989); and *Martin Luther: Selections from His Writings*, ed. John Dillenberger (New York: Anchor, 1958).
15. For Luther, the human "soul" is Christ's "bride."
16. Luther's commentary on Galatians (1535) can be found in WA 40/1:33–688; 40/2:1–184. An English translation can be found in LW, vols. 26 and 27.

"flooded over him," "tormenting" and "destroying" him, indeed, even "overwhelming" him.

In the Pauline texts and "The Freedom of the Christian," this "interchange" or "exchange" is linked with a power that seeks reconciliation and the common good. By contrast, in Luther's commentary on Galatians, this "exchange" is linked with a profound experience of sin and death as God's wrath, not merely as a psychological experience but as something truly ontological that inheres in ultimate reality. According to Luther, Jesus experiences God's wrath not only "adjectivally" or "concretely" but "abstractly" and "substantively." Drawing on Isaiah 53 to describe this experience ("God has laid on him the iniquity of us all"), Luther also invokes the Psalms, for example, Ps 40:12 ("My iniquities have overtaken me"); Ps 41:4 ("O LORD, be gracious to me; heal me, for I have sinned against thee!" KJV), and Ps 69:5 ("O God, thou knowest my folly; the wrongs I have done are not hidden from thee" KJV). Not merely the cries of an innocent prophet, these are the cries of one upon whom the sins of the entire world—past present, and future—"attack" and "damn." Luther also has Jesus cry out in lament. In Ps 88:7 and 16, Luther notes, "The prophet laments in Christ's name": "Thy wrath lies heavy upon me, and thou dost overwhelm me with all thy waves," and "Thy wrath has swept over me; thy dread assaults destroy me."

Moreover, in his commentary on Gal 4:6 (Paul's paradigmatic passage, along with Rom 8:15-17, dealing with "adoption"), Luther draws parallels between Christ's cry on the cross and the believer's cry amidst the "cross and suffering" of daily life. If we believed we were in a state of grace, Luther avers—that is, that our sins are forgiven—we would be happy and thankful (2 Cor 9:18). Nonetheless, we usually experience the opposite—fear, doubt, sorrow, and so on. The "feeling in our hearts" is one of "terrible" and "frightening" voices, which we do not even hear. We experience "clouds, the devil roaring, heavens bellowing, and earth quaking," and a sense that "evil and hell" are "opening up" in order to "swallow" us up. In these terrors of conscience, we are tempted to call God a "tyrant," an "angry judge," and a "tormentor." We feel forsaken by God: "I am driven from thy sight"; "I have become a broken vessel" (Psalm 31). By enabling us to cry, "Abba, Father!" in these moments, the Holy Spirit overpowers the "horrible" torments of the law, sin, death, and the devil. "It is not without purpose," Luther observes, "that Paul calls this sigh of the pious and afflicted heart" the "indescribable sighing of the Spirit." But, it is an effort and a labor to cling firmly to this when Christ is not "visible" to us and, indeed, can at times "appear wrathful towards us." In such moments, the "cry of the pious" is heard—as in the parable of the unjust judge (Luke 18:1-8) or Moses' "cry" at the Red Sea (14:15).

Making Sense of the "Wrath of God" in Luther

As we have seen, Luther retrieves dimensions of the Old Testament prophets and psalms of repentance and lament in ways that Paul does not. In his early commentaries on the psalms, Luther uses Dionysius's conception of God's incomprehensibility as a means for interpreting psalms that speak of God's "hiding his face."[17] From that point on, Dionysius's apophatic God, the God beyond visible and audible signs, is transmuted into the *deus absconditus* (the hidden God) against whom only Jesus in the manger and on the cross is a comfort.[18]

This image of God, of course, contrasts sharply with Paul's. Yes, Paul as well speaks of a divine power beyond the law's demands. The power and wisdom of God is greater than human power and wisdom (1 Cor 1:18—2:5). The "curse" of Jesus' death ushers in a new age of the Spirit that undoes basic antinomies—not only between circumcision/uncircumcision and bless-ing/curse but also Jew/Greek, slave/free, and male/female (Galatians 3).[19] But Paul's focus is not on the terror of this power but on its abundance. Paul tells the Corinthians that "all is yours" in Christ—not only past, present, and future, but life and death itself. His logic is that this surplus—"all is yours"—enables them to shift their focus off of their need to secure their egoistic and factional interests and attend instead to the common good. Further, the questions of why God allows evil and whether God is trustwor-thy do not trouble Paul. He does not go into extensive descriptions of the tra-vails and torments of conscience. His is a robust conscience; he assumes the goodness of God and the world around him.[20] Unlike the Gospel writers, Paul does not interpret Jesus' death in relation to psalms of laments and the cries of innocent sufferers.[21] The only place where he seems to wrestle with God's providence is in Romans 9–11, where he wrestles with why the Jews rejected Christ—but even there he does not seem to question God's trust-worthiness. Finally, his is a very different depiction of the sufferings of the Christian.[22] Suffering for Paul is voluntarily chosen by the apostle and is

---

17. On God's hidden face, see Pss 10:1; 22:24; 27:9. Luther speaks of the "hidden God" or God's "hiddenness" most frequently in his commentaries on the Psalms, Romans, Genesis, and Isaiah.

18. See Luther's appropriation of Dionysius the Areopagite (Pseudo-Dionysius) in his com-mentaries on the Psalms.

19. On these basic "antinomies" and how the cross ushers in an apocalyptic age that undoes them, see J. Louis Martyn, *Theological Issues in the Letters of Paul* (Nashville: Abingdon, 1997).

20. See Krister Stendahl, "The Apostle Paul and the Introspective Conscience of the West," *Harvard Theological Review* 56 (1963), 199–215; reprinted in *Paul among Jews and Gentiles and Other Essays* (Philadelphia: Fortress Press, 1976).

21. Note, e.g., how Psalm 22 is appropriated in Mark 15:24, 29, 34; Matt 27:35, 39, 43, 46; Luke 23:34, 35; see also John 19:24.

22. See 2 Cor 4:8-9; 6:4-10; 11:23-28; 12:10; Rom 8:35-39; 1 Cor 4:9-13; Phil 4:11-12; 2 Tim 3:11.

linked with joy.[23] Even his discussion of the "thorn in his side" is a confident affirmation of his apostolic ministry and Christ's presence in his life.[24]

Why this contrast between Paul and Luther? Paul Ricoeur's distinction between the Pauline "Adamic" myth, on the one hand, and the "theogonic" and "tragic" myths found in the Old Testament (and Greek myths and other literature), on the other, may help us tease apart what is going on here.[25] (1) Paul's "Adamic" myth locates the responsibility for evil with Adam's sin and not with God and God's good creation. As we have noted, for Paul, God and creation are always good and trustworthy. Christ, the second Adam, is unwaveringly identified with redemption, the "free gift" that brings justification and adoption. By contrast, (2) the "tragic" myth (of which the lament psalms contain aspects) presents individuals overwhelmed with suffering and evil but offers no ultimate solution to the problem of evil. (3) The "theogonic" myth, in turn (which originated with Babylonian and Greek creation myths and influenced the Genesis accounts) assigns the "tragic" to the act of creation, making it coincident with a logic of being or of ultimate reality.[26]

Luther incorporates dimensions of the "tragic" and "theogonic" into a Pauline "Adamic" understanding of redemption from evil by way of his reading of Paul through postexilic prophetic texts and the Psalms. The Son's lament on the cross—and by implication our lament, given our "adoption"—contains tragic elements. The Father's "hiddenness"—and, also, in some instances in Luther's commentary on Galatians, Christ's "hiddenness"—contains "theogonic" elements. This *deus absconditus* is a God beyond rational constraints, a God of infinite power, whose dark and incomprehensible form is as much an object of terror as it is of comfort.[27] Although Luther's, like Paul's, conception of evil and redemption is finally "Adamic," as evidenced in "The Freedom of a Christian," in the *Commentary on Galatians* (and I might add, a text like *The Bondage of the Will*), a tragic and theogonic conception can predominate at times.[28]

Why? Some historical context may help.[29] Luther writes after Anselm, whose influential *Cur Deus Homo?* focused attention on the death of Jesus as

---

23. L. Ann Jervis, "Accepting Affliction: Paul's Preaching on Suffering," in *Character and Scripture: Moral Formation, Community, and Biblical Interpretation*, ed. W. P. Brown (Grand Rapids: Eerdmans, 2002).

24. 2 Cor 12:7.

25. Paul Ricoeur, *The Symbolism of Evil*; trans. Emerson Buchanan (Boston: Beacon Press, 1967).

26. See Gerhard Forde, "The Power of Negative Thinking: On the Principle of Negation in Luther and Hegelianism," *Dialog* 23 (Autumn 1984): 250–56.

27. Michael Gillespie, *Nihilism before Nietzsche* (Chicago: Univ. of Chicago Press, 1996), 24.

28. Marc Lienhard, *Luther: Witness to Jesus Christ: Stages and Themes of the Reformer's Christology*, trans. Edwin H. Robertson (Minneapolis: Augsburg, 1982).

29. Gerard S. Sloyan, *The Crucifixion of Jesus: History, Myth, Faith* (Minneapolis: Fortress Press, 1995).

"satisfaction." Prior to Anselm, a much more complex understanding of redemption was predominant, for example, Irenaeus's notion of "recapitulation" (which situates Jesus' sacrificial death within an eschatological restoration of creation). Further, the experience of Jesus' passion was a central focus of the mystical theology and popular piety of the late medieval period.

But Luther adds a distinct twist to Anselm's and the mystics' focus on the death of Jesus. Anselm and the mystics would have thought it blasphemous to infer that God might be perceived as evil. Even laying stress on the accursed nature of Christ's experience on the cross would have seemed impious.[30] By contrast, instead of stressing how Christ satisfies God's "honor" with his obedient suffering, Luther not only stresses how Christ became "the curse" of God's wrath, but how he laments over and protests the attacks he experienced.

As Michael Gillespie has pointed out, the figure of a dark, "hidden" God emerges with the rise of nominalist philosophy and its critique of Aristotelian metaphysics—along with the devastation of the Black Death and the papal schism that brought the medieval world and the coherence of its worldview to an end.[31] What emerges is a new (nominalist) idea of God as a God who overturns all eternal stands of truth and justice and puts the will in place of reason and freedom in place of necessity and order. This God's *potentia absoluta* (absolute power) is greater than his *potentia ordinata* (ordained power). Indeed, Gillespie argues, one might trace contemporary nihilism's intellectual and spiritual origins not to Nietzsche's assertion of the death of God but to the new idea of God that emerges in the late medieval period—and, we might add, finds expression in Luther.

In the nineteenth and twentieth centuries, major European thinkers echoed Luther's themes in their somewhat analogous loss of confidence in Enlightenment rationality and its premise of historical progress. The most obvious is Søren Kierkegaard's conception of "anxiety," "dread," and the human "sickness unto death,"[32] but resonances can also be heard in Heidegger's notion of "anxiety," which, unlike regular fear, is not experienced in the face of this or that particular thing.[33] Finally, Nietzsche's suspicion of morality as a guise for the "will to power" is perhaps a secularized echo of Luther's own suspicion of the way "human beings misuse the best in the worst of manner."[34]

30. Compare St. John of the Cross and Luther.
31. Gillespie, *Nihilism before Nietzsche*, 24–25.
32. Søren Kierkegaard, *Concept of Anxiety: A Simple Psychologically Orienting Deliberation on the Dogmatic Issue of Hereditary Sin*, ed. and trans. Reidar Thomte (Princeton: Princeton Univ. Press, 1980); and *Sickness unto Death: A Christian Psychological Exposition for the Upbuilding and Awakening*, ed. and trans. Howard V. Hong and Edna H. Hong (Princeton: Princeton Univ. Press, 1980).
33. Martin Heidegger, *Being and Time*, trans. John Macquarrie and Edward Robinson (San Francisco: HarperSanFrancisco, 1962).
34. Gerhard Forde's translation of thesis 24 of the *Heidelberg Disputation* (1518) in *On Being*

Interchange and Two Kinds of Hiddenness in Luther

I have analyzed two different ways Luther depicts the "joyous or happy exchange." These two ways correspond to the two kinds of "hiddenness" Brian Gerrish has identified in Luther's theology.[35] On the one hand, like Paul, Luther has a *theologia crucis*: God works in Christ in a paradoxical mode *sub contrario*—his wisdom is hidden under folly, his strength under abject weakness, his life given through death, and his salvation through judging and damning (what Gerrish calls "hiddenness 1"). This is the "hidden God" as God incarnate, crucified, and hidden in suffering (*deus incarnatus, deus crucifixus, deus absconditus in passionibus*). Nonetheless, suffering and terror are not the last word in this understanding of hiddenness. Although the cross is a cipher for a different kind of power than that of the justice of legal satisfaction—the cross ushers in a new "age," in Paul's terms—this new age is linked with a fecundity of power that finally is defined by love, a self-giving love that seeks the interests of others out of its own abundance.

On the other hand, Luther also speaks of God's hiddenness in another way (what Gerrish calls "hiddenness 2"). This kind of hiddenness is linked with the inscrutable will of God that lies "behind" the manger and the cross, a *deus absconditus* whose goodness is not apparent but appears at times as tormenting and terrifying, bringing down wrath and hiding its face even from the pious who cry out in despair.[36] This notion of divine power is also different from the justice of legal satisfaction, but it does not derive from the fecundity of goodness; it is, rather, the power of an inscrutable God. This second kind of hiddenness offers a complex account of the relationship between divine judgment against sin and human repentance, on the one hand, and human lament and protest against evil, on the other.[37] It grapples with the reality of evil and death—and God's involvement with them—and, like the book of Job, offers no easy resolution.[38] Indeed, its insight into the profoundly ambiguous character of our experience of reality has been

---

a Theologian of the Cross. Compare Friedrich Wilhelm Nietzsche, *On the Genealogy of Morals*, trans. Walter Kaufman (New York: Vintage Books, 1989).

35. B. A. Gerrish, "To the Unknown God: Luther and Calvin on the Hiddenness of God," *Journal of Religion* 53 (1973), 263–93.

36. In addition to the *deus absconditus*, Luther speaks of the *deus nudus* ("the naked God," a strange, terrifying, indeterminate presence), the *deus absolutus* (God not in relation to the world), and the *deus revelatus* and *deus indutus* (the God who is not naked but clothed in his word). See Gerrish, "To the Unknown God."

37. Feminist theologians discuss the complex ways sin manifests itself as despair and the loss of self. See Judith Plaskow's now classic *Sex, Sin, and Grace: Women's Experience in the Theologies of Reinhold Niebuhr and Paul Tillich* (reprint, Lanham, Md.: Univ. Press of America, 2001).

38. On this, note the influence of H.-J. Iwand on Jürgen Moltmann's *The Crucified God* and Gerhard Forde's *On Being a Theologian of the Cross*. Moltmann discusses Iwand in *Experiences in Theology*, 70, 87ff.

echoed in late modern philosophers' analogues to its intuition of the "substantive" and "abstract" character of divine wrath.

But "hiddenness 2" can be distorted, especially when divorced from "hiddenness 1." One distortion takes a tragic form. God laments as the Son on the cross—and the Father who suffers with him—but is ultimately powerless in the face of radical evil. The other distortion, which may be more appealing in our century, takes a theogonic form.[39] Divorced from a deep sense of God's love "for us" in the incarnation and cross, Luther's picture of God can be terrifying—a tormenting, wicked god who creates and wills evil. Such a picture can especially be problematic if it reinforces a nihilism that is already well ensconced in contemporary intellectual and popular culture or a corresponding movement toward religious or political authoritarianism.[40]

To summarize, in the first part of the twenty-first century, we have witnessed not the disappearance of religious activity and interest in spirituality, as many had predicted, but their proliferation. Ever-changing forms of individualized expressions of spirituality have emerged alongside more conservative forms of communal belief and practice. Paul's and Luther's theologies of the cross offer highly fruitful ways of discriminating among these expressions of spiritual power. Their conceptions of the "interchange" or "joyous exchange" between Christ and human beings depict who Christ is as the "wisdom" and "power" of God and therefore, for Christians, what true spiritual wisdom and power are about. Nonetheless, in a way that moves beyond Paul, Luther incorporates a sense of the tragic and the theogonic into his theology of the cross. This heightens its subtlety and depth as an interpretive complement to Paul's interpretations on the death of Jesus. But these tragic and theogonic dimensions also have their distortions, which, if taken to be normative, contradict what one might call the "kenotic abundance" of the "wisdom and power of the cross."

---

39. Note the import of post-Holocaust reflection for Lutheran theology.
40. See, e.g., Mark Juergensmeyer, *Terror in the Mind of God: The Global Rise of Violence* (Berkeley: Univ. of California Press, 2001).

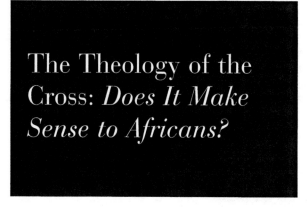

CHAPTER 8

The Theology of the Cross: *Does It Make Sense to Africans?*

Fidon R. Mwombeki

I t is well known that the cross may be the most important symbol of Christian faith and of the church. Great attention is paid to the "theology of the cross" within Lutheran circles. As an African, however, I have been puzzled by the dissonance between the understanding of the symbol of the cross in Africa and discussions on Luther's *theologia crucis*. Consequently, in this paper I will make three arguments. One, the theology of the cross is *not* central to Luther's theology and therefore it need not be central to African Lutheranism. Two, the theology as propagated does not make sense in the context of African realities of suffering. Three, a more appropriate theology of the cross for Africa is one associated with the theology of the blood, as a corrective supplement to *theologia crucis*.

Luther's Theology of the Cross

The early church used several symbols, including the fish and the cross. Indeed, the symbol of the cross in the time of the early church signified suffering and pointed to Jesus who died on it. It signifies suffering in the Gospels,[1] but it was not publicly used as the symbol of the church.

During and after Constantine, the cross appeared everywhere in public life. However, this time it was not to signify the suffering Christ, but the victorious, glorious one: *in hoc signo vinces* (in this sign you will conquer). The cross continued to be the symbol of Christ's power, even in the Middle Ages, as it obviously was during the Crusades against Moslem advancement in Europe.

The theology of the cross, which focuses on the suffering, helpless crucified Christ, was extensive in the monasteries, whereby a believer had to experience the agony of the cross. The cross has occasionally been seen as a symbol of suffering—even of Christians (consider the concept of the imita-

---

1. Mark 8:34 (and parallels); Luke 14:27. Paul does not use this symbol extensively in his letters, and never uses it to refer to suffering.

tion of Christ)—during difficult times, as we see in Germany during the time of Luther as well as during the two World Wars.

In a brief presentation of Luther's theology of the cross, Paul Althaus[2] says, "The theology of the cross permeates all of Luther's theological thinking and it is the measurement of the genuineness of all theology—the reality of God, of His grace, of His salvation, of the Christian life and of the church."[3] Luther introduced the terminology at his famous 1518 Heidelberg Disputation, as the essence of theology:

> That person does not deserve to be called a theologian who looks upon the invisible things of God as though they were clearly perceptible in those things which have actually happened.
>
> He deserves to be called a theologian, however, who comprehends the visible and manifest things of God seen through suffering and the cross.[4]

It is not difficult to affirm that "true theology and knowledge of God are to be found in the crucified Christ." The problem starts when Luther relates the suffering of God in Christ on the cross to the suffering of the Christian in the world. Althaus asserts that "the theologian of the cross knows him [God] from his [the Christian's] sufferings since he therein wishes to hide himself and be known through a discovery by suffering with and through Christ."[5] Althaus says this suffering "points to the deep correlation between the suffering Christ, in whom God makes himself known, and the suffering man [sic] who is the only man able to enter into community with God."[6]

Luther coined the phrases "theology of the cross" and "theology of glory" and juxtaposed them, demonizing the latter. His decision also to disregard creation as an inadequate source of revelation is obviously related to finding true revelation only in the cross, claiming that God must be hidden and only revealed in Christ on the cross. He even says that the church, the righteousness and holiness of the believers, the workings of God in the means of grace, the Word of God in proclamation, and the actual presence of God, are all hidden.[7]

However, at the Heidelberg Disputation, which is taken as a springboard for the theology of the cross, the issue was not suffering of Christians

---

2. Paul Althaus, *The Theology of Martin Luther*, trans. Robert C. Schultz (Philadelphia: Fortress Press, 1966), 25–34.

3. Ibid., 30.

4. Timothy F. Lull, ed., *Martin Luther's Basic Theological Writings* (Minneapolis: Fortress Press, 1989), 31.

5. Althaus, *Theology*, 26

6. Ibid., 27f.

7. Hermann Sasse, *We Confess Jesus Christ*, trans. Norman Nagel (St. Louis: Concordia, 1984), 42.

as such. Luther was basically responding to Erasmus on a more profound issue, the revelation of God: How do we know God? Luther opposed Erasmus, who claimed that we could see God revealing himself in creation (Scholasticism and Catholicism). Luther insists we must see God in suffering. His five main points are summarized by Walther von Loewenich:[8]

1. The theology of the cross is a theology of revelation and stands in contradistinction to speculation.
2. As a theology of revelation, revelation must be understood as hidden and indirect.
3. God's revelation is apprehended via the sufferings and cross of Christ, rather than in the works of creation and ethical works.
4. This knowledge of God who is hidden in (God's) revelation is a matter of faith.
5. God is ostensibly and definitively known in suffering.

While we may follow Luther in most of the claims, we need to have a good reason to take Luther as axiomatic in relation to the third and fifth points.

Examining Luther's foundation for the claim that creation and positive things in life do not contain any of God's revelation, we find that on other occasions, he is very different. For example, while expounding Rom 1:19-21, he does not argue that it is impossible to know God through creation. He instead says:

> From the beginning of the world to its end, He has always done and does such great things that people, if they would only use their understanding beyond what their senses show them, could easily and clearly recognize God. Thus it was from the beginning of the world, even though gradually the godless more and more obscured it on the account of their ingratitude as they went on to idolatry. Thus neither they nor their followers who have been deceived by them have an excuse, as is also the case with the Jews.[9]

With the concept of *imitatio Christi* (the imitation of Christ) in the background, Luther and others make a conspicuous shift from the suffering of Christ to the suffering of the followers of Christ, from the unique cross of Christ to the crosses of Christ's followers—shifts that he takes to be axiomatic. I argue below that this shift is dangerous, especially when it has

---

8. Walther von Loewenich, *Luther's Theology of the Cross*, trans. Herbert J. A. Bouman (Minneapolis: Augsburg, 1976), cited by Rudolph Featherstone in "The Theology of the Cross," *Theology and the Black Experience: The Lutheran Heritage Interpreted by African and African-American Theologians*, ed. Albert Pero and Ambrose Moyo (Minneapolis: Augsburg, 1988), 49.
9. LW 25:10.

been used to pacify people who are struggling and to convince them to accept their suffering.

In attempting to understand the difficulties of their time and their inability to effect changes, the believers declare that even God imposes the cross (suffering) on believers to discipline them[10] or to exercise them and to wipe out their lust so that the Spirit may awaken them.[11] So, in times of hardships and suffering God will "stand by us in every trouble, grant us patience, give us comfort, create hope, and provide a way out of all things so that we may be saved."[12] And every believer has predetermined "crosses and sufferings" designed to help them "conform to the image of Christ."[13]

In the period immediately after World War II, with the war and the fate of the Confessing Church as the context, we see such interpretation vividly. It was said then, "To believe in the cross always means also to carry the cross."[14] Pastors were asked to tell the people that the true people of God "must endure every misfortune and persecution, all kinds of trials and evils from the devil, the world and the flesh (as the Lord's prayer indicates) by inward sadness, timidity, fear, outward poverty, contempt, illness, and weakness, in order to become like their head, Christ."[15] They probably had Luther as their reference when he says:

> And the only reason they must suffer is that they steadfastly adhere to Christ and God's word, enduring this for the sake of Christ. . . . They must be pious, quiet, obedient and prepared to serve the government and everybody with life and goods, doing no one any harm.[16]

We must remember that Luther wrote these admonitions at the time he critically needed the rulers' protection from the wrath of Rome. But Luther himself not at all fit the description of the people he defines—quiet and obedient. He was far from that.

If the theology of the cross is occasional and not central to Luther's theology, it is not necessary for African Lutherans to adopt Luther's interpretation in order to understand and respond to their own suffering.

African Understandings of the Reality of Suffering

Suffering in Africa is a *skandalon* (scandal or stumbling block) to the whole globalized world. In most of Africa, pain and suffering is increasing.

---

10. *BC* 229f.
11. *BC* 213f.
12. *BC* 648.
13. Ibid.
14. Sasse, *We Confess*, 52.
15. Ibid.
16. LW 41:164–65. It is significant, however, that Luther is presenting this aspect of suffering, and carrying the cross as the seventh (last) of the signs of holy Christian people.

A theology that calls on Africans to "carry their crosses"—if that means to accept suffering and live with it or even to search for a revelation of God in it—is utterly flabbergasting. However, this suffering is caused by the peoples and structures we know and can change.

In June 2001, at the Danish Church Days, I offered a lament in my speech titled, "Africa! Africa! Africa!"[17] I lamented the unjust suffering of Africans (and other peoples of darker skin) specifically caused by other people. I lamented that Africans are walking "through the valley of the shadow of death."[18] The stench of death hovers over their villages and towns as more than 70 percent of all AIDS victims in the world are Africans. And there are equally disproportionate numbers of victims of malaria, TB, malnutrition, starvation, and water-borne diseases. Profit-hungry pharmaceutical companies are banking on these diseases, so they oppose every move that might make medications cheaper for the people of Africa.

Now we see African governments pressured to reduce their spending on provision of social services by the big powers in Washington, Brussels, and Geneva in the name of the World Bank, International Monetary Fund and their disastrous Structural Adjustment Programs, which impose on Africa conditions that would never be accepted in their own countries. Africa is systemically sidelined in the process of economic globalization, putting unending pressure on it to continue producing raw materials for export, causing even food insecurity in the process. At the same time, they are pressured to fully open up their markets and consequently are subjected to aggressive marketing ploys and insensitive rules that repeatedly cheat Africa.[19] Globalization is bringing multinational companies, armed with fraudulent, malicious contracts protecting them, to operate free of controls as they wantonly extract African nonrenewable resources. In a matter of just a few years, Africa will be a continent of empty pits, poisoned environment, and crushing poverty. The countries from which the companies take the wealth will continue to be given a few handouts, which these countries are to acknowledge as gifts from "benefactors."

At the same, time Africans increasingly face segregation as unwanted beggars all over the world. They are subjected to racist inspections at more and more airports in the world, and those who settle in foreign lands can be simply targeted, kicked out, attacked, or even killed. They are called "economic refugees" and are subject to deportation back to Africa, where nobody cares whether they live or die.

---

17. Fidon R. Mwombeki, "Africa! Africa! Africa!" *Danmission*, September 2001, 16–19. See also Fidon R. Mwombeki, "Are We of the Same God: A Pastor's Day Reveals Tanzania's Heavy Debt Burden," *The Lutheran*, August 2000, 50–51.

18. Psalm 23:4.

19. Looking at the proceedings in the World Trade Organization, it is clear that Africa has no chance to negotiate, as it does not have enough resources to put dozens of people in Geneva with enough capacity to participate meaningfully in the negotiations.

Under these circumstances, African theologians look at the reality of suffering from a hands-on experience and must respond to it theologically from this position. Many have tried to do so from different angles.

One of those presenting a scathing critique of an accommodating approach is Peter Kanyandago.[20] Kanyandago defines suffering as "the presence of physical or moral pain and deprivation as experienced by an individual or by a group of people, knowingly or unknowingly."[21] The objective of his essay is "to see how Jesus deals with his suffering and that of others, and then try to relate this to the African experience marked by suffering."[22] I regard his distinction between the way Jesus deals with his own suffering (the cross), which has a redemptive function, and the way Jesus deals with the suffering of those he is suffering to liberate to be very significant. A theology that fails to recognize this distinction and that assumes a correspondence between the two must be corrected. Throughout his article, Kanyandago presents Jesus in the Gospels as "uncompromising in his attitude and actions to liberate people from suffering."[23]

Kanyandago rejects as narrow an interpretation that calls on Jesus' followers to contemplate the suffering of Christ in order to "accept their own suffering as a form of participation in the passion of the Lord," since the passion of the Lord is in fact "a resistance to and non-acceptance of human suffering."[24] Jesus suffered and died in order to liberate humanity from suffering caused by those in power who abuse their authority.[25]

He says:

> The traditional understanding of the cross . . . has tended to keep the suffering people in their situation with the consolation that they are participating in the passion of the Lord. There is no way of defending this view, when we see that in the Gospels Jesus declares war on all forms of human suffering as exemplified in the way he fights against evil spirits.[26]

The theology of atonement, he continues, has had a "corollary spirituality that tends to justify human suffering as a meritorious participation in the suffering of Jesus."[27] Then the question is, For whom does the suffering of Christians play this redemptive role? When the political leaders kill innocent civilians in fights for power and wealth, for whom do the innocent die?

---

20. "The Cross and Suffering in the Bible and the African Experience," in *The Bible in African Christianity: Essays in Biblical Theology*, ed. Hannah W. Kinoti and John Waliggo (Nairobi: Acton Publishers, 1997), 123–44.
21. Ibid., 123.
22. Ibid.
23. Ibid.
24. Ibid., 124.
25. Ibid., 133.
26. Ibid., 124.
27. Ibid., 132.

When multinational corporations plunder the wealth of innocent peasants by removing them from their ancestral lands in order to excavate valuable minerals these people have been keeping for generations, leaving them homeless wanderers in their own land and languishing in dehumanizing poverty, whom does their suffering liberate? How is this kind of suffering a participation in the suffering of Christ? It just does not make sense.

According to J. M. Waliggo,[28] there are different types of suffering (self-inflicted, caused by others, accompanying an endeavor to succeed, on behalf of others, and mysterious suffering of the innocent). Most African suffering is caused by others, most of whom are well known. Kanyandago and others like him, including Manas Buthelezi,[29] would accept the interpretation and application of suffering of Christians only when it is for others, in order to liberate them.

What we have seen in Waliggo, Kanyandago, and others, is African theologians addressing the issue of suffering particularly through the once famous liberation theology. Even though the terminology used was not *theologia crucis* (maybe because most of its proponents were not Lutherans), the goal was the same.[30] The goal was to proclaim hope to the people suffering because of persecution and exploitation of the majority by the minority. The central theological motif was the Exodus—that God had heard the cries of the people and was going to come with might to deliver them from their tormentors. However, there was an irony in insisting that in suffering God was abundantly present and actually on the side of suffering people—sometimes indicating that those who suffer have a certain advantage in their relationship with God—while at the same time talking about delivering them from suffering. Who would want to be on the side where God is not?

According to the theology of the cross, one is tempted to say that God was actually manifesting (by hiding) himself in the life and experience of the suffering people who, as it were, were bearing their crosses. By suffering they were ironically experiencing the might and power of God.

When it comes to the suffering of the believers as a manifestation of the disguised mighty works of God, Africans must find it ridiculous and unethical. Our basic question is, Does God really stay on the side of and in solidarity with the suffering Africans? Does God pat their backs and say, "Live with it, my child; this is the way I show you my might! I am with you"? We currently ask ourselves what this God has been doing on the side of Africans when they are being obliterated through all kinds of evil—from slavery to colonization to exploitation and contemporary marginalization in the globalizing world. Is this how Africans should experience the manifestation of

28. J. M. Waliggo, "African Christianity in a Situation of Suffering," in *Jesus in African Christianity*, ed. J. N. K. Mugambi and I. Magesa (Nairobi: Initiatives Ltd., 1989), 94–98.
29. See Alan Boesak, *Farewell to Innocence* (Maryknoll, N.Y.: Orbis, 1977), 75.
30. It is crucial to say that there were differences between African and non-African liberation theologies.

the presence of the mighty God? Then we ask, why only Africans? Are they the most precious ones who have the privilege of experiencing God's wonderful presence and might by their suffering?

However, many boldly reject the notion of the God who helps us to suffer peacefully. Instead, they understand God as the "God who encounters us in human condition as the liberator of the poor and weak, empowering them to fight for freedom because they were made for it."[31] I could not agree more with James Cone when he writes:

> If God is unlimited both in power and in goodness, as the Christian faith claims, why does [God] not destroy the powers of evil through the establishment of divine righteousness? If God is the One who liberated Israel from Egyptian slavery, who appeared in Jesus as the healer of the sick and the helper of the poor, and who is present today as the Holy Spirit of liberation, then why are black people still living in wretched conditions without the economic and political power to determine their historical destiny?[32]

What is the relevance of the *theologia crucis* for the church as it lives and shares life in Africa, plagued by these human-caused sufferings?

African Theology of the Cross?

The cross has been received as the symbol or the flag of the church. As such, the cross has no image of suffering for the Africans. While it is supposed to be an image of suffering and death, like a hanging rope or executioner's ax, the cross comes to Africans as the symbol of the power and glory of God that brings deliverance from suffering. Instead of being the symbol of death, "the physical cross, like the staffs and stools looked upon as material representations symbolizing the presence of the ancestors, becomes the symbol of Christ's being *the ever-living*."[33] The church (and the cross) in Africa has from its genesis had as part of its mission the alleviation of suffering and human pain wherever it is found. The church takes the lead in feeding the hungry, healing the sick, raising the downtrodden, fighting for the weak, and so on. Consequently, the cross has the image of liberation. When a local pastor goes into the home of a very sick member of the church to administer Holy Communion, the placement of a small wooden cross on a table where the elements will be laid brings a sense of the presence of the Lord himself, who comes to alleviate pain and suffering—the Savior. I wonder how many would see—or would want to see—suffering in the cross at the

---

31. James Cone, cited in Featherstone, "Theology of the Cross," 50.
32. Ibid.
33. Kwesi Dickson, "The Theology of the Cross," in *A Reader in African Christian Theology*, ed. John Parrat (London: SPCK, 1987), 82–94 (91).

table of Holy Communion. When we go to visit them in their pain, how many sick people would we want to see pain and suffering in the cross?

Be it central or not, we need to join the Lutheran communion in contemplating the significance of the cross. How can African Lutherans present the cross as a symbol of suffering when it is a symbol of the church and of victory? What should then be the African theology of the cross? Where is our entry or point of departure as African Lutherans when we see a dissonance between Luther and us? Are the different attitudes toward suffering on the part of Western and African theologians theological, cultural, or social?

Luther was a product of his time, a prophet rooted in the realities of his context. We would be unfair to him, a rigorous contextualizer, if we positioned our theology in his medieval religious background. As he clearly wanted to break away from unintelligible Catholic archaism in order to make the gospel relevant to the German people, we would be truly Lutheran if we do the same for our people. On a number of things, Lutherans today have rightly moved away from Luther. Luther himself would have objected to anyone taking him to be infallible. We can no longer ally ourselves with Luther in labeling the pope of Rome as evil, nor in condemning Jews, Muslims, and Turks as messengers of evil, nor advocating injustice by asking slaves and subjects to be unquestioningly submissive to their "masters." In this regard, Rudolph Featherstone calls attention to one of the dangers facing theologians of today. This danger

> is expressed in the tendency of some scholars to ask and seek ancient solutions to contemporary problems. It is patently unfair to ask or expect from Luther answers to problems concerning Africa's children in America. Yet it is fair and right to inquire of Luther's concern for, interest in, and decision to be with those who, during his day, stood with their backs against the wall.[34]

I have argued that the theology of the cross in Luther was a reaction to Scholasticism and that it did not form the center of his theology. The slogans "theology of the cross" and "theology of glory" (with expressed disgust for the latter) and the emphasis on suffering as the right way are contextual in origin and should be treated as such. As we can see from Luther's lectures on Romans, it is not true that he saw nothing positive in creation, a subject related to "glory."

Second, I agree with Luther in emphasizing the cross as the ultimate act of God for the salvation of the world, and that God was actually in Christ on the cross reconciling the world to himself.[35] There is no objection to seeing God's revelation in Jesus on the cross. However, it is not the only way,

34. Featherstone, "Theology of the Cross," 50.
35. 1 Cor 15:17.

and Paul himself can speak of various modes of revelation.[36] The testimony of the Gospels and Acts makes the revelation of God in Christ much richer. In Acts, and even in Paul, the Easter experience is vital.[37]

Third, while the suffering of Christ and its salvific value are unquestionable, the value and necessity of the suffering of Christians as part of the cross of Christ are not at all established. There is ample evidence that Christians are susceptible to suffering because of their faith, but not as part of the salvific suffering of Christ.[38] Indeed, Luther insisted on this aspect of Christian witness. For Luther, the suffering and the cross (sometimes the same thing, sometimes both words used) refer and correspond also to the sufferings of Christians.[39] While the Bible supports the necessity for Christians to suffer, it is clear we are called to suffer *for* (because of our faith in) Christ. In this limited sense, Luther's understanding of suffering for Christians is acceptable. But he cannot be accepted when invoking this idea to silence the poor peasants of his time who were struggling for justice (liberation from exploitation) so that they would accept their position as impoverished servants of the wealthy aristocrats (who, incidentally, were providing for and protecting Luther himself).[40] It will not work to argue that by accepting to suffer under the yoke of landlords, the peasants would be suffering *for* or because of Christ. This was sheer exploitation that stemmed from greed and the desire to preserve the economic, social, and cultural status quo. Can we imagine that God was revealing himself in the plight of these poor peasants? Was God on the side of the peasants? We know he was in and with Christ on the cross. We know what he was doing there—reconciling the world to himself. The result was the shedding of the blood, giving himself on our behalf, the result of which is that we have salvation. We can find nothing good that God might have been doing with the peasants who, with Luther's endorsement, were crushed and killed mercilessly by the landlords who controlled their lives.

A Case for the Theology of the Blood

Having established that the cross does not symbolize suffering in the African church, and that we need to be contextual, we have three options. First, we may struggle to teach the people about the cruelty of the cross as

36. Even 1 Cor 2:1-2 should not be understood as Paul's approach everywhere, but expressly at Corinth, as depicted in the first chapter (similar to Luther at Heidelberg).

37. 1 Cor. 1:18 notwithstanding. See Acts 1:22; 1 Cor 15:1-22. See also a discussion on the factor of the resurrection in Kwesi Dickson, "Theology of the Cross."

38. Romans 12:12; 2 Cor 1:5-7; Phil 1:29; 3:8; 1 Thess 2:2, 14; 2:14; 3:4. Exceptions that might imply that believers suffer as part of Christ's suffering include Rom 5:3; 8:17; and Phil 3:10.

39. Von Loewenich, *Luther's Theology*, 113ff.

40. In his "Admonition to Peace: A Reply to the Twelve Articles of the Peasants in Swabia"; LW 36:5ff.

it was in the time of Paul and about Luther's theology of the cross. Second, we may leave the cross as it is for Africans and look for another symbol that communicates the important concepts in Luther's theology of the cross. Third, we may supplement Luther's theology of the cross in a contextually fruitful way.

I think the first option is tedious, unpredictable, and certainly unnecessary. As much as we are Lutherans, we need to know that the most important factor in Luther's theology was to make God's salvation known and understandable to the German people of his time. And of course, our time and place are extremely different. As Rudolph Featherstone states, many Lutheran scholars would maintain that "Luther relied heavily upon the reality of his own experiences and struggles, his understanding of 'the righteousness of God,' and, among other things, on the scriptural testimony of Paul in formulating what he called the *theologia crucis*, the 'theology of the cross.'"[41]

Some prominent African Lutherans have begun to question the essence of our Lutheranism as Africans. Ambrose Moyo goes so far as to question the legitimacy of maintaining that there are only three sacraments; he wants to find a way for the African Lutheran church to "respond concretely to the needs expressed in our African Christian spirituality."[42]

With the commendable emphasis of contextualization of theology, I argue that Africans must find a way to enrich the theology of the cross to communicate the important message of God's revelation in Christ as well as our experience through suffering. I propose *the theology of the blood*.[43]

While this theology will explicate fairly the salvific purpose of Jesus' death on the cross, it will restore the blood on the cross. It is a paradoxical symbol of death and life, suffering and healing, conflict and reconciliation, defilement and cleansing. The connection between the cross and the blood, even in the theology of Paul, is clear, though Lutheran theologians have long neglected it.[44]

Once, in an American congregation, I displayed a drawing of a crucifix with blood dripping from the side and hands of Jesus. The drawing was so grotesque that people would not look at it. Of course there were dozens of crosses everywhere in the church—in the building, on furniture, on robes, on stoles, on linens, and at the altar. None of them was offensive. With blood on the cross, I created a stir.

41. Featherstone, "Theology of the Cross," 45f.
42. Ambrose Moyo, "A Time for an African Lutheran Theology," in *Theology and the Black Experience*, 92f.
43. I have called for the need for the hermeneutic of resonance, demonstrating its efficacy and richness in my doctoral dissertation: Fidon R. Mwombeki, "Biblical Interpretation in a Current African Situation: The Case of Blood" (unpublished doctoral dissertation, Luther Seminary, 1997).
44. The liturgy and hymns of Lutheran tradition are rich in the symbolism of blood on the cross.

The cross is clean and nice, golden, adorned, and glorified, to the extent that all talk of the cross is a talk of glory. How do we make the cross a real, grotesque stumbling block? As our crosses are empty, so may our understanding of its efficacy become. To provide a corrective we must restore blood on the cross and talk as much about blood as the cross, insofar as they are both symbols with sufficient biblical grounding.[45]

The language of blood in African settings would resonate with the message of the death of Christ, adequately complementing the language of the cross. We have discovered that blood is paradoxical in the fact that it presents different messages.[46] It is a symbol of life (existence, suffering, death), cements covenants between people, is sacrificial for cleansing and protection, and is significant in reconciliation (or revenge), as well as in thanksgiving.

The theology of blood would help us in Africa, and thereby contribute to the global church, a new dimension to understanding the event of Christ's death and resurrection in a new and rich way. Several aspects of this theology relate to the death of Christ.

First, the death of Christ as sacrificial and for us. The cross, void of the blood, could not visually present to us the understanding of the work of Christ as pouring out life for us, without much explanation. But shedding of blood signifies death, the pouring out of life itself.[47] As we practice the ritual of Holy Communion, we are reminded daily as we receive the wine, "This is the blood of Christ, shed for you." Certainly, we know it is "the blood of his cross."[48] Focus on the blood shed on the cross makes the cross what it really is, the place where God gave life itself for our redemption, a priceless gift for all of us who now can believe and follow him.

The second aspect is that of the covenant of relationship among believers. Featherstone and Cone rightly differentiate between those who raise the question of suffering in an abstract, individualistic, rational and theoretical way (spectators), on the one hand, and those who raise it in an experiential way (participators), as the reality of their being, on the other.[49]

We have seen how Luther, while in aristocratic castles protected from death and suffering, never cared about the plight of the poor peasants. They could go on suffering, unto death, without disobeying their "masters." This is where the social impact of the spectator's position is so blasphemous. And here the classic theology of the cross does not help us much. It must be transformed. Precisely here the theology of the blood is enriching.

---

45. See further discussion in Mwombeki: *Biblical Interpretation in a Current African Situation: The Case of Blood* (PhD dissertation, Luther Seminary, 1997), 83–125.
46. Ibid., 145ff.
47. Biblical references to this effect are many. From the Old Testament, on which Paul builds his theology, blood is life itself.
48. Col 1:20.
49. Featherstone, "Theology of the Cross," 51.

The theology of the blood would emphasize that those who are in Christ are brothers and sisters, bound in covenant by the blood of Jesus, as we all share the cup in Holy Communion.[50] By partaking of it, we become one. When one suffers, we all suffer; when one rejoices, we all rejoice. This theology would put away the present trends, which are individualistic, nationalistic, and careless.

One of my favorite verses in relation to other people in the faith has always been Gen 4:9, where God asked Cain: "Where is Abel, your brother?" Cain, knowing where Abel was, lied: "I do not know; am I my brother's keeper?" When I presented this verse in an American congregation recently and argued for an attitude of "caring" about our brothers and sisters in the Lord, an elderly woman came to me afterwards and whispered to me: "I agree, but very few people here think that Africans are our brothers and sisters." And this is where the theology of the blood could help.

The theology of the blood calls for the entire world to know that we are one, to know that the sacrificial blood of Christ has bought us all. When we share the bread and wine at the Lord's Table, whether together physically or in spirit, we become one, and we are in covenant with one another in the Lord. It therefore calls us to real suffering, but suffering with a purpose—suffering for others in the process of liberation. It is significant that theology in the West legitimized slavery—even genocide—in the quest for acquisition of property. Theology, even Luther's in the case of peasants, sided with the rich for the safety of self. Not so many times do we hear of the heroic suffering of Moses, who refused to stay in the palace of Pharaoh and chose to suffer with his blood-kin. And the cross is nothing less than God "emptying" Godself for the deliverance of sinners. In the same spirit, the theology of blood is the reductio ad absurdum of ideologies called theologies that do not recognize and take practical steps to participate in the suffering of others. Theorizing that those who suffer have God on their side is empty and hollow. We need to be human believers who are ready to go all the way with the sufferers in their struggle to overcome the suffering. This is the proper understanding of the cross. The cross was not suffering for its own sake. It was suffering that shed the blood that brought salvation to the world.

The theology of the blood of the covenant is also the theology of the blood of reconciliation. This theology calls for practical steps to be taken not only to reconcile individuals in the congregation who need it and not only to reconcile an individual sinner with God. It is a powerful message of reconciliation in communities, between the sufferer and the torturer, the necessity of which has been obvious after traumatic situations worldwide. What is the message of the cross in Iraq, in Rwanda, in Zimbabwe, in South Africa, or in New York? It is a message about the blood that cleanses and

---

50. 1 Cor. 11:25

binds together but also symbolizes the pricelessness of life, which some people disregard in their quest for power and glory.

The theology of the cross, enriched to become the theology of the blood
of his cross, can address our salvation as well as the call for solidarity in the
blood of Christ in a covenant to work to alleviate suffering and pain wherever it may be found.

JUSTIFICATION

THE DOCTRINE OF JUSTIFICATION was in the sixteenth century the dividing line between Lutherans and the Roman Catholic Church. The emphasis on justification expressed the Reformation understanding of the biblical witness of Christ and was the reason why the Reformers had to confess their faith over against the dominating authorities in church and society. This explains the strong doctrinal strain in Lutheranism and, accordingly, the importance of the confessional writings.

In modern times, however, there have been tendencies to diminish the role of the confessional writings and to regard them as bound to the context of the past. Their significance was mainly seen as drawing a line of exclusion rather than as expressing a treasure of insight and inspiration.

The doctrine of justification nevertheless maintained and even widened its importance in twentieth-century Protestantism, partly due to the modern interest in individual freedom and selfhood. This has raised discussions as to whether the modern understanding of justification covers the full spectrum of the Reformation understanding of scriptural witness. Does the doctrine of justification as "the article by which the church stands and falls" give due regard to the whole body of Christian doctrine centered in Trinity and Christology? Does it give justice to the bonds between God's act of justification on the one hand, and human renewal (often labeled the "forensic" and the "effective" aspects of justification) on the other? And what is the relation between justification and the sacraments, and between the overcoming of sin by God's word of forgiveness and our continuous struggle against the evil within us and around us? These discussions have been an essential precondition for ecumenical dialogues, the most important of which resulted in the *Joint Declaration on the Doctrine of Justification*, officially signed between The Lutheran World Federation and the Roman Catholic Church on October 31, 1999.

Simo Peura argues that Luther's understanding of justification has to be seen in connection with the Sacrament of Baptism, in which the sinful and faithful person is placed "in Christ." This means on the one hand—and against late medieval teaching—that the human person's sin, remaining after Baptism, really is sin. On the other hand—and much closer to the Roman Catholic standpoint—this remaining sin is treated as dominated by the real presence of Christ. The *Joint Declaration* was made possible by working out the interconnection between these two aspects of Luther's theology of justification. This line of thought may be continued in the future to reach an ecumenical consensus about issues as yet unresolved.

David G. Truemper wishes to regain a central place for the Confessional documents without falling back to mere repetition of the past. He suggests reading and using the confessions as resources and guides for faithful life and work. To this end, he applies a bifocal approach, reading the symbolic texts against the background of their time and also with a view toward our own contemporary situation. In this way, it will be possible to transcend the polarity of historical relativism and dogmatic absolutism.

—PETER WIDMANN

CHAPTER 9

Baptism, Justification, and the *Joint Declaration*

Simo Peura

Now we finally come to the point. A righteous and faithful man doubtless has both grace and the gift. Grace makes him wholly pleasing so that his person is wholly accepted, and there is no place for wrath in him any more, but the gift heals from sin and from all his corruption of body and soul. It is therefore most godless to say that one who is baptized is still in sin, or that all his sins are not fully forgiven.[1]

The Means of Justification

The Lutheran doctrine of justification has traditionally proclaimed that salvation is not based on human works but on God's grace and on the work of Christ. Furthermore, Lutheran theology has always tied in salvation inseparably and permanently with Christ's person (*solus Christus*) and the reconciliation effected in him on the cross. If a Christian apprehends Christ in faith, she or he is able to participate in Christ and the salvation effected by him, which now exists exclusively in him.

Because the death and the resurrection of Christ took place almost 2000 years ago, it becomes inevitable that Lutheran theology preconditions certain "means" that bring salvation to our time. If Lutheran theology wants to underline the Christocentric understanding of salvation, it must also emphasize sacramental realism. In Lutheranism the sacrament cannot be only a sign that refers to the object external to the sacrament. It is possible to bring salvation to human beings only if the sacrament includes the reality to which it refers and that it gives to its receiver.

Luther explains the means of salvation in his writing *Von Abendmahl Christi: Bekenntnis* (1528). According to Luther, the gift of salvation includes what God is as well as what God has done to save human beings. The salvation of an individual human being begins when the Holy Spirit reveals Jesus Christ and his work to us. When this is revealed to sinners, the

---

1. Luther, "Against Latomus," LW 32:229.

Holy Spirit helps them to understand salvation, to preserve it, to use it to their advantage, and to impart it to others, increasing and extending it. It is the aim of the Holy Spirit that the gifts of salvation are realized in the life of a Christian both "inwardly and outwardly."[2]

Luther's idea that salvation should become "inwardly" true means that a Christian participates in God and receives the spiritual gifts through faith. We might say that an incarnation takes place in the Christian. The other point, that salvation is provided "outwardly," refers to the means by which the Holy Spirit saves and justifies human beings. The three means are the proclamation of the gospel and the sacraments of Baptism and the Eucharist. Through these means, and in them, the Holy Spirit comes to us, "inculcates" the work of Christ in us, and actualizes in us what Christ once did on the cross and in the resurrection. He restores to life and righteousness that which was once corrupted.[3] In this way the death and resurrection of Christ benefits all individual Christians in all places and in all times.

If salvation is understood as participation in the Triune God who gives himself to a sinner,[4] we must conclude that Lutherans must take seriously their own theology of the Word and sacraments in ecumenical relations. Otherwise Lutherans give up the ontological preconditions of their theological thinking and doctrine. The external—the means of salvation—is always first and prior to the inward side—faith and the reception of the spiritual gifts. For this reason, the sacrament of Baptism offers a solid starting point to consider the doctrine of justification and its ecumenical implications.

Baptism as the Beginning Point of Justification

1. It is not possible to speak about the sacrament of Baptism until the Word of God, the proclamation of Jesus Christ, has connected itself with natural water and become one with it in a specific sense. In the Large Catechism (Baptism 18), Luther leans on the Augustinian definition of a sacrament: "*accedat verbum ad elementum et fit sacramentum*" (when the Word is added to the element, it becomes a sacrament). When the natural water in the rite of Baptism has been "consecrated," it is no longer simply natural water. God has combined with it a treasure greater and nobler than heaven and earth. God's commandment and God's name are joined to the baptismal water, and they cannot be separated from it. Therefore, baptismal water is "a very different thing" from all other water.[5]

We notice the realistic standpoint of Luther's theology of Baptism when he says that the baptismal water is actually "divine, heavenly, holy, and blessed water" or something even worthier of praise. The argument is simple

2. *StA* 4:251, 22—252, 2; LW 37:366.
3. *StA* 4:252, 3–5; LW 37:366.
4. *BSLK* 660, 63, 18—64, 4; 661, 36—662, 1. See *StA* 4, 251, 22–29; LW 37:366.
5. *BSLK* 694, 15–21.

and obvious: God has staked his honor, his power, and his might on the baptismal water. For this reason, Baptism contains and conveys all that God is and is able to do if it is used in accordance with its purpose.[6] Luther thus argues that Baptism is a real means of salvation. These statements are not accidental ones but must be seen in the wider context of the Large Catechism. Its core idea is that the Triune God, when he saves human beings, gives himself as the Father, as the Son, and as the Holy Spirit with all their spiritual gifts. When the idea is applied to Baptism, it means that God through his word includes in the baptismal water the treasure, that is, his honor and name, what he is, and what he does. Faith can believe this because God has implanted his Word in this external ordinance, that is, the water, and joined his name to it. The Reformer states: "Thus faith clings to the water and believes it to be Baptism in which there is sheer salvation and life."[7]

Thus, from the ontological point of view, Baptism is a union of God's Word and natural water. Therefore, we must speak about Baptism only on the condition that the Word of God and the water are not separated from each other. According to Luther, faith has to call all its attention to the baptismal water in which the Word of God exists. The Reformer is convinced that God offers the treasure of salvation only in an external ordinance, which means here the water of Baptism. When grasping the baptismal water in faith, a Christian grasps the treasure that the water contains and participates in it.[8]

2. The Reformer reflects on the *effects* of Baptism from two points of view in a way that is typical for justification, too. I begin by considering a quotation from his "Sermon on Baptism" (1519):

> Faith means that one firmly believes all this: that this sacrament not only signifies death and the resurrection at the Last Day, by which a person is made new to live without sin eternally, but also that it assuredly begins and achieves this; that it establishes a covenant between us and God to the effect that we will fight against sin and slay it, even to our dying breath, while he for his part will be merciful to us, deal graciously with us, and—because we are not sinless in this life until purified by death—not judge us with severity.[9]

Luther's standpoint is that Baptism and faith unite a Christian with Christ (*unio cum Christo*). Because of this union, a Christian becomes free from sin in earthly life. Even if he or she does not become completely sinless or totally righteous, the basic change is real, and it has already taken place. The renewal of a Christian is, however, something that begins in this

---

6. *BSLK* 694, 21–30.
7. *BSLK* 696, 37–43.
8. *BSLK* 696, 43–48; see also *BSLK* 697, 1–26.
9. *StA* 1:264, 13–19; LW 35:35.

life but does not reach completion until the day of resurrection. Second, God shows favor toward a Christian, because she or he has become one with Christ. This is the case even though there is still sin in the person and she or he will never become completely cleansed. A Christian is permanently an object for God's goodwill and favor, and the holy God will not condemn the person. The third point is penance. It includes the fight against sin and its mortification.

Correspondingly, Luther in the Large Catechism describes the effects of Baptism. Baptism means participation in the true reality of salvation. It effects a true change and renewal of a Christian. A Christian is radically transformed by being given grace, Spirit, and power through Baptism to suppress the "old person." However, in spite of true transformation, the "new person" is not yet complete. Dying and being raised with Christ must continue through one's entire life. For this reason, it is necessary that the "qualities" of the old person, that is, irascibility, spite, envy, greed, pride, and doubt, must be daily decreased so that the new person may come forth and grow strong. Thus the qualities of the old person must be replaced by that what belongs to the new life, that is, the fruits of faith. The old person must become weaker day by day and finally completely disappear.[10]

Luther's description contains the three points that we already know from his sermon on Baptism. The first is that the gift of salvation is something very real in a Christian's life, even if the gift has not yet caused a complete transformation. This fact by no means contradicts the other, that a Christian is not yet totally free from sin but transgresses against the will of God. In spite of sin, a Christian does not lose the gift and treasure once given in Baptism. Second, the forgiveness of sin is continuously necessary because the transformation is still incomplete. For this reason, Luther says, "As we have once obtained forgiveness of sins in Baptism, so forgiveness remains day by day as long as we live, that is, as long as we carry the old Adam about our necks."[11] God's favor toward a Christian does not change, even if there is still sin in him or her. Third, continuous repentance unavoidably belongs to the Christian life. Luther even calls it "the third sacrament." A Christian has to fight against sin so that new life begins and so that what had begun earlier in Baptism would be practiced.[12]

3. If we use the vocabulary of the doctrine of justification, Luther's first point is the same as the effective aspect of justification. According to the Lutheran view, a Christian is made righteous in a real but incomplete way during her or his earthly life. Furthermore, the effective aspect includes the idea that the transformation is something continuous and makes progress: the new person must grow daily and the old person diminish. Second,

10. *BSLK* 704, 25—705, 6; 705, 30–37; 705, 47—706, 30; 707, 14–28.
11. *BSLK* 707, 40–45.
12. *BSLK* 705, 47—706, 30.

forgiveness of sins refers to the imputative aspect of justification; it is something comprehensive. Even if a Christian is still partly a sinner, God does not condemn but declares the person righteous. Because of these two first points, it is possible, third, that a Christian live righteously. When the Christian fights against sin and repents, the new life with the fruits of faith can come into existence.

Justification

1. Luther expressly explained his understanding of justification in relation to Baptism in his writing "Against Latomus" (1521). Latomus, a late medieval scholastic theologian, had criticized the Reformer because of his view on sin.[13] Luther's defense and arguments were based on his theology of Baptism described above and on the conviction that Christ is given to a Christian in Baptism.

For Luther, all Christian righteousness is in Christ (Rom 5:15). Christ has become our righteousness, because he has defeated sin and other destructive powers through his own righteousness in death and resurrection. This means that God's saving righteousness exists for us only in Christ: he is at the same time God's favor (*favor Dei*) and God's gift (*donum Dei*). Although God the Father shows his favorable disposition primarily toward Christ, God also regards a Christian as righteous in spite of sin, because a Christian has become one with Christ. For the same reason, a Christian has Christ as God's gift, which renews and makes him or her righteous.

2. In Lutheran theology, it is possible to speak about justification only on the condition that both aspects of justification described above are taken into account. Forgiveness of sin is the necessary condition of the gift; otherwise the renewal of a Christian does not move forward. We can say that, in this sense, the imputative aspect of justification is a condition for the effective aspect of justification. However, the relation between the two aspects is reciprocal. God's favor is directed toward a Christian only if she or he has received Christ as a gift. This means that there is a reason for God to declare a sinner righteous, if Christ is, as God's gift, present in a Christian, and if Christ has begun the renewal in the person. In this sense, the effective aspect is the necessary condition for the imputative aspect of justification.

The latter claim has often been passed over in Luther research, but I refer to Luther's own argumentation, in which he points to the necessity of the gift and the renewal created by it. He says: "To be sure, for grace there is no sin, because the whole person pleases; yet for the gift there is sin which it purges away and overcomes. A person neither pleases, nor has grace,

---

13. I have considered Luther's view on justification according to his writing against Latomus in more detail in "Christ as Favor and Gift: The Challenge of Luther's Understanding of Justification" in *Union with Christ: The New Finnish Interpretation of Luther*, ed. C. Braaten and R. Jenson (Grand Rapids: Eerdmans), 52–63.

except on account of the gift which labors in this way to cleanse from sin."[14] As this shows, it is not possible to put the two aspects of justification in chronological order. The imputative and the effective aspects of justification are only valid concurrently and in conjunction with one other.

3. Luther makes it clear in "Against Latomus" that justification includes the transformation of a Christian into the likeness of Christ. The transformation is for him a process that continues during a Christian's entire life and does not reach its final point until the resurrection. The permanent basis for and the continuous condition of transformation is the faith that unites a Christian with Christ. The permanent union with Christ in faith is necessary, because only the righteousness of Christ is complete. A Christian is made only partly righteous, and there is progress only if he or she is united with Christ. Therefore, all righteousness of a Christian has its origin permanently in Christ, it comes into existence only through Christ, and it always turns toward Christ. When Christ draws a Christian into himself day by day, that person is finally transformed into the same form as Christ (*plane in Christum transformari*). During the process of transformation, the complete righteousness of Christ becomes the righteousness of a Christian. Moreover, we must keep in mind that Christ's complete righteousness has to protect a Christian against the wrath of God as long as her or his own righteousness is incomplete.[15]

Therefore we can conclude that Luther's view on justification includes the imputative aspect as well as the effective aspect: a Christian is made and declared righteous because of Christ and his righteousness. If we disconnect the two aspects from each other, the doctrine of justification disintegrates in Lutheran theology. In doing so, we would arrive at the point in which the renewal already effected in a human being is the reason for his justification, or in which the effective aspect is a kind of "appendage" of the declared righteousness. The Lutheran doctrine of justification keeps its logical consistency and wholeness only if we take the union with Christ effected in Baptism as the beginning point of our considerations.

4. There is still one noteworthy issue in Luther's critique of Latomus in the context of Lutheran–Roman Catholic ecumenical relations. The main controversy between Luther and Latomus concerned the question of the sense in which a Christian is a sinner after his or her Baptism (*post baptismum*). The two theologians did not dispute the idea that if a Christian transgresses the will of God *post iustificationem*, he or she thereby becomes a sinner. Both of them acknowledged that possibility, even though they argued in a very different manner. Luther and Latomus did not dispute the issue of the sins of a Christian *post iustificationem*, which result in God's

14. *StA* 2:494, 9–12; LW 32:229; see also *StA* 2:499, 31–32 (cf. the translation in LW 32:236).
15. *StA* 2:499, 11–34; LW 32:235–36.

condemnation, or if sin in this sense separates a Christian from God *post baptismum et iustificationem*. To these questions, both Luther and Latomus gave a negative answer: "the sins neither cause God's condemnation nor separate from God," but the responsive arguments were different.[16] There were at the core of the controversy two questions: about (1) the nature of sin according to its essence and (2) the way in which sin exists in a baptized person *post baptismum*.

Luther does not share the view of Latomus on the essence of sin, because the scholastic definition of sin makes righteousness by works possible. According to Luther, we must not consider sin as a quality within the framework of Aristotelian-scholastic metaphysics, as Latomus does. We must instead consider sin in its relation to God's mercy. In line with this understanding, Luther reflects on the question of how Baptism cleanses the baptized of sin. He makes a distinction between the two aspects: the removal of the essence of sin and the destruction of the effects of sin.

> It must not therefore be said that baptism does not remove all sins; it indeed removes all, but not according to their substance. The power of all, and most (*plurimum*) of the substance, are taken away. Day by day the sin is removed according to its substance so that it may be utterly destroyed.[17]

As we can see, Luther establishes a difference between the removal of sin *secundum substantiam* (with respect to substance) and the removal of sin *secundum vires eius* (with respect to its power). He states first that Baptism removes most of the sin according to its substance. This means that there still remains a certain "amount" of sin or the remnants of sin (*reliquiae peccati*) in the baptized person. However, all sin that has remained in a Christian after Baptism is still in its nature true sin. In this sense, Luther wants to be faithful to Paul who said, "Sin lives in me."[18]

Luther's second point is that Baptism takes all the power away from sin. Because of Baptism, sin has been captured, condemned, and completely weakened so that it cannot carry a Christian to perdition. Luther describes sin as a robber who has been captured and is after that declared to death; one who is powerless, waiting for the fulfillment of the punishment. When sin is "included" in this way under grace, it loses its power to affect the baptized in a significant way (*praevalet*).[19]

Keeping in mind the different aspects of the doctrine of justification, Luther means that the remaining sin of a Christian (*peccatum manens*) consists of the remnants of sin (*peccatum reliquum/reliquiae peccati*) that are true sins in their nature. Therefore, a Christian is partly righteous and

16. *StA* 2:486, 19–33; LW 32:220–21. *StA* 2:500, 1–11; LW 32:236.
17. *StA* 2:476, 5–8 ; LW 32:207–8; see also *StA* 2:489, 27—490, 15; LW 32:225.
18. *StA* 2:470, 20–26; LW 32:203. *StA* 2:473, 37–40; LW 32:207.
19. *StA* 2:473, 23–474, 13; LW 32:206–7.

partly a sinner. However, because the Christian is in grace, that is, in union with Christ, the remaining sin is by no means a reason for God's wrath and it is not counted as sin. Because of the forgiveness of sin and the imputation of righteousness, the Christian is totally righteous, whereas in himself or herself, that is, without Christ, the person would be completely a sinner.

From an ecumenical point of view, the most challenging aspect of Luther's view on justification is that the remaining sin after Baptism is not the same sin as it was but is a "reigned sin" (*peccatum regnatum*).[20] When a human being is baptized and the power of God has been poured into the person, that is, Christ is given as God's gift and grace, the sin is subjected in the person and can no longer rule (*peccatum non regnans*). Therefore, a Christian can fight against the remaining sin. Because a Christian has received Christ as God's grace and gift and participates in Christ, Christ rules in the person and makes him or her able to resist the temptations of sin. A Christian does not have to consent (*consentire*) to the temptations of sin that still "live" in her or him: "So sin is truly sin, but because grace and the gift are within me, it is not imputed; not on account of its innocence— as if it were not harmful—but because grace and the gift reign within me."[21]

It is most important in Luther's argumentation that a Christian is *in* Christ. With this idea, the Reformer is able, on the one hand, to claim against Latomus that after Baptism the remaining sin is true sin according to its nature. On the other hand, the ideas of the real presence of Christ and the union with Christ help him to argue that the remaining sin is a *peccatum regnatum*. If the former expresses the difference between Lutheran and Roman Catholic standpoints, the latter brings the opinions much nearer to each other than we might assume.

The *Joint Declaration*[22]

1. The first draft of the *Joint Declaration on the Doctrine of Justification* was sent to the churches for their consideration in spring 1995. If compared with the first draft, the final text of the document was remarkably developed. As a result of the drafting process, the notions of the declared righteousness (the imputative aspect of justification) and the effective righteousness(the effective aspect of justification) became common to both churches. Besides this, the drafters built a bridge between the contents of

20. *StA* 2:470, 1–12, 20–26; LW 32:202–3. *StA* 2:471, 17–20; LW 32:204. *StA* 2:477, 9–27; LW 32:210. *StA* 2:479, 33—480, 13; LW 32:213–14. *StA* 2:481, 12–14; LW 32:215. *StA* 2:509, 13–17; LW 32:248. *StA* 2:509, 27—510, 2; LW 32:248–49. *StA* 2:511, 6–12; LW 32:250–51.

21. *StA* 2:509, 39—510, 2; LW 32:248–249; see also *StA* 2:470, 1–4; LW 32:202; *StA* 2:479, 5–14; LW 32:212; *StA* 2:502, 2–25; LW 32:239; *StA* 2:511, 6–12. LW 32:250–51.

22. The Lutheran World Federation and The Roman Catholic church, *Joint Declaration on the Doctrine of Justification* (Grand Rapids and Cambridge, U.K.: Eerdmans, 2000).

those terms. This was done by pointing to three basic convictions: (1) justi-fication has a Trinitarian-christological basis, (2) the righteousness of a Christian is bound together with Christ's person and work of salvation, which means that a Christian must become one with Christ to be justified, and (3) Baptism is a real renewal of the baptized.

First, the Trinitarian-christological basis is stated in Article 15. This section was expanded remarkably during the drafting process. Originally there was only a quotation from the document, "All under One Christ," which was produced by the International Lutheran–Roman Catholic Commission.[23] The original document did not consider justification as an activity of the Triune God. However, the final draft of the *JD* considers the works of the Holy Trinity as the basis of justification: "In faith we together hold the conviction that justification is the work of the triune God. The Father sent His Son into the world to save sinners. The foundation and pre-supposition of justification is the incarnation, death, and resurrection of Christ. Justification thus means that Christ himself is our righteousness, in which we share through the Holy Spirit in accord with the will of the Father."[24]

The change cited above shows that the doctrine of justification is not understood to be the core of the whole Christian doctrine. There is now a balance between the doctrine of justification and the other basic truths there. According to *JD*, justification is neither just one part or the most important part of all doctrine but "stands in an essential relation to all truths of the faith."[25] In spite of criticism from some Lutheran theologians, this description of justification and its relation to other truths of the faith is a very important one because it protects the Lutheran understanding of the doctrine against one-sided interpretations. If a very narrowly interpreted doctrine of justification is accepted as the norm over other truths of the faith, the understanding of the whole doctrine becomes distorted and thin. There are many other basic truths of the faith that belong to the very core of the Christian faith, for example, the doctrines of the Trinity and Christology. Moreover, these doctrines are in order "before" the doctrine of justification, and they must be understood as necessary conditions for its understanding and interpretation.

Second, the final document connects righteousness, by which a Christian is declared and made righteous, with Christ's person and work. It is stated in *JD* that if a Christian attains the righteousness of Christ, he has to be united with Christ in faith. This is the idea that brings the declared and effective aspects in connection with one another. In the first draft of *JD* (1995), the aspects were put in relation to each other in another way. It was

23. *JD* (1995), 14.
24. *JD* 15.
25. *JD* 18.

claimed that the two aspects of God's gracious action should not be separated; the connecting factor was only the agent of that gracious action, God.[26] In the final document (1997), the connection is based on the conviction that a Christian is united with Christ: that is why a Christian shares in Christ and his righteousness. When living in a Christian, Christ is for him or her the forgiveness of sins and God's saving presence.[27]

Third, the basis of the common understanding was strengthened by pointing to the sacrament of Baptism. This was necessary because of the differences in views on the justified as sinner. The disagreement was actually discovered during the drafting process, and it almost hindered progress and prevented the working out of the final document. The role of Baptism is emphasized twice in the common articles of the final text. The drafting group made the first amendment concerning Baptism to Article 25 in June 1996 in Würzburg. The text was honed once again in 1997, when the document was finalized. It was stated: "By the action of the Holy Spirit in baptism, they are granted the gift of salvation, which lays the basis for the whole Christian life."[28]

In January 1997, the other amendment to Article 28 was completed, in which the issue of "the justified as sinner" was addressed, because the previous draft was satisfactory for neither the Roman Catholic Church nor the Lutheran churches. Thus, the final draft of Article 28 emphasizes the union with Christ that comes into existence in Baptism, as well as the true renewal of a Christian effected by that union. The document states: "We confess together that in baptism the Holy Spirit unites one with Christ, justifies, and truly renews the person." In light of this understanding, it became possible for the churches to claim together that the struggle against the selfish desires of the old Adam and penance belong to the life of a Christian after Baptism.[29]

2. One can claim that Article 28 of the *JD* is a good compromise between two different approaches to the problem of defining how a justified Christian is a sinner. Indeed, Article 28 expresses the common understanding of the question as far as it is possible today for the Lutherans and the

26. *JD* (1995), 21. This means that the drafters actually gave up the precondition; there would be two different ways to express the same content: it is enough to understand justification either as the forgiveness of sins or as effective righteousness.

27. *JD* 22. *JD* 23, the Lutheran article in the issue, is a compromise of different Lutheran views on justification. It refers only superficially to Luther's "Against Latomus" and Christ as God's favor. The Lutherans had to be satisfied with another compromise concerning this issue in Article 26. In the end of the article, it is said: "Justification and renewal are joined in Christ, who is present in faith."

28. *JD* 25. Cf. *JD* (1995), 24. Baptism was mentioned in the draft of 1995 only in the Roman Catholic Article 26, whereas the Lutherans mentioned nothing about Baptism in their Article 25. However, the final text considers the justified as sinner in the context of Baptism in the Lutheran Article 29 and in the Roman Catholic Article 30.

29. *JD* 28. Cf. *JD* (1995), 27.

Roman Catholics. In spite of that we must ask, however, if the difference in views was specified clearly enough and whether the drafters used all the possibilities offered by Luther's disputation with Latomus.[30]

The Lutherans and the Roman Catholics in dialogue did not actually have differing views on the matters of whether sin still has negative effects on the baptized and of how the Christian should respond to the temptations of sin. In their ecumenical dialogue, both partners wanted to point to the fight against sin, which endures to the end of a Christian's life; conversion and penance are part of Christian life in faith. The difference of views on the doctrine of sin relate to the question of the specific way sin "exists" in a justified person after Baptism.

The Roman Catholic point of view is described in Article 30. There it is said that the grace of Jesus Christ imparted in Baptism takes away all that is sin "in the proper sense" and "worthy of damnation." Thus, there is no sin, in the strict sense of the word, in a Christian after Baptism, but an inclination toward sin, that is, concupiscence. Even if the inclination is objectively in contradiction to God and his "original design for humanity," it is not sin in itself. According to the Roman Catholic understanding, we cannot speak about human sin until a human being consents, by a voluntary act, to the inclination coming from sin. This means that the acting out of sin always involves a personal element. The sin after Baptism originally exists outside of the person but becomes his or her own sin at the moment the person voluntarily consents to the temptation.[31]

Lutherans have a different view of the justified person as sinner. They argue in Article 29 that a Christian is permanently a sinner, as affirmed in the classic statement of the Lutheran doctrine of justification: a Christian is *simul iustus et peccator* (at the same time justified and sinful). The Lutherans specify this statement with the help of the *totus* and *partim* aspects of justification, first considering the total aspect. When analyzing Article 29, we notice that it has become, in some sense, inwardly strained. This discovery shows that the article is a compromise between different Lutheran interpretations. According to the article, a Christian remains a total sinner when considered by the law (*usus legis*). After having made this claim, the drafters come to the conclusion that sin still lives in a justified Christian (1 John 1:8; Rom 7:17, 20). Besides the references to Scripture, the reason for the claim is the observation that a justified person repeatedly turns to false gods and does not love God with that undivided love that God as Creator requires from him or her.[32]

---

30. The Lutheran drafters used Luther's "Against Latomus" in Article 23, in which they try to define the common understanding on the two aspects of justification among Lutherans themselves. The issue of chapter 23 is "Justification as Forgiveness of Sins and Making Righteous."
31. *JD* 30.
32. *JD* 29.

3. In his disputation with Latomus, Luther considered the question of the justified as sinner in a partially different way from how it was considered in the Lutheran–Roman Catholic ecumenical dialogue at the end of the twentieth century. As already stated above, Luther discussed the problem of the remaining sin from the viewpoint that a Christian has become one with Christ in Baptism through faith. Because of this union, most of the sin is abolished according to its substance and all the sin according to its negative effects: condemnation, guilt, punishment, and God's wrath. God the Father has, for Christ's sake, a favorable attitude toward a sinner who has become one with his Son. The sin of a Christian after Baptism consists of remnants that are true sin in their nature but have already lost their ability to reign, to condemn, and to destroy the Christian. This means that the Reformer reflects upon the question from the *partim-partim* as well as from the *totus-totus* point of view.

Had the Lutherans in the ecumenical dialogue emphasized only the *totus* aspect of justification, the difference between Lutheran and Roman Catholic views would have been underlined needlessly and excessively. However, the Lutheran Article 29 also includes the *partim-partim* aspect. The Christian's opposition to God is based on the conviction that sin still lives in him or her (1 John 1:8; Rom 7:17, 20). It prevents undivided love of God and as such is truly sin. In spite of its nature as true sin, it is "ruled" by Christ, because the justified person is bound with him in faith. Therefore, a Christian can in part lead a just life.[33] This means that the *partim-partim* aspect of the Lutheran Article 29 refers in the first place to the actual righteousness of a Christian.

The Lutheran way of dealing with the question of the justified as sinner, as described above, leaves out one issue important to Luther. The Reformer stated, on the one hand, that Baptism has removed most of the sin from the justified. On the other hand, he argued that the remaining sin is true sin in its nature but the sin of a Christian who is one with Christ. Only the latter of Luther's two statements is mentioned in the Lutheran Article 29. It is said that a Christian is in faith bound with Christ, who "rules" her or his sin and, further, that despite this sin, a Christian is not separated from God.[34] However, Luther's idea that Christ has already removed most of the sin is not considered. The drafting process has proceeded here too quickly and stepped forward over to the "next" question, the question of the actual righteousness of the justified, that is, whether the Christian is able to lead a just life or not. Therefore, Luther's conviction that the condition of the baptized is very much different from that of an unbaptized person has not been emphasized enough in the dialogue.

33. Ibid.
34. Ibid.

Article 29 shows that the members of the drafting commission have been aware of the possibilities included in Luther's considerations on *peccatum regnatum*. Even if the drafters have not made good use of them in the common Article 28, the Lutherans state in their own article that they are in agreement with the Roman Catholics concerning the "ruled" sin. The common understanding on this issue could, however, be even greater. The Lutherans could have said that, according to their own opinion, Baptism has already removed most of the sin. In stating this, they would have dispelled some doubts of the Roman Catholics concerning the Lutheran understanding of justification. This is actually the Lutheran standpoint: a Christian is truly made righteous and is renewed in Baptism. The Lutherans state in Article 29 that a Christian has been born anew by Baptism, and the Holy Spirit has forgiven the person's sin.[35] The new birth does not mean only that the position of a Christian's relation to God has changed. Nor is the new birth the same thing as an ability to partly lead a just life and do righteous deeds. Rather, the new birth is a basic transformation of the baptized as a person.

If Lutheran theology takes seriously its own teaching that a Christian is united with Christ in Baptism and thereby made righteous, many of the questions that deal with the realization of the Christian life can be considered in the new light. Then it is possible to speak about the cooperation of Christ and a Christian renewed by God. Because of the union with Christ, a Christian can fight together with Christ against the remaining sin. Luther's understanding of Baptism also offers to modern Lutheran theology the possibility to reflect on the Sacrament of Penance much more unreservedly than is done in *JD*, which hardly addresses the issue. The same applies to the relation of faith and good works, which come into existence due to the cooperation between Christ and a Christian. Moreover, it would be useful to reflect on what the Christian life—the fight against sin, penance, confession, and the works of faith—means for justification. Does not Lutheran theology also teach that the union with Christ in faith deepens and that transformation to the form of Christ makes progress during our earthly life?

4. These questions must be discussed in the Lutheran–Roman Catholic ecumenical dialogue forum of the future. Even if there is no complete consensus on the question of how sin exists in a Christian, it might be that in many other questions concerning the doctrine of justification, the views are much nearer than we had once assumed.

Lutherans and Roman Catholics have reached a consensus in basic truths of the doctrine of justification. *JD* has shown that the core of the doctrine, as the basis of the consensus, includes not only justification but also other basic truths. In order that the basis might be steady enough to carry us further, it must be strengthened by some other truths, which refer to the doctrine of justification. After this there is reason to expect that we

---

35. Ibid.

can reach an adequate consensus on other issues—such as the ministry of the church—which are even more difficult to resolve than the problems of justification. At least for Lutherans, it is necessary to go back to reflect on Luther's argumentation in his writing against Latomus.

CHAPTER 10

The Lutheran Confessional Writings and the Future of Lutheran Theology

David G. Truemper

The Lutheran confessional writings (hereafter LCW) have become problematic for many if not most of the Lutheran churches. True, many of those churches have clauses in their constitutions binding themselves to the LCW as their doctrinal basis. Yet it is not at all clear just *how* those writings are supposed to function as constitutional doctrinal basis for a church's teaching and practice. The LCW are treated either as historical curiosities or else they are taken as timeless formulations of *the* Lutheran position on any and all of the topics addressed therein. But there is little in the literature or in the practice, at least of the American churches, that would suggest just how the normative function of the LCW is to be exercised.

If the LCW are taken merely as historical curiosities, churches will find it easy to dismiss them as documents of decreasing relevance in the contemporary situation. Historical relativizing works in just that fashion—so one thought and even confessed in 1530 or 1577—but today's issues are different or even completely new, and today's situation requires different language and different thought structures, so one can hardly expect to be instructed by them in such matters. And, as our distance in time and culture from the sixteenth century grows, we shall find less and less reason to refer to or to draw upon the LCW as resources for today's church. On the other hand, if the LCW are absolutized as timeless expressions of quintessential Lutheran formulations about doctrine and practice, churches will find it easy to abandon the rigorous demand for constructive theological reflection—in favor of a mere repristination of the formulae of the sixteenth-century confessors and reformers. Even when new problems and questions arise, one will seek to stretch the revered and ancient formulae over ever greater distances of meaning and relevance—until finally the absurdity and irrelevance of the implied logic becomes painfully and embarrassingly evident to all. And, as our distance in time and culture from the sixteenth century grows, we shall find less and less reason to draw upon the LCW as resources for today's church. On left hand and right, available approaches to the LCW do not seem promising.

Available literature on the subject during the later decades of the twentieth century does little to dispel the gloom of the picture just painted. In
what follows, I concentrate on literature that has enjoyed some popularity
and currency in the American churches. It appears that the discussion about
the LCW has been more vigorous in the German churches, as can be seen
from a cursory glance through the documentation in the introduction to
Gunther Wenz, *Theologie der Bekenntnisschriften der evangelisch-
lutherischen Kirche*.[1] Literature current in the American Lutheran churches
is almost completely silent on the question of just how the LCW are to be
resources for today's church. Among the few exceptions to this gloomy
observation are the following.

Günther Gassmann writes, "Commitment to the church's confession . . .
serves as an authoritative guide for the faith and life of the church and as a
hermeneutical means for focusing on the center of Scripture."[2] It is clear that
Gassmann thinks of the Confessions as resources, as he suggests that they
provided guidance to the churches for facing the problem of apartheid in
South Africa. But the promise is not developed in any kind of sketch of a theological procedure or method for deriving such guidance in new situations.[3]

Eric W. Gritsch and Robert W. Jenson come a bit closer when they call the
confessional teaching about justification by faith a meta-linguistic proposal of
dogma to the church catholic.[4] That is, the notion of justification by faith is a
"stipulation about what constitutes gospel speaking, whatever the content."[5]

Charles Arand, writing out of the tradition of the Lutheran
Church–Missouri Synod, seems to agree when he concludes his description
of the various approaches to the LCW by advocating what he calls a
"hermeneutical" approach. Such an approach, he writes, "would draw
attention to their continuing relevance as guides or maps for the further
study of Scripture," and it would draw "attention to the imperative for the
church to address the needs of its day. The church cannot be content merely
to parrot the past."[6] But Arand offers no constructive counsel about how to
accomplish this.

1. Berlin and New York: Walter de Gruyter, 1996, 27–44.
2. Günther Gassmann and Scott Hendrix, *Fortress Introduction to the Lutheran Confessions*
(Minneapolis: Fortress Press, 1999), 182.
3. Gassmann evidently has some sort of process in mind; he writes, "Lutheran identity is a
lived, dynamic reality that cannot simply be equated with this collection of texts. This identity
is shaped and sustained by fundamental theological and pastoral convictions, which are based
in the confessional texts but which are also shaped and nourished by the tradition and living
faith of the Lutheran church" (ibid., 180).
4. Eric W. Gritsch and Robert W. Jenson, *Lutheranism: The Theological Movement and Its
Confessional Writings* (Philadelphia: Fortress Press, 1976), 42–43.
5. The description is Gerhard Forde's, in *Justification by Faith: A Matter of Death and Life*
(reprint; Mifflintown, Pa.: Sigler Press, 1999), 95.
6. Charles Arand, *Testing the Boundaries: Windows to Lutheran Identity* (St. Louis:
Concordia, 1995), 266.

These writers seem to echo the point made in the early 1960s by Vilmos Vajta, who argued that the confessional writings have as their particular function "testing all presuppositions of scriptural interpretation."[7] Further, he suggests, the LCW come to function as "witness" to the biblical gospel; in the confessional witness, "the congregation accepts the Gospel as the message directed to them, but concentrates it toward its center."[8]

Finally, Carl Braaten argues for a similar function for the LCW. They have a hermeneutical significance, he writes, "because they point to the central message of the Scriptures as a whole. They are like a map giving directions on how to find the way through the Scriptures."[9]

Working It Out

It is one thing to name the LCW as the touchstone of Lutheran identity. It is quite another to use them effectively. One serious failure is to treat the Symbols in a "proof text" fashion, that is, as a source of orthodox utterances enforced on a "conform or perish" basis. Perhaps we could call this the "electric fence" theory of confessional loyalty. When an ecclesiastical cow is foolish enough to transgress the bounds of the pasture, she is zapped with a charge to keep her in bounds. Now that may be an effective way of keeping the herd together, but the cows soon learn to stay away from the fence and thus to have no contact with it. And the church learns only to avoid the symbolical books, to conduct its life and to do its care of souls unaffected, for good or ill, by them. Electric fences keep the herd together, but they don't nourish and feed. A fundamentalism of the Symbols may keep us from saying Zwinglian things in our liturgies, but it won't help us to say the gospel effectively in our day.

How may we take the LCW seriously as confessions of the faith for their time and place in the sixteenth century, and still—or perhaps precisely thus—find them helpful for our place and time? To continue the agrarian metaphor, I consider the LCW to be rather like the feed box, the source of nourishment for the ecclesiastical cows, located no doubt in the middle of the pasture or barnyard. Knowing the source of her life, what ecclesiastical cow would want to stray far from the feed box? One would want to stay in close and frequent contact with the source of nourishment and life.

Essentially, I am suggesting a kind of bifocal approach to the LCW, one that tries to read the Symbols and the contemporary situation together in such a way that the evangelical witness of the Symbols might be transmitted into the church's present situation as a resource and guide to faithful life

7. Vilmos Vajta, "Confession as an Ecumenical Concern," in *The Church and the Confessions* (Philadelphia: Fortress Press, 1963), 168f.

8. Ibid., 169.

9. Carl E. Braaten, "Prolegomena to Christian Dogmatics," in *Christian Dogmatics*, ed. Carl E. Braaten and Robert W. Jenson (Philadelphia: Fortress Press, 1984), 1:53.

and work.[10] True, there is a certain amount of untidiness in this approach, and it is hardly a foolproof operation. It assumes an open-ended struggle, not a foregone conclusion. It calls for trust as we wrestle together for ways to witness to the gospel in our world. Since in this view the Symbols are not an answer book, nor a set of preplanned decisions for "what to say when . . ." but are rather evidences of "how at various times the Holy Scriptures were understood in the church of God by contemporaries,"[11] they can help us really in no other way.

It is hardly my intention to denigrate the work of Robert Jenson in his essays exploring the theological workings of the LCW.[12] These essays are wonderfully creative and are surely exemplary and instructive; if you wish to theologize like the LCW, there is hardly a better unpacking of that theology available to English-speaking churches. My purpose is analogous but slightly different. Rather than explicate the theological method of the LCW, I seek to sketch a theological method for the positive use of the confessional writings by today's church and its theologians, pastors, and catechists as they go about the task of making the LCW into a resource for today's church.

Confession and Witness

To begin, one treats the Confessions as what they are, confessions of faith in the promises of God and witnesses to the biblical gospel that authoritatively offers those promises to a world of sinners. Of course, the LCW didn't for the most part start out as confessions, strictly speaking; they were catechisms, defenses of theological arguments, settlements for inner-Lutheran controversies. And even the Augsburg Confession began life as a political document, however much it became also a confession of faith. Nevertheless, each of the documents in the *Book of Concord* is also properly understood as a confession of faith, in the sense in which that was articulated in the previous section of this essay: they state faith's confidence in the promise of the gospel and in so doing they share in a confession's most significant attribute, namely, they bear witness to the biblical gospel.

The LCW are written as documents that hear and respond in faith to the gospel promise. The CA aims to say, formally and officially for the

---

10. G. Wenz writes, "Dass dies so ist, lässt sich freilich nicht ein und für allemal theologisch und kirchenrechtlich dekretieren; es muss sich vielmehr nach Massgabe des Gewissensgewissheit begründenden Evangeliums Jesu Christi, wie es in der Schrift beurkundet ist, je und je neu erweisen" (*Theologie der Bekenntnisschriften* [Tübingen: J. C. B. Mohr, 1994], 24). A few pages later he adds, "An der rechtlichen Verbindlichkeit der Bekenntnistexte lässt sich sinnvollerweise überhaupt nur dann festhalten, wenn von ihnen primär kein lehrgesetzlicher, sondern ein auf theologische Verständigung abzielender Gebrauch gemacht wird" (37).

11. FC, Ep Rule and Norm 8.

12. I refer to the constructive theological chapters and sections that Robert Jenson contributed to the volume he co-authored with Eric Gritsch, *Lutheranism*; see n. 4 above.

confessors, "This is in fact the catholic faith, is it not?"[13] The Apology defends and expands the lesson in hearing the biblical gospel that the CA offered. The Catechisms aim to support the teaching of the faith and the Christian life in home and school. The Treatise and the Smalcald Articles articulate the faith on the occasion of the prospective Mantua Council. In each case, the confessional writing brings to expression the faith of the church in relation to the topic(s) being addressed. Moreover, this view of the documents is supported by the Formula of Concord, both explicitly in the section on the "Rule and Norm" for theological statements and implicitly by the way it speaks about the understanding of the gospel among the Reformers, for example, in SD X. 31 where it speaks of agreement "in der Lehr und allen seinen Artikeln" (in the doctrine and in all its articles). Here "the doctrine" means as much as "the gospel as we have come to understand it," and "all its articles" as much as "all the ways one might articulate" our reformatory understanding of the gospel.[14]

In the CA this point stands out, despite the almost bewildering complexity and multiple purposes of its creation and its history after the presentation in June 1530.[15] Not least because the legal burden of the confession was to meet the requirement of showing that the reforming princes had not departed from the catholic faith (lest they be found culpable under the Justinian Code of having so departed and therefore in jeopardy of losing title, property, and life itself), the CA goes out of its way to show, in topic after topic, the catholicity of its confessed faith. And even a casual rhetorical analysis of the doctrinal articles suggests that the document leans in the direction of an ample confession of faith rather than a mere recitation of or summary of crucial orthodox theological points. That is to say, the CA is not so much a summary of catholic teaching as it is a summary of catholic believing.

---

13. "Here we are concerned with the one Gospel of Jesus Christ, as it is *recorded* in the Holy Scriptures and *witnessed* to in the confessions. In the witness, the congregation accepts the Gospel as the message directed to them, but concentrates it toward its center" (Vajta, "Confession as an Ecumenical Concern," 169).

14. "In gewisser Hinsicht war für die Reformation die Verankerung des neuen Verständnisses des Evangeliums von wesentlicher Bedeutung. Hier kam neben der Predigt dem Katechismus und dem Katechismusunterricht eine entscheidende Rolle zu. Er war das verstehbare Lehrbekenntnis der Gemeinde" (Martin Brecht, "Bekenntnis und Gemeinde," in *Bekenntnis und Einheit der Kirche: Studien zum Konkordienbuch*, Martin Brecht and Reinhard Schwarz [Stuttgart: Calwer Verlag, 1980], 53).

15. Christoffer Grundmann has summarized this complexity in brief fashion: "Aus einem Rechenschaftsbericht über die Rechtgläubigkeit wurde so im Verlauf der Ereignisse ein reichsrechtliches Dokument und verpflichtendes Bekenntnis für protestantische Amtsträger, das darüber hinaus in den verschiedenen Druckausgaben nicht nur mehrfach grosszügig redigiert wurde, sondern auch andere Texte ähnlicher Art wie die Confutation und Apologie provozierte, und damit ein ganz neues Genre schuf, eben das der Bekenntnisschriften" (Christoffer Grundmann, "Die ökumenische Wirklichkeit neu bedacht," *Ökumenische Rundschau* 46:4 [October 1997], 426–44; the quotation is from p. 433).

A few illustrations from the CA will have to suffice for this point. Article
IV makes its theological/doctrinal point, to be sure, but it does so in language that is very much confession of faith: "We receive forgiveness of sin
and become righteous before God out of grace for Christ's sake through
faith when we believe that Christ has suffered for us and that for his sake
our sin is forgiven and righteousness and eternal life are given to us."[16] The
focus on faith is evident in Article V, as well: "To obtain such faith God
instituted the office of preaching, giving the gospel and the sacraments.
Through these, as through means, he gives the Holy Spirit who produces
faith, where and when he wills, in those who hear the gospel. It teaches that
we have a gracious God, not through our merit but through Christ's merit,
when we so believe." These concerns are echoed in Article XX: "This happens through faith alone when a person believes that our sins are forgiven
for Christ's sake, who alone is the mediator to reconcile the Father."
Instructively, the CA adds: "We must also explain that we are not talking
here about the faith possessed by the devil and the ungodly, who also believe
the story that Christ suffered and was raised from the dead. But we are talking about true faith, which believes that we obtain grace and forgiveness of
sin through Christ."[17]

At the same time, the CA functions, and understands itself, as witness
to the biblical gospel. The biblical citations alone could stand as evidence of
this point. Reference is made to key passages in Romans 3–4; Ephesians 4;
Matthew 3; Acts 5; 1 Corinthians 2. And the spirit behind the document is
made clear in the conclusion to the first part, the doctrinal articles (following Article XXI, German text):

> For we certainly wish neither to expose our own souls and consciences to
> grave danger before God by misusing the divine name or Word nor to pass
> on or bequeath to our children and descendants any other teaching than
> that which accords with the pure Word of God and Christian truth. Since,
> then, this teaching is clearly grounded in Holy Scripture and is, moreover,

16. CA IV, German.
17. Forde, *Justification by Faith*, 95: "What they [the Reformers] sought was a language that
does the speaking of the gospel directly and does not merely give descriptions of it." Forde continues: "Justification by faith alone does not limit us to one particular content but is rather a
stipulation about what constitutes gospel speaking, whatever the content" (ibid.). And he con-
cludes: "We cannot be content merely to *report about* God or the text, we must *do* it, do what
the text authorizes us to do in the present, exercise the office. That is the word of life" (97).
Gunther Wenz speaks similarly of biblical authority and confessional concentration on the
gospel: "Die Autorität der Schrift besteht allein in ihrem Sinngehalt. . .. Dieser Sinngehalt ist
nach dem Urteil der Reformatoren offenkundig begründet und gegeben in dem Rechtfertig-
ungsevangelium, das Jesus Christus, der auferstandene Gekreuzigte, in Person ist. . .. Die
Summe der Schrift ist das Evangelium. Vom Evangelium her begründet sich daher die
Normativität der Schrift, so dass gilt: 'Die heilige Schrift ist Norm als prophetische und apos-
tolische Bezeugung des Evangeliums.' [quoting Schlink]. Weil sie Zeugnis des Evangeliums ist,
ist sie kanonische Norm aller kirchlichen Lehre" (*Theologie der Bekenntnisschriften*, 179f.).

neither against nor contrary to the universal Christian church—or even the Roman church—so far as can be observed in the writings of the Fathers, we think that our opponents cannot disagree with us in the articles set forth above.

The conclusion to the CA offers more evidence of the confessors' readiness to be understood as bearing witness to the biblical gospel: "In keeping with the summons, we have desired to present the above articles as a declaration of our confession and the teaching of our people. Anyone who should find it defective shall willingly be furnished with an additional account based on divine Holy Scripture."

The evident self-understanding of the CA is that it is both a confession of faith and a witness to the biblical gospel. Only as such does it function also as a summary of doctrinal points.[18]

Historically Conditioned

A simple awareness of the LCW as confession of faith and witness to the biblical gospel, however, will not suffice if they are to function as a resource for the church today. For the confessional writings are every bit the product of their times. The issues they address are those of the churches of the sixteenth century. They use the language and conceptual forms of theology developed under the influence of Renaissance humanism. They are occasional documents, written to address the circumstances of a particular moment or circumstance. The Catechisms address the situation disclosed by the Saxon Visitations. The Smalcald Articles address the possibility of a Council at Mantua. The Augsburg Confession, in particular, is the offspring of the circumstances created first of all by the imperial summons to the Augsburg Diet, then by the challenge posed by the publication of Eck's *404 Articles*. In addition, the CA reflects the situation in the law of the Holy Roman Empire and its requirement under the Code of Justinian that estates of the empire not depart from the catholic faith.

In such historical conditionedness, the LCW are not unlike the biblical documents to whose gospel they bear witness. Though the church has regularly received the epistles of the New Testament as authoritative Word of God for subsequent centuries, it has (at least at its best) noticed that the truth of the Word of God addressed to the legalists in Galatia sounds radically different from the truth of the Word of God addressed to the libertines in Ephesus. Imagine the chaos that would have resulted had those two epistles, for example, been delivered to the other's addressee. True Word of God

---

18. Cf. G. Wenz, who asserts (contra H. Fagerberg, who denies that the distinction between law and gospel is in any sense an "übergreifendes hermeneutisches Prinzip") that the Confessions' focus on the gospel has "eine hermeneutische Leitfunktion für reformatorisches Schriftverständnis"; in fact, he argues, it is this distinction that "in die ganze Bible allein die Tür auftut" (Wenz, *Theologie der Bekenntnisschriften*, 180).

would then, inappropriately and nonrelevantly, have encouraged the legal-ism that was making inroads in the Galatian churches, and the same true Word of God would then, inappropriately and nonrelevantly, have encour-aged the irresponsibility and libertinism that was corrupting the Ephesian churches. Accordingly, the historical situation gets taken into account even as one seeks to receive the biblical document as the truth-bearing Word of God. Minimally this means that the Galatian manifesto for Christian liberty is used when there is a threat to such freedom in the gospel, and not when uncaring irresponsibility is afoot in the church—and vice versa in the case of the letter to the Ephesians. The person who would faithfully *use* the bib-lical record of the gospel will thus need to attend to the situation addressed in the original setting of the epistle, lest the truth be turned into a lie by mis-directing that Word of God. Much the same argument could be made regarding, say, the Gospel of Mark and the Gospel of John.

The emerging principle is that to receive the biblical gospel one needs to be attentive to the original setting so as to retain the kerygmatic edge of the apostolic *paraenesis* for the contemporary situation. Such is the value of minding the historical relativity of the biblical documents. And the same is true of the confessional witness to the biblical gospel. Only when the cir-cumstances of Augsburg in the first half of 1530 are kept in mind does the language and the content of the CA yield its true sense. Only when the new situation created by the publication of Eck's charges against the Reformers is attended to does it begin to make sense why the confessors prepended the first twenty-one articles to what was to have been a defense of the most important of the reforms that had been introduced into the churches in Saxony (and the other reformation territories). Only when the language of the Code of Justinian is kept in mind does much of the language—to say nothing of the condemnations of heresies ancient and modern—in the first part of the CA yield its sense.

Far from rendering the LCW irrelevant to the church of today, minding their historical situatedness in the circumstances of church and state in the sixteenth century provides the only possibility for hearing these documents as confession of faith and as witness to the biblical gospel. Thus does one hear the homology of faith's confession and the clarity of evangelical teaching.

Exemplary Confession and Witness

Next we add the notion of "exemplary" to our emerging thesis about the resourcefulness of the LCW for today's churches. For all the historical con-ditionedness of the confessional writings, and necessary as it is to be mind-ful of that historicality, we would not care about the question of the resourcefulness of the LCW for today's churches if we did not regard their confession of faith and their witness to the biblical gospel as fundamentally *exemplary*. Just as the CA sought to say to the estates of the empire, "in order to get the catholic faith in its right and authentic shape, you need to understand the gospel always and only as unconditional promise from God made on account of the crucified and resurrected One, a promise that is received precisely and only when one hears that gospel story as good news addressed directly to the hearer—which hearing is precisely the hearing of faith," so the Lutheran churches of subsequent eras and different cultures seek to use that confession and witness as *exemplary* focus on the promise-and-faith nature of authentic catholic Christianity.

The continuity of Lutheran identity that one seeks from the LCW is thus to be found in the continuity of confession and witness to that radical understanding of the gospel as promise to be received by trust, by faith. Such identity does not consist in mouthing the same formulae, nor in condemning the same ancient and "modern" heretics—as if the quality of one's claim to authentic Lutheran identity could be determined by the quantity of confessional formulae that were in circulation in a given church (any more than the quality of one's grasp of the apostolic gospel could be maintained without keeping the contrary currents of, say, Galatians and Ephesians, or of Mark and John, distinct and separate from one another). No, continuity of Lutheran identity will be grounded in discerning the inner theo-logic of the LCW's confession and witness and learning therefrom to speak out of an understanding of radical and unconditional promise in the contemporary situation. We don't add up all the confessional assertions; we learn from their exemplary gospel-serving how to serve up gospel to the contemporary issues and problems we face in today's church. "Do it in this manner!" Such is the promise of taking the LCW as *exemplary, paradigmatic* confession and witness.[19]

Problem-Solving Literature

There is one more dimension to be added to the developing understanding of the resourcefulness of the LCW for today's churches. The confessional writings are not only confessions of faith and witnesses to the gospel; they are not only historically conditioned and situation-specific; they are not only exemplary or paradigmatic; they are also, like the biblical documents to whose truth and gospel they bear witness, best taken as "problem solving" literature. There is a diagnosis/prognosis dimension to the biblical documents, and there is a similar diagnosis/prognosis dimension to the LCW. That this is true in the case of the biblical documents requires little demonstration. Galatians addresses the problem of creeping legalism in the Galatian churches, and it provides exemplary diagnosis of how such legalism corrupts and vitiates and finally loses the gospel, while at the same time

---

19. The very point is made in CA VII in its specification of what is "sufficient" for the true unity of the church when it argues that alongside a pure understanding of the word it is required that the sacraments be administered "lauts des evangelii" (according to the gospel). The whole theological enterprise, I contend, needs to be done "according to the gospel," that is, according to the Reformation insight into the nature of the gospel as sheer promise.

providing paradigmatic gospel-proclamation. The one way to repair the problem of creeping legalism is to make available ringingly clear gospel, so that faith can once more hear the good news and so receive the precious gift of freedom from the obligation to work one's way into divine favor.

The plea of the present essay is to understand the LCW in similar fashion. The CA addresses the situation of a legalistic application of the Justinian Code's requirement of adherence to the catholic faith, seeks to show how such a slavish and legalistic application makes room in the church (and consequently in the empire as then constituted) for sub-evangelical and even gospel-destroying theology and practice, and finally proposes fresh articulation of the gospel and of the faith that trusts the gospel as the authentic and life-restoring antidote. The Apology addresses the situation of the biblicistic and sub-evangelical reading of the scriptures that Melanchthon found in the *Confutatio Pontificia*, seeks to show how such a misreading of the scriptures vitiates and destroys the gospel, and (especially vividly in Article IV) vigorously puts forth a reading of the biblical material that is at once informed by its gospel content and at the same time yields fresh gospel content to one who so reads the scriptures.

An "evangelically analogous" approach to the LCW is being commended here. Instead of being restricted to those topics that the sixteenth-century situation put before the confessors, our proposed quest for exemplary problem-solving can take up any number of new and as yet unaddressed issues or problems and seek to provide the sort of evangelical diagnosis and prognosis that the LCW embody. It is then no disadvantage, for example, that there is hardly any explicit treatment in the confessions of the locus *de scriptura*; if and when that becomes an issue in the church, let the theologian realize that the LCW are providing exemplary diagnosis and prognosis in other areas, and seek to engage in similarly evangelical diagnosis and prognosis. There is then really no boundary or limit to the applicability of the theological analysis of the confessional writings; Lutheran identity and continuity therein are assured when like problem-solving is carried out. And, when one takes the LCW precisely as problem-solving documents, there is in fact positive impetus to engage in the creative and contemporary problem-solving, that is, in evangelically analogous diagnosis and prognosis for today's church and the new and distinctive issues that it faces as it seeks to live and confess and believe "Lutheranly" in the new millennium.

A Sample from the Feed-Box: Grounding the Church and Its Unity Eschatologically

One sketch will have to suffice to illustrate the point(s) being advocated. It is keyed by the Augsburg Confession, and it addresses a contemporary issue that is not directly addressed in the confessional writings.

Left to its historical situation in the sixteenth century, the seventh article of the CA would afford little by way of resource for today's church as it confronts the contemporary ecumenical situation. In 1530 in the Holy Roman Empire, the issue was simply (!) one of demonstrating that the confessors had not departed from the catholic faith; then it was enough to point out that recognizably authentic saying and doing of the gospel was sufficient (*genug, satis*) for the true unity of the church. In the modern ecumenical or postecumenical setting, however, where the Justinian Code is not the law of the ecclesiastical landscape, we need something more than a potentially minimalist set of requirements. What was enough to maintain the unity of the church in 1530 may not be enough to recover the unity of the church in 2003; or, to anticipate the result of these reflections, it may already be too late to treat the church as anything but truly unified.

Read in its historical setting, CA VII pleads for a minimum standard for meeting the demands of the Code of Justinian, requiring that the essential unity of the church not be compromised by the action of any of the estates of the empire. Not only does the church have the divine promise that "one holy church will be and remain forever," but "this is enough for the true unity of the Christian church that there the gospel is preached harmoniously according to a pure understanding and the sacraments are administered in conformity with the divine Word." Little help seems to be provided for the modern situation, when the whole ecumenical discussion is about the *criteria* for "pure understanding" and "conformity with the divine Word."

That would be the end of the use of CA VII by today's church unless we reorient ourselves to the way in which that article addresses exemplary problem-solving gospel to the situation and in which it brings to expression the church-making trust in the unconditioned promise of the gospel. I propose we tune into that by means of a layering of the end-time logic of the New Testament, the "eschato-logic" so evident in the biblical period and allegedly so absent from the theological work of the sixteenth century. As I see it, the vision of the New Jerusalem in Revelation 21 and 22 is an eschatological, apocalyptically colored portrait of the assembly of believers saying and doing the gospel; put the other way round, the assembly of believers saying and doing the gospel is the proleptic enactment of that Holy City come down out of heaven from God, all bedight with jasper and pearl and carnelian, all nourished by the river that flows from the throne of the Lamb, all illuminated by the light that comes directly from the throne of God and of the Lamb. That is not a new thing, not a future thing, but this present thing, this assembly around the gospel said and done, seen from the point of view of God's consummation of the world's salvation. As if the church could be about anything less in its Eucharist!

Jesus' prayer in John 17 works out the same kind of eschato-logic. Though set in the narrative of the upper room in John, it is rather evident that John's Gospel is really addressing the church at the turn of the first to the second century and the continuing dividedness of the Christian community at that time, with the resulting risk to the credibility of the church's missionary enterprise. The evangelist's concern is for "those who would come to believe on [Jesus] through their word," that is, through the word of the contention-laden second or third generation of witnesses to the apostolic gospel. John's Jesus speaks to that generation via his prayer for those turn-of-the-century witnesses, that they may be one with one another, one with those to whom they witness, one with Jesus, one with the Father.[20] Now, Jesus' prayer-language thus amounts to promise-language to the community, declaration-language of the will of God for the community. The result of that promise, that divine declaration, may not have been apparent for the community of the beloved, but it is no less real. What is true and real in the heart of God may be treated as true and real by the beloved community, already here, already now (i.e., at the turn of the first century to the second, and also now as the second millennium turns to the third!).

We can see the force of the eschatological perspective in the important language that we use about Easter, the great feast of the eschaton. Easter-talk is full of eschato-logic.[21] We can hardly turn around without bumping into it. Thomas, getting an eyeful and a fingertip full of the risen crucified one, catches it: "My Lord and my God!" Mr. and Mrs. Clopas, grief-stricken residents of Emmaus, catch it (via Word and sacrament, no less!): "We have seen the Lord!" Mary of Magdala catches it, not so much in her "Rabbouni!" as in her dash to the disciples to announce, "I have seen the Lord!" G. F. Händel caught it from St. Paul: "Death is swallowed up in victory!" Not just "will be" swallowed up, but "is" swallowed up, already here, already now. And Luther caught it in his great Easter hymn, "Christ Jesus Lay in Death's Strong Bands"; though an Easter hymn, it is really a meditation on what Easter discloses about Good Friday: Jesus Christ in his dying has "done away with sin," has "taken away from death all its right and power," so that "there remains nothing but death's form/image," and "death has lost its stinger" and "the strangler can no longer harm us." Now, perhaps it is easy to sing that during the Great Fifty Days of Easter. But try

20. What I. U. Dalferth comments in connection with the Gospel of Mark is true of John, when he speaks of a post-Easter perspective in the Gospel, "die belegt, dass der Autor (und damit der aufmerksame Leser und Hörer) des Evangeliums mehr weiss als die Akteure seiner Erzählung" (*Der auferweckte Gekreuzigte* [Tübingen: J. C. B. Mohr, 1994], 94).

21. My use of the notion of eschatology is indebted to the discussion by Dalferth, *Der auferweckte Gekreuzigte*. He writes, "Die Eschata sind also nicht nur die letzten Dinge im chronologischen Sinn, sondern zugleich die wichtigsten Dinge im Sinn gegenwärtiger Lebensorientierung. . . . Sie handelt vielmehr von der grundlegenden normativen Orientierung unseres Lebens durch Hinweis auf dessen letzten Zweck und ultimative Rahmenbedingungen" (198). "Alles musste daher theologisch in eschatologischer Perspektive behandelt werden, nicht nur die traditionellen Eschata" (199). "Die Theologie muss sich also nicht mit einer Reihe eschatologischer Lehrstücke beschäftigen, sondern mit der einen eschatologischen Realität des auferweckten Jesus Christus" (200).

singing that hymn over the grave of a beloved parent or spouse or child; tell me then that death is just an empty form and that it cannot sting us any longer. Pious balderdash, it would seem. And yet with eschato-logic we sing as we can and through tears as we must, "One death has devoured the other, and has made a joke of death"—already here, already now.

One more example. The gospel of our Baptism speaks to each of us God's final verdict upon us: "You are forgiven; you are mine; I love you for Christ's sake, and I will never let you go!" Now, consider what that means for our dealing with one another. If God's ultimate verdict on you is that you are for-given, righteous, God's own child, then it is already too late for me to treat you as if that were not in fact God's own last word about you and to you. If I hold a grudge against you, or if I refuse to forgive you, why, look whose "last word" I am thereby opposing, whose "final verdict" I would thereby disallow! God's end-time word about you and to you is forgiveness; how can I oppose that and nevertheless claim God's love myself? No, by the eschato-logic of forgiveness, it is too late to treat you as unforgiven, too late to nurse a grudge, too late to pretend that I could rule you out of the kingdom! The eschato-logic of baptismal forgiveness is true, already here, already now. That is why "it is not necessary" for human creations—formulae, contracts, declarations—to be made universal. *It is too late for that.* Christ's church is Christ's church, already here. Christ's one church is Christ's one church, already now. It is too late to act otherwise, and it is most dangerous to put one's own standing before God in jeopardy by opposing God's end-time ver-dict. Enough, already, is enough.[22]

Conclusion

I have proposed to transcend the polarity of historical relativism and dog-matic absolutism in one's reading of the LCW by means of what I have called a principle of "evangelical analogy," a principle in four parts: (1) take the LCW seriously as both confession of faith and witness to the biblical gospel; (2) honor the historical situation in which the particular confession and witness of the LCW was first made; (3) treat the LCW as *exemplary* confession and witness; and (4) understand the LCW as problem-solving literature. This approach opens the way to vigorous contemporary theolo-gizing and to lively and gospel-focused interchange among the faithful. And that will surely be required in this new millennium, when the church faces

---

22. These reflections are drawn from my presentation at the Institute of Liturgical Studies at Valparaiso University, 11 April 2002; it is currently available at www.valpo.edu/theology/ils/EnoughILS.pdf. They draw inspiration from two works by the author's teachers: Robert W. Bertram, "Christ's Resurrection: Only Secondarily Saving?" (unpublished sermon from Eastertide, 1972); Arthur Carl Piepkorn, "The Urgency of Dialogue" (unpublished manuscript of a lecture delivered at Augustana College, Sioux Falls, S.D., August 1967).

questions about the nature of church law, when ecumenical dialogue (as, for example, with the Mennonites) raises questions about the historical accuracy of the condemnations in the LCW,[23] and when we shall be facing as yet unrecognized issues where the LCW are silent.

23. See David Truemper, "The Role and Authority of Lutheran Confessional Writings: Do Lutherans Really 'Condemn the Anabaptists'?" *Mennonite Quarterly Review* 76/3 (July 2002): 299–314.

JUSTICE

Part IV

FROM THE VERY BEGINNING, Lutheran responses to political reality were complex but also problematic. One could mention Luther's highly questionable attitude in the Peasants' Revolt, the problematic alignment of the Lutheran movement with the political authorities, as well as the sharp but unrealistic critique of usury. When Luther burned the canon law, justice in legal matters was no longer an ecclesiastical affair. Instead, a new way of organizing society began to develop. Lutheran theology has, on the one side, directly and indirectly nurtured the creation of welfare states and, on the other side, has to respond to sharp accusations concerning its responsibility for political passivity.

In contemporary theologies from the South, the relation between a theology of justification and a theology of social justice is intimate. In the essay "Reconciliation and Forgiveness in an Unjust Society," Bishop Ambrose Moyo argues that justice is a precondition for reconciliation. Zacchaeus and Nehemiah become role models for an authentic theology in which justification never leads to the acceptance of oppression by the oppressed. The engagement of the church in social issues is for Moyo the direct consequence of the church's self-understanding as a communion of justified sinners. Accordingly, the Lutheran principles of "faith alone" and "grace alone" should never be emphasized at the cost of the actualization of God's justice in the social world.

Without discounting this point, Guillermo Hansen, in his response to Moyo, asks for a clearer distinction between ultimate reconciliation and what can be achieved penultimately. Addressing the role of churches in creating social justice, Hansen argues for a prophetic responsibility of the churches that does not identify the church with God's own dominion over the world. Rather, churches should interact with governmental institutions and nongovernmental organizations in creating a healthy civil society.

In chapter 13, Vítor Westhelle critically examines the so-called two-kingdoms doctrine, which has played a crucial role in Lutheran discussions since Franz Lau coined the phrase in 1933. Luther scholar Johannes Heckel once compared this doctrine with an ingenuous labyrinth. Westhelle argues, however, that Luther's view on the political order does not coalesce into a doctrine, but rather serves as an epistemic principle that teaches the faithful that knowing Christ is knowing justice. Justice always begins by allowing the other to have a voice and a face.

In the different contributions to this book, one can see the emergence of a new Lutheran theology of communicative grace. The different emphases on the inclusive gift of grace and its community-forming dimension seem to have the potential of establishing a platform for discussions between the North and the South and, in this section, also internally among theologians of the South. If grace is understood as eliciting a social structure of participation and mutuality, the negative consequences of a theological emphasis on passivity, criticized by Lutherans of the South, may be addressed without stepping outside of Reformation soil.

—Bo Holm

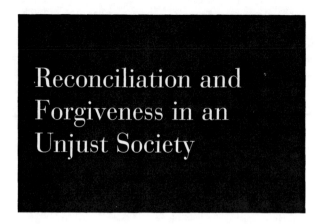

CHAPTER 11

Reconciliation and Forgiveness in an Unjust Society

Ambrose Moyo

The message of reconciliation and forgiveness through faith in Jesus Christ is at the core of the life and ministry of the church.[1] The church is that instrument through which God chooses to be reconciled with creation as a whole, but more so with people, and to reconcile people with one another regardless of race, color, or creed. In other words, that message constitutes the core business of the church and is not only to be proclaimed, but must also be lived out both in church and in society. The basic question that this article seeks to address is whether our Lutheran theology has anything to offer to a world that hungers for justice, reconciliation, and forgiveness.

Recent developments in postapartheid South Africa pose a challenge to theological reflection on the issues of justice, reconciliation, and forgiveness in the region. How do we strike a balance between the demands of justice, on one hand, and the need for reconciliation and forgiveness and the search for national unity, on the other? What is the contribution of churches to a circular process that is focused on implementing concepts that are central to the gospel? How do we as a church of Christ and as individual Christians respond to the cry for reconciliation? On what grounds can the church participate in the dialogue on reconciliation and forgiveness, which was opened up with the transitions from colonial or repressive regimes to new democratic dispensations?

My task is to present a theological reflection on reconciliation and forgiveness from the perspective of those who suffer as a result of bad governance, unjust and discriminatory laws, ethnic conflicts that have led to gross human rights violations, and unjust societies. How do you reconcile someone to a neighbor who is known to be responsible for torturing and killing one's father or brother or mother or sister or child? How do you remove the hate or the guilty feeling? How do you deal with the perpetrators of injustice or

1. Originally published as "Reconciliation and Forgiveness in an Unjust Society," *Dialog* 41/4 (Winter 2002): 294–301.

violators of human rights who have no feeling of remorse and openly say that, given similar situations, they would not hesitate to do the same? How do you bring about healing of broken relationships in societies that have been riddled with such terrifying conflict over the years? Can there be reconciliation without forgiveness, and can there be forgiveness without repentance and confession? Can reconciliation be achieved within a context of unjust social, economic, and political structures of the past? How can these structures be reordered so as to create an environment in which reconciliation and forgiveness are possible? These are difficult questions that must be faced if we are going to make a contribution to the creation of a just society in our world. I cannot speak for all persons living in unjust societies, but I can speak from my experience as a male church leader and pastor in Southern Africa. How do I as a Lutheran pastor and theologian translate that message into reality among my people in Southern Africa, and in Zimbabwe in particular? Relevance and contextuality draw me to Southern Africa as I engage in theological reflection on reconciliation, forgiveness, and justice.

The Social, Economic, and Political Context

In his inaugural speech on Independence Day in 1980, Zimbabwe prime minister Robert G. Mugabe surprised the world when he announced that reconciliation would be the cornerstone of his policy to bring about national unity. Fourteen years down the road, South Africa became a democratic state. The new government, under the leadership of President Nelson Mandela, immediately established a Truth and Reconciliation Commission (TRC). After many years of racial conflict, it was clear to these two national leaders that the only viable way forward was through a program that would reconcile warring groups and promote national unity. In this regard, the TRC defined reconciliation as "the ending of division or enmity between people or groups . . . understood not as something that occurs once or instantaneously, but as a goal and a process. It is recognized that there are different levels of reconciliation, including coming to terms with painful truth, reconciliation between victims and perpetrators, reconciliation at community level, promoting national unity and reconciliation, and reconciliation and redistribution."[2] It was clear that only a holistic approach to the issue of reconciliation and national unity could produce the expected results.

The difference between Zimbabwean and South African approaches is that the former did not adopt a holistic approach to the question of reconciliation. The president knew that the way forward was reconciliation, but

2. Iain S. Maclean, "Truth and Reconciliation: Irreconcilable Differences? An ethical Evaluation of the South African Truth and Reconciliation Commission," in *Religion and Theology* 6 (1999): 276.

he apparently did not recognize the need to develop new systems that would address the social and economic imbalances that had led to the armed conflict. The resource bases of the local communities had been exploited to create a very high standard of living for a few former immigrants at the expense of the majority. People had lost their properties, their land, their human dignity, their culture, and their wealth during the years of colonialism. Their bitterness fueled the war of liberation. Expectations were high at the time of independence, but twenty years down the road, their hopes had not been realized. The white communities and a few blacks continued to enjoy a high standard of living. Prime Minister Robert G. Mugabe had proclaimed a policy of reconciliation but had not in the subsequent years addressed the question of the socioeconomic imbalances as part of the process toward reconciliation. The people felt cheated, and the whole reconciliation policy was seen to have benefited the whites with the exception of a few black Zimbabweans.

This simply underlines the question raised by Tinyeko Sam Maluleke as to whether reconciliation is possible "while the gap between rich and poor is not only widening but also retaining its essentially racial nature."[3] There was talk of bridging the gap between rich and poor, but no effective strategies were developed. The 150,000 white Zimbabweans (as against the 12 million black Zimbabweans) who chose to remain in the country after independence continue to control most of the commerce and industrial sectors, and own nearly 90 percent of the land. Independence seems to have changed very little more than the bringing in of a black government.

On the other hand, the South African case has attracted great attention and stimulated a great deal of discussion both nationally and internationally. Its Constitution, which was effective from 21 October 1993, recognized the divisions caused by apartheid and laid a foundation for the process towards reconciliation when it stated: "This Constitution provides a historic bridge between the past of a deeply divided society, characterized by strife, conflict, untold suffering and injustice, and a future founded on the recognition of human rights, democracy and peaceful coexistence and development opportunities for all South Africans irrespective of color, race, belief or sex."[4]

A parliamentary act called the "Promotion of National Unity and Reconciliation Act of 1995" led to the establishment of the Truth and Reconciliation Commission (TRC). It was given a clear mandate, namely, to promote national unity and reconciliation by establishing as "complete a picture as possible of the nature, causes, and extent of gross violations of human rights" between March 1963 and the end of 1993 (later extended to

3. Tinyeko Sam Maluleke, "Can Rabbits and Lions Reconcile? The South African TRC as an Instrument for Peace Building," *The Ecumenical Review* 53/3 (2001): 192.
4. Maclean, "Truth and Reconciliation," 274.

May 1994). Second, it was empowered to grant amnesty to "people who make full disclosure of all the relevant facts to acts relating to acts associated with a political objective."[5] The reference here is to those who openly confessed their politically motivated crimes and by so doing pleaded for pardon. And, third, it was to provide a platform for victims or their survivors to tell their story to the nation and for the TRC to recommend reparations. It was an opportunity to share their grief with the nation and by so doing expose the inhumanity of the apartheid system.

The TRC represents a commitment on the part of the South Africans to hear "the wounds of the people"[6] and thus promote reconciliation, forgiveness, and national unity. The preamble to the Constitution clearly reflects a commitment to redress past injustices and to create a just society through the recognition of the contribution of each South African group: "We, the people of South Africa, recognize the injustices of the past; Honor those who suffered for justice and freedom in our land; Respect those who have worked to build and develop our country; and Believe that South Africa belongs to all who live in it, united in our destiny."[7] The setting up of the TRC was received enthusiastically by many commentators declaring, "Never before in modern history has a people told their story so fully and movingly."[8] So Bishop Desmond Tutu, in his foreword to the report, states that through the TRC the people of South Africa have been enabled to "look the beast of the past in the eyes," and confidently suggests, "Let us shut the door to the past."[9] With the establishment of the TRC, South Africa rejected the idea of revenge and vengeance as a way of solving conflict and creating a just society. For them the way to deal with the past is not amnesia, but truth telling and confession, which form the basis for forgiveness and reconciliation and for dealing with injustices. The truth must be told, and only then can the repentant sinner be pardoned, the victim be compensated, and society restructured to remove the injustices.

Reconciliation and Renewal

The period of the struggle for liberation in Southern Africa was also a period of reflection on the nature of apartheid for Southern Africa and on issues of reconciliation and forgiveness. The authors of the celebrated *Kairos Document* spelled out their vision of reconciliation when they wrote:

5. *Report of the Truth and Reconciliation Commission of South* Africa; 5 vols., 1:4, Section 31/3b (Hampshire, England: Macmillian, March 1999).

6. See Tinyeko Sam Maluleke, "Dealing Lightly with the Wounds of my People? The TRC Process in Theological Perspective," *Missionalia* 25 (1997), 324–43.

7. Cited from Jonathan Allen, "Between Retribution and Restoration: Justice and the TRC," *South African Journal of Philosophy* 20 (2001), 2.

8. Tinyeko Sam Maluleke, "Can Lions and Rabbits Reconcile?" 190–99.

9. Ibid., 195–96.

In our situation in South Africa today it would be totally unchristian to plead for reconciliation and peace before the present injustices have been removed. Any such plea plays into the hands of the oppressor by trying to persuade those of us who are oppressed to accept our oppression and to become reconciled to the intolerable crimes that are committed against us. That is not Christian reconciliation, it is sin. It is asking us to become accomplices in our own oppression, to become servants of the devil. No reconciliation is possible in South Africa without justice.[10]

The movement toward reconciliation presupposes an equally important movement toward the creation of a just society. In other words, there can be no reconciliation without a visible effort to bridge the gap between the impoverished majority and the rich. A new social order has to be created. This is the lesson learned from Zimbabwean experience, which failed to address these issues from the beginning. National reconciliation cannot be achieved in such situations without addressing the question of reparations within a reasonably short period. That is a Christian principle rooted in the biblical ethic, which requires that those who have accumulated wealth by cheating or exploiting fellow human beings must redistribute or return a much higher portion of what they stole or robbed to its rightful owners.

The story of Zacchaeus the tax collector is a classic lesson on restitution or making reparation (Luke 19:1-9). Zacchaeus's encounter with Jesus led to a conversion, which enabled him to declare: "Look, Lord! Here and now I give half of my possessions to the poor, and if I have ever cheated anybody of anything, I will pay back four times the amount" (19:8). Zacchaeus voluntarily gave up some of his riches as his contribution toward creating a just society. Reconciliation with God meant for him reconciliation with those he had dehumanized by impoverishing them through the exploitation of their meager resources. Zacchaeus was prepared to make reparation. Only after he had taken that gigantic step did Jesus acknowledge that "Today salvation has come to this house" (19:9). Salvation only comes through reconciliation with God and with fellow human beings. Zacchaeus made a public confession of his sin and took the necessary steps to improve the quality of the lives of those he had exploited.

Zacchaeus's response to God's forgiving grace offered to him through faith in Jesus Christ is indeed a commitment to social justice. An even more radical approach is the one adopted by Nehemiah in response to the cry of the people (Neh 5:1-19). Nehemiah 5 describes a crisis situation that had hit the Jewish community. A situation of oppression had arisen whereby the

---

10. Cited by John W. de Gruchy, "The Dialectic of Reconciliation: Church and Transition to Democracy in South Africa," in *The Reconciliation of Peoples: Challenge to the Churches*, ed. Gregory Baum and Harold Wells (Geneva: WCC Publications and New York: Orbis, 1997), 17. Essentially the *Kairos Document* was a critique of "church theology" and in particular what is referred to as "cheap reconciliation."

poor were not oppressed by an external power but by their own kindred. The poor complained that their desperate food situation had forced them to mortgage their fields, vineyards, and homes and to borrow money at high interest rates from their rich kindred to obtain grain during famine and to pay the state tax. The cry of the people reached Nehemiah: "Our flesh is the same as that of our kindred; our children are the same as their children; and yet we are forcing our sons and daughters to be slaves, and some of our daughters have been ravished; we are powerless, and our fields and vine-yards now belong to others" (5:5). Nehemiah was moved to call an assem-bly of all the inhabitants at which he reprimanded the rich people and the corrupt officials for allowing the situation to degenerate that far and to agree on action to be taken to address the crisis. It is interesting to note that Nehemiah includes himself and his servants among the rich people who were lending money and grain to the poor (5:10).

Jose Soverino Croatto has argued that the center of the text lies in v. 11, which, as he points out, contains a detail that is generally overlooked.[11] Nehemiah made a concrete proposal, which included returning a *me'at hakkesep* of the money, grain, and oil, which had been lent. The NRSV trans-lates this verse as follows: "Restore to them, this very day, their fields, their vineyards, their olive orchards, and their houses, and the interest on money, grain, wine, and oil that you have been exacting from them." *Me'at hakke-sep* is paraphrased as "interest." In other translations, *me'at* is translated as "a hundredth part," which means they must return the capital plus one per-cent interest.[12] Others would interpret this as a proposal to cancel a part of the debt. However, after a linguistic analysis of the expression, Croatto con-cludes that the Hebrew text actually means that the demand was to return the capital plus "a hundred (for one) of the money, which you have lent" and not a "hundredth part" or a certain percentage of the interest or a debt reduc-tion.[13] The rich people addressed accepted the proposal, and structures were put in place to ensure that they all implemented the decision. What this means is that "the creditors had become so exceedingly wealthy that they could do what Nehemiah was insisting that they do."[14] What needed to be done, as far as Nehemiah was concerned, was not some cosmetic action on behalf of the poor but to empower them by returning to them their means of production. Nehemiah insisted that, in situations of exploitation and oppres-sion such as the one he faced, the way forward is to help the wealthy (credi-tors) to recognize that they are indebted to the poor and that it is their moral

11. Jose Soverino Croatto, "The Debt in Nehemiah's Social Reform: A Study of Nehemiah 5:1–19," in *Subversive Scriptures: Revolutionary Readings of the Christian Bible in Latin America*, ed. Leif E. Vaage (Valley Forge, Pa.: Trinity Press International, 1997), 39–59.

12. See the NRSV. The Septuagint translates it as *apo tou argyriou* (v. 11) so as to translate as "part of the money."

13. Croatto, "The Debt," 44.

14. Ibid., 45.

responsibility to restore both the capital or the means of production plus a substantial amount of interest gained over the year. This was a basic step in the restoration of broken relationships and bringing about reconciliation.

For those living in my region, this means that a situation in which the poor continue to watch the rich eat sumptuously at their tables makes the poor angrier and more hateful. In Zimbabwe this led to the "third chimurenga," which focused on taking back the land that had been violently grabbed from the Africans by the colonial regimes on behalf of a foreign majesty who freely gave some of the land to his or her loyal subjects who were willing to move to the new colony. The white commercial farmers failed to recognize the need to economically empower the poor majority by returning to them most of the land that their ancestors had illegally seized from the Africans—most of which was not being used. To this day in South Africa, Namibia, and Zimbabwe, the wealth of the nation is basically under the control of a small minority. This is not just, and there can be no hope for reconciliation under such circumstances.

The land in African traditional religious beliefs is sacred; it belongs to the nation, and no one person can claim ownership to any piece of land. Displaced Africans will always feel bitter about their land and will always look for means to repossess their land. King Lobengula did not give the land to Cecil John Rhodes, but allowed him to live on his (Lobengula's) land. It was a lease agreement. What this means is that reconciliation between black and white in Zimbabwe cannot be achieved without solving the issue of land ownership. If the willing-buyer and willing-seller approach could not be implemented, the poor majority was bound to demand compulsory acquisition or nationalization of the means of production, beginning with the land. However, unjust agrarian reform methods can never create a just society, let alone promote reconciliation. The land issue is a justice issue, and as such the church cannot and should not adopt a neutral position.[15]

From Justification to Justice

The church's involvement in justice and reconciliation issues must be seen from its self-understanding as a community of sinners who have been justified through faith in Jesus Christ. It is a community of believers who have

15. From an ethical point of view, the Zimbabwe government was doing the right thing by engaging in the redistribution of land, which is a God-given resource essential to sustain life on earth. Regretfully, the exercise came too late and was done for the wrong reasons and in the wrong way. Political analysts have observed that turning to the land issue was the last card that the ruling party could play to perpetuate its leadership in power when it was rudely awakened by the referendum on the draft constitution in 2000 and for the first time realized that it had lost the support of the majority because of its failure to meaningfully address the socioeconomic imbalances inherited from the nation's colonial past. Agrarian reform to appease the peasants was the only way to impress them. Second, this had to be done quickly in order to win the forthcoming elections, and the only way to do it was through the use of violence and disregard for

experienced the justice of God in his dealings with them. The doctrine of justification by faith alone is, needless to say, the cornerstone of Reformation
theology and in particular the Lutheran tradition. The *sola fide* or *sola gratia* aspect of this doctrine has often been emphasized at the expense of how
the believer lives out God's justice not only as an individual but also in community with others. Only the one who is justified through faith in Jesus
Christ can produce the book of James, whose message the Lutherans need to
rediscover after it was dismissed as a piece of straw by Martin Luther.

The African understanding of being is that "I am because you are."
Being in community with others is what makes one human. In the midst of
hunger and starvation, of poverty and untold suffering and pain as a result
of human greed for power and wealth, those who labor for God's justice,
those justified by God, cannot rest until Christ's vision of the justice of God
is realized. Being justified by faith in Christ means you commit yourself to
working for justice for all of God's people and for their justification by God
as they participate in the justice of God. This means that God's justice
demands not only the right vertical relationship but also its horizontal manifestation in community as we live out the philosophy of *ubuntu*.[16] If we
believe that the justice of God is revealed in Jesus Christ (Rom 1:17) and
that we are Christ's disciples, our task cannot be divorced from creating a
just society, because that is what the death and resurrection of Christ are all
about. The church therefore can only be an instrument of God's justice and
is called upon to work for social justice and in that way manifest God's justice in all spheres of human existence. The African philosophy of *ubuntu*
helps me as an African to understand faith not as something that is
"restricted or limited to an individualistic relationship to God, but necessarily includes the neighbor, and thus concern and responsibility for the
social and indeed political dimensions of life."[17] *Ubuntu* is, as observed by
Maclean, "The African functional equivalent of the traditional Christian
concept of *imago dei*."[18] The concept emphasizes our common humanity
and our common responsibility as essential parts of our being Christian.

Justice North and South

In concrete terms, the story of Zacchaeus and that of Nehemiah are a call for
the church and the religious leaders to realize that it is their duty to call upon
those who have acquired riches through the exploitation or impoverishment

---

human rights. Such an approach can only produce further divisions, bitterness, and conflict and
increase the misery of the poor, as they now have to grapple with hunger and starvation.

16. On the philosophy of *ubuntu*, see Desmond Tutu and Michael Jesse Battle, *Reconciliation:
The Ubuntu Theology of Desmond Tutu* (Cleveland: Pilgrim Press, 1997). Ubuntu is an
African term almost translatable with "humaneness" (Editor's note).

17. Maclean, "Truth and Reconciliation," 282.

18. Ibid.

of others as the case in Southern Africa to voluntarily return some of the wealth they control to its rightful owners. The contribution of the African slave to the wealth and prosperity enjoyed by the North is still to be recognized and rewarded. The history of slavery and colonialism is characterized by some of the most cruel violations of human rights and dehumanizing activities, which have left two-thirds of the world in poverty. The stories of Nehemiah and of Zacchaeus are a challenge to the rich North to consider restitution or reparations for the damage done to Africa, to the Australian aborigines, the Maoris in New Zealand, the Native Americans, and other groups in the Two-Thirds World.

This is what the justice of God is all about. The truth of the matter is that the North is indebted to two-thirds of the world—and not the other way around. This includes the churches in the North, which blessed the plundering of the wealth in the colonies and received their share of the loot. African churches as well as other churches in the Two-Thirds World are struggling for survival with their church leaders, pastors, and others workers living on crumbs falling from the tables of their sister churches in the North. Is this not a mockery of justice of God even within the church, which is the carrier of that message? Mission societies or the boards for global mission will rejoice when they see the large numbers of new converts to Christianity. But the question is whether these people are seeking religious refuge from the hunger, starvation, disease, and ignorance they experience because of poverty.

The way forward is to listen to the message of Nehemiah and the story of Zacchaeus in Luke and create an environment where reconciliation is possible in both the church and society. Globalization is not the answer, as it is a new form of colonialism that creates new oppressive structures that make poor people even poorer. In societies where there has been conflict, reconciliation should not be understood as something that must be accomplished at the level of individuals only but as something that must take place at the societal level and "as a step towards social and economic equality."[19] There can be no equality as long as the gap between rich and poor keeps widening. Globalization, with all its negative manifestations, has also brought us closer to each other, and we are all affected by conflicts in other regions. A reconciliation process that goes hand in hand with efforts to establish a just society will create a global environment that unites humanity in a common destiny.

Two Kingdoms in One World

The cry for justice and the connection to reconciliation must also be viewed from the perspective of the Lutheran doctrine of the two kingdoms. It

---

19. W. Kristner, "The Biblical Understanding of Reconciliation," cited by Maclean in "Truth and Reconciliation," 284.

affirms that there is no sphere in the whole of God's creation that lies outside of God's control. This gives the church the authority to carry out a prophetic ministry—to be involved in the creation of a just society that mirrors the justice of God.

The poor people are created in the image of God. Jesus stands in their midst demanding their recognition and justice for them. That is where the church should be, showing God's justice in the redistribution of the God-given wealth to the nation. The two-kingdoms doctrine calls on us to be good stewards because all we have belongs to God who is sovereign over all, including our wealth, some of which was stolen from others. If this is our understanding of God's two kingdoms, then it is our duty to call for the redistribution of the resources available to the nation.

This may, within the context of respect for basic human rights, call for an orderly compulsory acquisition of some wealth from those who have greedily amassed it at the expense of others and for it to be equitably distributed to the needy to meet everybody's basic needs without impoverishing others. If we believe God is in control and that we are instruments of God's justice on earth, it is then our duty to call for restitution or reparations by supporting different initiatives such as debt cancellation. This is what God's justice or our justification by faith is all about; we are saved to save others, including saving them from dehumanizing poverty situations. The process toward reconciliation must include the creation of a just society.

Healing the Wounds through Forgiveness

Forgiveness is an essential component in the process toward reconciliation. Efforts have to be made to heal both the physical (material) and the spiritual wounds. The physical can be dealt with through restitution or reparations to create a just society. It is, however, essential that the emotional aspects, the anger, hatred, and trauma created by the gross human rights violations need to be addressed. In this respect there are lessons to be learned from the TRC in South Africa.

The mandate of the TRC, as noted above, includes providing a platform for both perpetrators of human rights violations and the victims to tell their story. Those perpetrators who confessed their contribution to the atrocities of the apartheid period in question were granted amnesty. They were pardoned. The victims were able to look into the faces of those who made them suffer so that their oppressors could see and feel the pain they caused and hopefully come to repentance. This is in line with the injunction in Matthew:

> If another member of the church sins against you, go and point out the fault when the two of you are alone. If the member listens to you, you have regained that one. But if you are not listened to, take one or two others along with you, so that every word may be confirmed by evidence of two

or three witnesses. If the member refuses to listen to them, tell it to the church; and if the offender refuses to listen even to the church, let such a one be to you as a Gentile and a tax collector. (Matt 18:15-17)

The opportunity to tell one's story as a perpetrator or as a victim also creates an awareness of the evil that human beings are capable of unleashing on fellow humans. To build a just society, truth telling and confession are necessities. Without forgiveness there can be no reconciliation. The question critics of the TRC have raised is about the nature of that forgiveness. Apartheid was very costly both spiritually and physically; hence there are voices to the effect that forgiving perpetrators of the violent and unjust system is nothing other than an administration's "cheap grace." It may be easier to reconcile individuals, which is a necessity even in situations of national conflicts, but how does one reconcile communities? Yet it is essential to work for reconciliation at the community level if we are to create a just society. The well-being and health of the community have to be restored in order to promote national unity. To balance the demands for justice and reconciliation for the restoration of the community, the TRC opted for the path of confession, penitence, and forgiveness rather than for a blanket pardoning of perpetrators of injustice. As pointed out by Maclean, "forgiveness has to include not only true knowledge of the situation, but also repentance leading to change. Only a turning away from sin, from patterns of the past, can enable forgiveness to avoid the charge of 'cheap grace.' In fact forgiveness without repentance leads but to the continuation of sin."[20]

Theologically speaking, reconciliation can be defined as God's initiative in restoring relationships between God and humankind and between people. God has given that mission to the church, which is called upon to support and strengthen human initiatives toward reconciliation by bringing a religious face into the process through active participation. God in Christ reconciled the world to himself and in that way created a new being and a new society in the image of God. Our understanding of the two kingdoms of God demands our involvement in the restructuring of human society, removing the structures of injustice to create a just society. The process toward reconciliation demands the creation of a just society, one that is truly reconciled to God and is based on genuine repentance and forgiveness.

20. Maclean, "Truth and Reconciliation," 290.

CHAPTER 12

Reconciliation and
Forgiveness:
*A Response to
Ambrose Moyo*

Guillermo
Hansen

General Comments

I begin with a note of deep appreciation for Ambrose Moyo's thoughtful, vivid, and creative presentation that emphasizes the biblical notions of reconciliation and the concern for justice. His work echoes the "Official Common Statement of the Joint Declaration on the Doctrine of Justification" when it calls to "interpret the message of justification in language relevant for human beings today . . . with reference both to individual and social concerns of our times."[1] By taking us to the test case of the critical sociopolitical process of reconciliation that still goes on in South Africa, Moyo skillfully places us at a juncture were the rubber of justification meets the road of justice. The meta-message of Moyo's chapter is that only at the foot of the cross is the significance of justification and reconciliation intelligible at all.

Second, as I read Moyo's essay, a plethora of images crept into my mind that took me back to the 1980s, the years of transition from military dictatorship to democracy in Latin America, especially in the countries of the Southern Cone. The issue of social forgiveness and reconciliation in face of the atrocious human rights violations is still a matter to be grappled with—especially after experiencing political processes that backtracked from exemplary judicial measures to indiscriminate amnesty for the perpetrators of human rights violations. When impunity sets in, sooner or later social and political destabilization follows. Moyo's questions as to how to be reconciled with persons who are responsible for torturing, killing, or collaborating with torturers renews the questions of how we are to love in a Christian way without positing—as Sigmund Freud would say—"a positive premium on being bad."[2]

1. The Lutheran World Federation and The Roman Catholic Church, *Joint Declaration on the Doctrine of Justification* (Grand Rapids and Cambridge, U.K.: Eerdmans, 2000), 42.
2. Sigmund Freud, *Civilization and Its Discontents*; trans. James Strachey (New York: W. W. Norton & Co., 1961), 58.

In this regard, the experience of South Africa, which Moyo contrasts with Zimbabwe, presents an illustrative case in which forgiveness struggles with the limits of its own radical nature. This leads us to explore to what extent forgiveness can accommodate itself to social and political expediency. Moyo implicitly demonstrates that responsible theological language must always be accompanied by an ethical evaluation of the social, cultural, and political impact of religious speech and action. Indeed, forgiveness without a call to repentance *and* reparation is, in the social arena, a formula for an impending catastrophe.

Third, Moyo's proposals also face one of the issues that have plagued the Lutheran tradition, namely, the dualistic hiatus between justification by faith and social justice, between a forensic declaration and the inhabitation of Christ, between the *Christus pro nobis* (Christ for us) and the *Christus in nobis* (Christ in us), between the kingdom of the right and the kingdom of the left. He develops his thought along the post-Helsinki trend in global Lutheran reflection, where the debate is no longer over the centrality of justification but how its relevance is spelled out in daily life.[3] The Helsinki Assembly of the Lutheran World Federation (1963) did signal the beginning of a paradigm shift, a widening search for language relevant to contemporary experience. But the impasse and dissonance represented by Helsinki's lack of a clear consensus encouraged other Lutheran voices, particularly from the South, to introduce social-analytical perspectives in correlation with the doctrine of justification. From there on, the accent fell not only on discerning the preconceptions that we bring to the interpretation of any doctrine but also on clarifying the social and political dimensions of theological discourse. Thus, between 1963 and today there have been an increasing hermeneutical pluralization and a growing emphasis on the socioethical consequences to be drawn from the doctrine of justification.[4]

Moyo's chapter is another important contribution in this direction. Highlighting a concern for reconciliation and forgiveness in church and society must be seen as a part of this post-Helsinki trend that has decisively changed the face and impetus of global Lutheranism. In this particular case, Moyo invites us to review a sociopolitical experiment in light of the gospel message of forgiveness and reconciliation, disclosing at the same

3. The 1963 LWF Assembly in Helsinki attempted to reexamine, reformulate, and restate the doctrine of justification vis-à-vis the new reality signified by the experience of "modern man" (*sic*) in a secularized world. At the same time, the debate revealed the difficulties in defining the modern experience and its relation to the message of justification, since no common or unified language was found to speak to the hearts and minds of "the man of today." One problem was that this "man" was defined in a thoroughly Western and male-centered way, reflecting the perceived challenges of only some of those who compose the LWF. A second problem was that contextuality, ecumenicity, and plurality were not sufficiently recognized as dynamic components of theological reflection. Cf. Jens Holger Schjørring, ed., *From Federation to Communion: The History of the Lutheran World Federation* (Minneapolis: Fortress Press, 1997).

4. See Wolfgang Greive, ed., *Justification in the World's Context* (Geneva: LWF, 2000), 11.

time alternative modes of conflict resolutions between the Scylla of a "blanket pardoning" and the Charybdis of punitive justice. At this juncture, the church and its praxis of reconciliation and forgiveness have an important experience and perspective to offer in the social and political arena. Displaying a deep pastoral concern for all those involved in this painful process (a very Lutheran notion, considering Luther's understanding of the relation between theology and the "comforting of conscience"), he also suggests that achievements based on the gospel-grounded values—important as they may be in the interpersonal and societal healing between victims and perpetrators—may run aground if the sociopolitical foundation remains unchanged. Redressing injustices is part and parcel of Moyo's understanding of social forgiveness and reconciliation.

Some Critical Remarks

I understand Moyo's essay as a valuable pastoral reflection and encouragement for the process of reconciliation in Southern Africa. The focus on the theme of healing both the physical and spiritual wounds (which also anticipates the central theme for the 2003 assembly of the LWF in Winnipeg, Canada) further underscores this pastoral drive. But Moyo's essay is also a theological reflection that invites one to ponder and observe the *extent* and *limits* of forgiveness and reconciliation in the social and political arena. Therefore I will comment with the aim of deepening lines already opened by this presentation. I shall do so by taking note of what appears to me as being "crevices" in the development of Moyo's argument, touching upon two concepts central to Lutheran theology that are already present in his work. My hope remains that in doing so I do not displace one of the main emphases of this paper, namely, that true social reconciliation implies the redress of injustices.

My first comment has to do with the kind of relationship established between justification and justice, and the second with the use of the doctrine of the two kingdoms and twofold governance. Overall, I agree with the direction of Moyo's reflection, but it seems to me that a lack of eschatological *tonos* or tension leads some of Moyo's statements to the edge of collapsing the gospel with a sociohistorical achievement and to a not altogether clear distinction between the kind of reconciliation that is ultimate and that can be achieved penultimately.

1. To weave our theological discourse with processes pertaining to the sociopolitical realm does not entail that we remain unaware of the transition that is implied between discourse ruled by the symbol of justification and our concern for justice. There is no doubt in my mind that the relationship between justification and justice is grounded on the promise given to real people in real space and time that we recount in the Gospel stories about Jesus and that we confess through our Trinitarian faith. For that reason, I

deeply sympathize with Moyo's critique of a merely forensic understanding of justification and therefore with his stress on the communal aspects involved in justification (his reference to *Ubuntu*). I also agree with his assertion that "being justified by faith in Christ means that you commit yourself to working for justice for all."[5]

Yet I cannot go all the way with Moyo and affirm with him that our task as justified sinners is to create a just society "because that is what the death and resurrection of Christ is all about."[6] This sounds to me like a too direct rendition of justification into justice, which may lead us to believe that life and its achievements constitute a commentary on or a corroboration of salvation (the perennial problem of confusing necessary demands with unqualified promises). To find the right equilibrium is certainly not easy, and enough credit has to go to those who—like Moyo—insist on the necessary relationship between justification and justice. But at the same time, a balance must be sought whereby the significance of Christ, which transcends our social commitment and ethics, does not lead to a downplaying of Christian social commitment. The eschatological *tonos* applied to our historical achievements must not become a fainthearted excuse for dispensing from serious moral deliberation; it is in fact its ground, but it also sets its limits on such deliberation.

Certainly, in the Christian faith, ethics is not something that is added to the primary significance of religious myths only at a secondary stage; it is rather constitutive of this significance.[7] Therefore the outlook that Christian symbols and rites open up to life and existence is unquestionably carried over through our ethical action in daily life. But a direct identification of justification with justice may overlook the complex transition that accompanies the elucidation of eschatological values—packed in mythological affirmations and ritual practices—into concrete moral action and political options. For example, if we take the life, death, and resurrection of Christ as the basis for justification, we must also notice that this notion is deeply tied to a sacrificial concept of life (*agape*), which may or may not have a function in the pursuit of social justice. Although the latter indeed falls under the central value of love of the neighbor, this selfless love flowing from justification finds itself in tension with the common experience in which one must balance claims and counterclaims making discriminate judgments about competing interests: the "nicely calculated less and more" that social and political expediency requires (Reinhold Niebuhr). It is a tension not so much in the order of ends but of means. I believe that this is the tension that Luther faced following 1520 as the Reformation became a

5. Ambrose Moyo, "Reconciliation and Forgiveness in an Unjust Society," *Dialog: A Journal of Theology* 41/4 (Winter 2002): 298.
6. Ibid.
7. Cf. Gerd Theissen, *The Religion of the Earliest Churches* (Minneapolis: Fortress Press, 1990), 93.

program involving the body politic, and it resembles what Max Weber described as the difference between the ethic of convictions and the ethics of responsibility. Curiously, both dimensions must be present if the love that we talk about translates as love of the neighbor.

The tension that exists between justification and justice, therefore, needs to be explicitly stated. Unclarity on this matter may lead either to ignoring the concern for justice in the name of justification or to over-emphasizing justice at the expense of justification, thereby creating a worse scenario than the one sought to be redressed. While justification signals crit-ical values, justice is the search for means that seeks a historical and rela-tive balancing between these values (and others), self-interest and group interests, and the possibilities offered by a historical context. For Christians it is also the tension between selfless love and the preservation of the self, since as believers and citizens we live with both a calculating love in the form of justice and a sacrificial love that exceeds the demands of the law. Thus the line that unites justice (which is always a balance between differ-ent interests and values) with justification (which is the abolition of the self-centered logic) is rather an oblique and fluctuating one. The *saeculum* cannot become a mirror of eternal values but a refraction mediated by our different attempts to establish temporary arrangements of justice. In a fallen world, ethics must be satisfied with the imperfect second best.[8]

The development of Moyo's arguments somehow uncovers this tension when he speaks, on the one hand, of situations that may need "an orderly compulsory acquisition of some wealth from those who have greedily amassed it at the expense of others,"[9] i.e., expropriation and land redistribu-tion. Yet, on other hand, by quoting the story of the tax collector Zacchaeus in the New Testament and of Nehemiah's response to the cry of the poor in the Old Testament, Moyo seems to be calling for a "voluntary return" of some of the wealth expropriated by the wealthy to its rightful (original) own-ers. "Compulsory" is certainly different from "voluntary." What, then, is the teaching of the Bible? Is justice the result of compulsion or the conformation of the self to Christ? Can either means be equally associated with the gospel of justification by grace through faith? What happens when people do not want to give up what we consider is not rightfully theirs?

Moyo is absolutely right in implying that the redistribution of power and possession is one of the sociopolitical boundaries crossed by the central value of Christian love. Yet society cannot be directly ruled by the same means that we commonly associate with "gospel." Can one really directly translate biblical attitudinal modeling into the large and complex realm of (pluralistic and secularized) society? It cannot escape us that the biblical texts quoted by Moyo addressed either the covenantal community of Israel

---

8. See William Lazareth, *Christians in Society: Luther, the Bible, and Social Ethics* (Minneapolis: Fortress Press, 2001), 168.
9. Moyo, "Reconciliation and Forgiveness," 299.

or the communities of Christian believers, whose psychological and moral profile were already shaped by the "cultural sign language" grounded in the proclamation of a communion with God. This we may call a "gospel experience" whose consequences were, among other things, a "voluntary" and liberating participation in God's justice by fulfilling God's law (of love). Yet we must not overlook the transition existing between language and practices referring to compulsion and exacting and those referring to the voluntary and spontaneous dispositions that surface in the encounter with grace and the gratuitousness of the gospel. In short, justification points directly to justice, but it does not lead directly into it. By misplacing their places, we may end up misreading and misleading either church or society, or both.

Perhaps it is at this point that the category of "law" could become a useful complement for Moyo's central reference to the issue of justice and the redressing of injustices. Here I understand the category of law as holding three notions together: it expresses the love of God, it is "written" in creation as an order of love (all things exist for others), yet it is distinguished from the gospel not in its content but in its relation and effects upon creatures. While society and this world certainly belong to the order of love of God's triune economy, it is also true that in this world some form of coercion—not necessarily violent—is needed to open up our works to the care of others.[10] A minimal social practice is forced out of unbelief for the sake of life together. In this fashion, realities such as justice, repentance, forgiveness, and reconciliation can be understood as social and political realities that not only flow from our justification in Christ (good works) but also are realities that are exacted from us—with a rational and/or "lovingly" applied coercion. Yet, precisely for that reason, it can be positively related but not confused with these same realities, which flow spontaneously from believers due to the indwelling presence of Christ (or the Holy Spirit, as Luther sometimes remarks). The latter is the "faith" aspect that Moyo noted in the biblical passages quoted above. It goes well beyond a mere external accommodation to whatever is required from us, pointing instead to an integral involvement of our persons with the triune praxis of God. Yet, as Luther well knew, this is not something that guides the logic of most persons in the social body.

In brief, justification does not necessarily lead to justice in society, because the latter—confined in our experience by the limits of space and time—requires measures and means whereby attitudinal aspects analogous to "love" have to be exacted from us in order to establish a minimal frame for life. One simply cannot count on people and societies to confess and repent so that justice may prevail and be established. Even if this were to happen, it would be no guarantee that injustice would be redressed; societal

10. See Antti Raunio, "Natural Law and Faith: The Forgotten Foundations of Ethics in Luther's Theology," in *Union with Christ: The New Finnish Interpretation of Luther*, ed. Carl E. Braaten and Robert W. Jenson (Grand Rapids: Eerdmans, 1998), 109.

dynamics and needs for justice well transcend subjective motivations and inner convictions.

I believe that the law-gospel relation and distinction serves not to undermine but to underscore Moyo's point and, at the same time, gives more room to understand a societal rationale for forcefully redressing the root causes of social injustices. In doing so, we probably will not have a "gospel experience" but an experience of God's judgment (coercion, exacting), which seeks to create room for creation. On the other hand, our urge for a practical and achievable means for establishing justice should not lead to the familiar divorce between law and gospel. For the Christian, what legitimates the social practice of justice is the same care and love of God that the believer identifies unambiguously in the gospel event. Behind Christian righteousness and social righteousness stands the same reality: love. The nexus between both means is given by the Gospel's paraenetic function, which ties the telos—although not the means—of gospel and law.[11] This function is what interpenetrates the political function of God's law and serves as criteria for moral deliberation as well as for the character formation of the Christian community.[12] New concepts for what is "just," therefore, are thoroughly informed by the gospel, but often we will have to search for means that uncomfortably coexist with what we deeply believe.

2. This leads to my second comment, which has to do with the understanding of the so-called doctrine of the two kingdoms and the interpretation of the church's role in the context of the South African process. Moyo rescues Luther's doctrine of the two kingdoms, arguing that it "gives the church the authority to carry out a prophetic ministry [and] to be involved in the creation of a just society which mirrors the justice of God." Basically, this doctrine "affirms that there is no sphere that lies outside of God's control."[13] Granted, but what kind of control is Moyo speaking about? It seems to me that in the semantic field of his presentation, this "control" is directly tied up with the church, serving thus to legitimate a sort of all-encompassing, holistic, all-embracing ecclesiastical organization. The church appears so identified with God's rule and dominion that one wonders whether anything is left outside of it. This feeling can change into open suspicion when one reads that "we [the church?] are instruments of God's justice on earth" or "the church. . . can only be an instrument of God's justice and is called upon to work for

---

11. It is the Trinitarian "corrective" that holds together that which in Luther's unsystematic statements can easily be set asunder. Regarding the paraenetic use of the gospel, see Lazareth, *Christians in Society*, 224ff.

12. Space does not allow me to expand on an interesting concept presented by Vítor Westhelle, that of the "munus theologicus evangelii" (the theological use of the gospel) and the "munus civilis evangelii" (the civil use of the gospel). I believe that here lies an important clue for the problem that I am discussing. See "Luther and Liberation," *Dialog: A Journal of Theology* (Winter 1986): 55.

13. Moyo, "Reconciliation and Forgiveness," 299.

social justice and in that way manifest God's justice in all of human existence."[14] Although I doubt that Moyo will side with either neo-Calvinistic views or with Roman Catholic twentieth-century integrism, some of their traces are found among his assertions. I agree with the author's concern to clearly state the social responsibility of the church, but I have to confess that the inflated portrayal of the church that emerges makes me uncomfortable. This is so, not because I deny the need for its commitment to peace and justice, but rather because I sense that little room is left for other instruments and institutions besides the church for the establishment of justice in the world.

At this point, I want to carefully distinguish a theological issue from a contextual-cultural one. It may be the case that I am missing something important of the African worldview related to the notion such as that of *Ubuntu* developed by Moyo. Yet, in my limited knowledge and conversations with African churches and theologians, I have repeatedly come across a similar conception as to the place of the church in society. There is a de facto tendency to highlight the church as almost the only critical protagonist in all spheres and areas of life that have do with the development of the "whole" human being. While this concern is undoubtedly in tune with the gospel's goals, it seems to me that it confuses the means by which these promises may be proleptically and partially realized. There certainly can be no objection that the church can and must undertake different responsibilities in the social field; the problem is when by so doing the church either impoverishes civil society and the state (for removing some of its responsibilities) or becomes a hindrance to its own credibility by overstepping boundaries. There is another way to realize the prophetic and catholic call of the church when the church is seen as called to empower other institutions and groupings that may have other immediate goals but that are indispensable for the creation and maintenance of a strong and healthy civil society. In brief, one has to ponder whether this "all-embracing" character of the church is an expression of the "holistic" African soul or is the result of failed and/or thwarted attempts of states and civil societies to set the foundations for viable economies and democratic regimes.[15]

The words of an African theologian appear to me to constitute a good foundation for a contemporary hermeneutic of the two kingdoms and twofold governance in the African context. Anna Mghwira states that in her Tanzanian experience the role of the church should not be to replace the social responsibilities of the state but to remind the state of its duties and at the same time strengthen the institutions that build up civil society. Quoting Dietrich Bonhoeffer's *Ethics*, she reminds us that "the space of the church is

14. Ibid., 298.
15. See Guillermo Hansen, "On Boundaries and Bridges: Lutheran Communio and Catholicity," in *Between Vision and Reality: Lutheran Churches in Transition*, ed. Wolfgang Greive (Geneva: LWF, 2001), 392–95.

not there in order to try to deprive the world of a piece of its territory, but in order to prove to the world that it is still the world which is loved by God. . . ." Interestingly, Mghwira found in Bonhoeffer's repristination of Luther's hermeneutics of the twofold governance an important tool for addressing and redressing the lack of clear boundaries in the social responsibilities and engagements of her own church. She understood that Luther's and Bonhoeffer's doctrine of the two kingdoms and governance was also a call for institutions other than the church to fulfill, by their own institutional means, the law of love that stems from the Triune God.

In sum, the hermeneutic of the twofold governance teaches us that it can be either a deficit or an excess that leads the church to speak and act prophetically: either when there is too little of church or state or when there is too much of them both. One never knows when the necessity will arise to raise one's voice for or against either church or state or for or against both. This is the Spirit's call.[16]

---

16. Cf. Dietrich Bonhoeffer, "Die Kirche vor der Judenfrage" (1933), in *Dietrich Bonhoeffer: Gesammelte Schriften*, ed. Eberhard Bethge (Munich: Chr. Kaiser, 1959), 2:52f.

CHAPTER 13

The Word and the Mask: *Revisiting the Two-Kingdoms Doctrine*

Vítor
Westhelle

The so-called two-kingdoms doctrine is the label under which a particular framing of the relationship between God's grace and everyday life in the midst of its institutional realities has been presented in twentieth-century Lutheranism. For more than half a century it has been the way Lutherans framed the relationship between justification and justice. How is it that this doctrine came to be regarded as a central piece in Lutheran theology when it has such a remarkably short history as a "doctrine" and for the last decades has even faded into oblivion?[1] The reasons for this phenomenon are closely connected to a particular modern (Western) agenda fraught with the crisis of legitimacy of modern institutions.[2] And here we can be even more specific and locate the discussions within the German context from the end of the Weimar Republic through the post–World War II reconstruction. At the core of it lies, obviously, the experience with Nazism. Regardless of the answer, the question remains the same: In the face of the increasing awareness of the erratic and potentially volatile character of modern institutions, how is the Christian faith to relate to them? The question has been one of legitimacy. Under which conditions can institutions claim the right to exercise dominion?[3] The Lutheran answer to the legitimacy question often was to grant these institutions autonomy vis-à-vis theological demands.[4] If the advantage of such a separation of

---

1. "For the last two or three decades, the 'doctrine of the two kingdoms' has been one of the most debated aspects of Luther's theology." Heinrich Bornkamm, *Luther's Doctrine of the Two Kingdoms in the Context of His Theology*, trans. Karl H. Herz (Philadelphia: Fortress Press, 1966), 1. Gerhard Ebeling sees expressed in "the doctrine of the two kingdoms . . . the fundamental problem of theology"; see *Word and Faith* (Philadelphia: Fortress Press, 1963), 389.
2. See Jürgen Habermas, *Communication and the Evolution of Society* (Boston: Beacon, 1979), 178–205.
3. It is important to notice that the question behind it was not one of authenticity (What are the practices by which subjects truly constitute themselves—*authenteo*?). See Jürgen Habermas, *Legitimation Crisis* (Boston: Beacon, 1975).
4. To focus its criticism on this point of the Lutheran heritage is the great merit of the Barmen Declaration.

competencies is to avoid theocratic tendencies, exclusivism, and other "isms," it has also often proved disastrous under the particular conditions in which it was historically applied.[5] Further, its recent demise (who still discusses this doctrine today?)[6] is certainly linked with a thesis that dominated the sociology of religion throughout most of the twentieth century but is now generally accepted as wrong, namely, that modernization leads inevitably to secularization.[7] The clear distinction between the spiritual and the earthly was thought to be the articulation of a theology for a secularized world in which religion and everyday life could and should be kept apart.

My task here is to address the question of justification and justice in the context of the two-kingdoms doctrine and draw implications for its relevance in contemporary theology and ethics. I shall address the following questions. How and where did this doctrine emerge, and what are its problems? Can these problems be traced back to Luther himself? Is there something that ought to be retained from this "doctrine"? And, finally, can it be relevant for a global multicultural reality?

The Genealogy of a "Doctrine"

The two-kingdoms doctrine (*Zwei-Reiche-Lehre*) is a twentieth-century creation insofar as its formal status and acclaim as a doctrine are concerned. As it is used as a technical term in contemporary discussions, this concept was coined by Franz Lau in an essay published in 1933.[8] The main thrust of the argument is the distinction between the spiritual reality (*spiritualia*) and the earthly institutions, as the *carnalia* are defined. The *carnalia* are for Lau the expression of the *lex naturae* (natural law) but conditioned to change according to the *jus positivum*, the positive law that adjusts itself to changing circumstances: *tempora mutant leges et mores*

5. This was the case not only in Germany but also in South Africa under Apartheid, in Chile under Pinochet, and in some East European countries under Soviet régime or influence. See Ulrich Duchrow, ed., *Zwei Reiche und Regimente: Ideologie oder evangelische Orientierung?* (Gütersloh: Gerd Mohr, 1977).

6. To my knowledge, the exception for over two decades is Silfredo Dalferth, *Die Zweireichelehre Martin Luthers im Dialog mit der Befreiungstheologie* (Frankfurt and New York: Peter Lang, 1996). But see also Adolfo Gonzalez Montes, *Religión y nacionalismo: la doctrina luterana de los dos reinos como teologia civil* (Salamanca: Universidad Pontificia, 1982). I thank John Stumme for calling my attention to this work.

7. Peter Berger, "Protestantism and the Quest for Certainty," *Christian Century* (August 26—September 2, 1998): 782.

8. Franz Lau, *"Äusserliche Ordnung" und "weltlich Ding" in Luthers Theologie* (Göttingen: Vandenhoeck & Ruprecht, 1933). Others would date it to the publication of Hermann Diem's seminal work on Luther's hermeneutics, "Luthers Lehre von den zwei Reichen untersucht von seinem Verständnis der Bergpredigt aus: ein Beitrag zum Problem 'Gesetz und Evangelium,'" in *Zur Zwei-Reiche-Lehre Luthers*, ed. G. Sauter (Munich: Chr. Kaiser, 1973). See Martin Honecker, *Soziallehre zwischen Tradition und Vernunft* (Tübingen: J. C. B. Mohr: 1977), 176.

(time changes laws and costumes).[9] Lau called this particular way of framing the issue in theological terms the "two-kingdoms doctrine" (*Zwei-
Reiche-Lehre*).

Lau's essay is an attempt to address and overcome the dispute within the
Luther Renaissance early in the twentieth century between Ernst Troeltsch
and Karl Holl on the question of Luther's understanding of the relationship
between the divine law and natural law and how they are institutionally
embodied or positively expressed. For Troeltsch, the "early Protestantism" of
Luther or Calvin was "simply a modification of Catholicism, in which the
catholic formulation of the problems was retained, while a different answer
was given."[10] Early Protestantism, argues Troeltsch, "exactly like the Middle
Ages, everywhere subsumes under itself the *Lex Naturae* as being originally
identical with the law of God."[11]

Although Holl accepts Troeltsch's dating of the beginning of modernity
to the end of the seventeenth century, he sees in Luther the opposite of
what Troeltsch has found. For Holl, "Luther did not appeal to a natural
law."[12] Despite using terminology akin to natural law arguments, which
admittedly causes some confusion, Luther is seen by Holl as a forerunner
of Hume, setting apart the fundamental connection between "is" and
"ought" that sustained the medieval doctrine of the natural law along the
lines of Aristotelian entelechy.[13] If Troeltsch's Luther is a "restored" relic of
medieval Catholicism, Holl's is the beacon of modernity. Here the problem
became one of adjustment or nonadjustment to the earthly stations
(*Stände*) of the state, family, economy, and the church, as they were
defined in medieval times and by Luther himself. If Troeltsch saw in
Luther a fundamental adjustment, Holl sustained a theonomic principle at
work in Luther's understanding of Christian morality, for which the norm
was *lex caritatis* (the law of love) and not *lex naturae*.

However, in spite of the theonomic orientation of Holl's exposition of
Luther, the way in which he insisted on Luther's break with the natural law
tradition and on the separation between "is" and "ought" brought the suspicion that, for Holl, Luther would be defending the autonomy of institutions in the tradition of Kant's definition of the private use of reason by
which one is compelled to accept their internal rules.[14] This led to an interpretation of the Lutheran theory of law along the lines of the notion of
divine ordinances or mandates and a rejection of an abstract normative

9. Lau, *Äusserliche Ordnung*, 38.
10. Ernst Troeltsch, *Protestantism and Progress* (Boston: Beacon, 1958), 59.
11. Ibid., 45.
12. Karl Holl, *The Reconstruction of Morality* (Minneapolis: Augsburg, 1979), 103.
13. Ibid., 145–47.
14. See Immanuel Kant, *On History*, ed. Lewis W. Beck (Indianapolis: Bobbs-Merrill, 1963),
5–7 (on the essay "What Is Enlightenment?").

concept of natural law.[15] So the question became one of relating freedom with legal obligation in the sense of the "first (viz., political) use of the law."

Lau's conceptualization of the two-kingdoms doctrine was in fact an attempt at rescuing the uniqueness of the Reformation (over against medieval Catholicism) without succumbing to modern secular autonomy (*Eigengesetzlichkeit*). But, if the solution seems so simple, how do we get to what a quarter of a century later was defined by Johannes Heckel as a maze? For Heckel, "Luther's doctrine of the two kingdoms, as it has been articulated in protestant theology, is like an ingenuous labyrinth whose creator lost its plan in the middle of the work, so that [one] cannot find the way out."[16]

The Design of the Labyrinth

Fifty years of intense debate followed this initial argument. But the parameters of the debate would remain basically the same and would become, particularly in the 1970s, the litmus test for diagnosing a Lutheran's stance on any social issue. Flanked by the classical Reformed tradition of a "third use of the law," on the one side, and the Roman Catholic natural law tradition on the other, the two-kingdoms doctrine became the Lutheran identifying badge. Yet within its own ranks, the divisions were not less relevant. On the one side were the "Barthians" in the Lutheran camp, who called for the primacy of the lordship of Christ in dealing with questions of justification and justice. On the other side, we find an array of liberal-inspired and confessionally framed theologies proclaiming a hands-off approach to Christian claims over what were regarded as autonomous spheres of public life. The issue was not settled; it was evaded by exhaustion.

Now, after two decades of only faint murmurs about it being heard, it might be time to revisit the issue in a different light, within different contexts, and with a new agenda. When the debate ebbed, the theological scenario worldwide changed. It was at the eclipse of the "two kingdoms" debate that two interrelated factors came into play in theological discussions, factors that pertained to the issues and problems plaguing that debate. The first, briefly mentioned above, is that the parallelism between modernization and secularization is a particular and localized phenomenon and not a universal one. The second is that voices from around the world started to be heard in the theological arena. The traditional dissemination centers of theology have since become aware of their own location as a

---

15. Hence there was a compromise; mandates and the "stations" (*Stände*) were neither under natural law, nor were they autonomous. Oswald Bayer, "Nature and Institution: Luther's Doctrine of the Three Orders," *Lutheran Quarterly* 12/2 (Summer 1998): 125–59, particularly 129–31. See also Wolfhart Pannenberg, *Ethics* (Philadelphia: Westminster, 1981), 26f.
16. Heckel, "Im Irrgarten der Zwei-Reiche-Lehre: Zwei Abhandlungen zum Reichs- und Kirchenbegriff Martin Luthers" *Theologische Existenz heute* 55 (1959): 317

methodological and theological issue. And it is not by chance that these centers were largely the same in which the link between modernization and secularization was being promoted. Christian theology in its Western and Northern manifestation has become aware of its particularity in a multireligious world, albeit modernized and globalized. Under these circumstances, it is indeed interesting to probe how one would revisit the quandary plaguing the two-kingdoms doctrine.

Tracing the problem back to Luther, we can observe that it stems from two different models that are unevenly blended in Luther's own musings over some theological insights that neither he nor the Confessions framed as a doctrine as such. Luther was working simultaneously with two theological blueprints of very different origins—two informing theories, as philosophers of science would call them. It was almost like trying to get orange juice by squeezing together apples and bananas. The first is related to Luther's understanding of the relationship between law and gospel. The gospel is the end of the law in the sense of bringing the power of the law to termination. The second was predicated upon the way earthly institutions (*carnalia*) were connected to natural (and divine) law. The gospel is seen here as restoring the law to its fullness, bringing it to fulfillment, which is the other sense of "end" or telos. Out of these two sets of issues, a systematic reconstruction of Luther's understanding of the relationship between justification and justice has been attempted. In general, these two models are distinguished by a somewhat consistent use of terms in his German texts: "kingdoms" (*Reiche*) and "governances" or "regiments" (*Regimente*).[17] The first model (when "kingdom" is the dominant category) goes back to the Augustinian tradition of the two cities (*civitates*), implying an axiological distinction, while the second (when "governance" language is more often used) retrieves the main elements of the medieval theory of two powers (*potestates*) or swords (*gladii*), implying a distinction of competencies.

Depending on the way Luther is read, emphasis on one or the other of these informing theories is going to have a bearing on how the two-kingdoms doctrine is interpreted and presented. Some lean toward one end of the spectrum and could be characterized as having an "Augustinian" reading of Luther, with emphasis on the negative attitude toward institutions.[18] On the other end of the spectrum are the more conventional interpretations that see

17. Even these terms are not consistently used by Luther. While in German *Reiche* and *Regimente* suggest a clear distinction between conceptual schemes, in Latin the term used for both is *regnum*. For the best description of the formation of these two traditions, see Ulrich Duchrow, *Christenheit und Weltverantwortung: Traditionsgeschichte und systematische Struktur der Zweireichelehre* (Stuttgart: Ernst Klett, 1970), particularly his main thesis on p. 440.

18. See, e.g, Ernst Wolf, "Die 'lutherische Lehre' von den zwei Reichen in der gegenwärtigen Forschung," *Zeitschrift für evangelisches Kirchenrecht* 6 (1958/59): 255–73; Hermann Diem, "Luthers Predigt in den zwei Reichen" in *Zur Zwei-Reiche-Lehre Luthers*, ed. Gerhard Sauter (Munich: Chr. Kaiser, 1973), 178–214; Heinrich Bornkamm, *Luther's Doctrine*.

the two kingdoms mainly along the lines of the medieval understanding of the two swords, which emphasizes Luther's positive appreciation of the human institutions as founded in an original divine ordinance.[19] While the Augustinian emphasis sees Luther's concern in the efficacy of the gospel in instituting the law of Christ, in conforming reality to the lordship of Christ, the medieval reading sets the emphasis on the adjustment of Christian life to the orders of creation. While the former has a christological emphasis, the latter has a social and institutional agenda. But both express the same concern with social ethical criteria that shape institutional commitments in politics, economy, the church, the family, and so on. Both are concerned in defining how justification is related to justice.

Trying to "edit" Luther out of his methodological eclecticism suggests that there is a theoretical blunder that ought to be cleared of its unsystematic elements or harmonized under a single paradigm. However, I contend that there is more to it than the apparent inconsistencies suggest. By combining the two traditions, Luther was attempting to ensure two things simultaneously; first, to affirm the radical crisis that the Word represents in the midst of the world and its régimes;[20] second, to uphold also that this world with its ordinances, institutions, and régimes is still part of God's good creation, however much sin has corrupted them.[21] What once was an exception (the Fall) is now disguised as the rule and has spread itself from humans through their institutions to nature itself.[22]

---

19. See, e.g., Werner Elert, *Morphologie des Luthertums*, vol. 2 (Munich: Beck, 1931), Paul Althaus, "Luthers Lehre von den beiden Reichen im Feuer der Kritik," *Luther-Jahrbuch* 24 (1957): 40–68; and Lau, *Äusserliche Ordnung*.

20. For reasons that later will become clear, I find "regime" the best way to translate either *Regiment* or *Reich*, avoiding some of the connotations that "regiment," "governance," or "kingdom" carry. "Regime" is a regulated social system or pattern that includes institutions and also hegemonic patterns of thought. It combines power and knowledge.

21. In the case of the state (*politia*), unlike the other orders (*ecclesia* and *oeconomia*) some would defend the prelapsarian origin of the state. See Lau, *Äusserliche Ordnung*, 13–14; Werner Elert, *Morphologie des Luthertums*, 2 vols. (Munich: Beck, 1931), 2:49–65; and, in a unique interpretation that will be discussed later, Gustaf Törnvall, *Geistliches und weltliches Regiment bei Luther* (Munich: Chr. Kaiser, 1947), 38. Others, almost in a Hobbesean manner, would argue that it was an outer medicine (*externum remedium*) instituted as a result of the Fall. See Diem, *Luthers Lehre*, 56–59, 70–72; Heckel, "Im Irrgarten der Zwei-Reiche-Lehre," 343–45; Bornkamm, *Luther's Doctrine*, 34–35; Oswald Bayer, "Law and Morality," *Lutheran Quarterly* 17/1 (Spring 2003): 64.

22. The metaphor of the mask (*larva*) Luther takes from the medieval carnival, in which the mask was a disguise but also an allegory to unveil the real situation that in fact was more masked than the mask itself. Unlike Luther and his contemporaries, we presuppose a divide between nature and institution. For Luther the distinction could be compared to the one between the buffoon and the costumes he wears, while the modern ditch corresponds to the crisis in natural law thinking since Hume. But for Luther such a distinction could not be taken for granted, even if Holl is right that he did not rely on the medieval concept of natural law. Nature and culture are both "institutions," and only as such are they also creation. For Luther the being of the world as creation is nature and institution, institution and nature, at the same-time (see Oswald Bayer, "Nature and Institution: Luther's Doctrine of the Three Orders,"

So here we are in the midst of the maze or labyrinth that Heckel diagnosed in 1959: Luther tried to bring together apparently incompatible theological constructions and ended up either in a fossilized idea of the
"orders" of creation, incompatible with modern-day institutions, or in a system incapable of unfolding a social ethics out of its own premises, surren-
dering ethics and morality to autonomous spheres in secular existence.

The Mask and the Word

A careful examination of this problem and an insightful Ariadne's thread out
of the labyrinth is offered by an unfortunately little known albeit important
work by Gustaf Törnvall.[23] Breaking with the dominant institutional
approach to the two-kingdoms doctrine, Törnvall appeals to a functional
interpretation of Luther's categories that refer to what is being discussed
under "two kingdoms." Showing Luther's inconsistent use of terms to refer
to these realities,[24] he argues that the institutional and substantive language
that is used only reveals Luther's concern with being concrete in his
imagery.[25] The two governances are fundamentally expressions of the
Creator/creature theme in God's self-revelation, through the invisible Word
of God (*verbum dei*) and the visible world as masks of God (*larvae dei*). The
result, for Törnvall, is that the two kingdoms are two functional aspects of
God's revelation: a kingdom of listening (*Hörreich*) and a kingdom of seeing
(*Sehereich*). They are perspectives or dimensions of the single act of God's
creation and revelation and only derivatively institutional realities.[26] The
question then is how to relate the visible with the audible in the midst of existence and recognize them in their relationship.

Hence, the basic distinction that is operative in Luther, at least since the
Heidelberg Disputation of 1518,[27] is the one between the visible and the
Word, between creature and Creator, the outer and the inner, between what
the senses register and reason draws together, and what grace reveals to the

---

Lutheran Quarterly 12/2 [Summer 1998]: 125–59). To put it still in other terms, nature was,
for Luther, artificial, while the reverse then was also true: institutions are natural. The modern
understandings of institutions, in the definition of Anthony Giddens, "create settings of action
ordered in terms of modernity's own dynamics and severed from 'external criteria'. . . day-to-
day social life tends to become separated from 'original' nature"(*Modernity and Self-Identity*
[Stanford: Stanford Univ. Press, 1991], 8. Under these conditions the main question plaguing
Lutheran social ethics has been the one of relating God's justifying word, cast in a forensic
sense, to a reality of quotidian existence in which the juridical sense for even grasping the passive character that this justification implies is missing.

23. Törnvall, *Geistliches und weltliches Regiment.*
24. Ibid., 94–95. He quotes thirty-eight different pairs of terms to frame the distinction.
25. Ibid., 38.
26. Cf. ibid., 17. In his interpretation of the law in Luther, Gerhard Forde follows a similar
insight: "'law' is to be taken in a functional rather than a material sense." See his locus on
"Christian Life" in *Christian Dogmatics*, ed. Carl Braaten and Robert Jenson (Philadelphia:
Fortress, 1984), 2:400.

spirit. Between these sets of categories, there is a paradoxical and asymmetric relationship with which Luther operates to formulate his understanding of God's revelation.

It is paradoxical in the sense that one (the visible) points to the other (the Word) but is in it simultaneously negated. This implies the rejection of analogical reasoning while keeping the appearance of analogical correspondence, that is, Luther's mode of argumentation entails elements of irony, the breakdown of analogical correspondence. It is impossible to read Luther without constantly being faced with ironic moves that break up continuities and systems of correspondence. It is asymmetrical because what appears to be the case in one set of categories that belong to one of the régimes (spiritual or earthly) is not simply reflected in the other but is shaped in it in unexpected ways. Luther's use of two different theoretical models to articulate this issue of relating the Word to the mask and vice versa is what allows him to keep the ironic tone alive and not succumb to the dominant analogical method and yet keep the search for correspondences. His theology is neither synthesis nor a diastasis yet simultaneously both: irony breaking into the tranquil realm of analogy. What the mask reveals is the very Word hidden in its cracks, to keep Luther's metaphor of the mask.

The Epistemological Turn

Between the mask and the Word, between what the eyes see and the spirit hears, lies language—a strenuous search to convey a theological view for which there is not a grammar readily available (after all, he believed that the Spirit has its own grammar). How would this help us to frame the question of God and justice?

The dramatic dimension of Luther's own anguish over a text of Paul on the justice of God comes to a sharp, if enigmatic resolution in these words in his commentary on Isaiah 53: "Behold the new definition of justice (*definicionem novam iusticiae*): justice is the knowledge of Christ (*iusticia est cognicio Christi*)."[28] The insight to understand this came when I once read the Heidelberg disputation backwards, from the "philosophical" theses at the end to the theological ones at the beginning. Such a reading allows one to realize that, as Gustaf Aulén and others already noticed,[29] Luther is struggling with language in order to bring to light something new, some

27. WA 1:353–74; LW 31:39–70.

28. This is my translation from WA 31/2:439, 19–20. The standard English translation (LW 17:230) reads: "You must therefore note this new definition of righteousness. Righteousness is the knowledge of Christ."

29. Anders Nygren, *Meaning and Method* (Philadelphia: Fortress Press, 1972), 243–64; Dennis Bielfeldt, "Luther on Language," *Lutheran Quarterly* 16/2 (Summer 2000): 195–220; Vítor Westhelle, "Communication and the Transgression of Language in Martin Luther," *Lutheran Quarterly* 16/1 (Spring 2003): 1–27.

good news, while being a child of his old world with its rhetoric in all the realms institutionally recognized.

His attack on philosophy (with its "reason"), the economic system (with its "markets"), jurisprudence (with its "justice"), the territorial states (with their "politics"), and the church (with its "polities") was not to remodel them. The Reformation was not about "reforming," as when one restores a building or remodels a house, but it is about a *new* formation. He was well aware of the inefficacy of interweaving the new with the old (Luke 5:36). He wanted to find or even provoke a crack, a crisis, in the systemic arrangements that controlled, ordered, and regulated those institutions that Luther took as basic following a general consensus: *ecclesia, oeconomia,* and *politia*. The new definition is not only redressing the old, mending the fractures; it is something new, a gift. It cracks the surfaces, opens up the wounds behind the mask, and reveals the crisis. Luther's "new" definition sets itself against the old, which he explicitly mentions in the same text: the proverbial *suum cuique* (to each what is due). The classical definition presumed a correspondence between the order of things (the *Stände*) and God's mercy toward us. The *cognitio Christi* (knowledge of Christ) is precisely this new knowledge, this new way of knowing that erupts through the very cracks of the systems of this world. The genitive in *cognitio Christi* means to know Christ, but it also means to have the *cognitio* of Christ, to have Christ's knowledge and Christ's mind; it is a double genitive. And this is a different knowledge of the order of things in the régimes of this world.

It is in the same context of the commentary on Isaiah 53 that Luther talks about how this is accomplished: it is a "wonderful exchange" (*mirabilis mutatio*).[30] For the Reformer, the danger in the interpretation of this expression is to make the "wonder" of this exchange into a temporary readjustment of relations into a new hegemonic arrangement, thus only reinstating the integrity of the old rule. This for him would be sophistry: "The sophists say that righteousness is the fixed will to render to each his own."[31]

The justice of Christ, then, has two interrelated aspects. It entails the grace of God toward us in the midst of our condition, although it does so not by supplementing or even mending the systems in the world. It does this by disclosing the fissures in the systems of knowledge and power. The new justice, the knowledge of Christ, is indeed foolishness. The power of Christ is indeed weakness. Paul's antitheses of 1 Corinthians 1 are examples of the search for this language that breaks through and breaks forth. Hence, it is not by chance the first "philosophical" thesis of the Heidelberg Disputation says: "The one who wishes to philosophize by using Aristotle without danger to his soul must first become thoroughly foolish in Christ." Luther himself could praise Aristotle on questions of ethics, for example, which cannot entail

30. LW 17:225; WA 31/2:435, 11.
31. LW 17:229; "Iusticia est constans voluntas reddenti cuique, quod suum est." WA 31/2:439, 5–6.

the meaning that the philosophy of Aristotle per se is anti-Christian. This first philosophical thesis makes sense only once one realizes that "Aristotle" functions here as a metonymy for the standards of valid rationality, for the accepted régime of truth, which for the most it was.

While on our pursuit to be righteous, to have our due share and pay our dues and yet not achieve it, the justice of Christ breaks in and fragments the systems of the world, its philosophy, ecclesial structures, legal rules—in short, economies and régimes. The possibilities of justice in the midst of this world manifest themselves precisely where these economies and régimes break down. However, this is still a negative if not apocalyptic definition of justice. We need to know more than the power of fragmentation; we need to know that which brings about justice in the midst of everyday life in and in spite of the powers and the knowledges (*epistemai*) that rule the world.

The old quest for the Lutheran relation between justification and justice has been a search for a doctrine, when the very point is that—ironically—it is a "doctrine" that brings doctrines (insofar as they are human constructions) themselves into question. Addressed often from a moral theological standpoint (What ought we to do in society in accordance to our faith?), or from an ontological standpoint (How is the creature related to the creator?), what is overlooked in the discussion is the epistemological question about the conditions of possibility for stating the problem (Where are we to look to find the truth?). Luther's insight brings into question the relation between revelation and the régimes that control knowledge, establish rationalities, norm the market, and rule the church (the visible church is an earthly régime, just like the state or "economy"). This reading of the two-kingdoms doctrine suggests that knowledge of Christ can emerge only when we understand that it is in the fissures and ruptures in the order of things that a new justice can be shaped. And this is a renewed, newly formed justice—not a particular Christian justice or a Christian alternative to the world but the alterity of Christ in the midst of the world.[32]

If there was a failure in the interpretations of Luther's thought on justification and justice, it was not to recognize that when and where the two meet we are in an eschatological dimension.[33] The irruption of justice comes from the ends of this world (the outer ends, but also the ends in the midst of the world), precisely where another world comes about and we have the

---

32. The "third use of the law" is excluded. Although Luther can say that we can create new Decalogues (WA 39/1:47; LW 34:112–13) it is always within the context of the inherited tradition. Thus he writes from Coburg in 1530 a letter to Justus Jonas, saying, "et coepi judicare, decalogum esse dialecticam evangelii, et evangelium rhetoricam decalogi, habereque Christum omnia Mosi, sed Mosem non omnia Christi" ("to begin with a distinction, the Decalogue is the logic of the Gospel, the Gospel the rhetoric of the Decalogue, so that we have in Christ all of Moses, but in Moses not all of Christ").

33. To stress Luther's eschatological thinking in connection with the "two kingdoms" is the merit of Ulrich Duchrow's comprehensive study, *Christenheit und Weltverantwortung*.

courage not to disguise it for the sake of the old. The kingdom of God, which Paul translated as "justification," comes to us exactly at that point in time and space where our work, reasons, and régimes end or break down. There, where there is nothing, God creates. And this creation is also the introduction of another knowledge that comes through another way of reasoning, which Paul called the *apokalypsis Iesou Christou* (revelation of Jesus Christ).[34]

Justice as Difference

In its attempt at apologizing for the rightfulness of its order, the system hides its cracks. In his sermon on the "Two Kinds of Righteousness" (1518 or 1519),[35] Luther claims the priority of the alien justice of Christ over our justice, which is also God's doing and can only be truly accomplished in divine-human cooperation. Later, in *The Bondage of the Will*, the reformer reflected on this distinction between the realm in which God works alone through grace and the other in which we cooperate with God (*cooperatio hominis cum Deo*), using our reason, work, and institutions.[36] However, there is a necessary logical priority between the first realm and the second. Luther's attack on works, as much as on reason (power and knowledge, as we would say it today), when framed in this context, should be able to dispel the recurring suspicion of a Lutheran inherent quietism. This is so because the earthly régimes (with their second form of justice, according to Luther's sermon on the "Two Kinds of Righteousness") in which we are called to cooperate with God are a logical result of God's work in Christ, conforming us to him and not displacing us into an alternative realm.[37] In the régimes of power and knowledge, of work and reason that are in place in this world, Luther's spiritual governance is a difference, a counterpoint in the order of things; it is another régime in the sense of being a different régime and not an alternative one. In his late (1541?) sermon on Psalm 1, he phrased it like this: "When I say, 'Heaven' of the heaven of the Lord, I do not mean heaven as a site and a place in distinction to the Earth, I mean by it a régime."[38] God's régime functions as an antithetical factor in the midst of the régimes that our reason and work erect, which are both part of God's good creation yet also defiled by sin. Luther's understanding of revelation is indeed what the word

34. See Alexandra Brown, *The Cross and Human Transformation* (Minneapolis: Fortress Press, 1995), and the insightful epistemological study on the theology of the cross by Mary Solberg, *Compelling Knowledge* (New York: SUNY Press, 1997).

35. WA 2:145–52; LW 31:297–306.

36. WA 18:754, 1–16; LW 33:242–43.

37. Herein lies a further problem with the forensic understanding of justification. The first was to conform the logic of grace to juridical models. The additional problem is that it does not link causally and positively the work of redemption with human emancipation. At most, it does it negatively by the fact the forgiven person is set free to act.

38. "Quando dico: Celum celi domini, non intelligo celum situ et loco distincto terra, sed ich meine das regiment mit"; WA 49:224, 30.

"apocalypse" means in Greek. Luther's thinking on the two-kingdoms motif is an invitation to recognize otherness, the difference that emerges in the midst of our platitudes, as the locus for the insurgence of justice.

What such a reading of the two-kingdoms motif allows for is a theological practice in which the voices and knowledge of those who are subjugated can come to the fore. If justification is the Word embodying forgiveness, this forgiveness will produce words; it will authenticate the self-expression of those who have been defiled under the weight of sin and oppression. Justification is the word of the Author who authorizes. It authorizes the emergence of other voices dissonant from the prevailing régimes of truth and power. Justice begins here; it begins not by fulfilling the requirements of the prevailing régimes, but by setting other conditions, other parameters, which indeed sound foolish or inane.

Instead of outrightly rejecting the two-kingdoms doctrine in its classical twentieth-century formulation as a useless relic of a superseded social and theological problem in the West, we can read it as a frail attempt to articulate Luther's own conviction that if justice is to be done, it will have to come from the other, and every "other" is ultimately irreducibly the other.

By this new definition, justice not only addresses the marginalized, heals the wounds of our world, and cares for the poor, but above all listens to their plea (Pentecost is after all also a miracle of listening) and sees the faces of the excluded ones. This is all the more relevant because their plea and faces reveal the fissures in the mask of God in the midst of the crude realities of this world that the régimes constantly try to hide, norm, and regulate. Hiding the margins is the oldest of strategies for maintaining power, for that is where the frailty of power is made manifest.

In sermon 45 of the "Homilies on the Acts,"[39] Chrysostom illustrates what I am trying to explain here. The church, recognizes Chrysostom, has plenty of "money and revenues." This was, after all, the early Constantinian church. Institutions for the care of the poor and strangers were created; *xenodocheion* they were called. With his thundering, golden mouth, Chrysostom launches an attack on them, for they were being used by the now well-off Christians to avoid the face of the poor themselves. The incisiveness of Chrysostom's argument reveals someone who was ashamed of his fellow Christians and who knew where justice started; it begins by allowing the other, the poor, the stranger to emerge, to have a voice, to have a face. The two-kingdoms doctrine is not a doctrine. It is an epistemic principle that teaches the faithful that to know Christ is to know justice. And, conversely, where justice cries out, there we find Christ. And so Luther: "Thus the world is full of God. In every alley, at your door you find Christ; stare not at heavens."[40]

39. *The Nicene and Post-Nicene Fathers*, ed. Philip Schaff (reprint: Peabody, Mass.: Hendrickson, 1995), 11:272–77.
40. "Also ist die welt vol von Gott. In allen gassen, fur deiner thur findest du Christum. Gaff nicht ynn himel"; WA 20:514, 27f.

COMPARISONS

Part

V

FROM THE OUTSET LUTHER had many followers who eventually developed new directions or turned critically against him. This is especially true of the paragons of the later so-called Reformed Church, most notably John Calvin. Also within Lutheranism the most important thinkers could not maintain their faithfulness to the central Reformation ideas without also correcting certain views of Luther. This point can be studied in the two outstanding personalities of nineteenth-century Protestantism, N. F. S. Grundtvig and Søren Kierkegaard.

George Hunsinger examines the controversy between Lutheran and Reformed theology about the Eucharist from the background of the Reformation protest against the Roman Catholic understanding of the mass, not least of all in Thomas Aquinas. Hunsinger argues, however, that when read in light of the Chalcedonian formula of the two natures of Jesus Christ, the positions on real presence of Christ in Aquinas, Luther, and Calvin can no longer be regarded as mutually exclusive; rather, the three theologians may be seen as challenging and enriching one another. By applying the rule of mutuality in ecumenical dialogue, mutual acceptance of all traditions involved can be reached, so that all parties can come to understand themselves in a new way.

Theodor Jørgensen portrays Grundtvig as a successor of Luther who at the same time regarded himself as Luther's equal and peer. Faithful to the church reforming ideas of Luther, Grundtvig felt free to continue the Reformation process. Inspired not least by the early Greek fathers, Grundtvig's thinking was centered in the sacramental and liturgical community, fed by the living Word of Christ. On this basis, he criticized the *sola scriptura* principle and reached a new understanding of the connection between Christianity and humanity, church and people.

Hermann Deuser describes the growing tension between Reformation legacy and the actual demand of Christianity in Kierkegaard's thinking and activity as a public writer. The more Kierkegaard stressed the importance of a subjective appropriation of faith, the more he became suspicious of Reformation preaching and teaching. In spite of the Reformation emphasis on personal faith, its effect comes down to supporting the great delusion of an already existing Christianity, against which Kierkegaard set his "one thesis": Christianity no longer exists! In Deuser's view there is nevertheless a near connection between Luther's and Kierkegaard's thinking, which cannot be encapsulated in a single thesis.

—PETER WIDMANN

Aquinas, Luther, and Calvin: *Toward a Chalcedonian Resolution of the Eucharistic Controversies*

George Hunsinger

N o point of division in the ecumenical church has been more vexing than the disunity that so ironically surrounds the Eucharist, the very sacrament of unity itself. "The Eucharist tastes bitter," declared George Lindbeck, "in a divided church." If no issue could be more pressing, perhaps none is more intractable at the same time. For the divisions that surround the Eucharist are not only profound in themselves, but they also intersect with equally divisive questions about ministry, about the church, and about the meaning of salvation itself—to name only a few. To submit that there is more actually existing unity about the Eucharist than is commonly supposed and that the potential for unity may be even greater still is bound at first glance to seem quixotic. Yet that is what I propose.

My proposal is at once descriptive and constructive. I examine representative figures from three ecumenical communions: the Roman Catholic, the Lutheran, and the Reformed. While the unity to be unearthed among them is far from perfect, the convergences, I contend, are significant. Some of these convergences will be actual, others merely potential. The more potential they are, the more the weight will have to fall on the constructive side of my proposal. An analogy will be drawn between the incarnation and the Eucharist. While this analogy is hardly unprecedented, it has not been exploited, it seems to me, as fully as might be useful. Like the Chalcedonian definition itself (two natures, neither separated nor confused), which did not stabilize the church's understanding of the incarnation without also generating lasting dissent, the incarnational analogy I propose for understanding the real presence of Christ in the Eucharist will also undoubtedly leave dissent in its train. But it may also lay the groundwork for an unexpected measure of convergence.

Real Presence according to Aquinas

As a point of entry into the Roman Catholic tradition, I begin with Thomas Aquinas. Aquinas was able to accomplish something that neither Luther nor

Calvin ever quite managed to pull off. He was convincingly able to hold together a robust understanding of "real presence" with an equally robust stance on "local presence." He was able, that is, to satisfy two conditions that are indispensable for any Eucharistic proposal that hopes to be viable in the larger ecumenical church.

When it comes to technical precision and unequivocal affirmation, Aquinas's definition of Christ's real human body in heaven—its local presence—left nothing to be desired. Yet this definition served merely as background for the point that really mattered to him—the real presence of Christ in the Eucharist under the specific form of his body and blood. Real presence was the sacramental means by which the risen Christ drew near in order to unite us with himself in love. "He joins us to himself in this sacrament," wrote Aquinas, "in the reality of his body and blood. . . . Hence this sacrament, because it joins Christ so closely to us, is the sign of his supreme love and lifts our hope on high."[1]

Real presence, Aquinas continued, must be kept logically distinct from local presence. "The body of Christ is not in this sacrament in the way a body is located in a place. The dimensions of a body in a place correspond with the dimensions of the place that contains it. Christ's body is here in a special way that is proper to this sacrament."[2] Or again, Christ's body is in the sacrament "[not] as if it were present in the way that is natural for a body to be present, that is, visibly in its normal appearance . . . [but] a spiritual, nonvisible presence, in the way of a spirit and by the power of the Spirit."[3]

Christ's bodily presence, Aquinas affirmed, is spiritual, and it comes about only by the power of the Holy Spirit. Nevertheless, although lacking in spatial dimensions, it is also substantial. "The substance of Christ's body or of his blood is in the sacrament as a result of the sacramental sign; not so the dimensions of his body or of his blood. . . . The whole substance of the body and the blood of Christ is contained in this sacrament."[4] Real presence, reiterated Aquinas, meant nothing less than substantial presence—the actual presence of Christ's body, though in a spiritual mode without dimensions. "The body of Christ is here as if it were just substance, that is, in the way that substance is under its dimensions, and not in any dimensive way. . . . The manner of presence is controlled by considerations of what it means to be there just as substance."[5] Aquinas's point was that substantial presence did not require local presence but occurred precisely without it. "The body of Christ is not under the dimensions of the bread locally. . . . Hence,

1. *STh* 3a. 75, 1. Thomas Aquinas, *Summa Theologiae*, 1964–1980, ed. Thomas Gilby (New York: McGraw-Hill Black Friars, and London: Eyre & Spottiswoode). The following quotations are from this work.

2. *STh* 3a. 75, 1.

3. Ibid.

4. *STh* 3a. 76, 1.

5. *STh* 3a. 76, 3.

Christ's body in this sacrament is in no way localized."[6] Christ's body was, as it were, in but not of the sacrament; that is, properly speaking, it was in heaven yet also sacramentally present at the same time.

Christ's body is not in this sacrament in the sense of being restricted to it. If that were so, it could only be on that altar where the sacrament is actually being consecrated. But it is always in heaven in its proper appearance, and it is on many other altars under its sacramental appearance. . . . So it does not follow that the body of Christ is in this sacrament as localized.[7]

In his *Summa Theologiae*, Aquinas did not reach for an incarnational analogy to explain how the substance of Christ's body was related to the sacramentally consecrated bread, or his blood to the consecrated wine. When he did think about the incarnation in relation to the Eucharist, it was to establish his doctrine of concomitance. According to that doctrine, "wherever the body of Christ may be, you must have the godhead with it."[8] Concomitance thus establishes the presence of the whole Christ in the Eucharist, his deity in and with his humanity. But the possibility of an analogy between two different relationships—between Christ's deity and humanity, on the one hand, and between Eucharistic sign and reality, on the other—was not considered.

Instead, the analogy Aquinas drew was, rather strikingly, to the doctrine of creation. The famous doctrine of transubstantiation was conceived as a miraculous change comparable only to the divine work of *creatio ex nihilo*. In fact, Aquinas noted, the extraordinary change, or *conversio*, that occurs in transubstantiation involves "far more difficulties than does creation."[9] For whereas creation involves "just the one difficulty that something comes from nothing"[10] transubstantiation involves at least two difficulties. First, the substance of one entity, the consecrated element, is totally transformed into that of something else, namely, the body or the blood of Christ. The second difficulty is that nonetheless the "accidents" or appearances of the consecrated element remain even after "their substance has disappeared."[11]

For my purposes, two points are worthy of note. First, the analogy to creation could not be drawn more explicitly. "This change," Aquinas explained, "does not occur because of passive ability in the creature to be this or that, but solely through the active power of the Creator."[12] Second, Aquinas believed that transubstantiation was the only possible way that real or substantial presence could occur in the Eucharist without local presence.

6. *STh* 3a. 76, 5.
7. *STh* 3a. 76, 6.
8. *STh* 3a. 76, 1.
9. *STh* 3a. 75, 8.
10. Ibid.
11. Ibid.
12. Ibid.

"There is no other way," he wrote, "in which the body of Christ can begin to be in this sacrament except through the substance of the bread being changed into it."[13] Because of this change, the body of Christ was substantially contained under the accidents of the consecrated bread.

The idea that the substance of the consecrated element did not remain but was changed into Christ's body, became, of course, the official teaching of the Council of Trent. It thus remains normative, in some sense, for the Roman Catholic Church right down to the present day. What that normative sense might be today will be taken up a little later. In official Roman Catholic teaching, however, the idea of real or substantial presence is always inseparable from two ideas: that of sacramental conversion and that of sacramental containment.

Before moving on, a glance needs to be taken toward the effect of the sacrament as Aquinas understood it. The Eucharist, he noted, looks to the past, the present, and the future. Looking back to the past, it commemorates Christ's passion and so is called a sacrifice. (Although the topic of Eucharistic sacrifice is immensely important, it is unfortunately too large to be discussed here, though a few points will be made later on.) Looking forward to the future, the Eucharist "prefigures that enjoyment of God which will be ours in heaven."[14] And looking to the present, the Eucharist establishes what it signifies and signifies what it establishes, namely, the unity of the church.[15]

In particular, the sacrament leads those who receive it toward "spiritual perfection" by bringing them into union with Christ and so with one another.[16] In other words, for those not in a state of mortal sin, it brings an increase of grace[17]—the grace that forgives venial sins, forms habits of virtue, and leads to acts of charity.[18] Grace is conferred and received according to the measure of faith and devotion in the recipient.[19] Through regular participation in the sacrament, the communicant is drawn gradually into an ever-greater conformity with Christ. "A person needs Christ's health-giving virtue," Aquinas explained, "every day."[20]

Finally, the question of efficacy can be illuminated by considering the case of reception by an unbeliever. Here Aquinas made a suitably complex judgment. Although sinners receive Christ's body sacramentally, he explained, they do not receive it spiritually. Sacramental reception seems to be objective, while spiritual reception, in turn, is subjective. Christ's body is

13. *STh* 3a. 75, 3.
14. *STh* 3a. 73, 4.
15. Ibid.
16. *STh* 3a. 73, 3.
17. *STh* 3a. 79, 1.
18. *STh* 3a. 79, 5.
19. *STh* 3a. 80, 2.
20. *STh* 3a. 80, 10.

indeed given and eaten objectively, under the species of the consecrated bread, but it brings no spiritual benefit and, indeed, tends only to destruction. In the absence of faith, the body of Christ can be received and eaten only improperly and in a sense is not eaten at all.[21] But with faith (understood as assent to the articles of belief), and especially with devotion, Christ himself is received and his health-giving virtue is conferred, both sacramentally and spiritually, under the species of the bread and the wine.[22]

Real Presence according to Luther

In contrast to Aquinas and Calvin, it was Luther who set forth the incarnational analogy. In doing so, he retrieved a long-standing patristic tradition that had gradually fallen into eclipse. For Luther the analogy functioned as an alternative to the doctrine of transubstantiation. In *The Babylonian Captivity of the Church*, he wrote:

> Thus, what is true in regard to Christ is also true in regard to the sacrament. In order for the divine nature to dwell in him bodily [Col. 2:9], it is not necessary for the human nature to be transubstantiated and the divine nature contained under the accidents of the human nature. Both natures are simply there in their entirety, and it is truly said: "This man is God; this God is man." Even though philosophy cannot grasp this, faith grasps it nonetheless. And the authority of God's Word is greater than the capacity of our intellect to grasp it. In like manner, it is not necessary in the sacrament that the bread and wine be transubstantiated and that Christ be contained under their accidents in order that the real body and real blood may be present. But both remain there at the same time, and it is truly said, "This bread is my body; this wine is my blood," and vice versa.[23]

Luther based the analogy, in part, on an interpretation of 1 Cor 10:16: "The bread that we break, is it not a participation [Greek: *koinonia*] in the body of Christ?" According to this verse, as Luther read it, the relationship of the body of Christ to the Eucharistic bread was one of participation or *koinonia*.

The formal pattern in the analogy thus consisted of two terms and a relationship. As in the incarnation, so also in the Eucharist, the relationship was one of participation or *koinonia*—a relationship that hinged on the mystery of mutual indwelling. Just as the divine nature dwelt in Christ bodily, so also did his life-giving flesh come to dwell, so to speak, in the consecrated bread, and vice versa. Regardless of whether reason could

21. *STh* 3a. 80, 3.
22. *STh* 3a. 80, 5.
23. LW 36:35.

understand it, both entities in the relation were simply there in their entirety. Consequently, just as one could point to the human Jesus and say without equivocation, "This man is the Lord," so also could one take the consecrated bread and say without equivocation, "This is the body of Christ." The predications were true by participation, and for Luther the idea of participation invalidated the idea that one substance was transformed into another. Real presence meant that Christ's life-giving flesh was substantially present in, with, and under the bread, whose substance remained that of bread.

Unfortunately, Luther did not exploit the incarnational analogy he had revived. Instead, he relied more heavily on two other arguments. The one we might call the argument from literalism, the other the argument from ubiquity. Let us take up the ubiquity argument first.

Although Luther never denied the idea of local presence, as it had been so carefully defined, for example, by Aquinas, his argument from ubiquity understandably undermined the confidence of his opponents in the Reformed theological camp. However, the Reformed never appreciated that Luther attributed no more to ubiquity than secondary importance. For him it was no more than a kind of background belief designed to show that real presence was not, as some had supposed, impossible. Luther's ubiquity argument was that if Christ is seated at God's right hand, and if God's right hand is a metaphor for God's power, and if God's power is ubiquitous, then Christ's body is also ubiquitous. Real presence, therefore, was not impossible.

To the Reformed, however, it looked as though the Lutheran position boiled down to the twofold error that Christ's body was locally present in the Eucharist, yet only substantially present in heaven. "Tell me," Zwingli asked at the Marburg Colloquy, "is the body of Christ in a place?" To which the Lutheran Brenz retorted: "It is without place." Luther, to my knowledge, never made such an unqualified statement. When Zwingli insisted, "Christ is finite as we are finite," Luther replied, "I admit that." It seems fair to say that in the highly charged atmosphere of those years, the Lutherans were so concerned to assert real presence in the Eucharist that the idea of local presence in heaven, so important to the Reformed, suffered by comparison. The Lutherans had a robust doctrine of real presence but—in contrast to someone like Aquinas—not an equally robust doctrine of local presence.

And yet the account cannot rest there. In a little-known proposal drafted hurriedly by Luther just before the Marburg Colloquy dissolved, the makings of an adequate solution were set forth. The sentence, "This is my body," Luther proposed, meant that Christ's body was present in the Eucharist truly but not locally. "Truly" meant "substantively and essentially," he explained, while "not locally" meant "not according to ordinary qualities" and "not quantitatively." The Reformed were asked to affirm real presence on these terms, while the Lutherans would reject local presence with respect to the Eucharist.

Luther's last-minute proposal rose nearly to the level of Aquinas. While it lacked the latter's careful analytical detail and made no mention of local presence in heaven, it nonetheless brought a degree of clarity to the Marburg Colloquy that had not been previously attained. Unfortunately, the proposal was not only rejected by the Reformed but also immediately discarded, apparently even by a figure like Bucer, who had himself been present at Marburg and who persisted long afterwards in striving for reconciliation, as if Luther's proposal had never been made.

What Luther wanted more than anything else was to take seriously Christ's statement, "This is my body." Although it is often said that Luther interpreted this statement "literally," it would be better to say that he interpreted it "realistically." For he explicitly described the statement as a synecdoche. While Luther wanted to rely on the words of Christ and nothing else, he knew that Christ's flesh was not literally present in the Eucharist, as he once colorfully put it, like pork on a plate. According to Luther, synecdoche is a figure of speech such that when two realities are present so that the one is contained in the other, either can be used to refer to the other. The statement "This is my body" is a synecdoche, because the word "bread" is used to refer to the body, yet the bread that does the containing is not identical with the body it contains, and vice versa. Together they form a unity-in-distinction, with the emphasis falling on their unity.

The efficacy of the Eucharist, according to Luther, is no different from that of the Word, because the content imparted by both is identical. For Luther, the Eucharist is a particular form of God's Word, not something independent of or alongside it. "The same thing is present in the sermon," he stated, "as in the sacrament."[24] "The sacraments . . . contain nothing but God's words, promises and signs."[25] As a visible form of the Word, the Eucharist testifies concretely that Christ came also for me (*pro me*). It gives me "a sure sign" that "Christ's death overcame my death in his death, that his obedience blotted out my sin in his suffering, that his love destroyed my hell in his forsakenness."[26]

What finally makes the substance of the Word and the Eucharist identical, according to Luther, is that each imparts "the entire Christ." Christ himself is mediated no less through the Word than through the sacrament. The Word of God, explained Luther, always "brings with it everything of which it speaks, namely, Christ with his flesh and blood and everything that he has and is."[27] Christ "has put himself into the Word," Luther continued, "and through the Word he puts himself into the bread [and wine] also."[28] Christ's real presence in the Eucharist is thus a special form of his

24. LW 36:348.
25. LW 42:109.
26. LW 42:109.
27. LW 36:278.
28. LW 36:343.

presence in the Word. Just as Christ is imparted to us through the Word, so is he also imparted to us, though in a different form, "corporeally in the bread and wine."[29]

Since Christ has only one body, Luther reasoned, it is the body that was born of the Virgin Mary and that suffered for us on the cross that is made present to us in the Eucharist. Luther followed the medieval tradition, as seen, for example, in Aquinas, to this extent: while rejecting the idea of *conversio*, he retained the idea of containment. In the Eucharist, the body of Christ appears to us in the form of bread. It cannot be eaten spiritually without also being eaten physically at the same time. Yet even this physical eating is somehow distinctively spiritual, since the substance of Christ's flesh cannot be "cut into pieces, divided, chewed, digested, consumed and destroyed."[30] While all who participate, whether believers or impious, receive Christ's flesh in the form of bread, faith (understood as *fiducia* more than *assensus*) is always necessary if Christ is to be eaten and received spiritually.[31] "As we eat him," wrote Luther, "he abides in us and we in him. For he is not digested or transformed but ceaselessly he transforms us, our soul into righteousness, our body into eternal life."[32] Through our Eucharistic union with Christ, we are transformed as whole persons, body and soul, that we might dwell with him and he with us to all eternity.

Real Presence according to Calvin

Whereas Aquinas had upheld a robust distinction between real and local presence and Luther had retrieved the incarnational analogy, Calvin made a distinguished contribution of his own. First, he assigned to the Holy Spirit a more prominent role in the Eucharist than had previously been common and, second, he introduced into the discussion what might be called the upward vector. That is, whereas theologians like Aquinas and Luther and the traditions they represented had thought primarily of a movement from heaven to earth, Calvin introduced the complementary idea of a movement from earth to heaven. For Calvin, the Holy Spirit served as the mediator of communion between heaven and earth. By the Spirit's operation, Christ was not only made really present to us in the Eucharist but at the same time we were really made present to him in heaven.

The mediation of the Spirit was, in effect, Calvin's alternative to Luther's idiosyncratic doctrine of ubiquity. Like Aquinas, and like the entire Reformed theological camp, Calvin was profoundly concerned not to undermine the idea of Christ's possessing a real, and therefore finite, human body. Also like Aquinas, Calvin sought a way to affirm the real presence of Christ

29. LW 36:343.
30. LW 37:130.
31. LW 37:132.
32. Ibid.

in the Eucharist without jeopardizing Christ's local presence in heaven. Unlike both Aquinas and Luther, however, Calvin distanced himself from the notion of containment. He agreed that real presence meant substantial presence but disagreed that substantial presence meant containment, in other words, that Christ's body was contained in the bread. Whether Calvin rejected this idea categorically, however, or only under a certain aspect is not easy to decide.

For Calvin, as for almost all the Reformed, the idea of containment veered too close to the idea of local Eucharistic presence. In effect, Calvin argued not so much that Christ's body was in the bread as that the bread was the instrument by which the Spirit presented and imparted the life-giving flesh of Christ to faith. Calvin's resort to the upward vector was closely related to his fear that containment meant local presence. He wrote:

> But greatly mistaken are those who conceive no presence of flesh in the Supper unless it lies in the bread. For thus they leave nothing to the secret working of the Spirit, which unites Christ himself to us. To them Christ does not seem to be present unless he comes down to us. As though, if he should lift us to himself, we should not just as much enjoy his presence! The question is therefore only of the manner, for they place Christ in the bread, while we do not think it lawful to drag him down from heaven. . . . Since this mystery is heavenly, there is no need to draw Christ to earth that he may be joined to us.[33]

At the moment of distribution, according to Calvin, the body of Christ was exhibited and offered to the recipient with the bread, although sometimes he could also say in and through it as well. The bread was therefore not an empty sign. In the act of reception, however, the bread alone was in the mouth, while the life-giving flesh of Christ, and so Christ in person himself, entered into one's heart by faith. We carry away from the Eucharist no more than we collect with the vessel of faith, Calvin explained. Those without faith were like an empty bottle that cannot be filled with liquid as long as it is corked and sealed. In other words, while the impious may receive the bread, they receive nothing of Christ's life-giving flesh.

Like Luther, Calvin believed that the content of the gospel and that of the Eucharist were the same—the living Christ himself—differing only in their forms of presentation and reception and therefore, to some extent, in their function. Roughly speaking, while the gospel's function was to awaken faith and instruct it, the Eucharist was designed to nourish faith and renew it. The Eucharist had to be seen, Calvin believed, within the larger context of the gospel. That meant within the context of our union with Christ, or

---

33. *Inst.* 4.17.31; John Calvin, *Institutes*, English Version: John Calvin, *Institutes of the Christian Religion*; trans. Henry Beveridge (Grand Rapids: Eerdmans, 1995).

participatio Christi, as established by the Holy Spirit through faith. As in Aquinas and Luther, the main point of the Eucharist for Calvin was union and communion with Christ:

> The Lord bestows this benefit upon us through his Spirit, so that we may be made one in body, spirit, and soul with him. The bond of this connection is therefore the Spirit of Christ, with whom we are joined in unity, and is like a channel through which all that Christ himself is and has is conveyed to us. For if we see that the sun, shedding its beams upon the earth, casts its substance in some measure upon it in order to beget, nourish, and give warmth to its offspring—why should the radiance of Christ's Spirit be less in order to impart to us the communion of his flesh and blood? On this account, Scripture, in speaking of our participation with Christ, relates its whole power to the Spirit. But one passage will suffice for many. For Paul, in the eighth chapter of Romans, states that Christ dwells in us only through his Spirit (Rom. 8:9). Yet he does not take away that communion of his flesh and blood, which we are now discussing (Rom. 8:9), but teaches that the Spirit alone causes us to possess Christ completely and have him dwelling in us.[34]

Although Calvin has been criticized for identifying the "substance" of Christ's flesh with its life-giving virtue or power, no difference would seem evident in this respect between Calvin and Aquinas, both of whom could use the terms *substance* and *virtue* interchangeably. Calvin clearly intended to affirm not only the real presence but also real reception of Christ's life-giving flesh in the Eucharist.

> The same body, which Christ has offered as a sacrifice is extended in the Supper.[35]

> In short, he feeds his people with his own body, the communion of which he bestows upon them by the power of his Spirit.[36]

> I freely accept whatever can be made to express the true and substantial partaking of the body and blood of the Lord, which is shown to believers under the sacred symbols of the Supper.[37]

It seems fair to say that Calvin agreed in principle with Aquinas and Luther on the fact of real presence but disagreed with them in various ways about the modes of presence and reception. For Calvin, unlike Aquinas and

34. *Inst.* 4.17.12.
35. *Inst.* 4.17.34.
36. *Inst.* 4.17.18.
37. *Inst.* 4.17.19.

Luther, reception took place, as we have seen, by faith alone—not also orally by the mouth. Reminiscent of Luther, however, Calvin at least hinted at the possibility of an incarnational analogy. Yet where Luther's christological sensibilities were Alexandrian, Calvin's were Antiochian. In describing how he thought Christ's body was related to the eucharistic bread, Calvin was fond of using the formula "distinction without separation"—a clear allusion to Chalcedon. As in Christology, so also with the incarnational analogy, Calvin seemed to differ from Luther in emphasis but not in principle. Where Luther stressed the inseparable unity, Calvin affirmed the abiding distinction. Yet with respect to the incarnation, both theologians arguably fell, despite their differing emphases, within the bounds of Chalcedonian orthodoxy. If we were to subject the incarnational analogy to a Chalcedonian interpretation, might not the same be said of their views of the Eucharist as well?

Conclusion

My ecumenical proposal for resolving the eucharistic controversies can be summed up under four headings: the efficacy of the Eucharist, the mode of real presence, the mode of rhetoric, and the mode of reception.

The Efficacy of the Eucharist

Every major tradition in the ecumenical church affirms that Christ himself is the central meaning of the Eucharist. Every tradition also agrees, beyond what I have been able to discuss here, that salvation has three tenses. Remembrance or *anamnesis* in the Eucharist looks back to the past and, as Aquinas noted, to Christ's priestly work of atoning sacrifice. Consecration and invocation or epiclesis look to the liturgical transfiguration of the present time by the Holy Spirit, as does the renewal of our union and communion with Christ (*koinonia*). Finally, joyful expectation looks to that future banquet of the great king, where the first shall be last and the last first, which the Eucharist actualizes, anticipates, and symbolizes. Within this broad common agreement, of course, many deep and divisive questions remain to be discussed and resolved. All ecumenical traditions will need to strive for a more balanced and also a more intensive understanding than has previously been achieved of salvation's three tenses in their proper ordering, unity, and distinction. Yet the broad consensus that exists here is reason for encouragement that real progress continues to be possible even beyond the very real ecumenical gains of the last fifty years.

The Mode of Presence

Following Aquinas, any viable ecumenical resolution would need to affirm that in the Eucharist no real presence occurs at the expense of the local presence of Christ's body in heaven, and that no local presence prohibits the real presence of Christ's life-giving flesh in the Eucharist. Both real presence and local presence must be upheld together. None of the major traditions I have mentioned—Roman Catholic, Lutheran, and Reformed—would have a problem with this affirmation.

In the proposed resolution, the mode of real presence is governed by the incarnational analogy. The bread that we break is itself a *koinonia* in the body of Christ. The bread dwells or participates in the body, and the body in the bread. The bread does not change into the body, nor does the body change into the bread ("without confusion or change"). Yet with the Eucharistic *epiklesis* and *anamnesis*, the two enter into the closest of sacramental unions ("without separation or division"). The sacramental union means that the body of Christ is really present in, with, and under the bread. The union is established by the Holy Spirit for the sake of imparting Christ's life-giving flesh to its faithful reception.

The Mode of Rhetoric

The incarnational analogy helps us to see how Jesus' statement, "This is my body," can be taken seriously without being taken literally. Luther saw the statement as a synecdoche, Calvin allowed for it to be either a synecdoche or a metonymy, and the Eastern Orthodox see it as a form of realistic symbolism or symbolic realism. Speaking of how the symbol of bread is related to the reality of Christ's flesh, Alexander Schmemann writes: "The symbol does not so much 'resemble' the reality that it symbolizes as it participates in it and therefore it is capable of communicating it in reality."[38] Here, too, the idea that the symbol (*signum*) participates in the reality (*res*) that it communicates is perhaps not impossible from a Roman Catholic point of view. If not, then for all four traditions, the false contrast between "symbolic" and "realistic" interpretations of the statement "This is my body" would in principle be overcome.

The Mode of Reception

Where consensus cannot be attained, convergence can sometimes be enough. Even if the Reformed could accept the idea of transelementation, they are not likely ever to accept the idea that Christ's flesh is received orally, even by unbelievers. Real presence as the transformation of the bread through its participation in Christ's life-giving flesh would still not necessarily entail the idea of oral reception. It would be logically consistent to maintain that Christ's flesh is received only as Christ himself is received—by faith alone. All four traditions would agree that whatever is visible of the bread is bodily consumed, but that the substance of Christ's flesh is not. If the only possible vehicle of reception were faith, as Calvin

---

38. Alexander Schmemann, *The Eucharist: Sacrament of the Kingdom* (Crestwood, N.Y.: St. Vladimir's Seminary Press, 1987), 38.

and Vermigli maintained, then Christ's flesh would be received by faith with the bread; but without faith neither Christ himself nor his flesh would be received. Since affirming real presence seems vastly more important than affirming oral reception, and since the former need not depend logically on the latter, it is conceivable that the Reformed position on reception would not ultimately be a barrier to intercommunion with churches of the other traditions.

In short, according to this proposal, the Roman Catholic tradition would contribute to a robust understanding of how real and local presence can be upheld at the same time, but it would rethink its traditional understanding of eucharistic conversion. The Lutheran tradition, along with the Eastern Orthodox tradition, would contribute the incarnational analogy and the idea of participation as the key to real presence; but the Lutherans would rethink their tendency to affirm real presence at the expense of local presence. Finally, the Reformed tradition, along with Eastern Orthodoxy, would contribute the idea of the Holy Spirit as the mediator of communion, not only between Christ and faith, but also between symbol and reality; but the Reformed would rethink their perception that real presence in the form of containment jeopardizes local presence.

If this proposal to resolve the eucharistic controversies along Chalcedonian lines is on the right track, then it points toward the fulfillment of the basic rule of mutuality in ecumenical dialogue: No tradition gets everything it wants, each tradition gets much that it wants, none capitulates to another, nor is any forced to make unacceptable compromises; but each contributes to the other, and all are invited to stretch to accept some things they might not at first have seen as possible.

CHAPTER 15

Grundtvig and Luther: *How Was Grundtvig Influenced by Luther?*

Theodor
Jørgensen

Throughout his life Grundtvig considered himself a successor of Luther and was concerned with the same cause as Luther was.[1] At the same time, however, he also considered himself Luther's equal and his peer. In an article entitled "Skal den lutherske Reformation virkelig fortsættes?" (Should the Lutheran Reformation really be continued?),[2] which he wrote in 1830 and had reprinted in 1863, Grundtvig answered yes to the question posed in the title. He believed the Reformation should be continued but should move forward in keeping with the nineteenth century and the realities of nineteenth-century life, and in this connection Grundtvig sets himself a task similar to the one taken on by Luther. Like Luther and Paul, Grundtvig was the sort of humble, self-conscious Christian whose self-judgment Paul very accurately expressed when he said: "But by the grace of God I am what I am, and his grace toward me has not been in vain" (1 Cor 15:10). Grundtvig possessed a prophetic self-consciousness. He felt called to be a seer for the Christian congregation in the Nordic countries, and by extension for the whole of Christendom, since the Nordic congregation held its own particular, significant place in the universal history of Christianity.

Grundtvig and the Lutheran Reformation

Grundtvig thought in terms of history, and he also saw himself as a historian. He was conscious of the fact that he was living in times of great change, as a part of modernity. He considered this era particularly challenging for the church—which had been taken captive by a new papacy, the

---

1. Originally published as "Grundtvig und Luther: Welche Bedeutung hatte Luther für Grundtvig?" in *Luther im Widerstreit der Geschichte*, Veröffentlichungen der Luther-Akademie Ratzeburg 20 (Erlangen, 1993), 97–108.
2. N. F. S. Grundtvig, *Værker i Udvalg*, vol. 3 (Copenhagen: Gyldendal, 1942), 219–93. Published by Georg Christensen and Hal Koch.

papacy of the philosophical theologians who had cast reason and nature in the role of pope.[3]

Grundtvig was not fond of Protestantism. He accused H. N. Clausen, a well-reputed professor on the Faculty of Theology at the University of Copenhagen whom he regarded as Protestantism's representative, of constructing the church solely on the basis of a doctrine and thereby turning it into a castle in the air. Clausen should instead remain faithful to the actual church, which always has been and always will be. Grundtvig liked to refer to Article VII of the *Confessio Augustana*, which served as the motto in his polemic essay against Clausen in 1825,[4] entitled *Kirkens Gienmæle* (the rejoinder of the church). Here, for the first time, Grundtvig presented his *kirkelige anskuelse* (church view): Protestantism had turned protest into its central principle. It had come to see the Reformation as renewal for renewal's sake. In this respect, Grundtvig felt, Protestantism significantly deviated from Luther. In Grundtvig's article on continuing the Lutheran Reformation, he set out his reasons for limiting himself to this reformation: "Not only because it is closest to us but most notably because only in this Reformation—if not theoretically, then at least practically—do I, as a Christian church historian, find that this fundamental assumption has been followed: that every significant element of which the Christian fellowship of faith consists should be retained unchanged during all of the upheavals."[5] Luther did not wish to create a new church but to remain faithful to the ancient church in the issues he defended, going against the religious leaders of his day. Grundtvig mainly found evidence of this in the way Luther did not reject the so-called baptismal creed of the ancient church, the Apostles' Creed, but retained this creed in common with the Roman Catholic Church. If this was supposed to be a continuation of the Lutheran Reformation— that is, not attempting to bring about any *significant* changes in the church—then it was certainly important to continue the Lutheran Reformation. Grundtvig spoke of the deep reverence in which Luther held all the "basic Christian qualities" (as Grundtvig called them), and he found this reverence expressed with outstanding clarity in Luther's Small Catechism, a work that Grundtvig treasured all his life, though he did raise a few critical objections. For one thing, Grundtvig would have preferred the work without its Decalogue, for the Christian is liberated from the law, and the Small Catechism lays claim to being what Grundtvig refered to as *Den kristelige Børnelærdom* (elementary Christian teachings). It was precisely the veneration expressed in the Apostles' Creed, which Grundtvig also found in Luther's interpretation of this creed, that should have led Luther to explain the Apostles' Creed in connection with Baptism, for in the very use

3. Ibid., 229f.
4. N. F. S. Grundtvig, *Udvalgte Skrifter*, vol. 4 (Copenhagen: Gyldendal, 1906), 395–429. Published by Holger Begtrup.
5. "Lutherske Reformation," 223.

of the Apostles' Creed as the baptismal creed, we would come to find most clearly expressed the matters dealt with in the Apostles' Creed.

What, then, in Grundtvig's perception, was so special about Luther's reformatory efforts, considering the fact that Luther wished to retain the basic Christian qualities? "Martin Luther was an incomparable church reformer, by the grace of God, for he found that those things lacking in the Christian church in no way included a new faith or anything new at all, but rather life and light in the age-old order of things."[6] It is important here to note the words emphasized by Grundtvig himself—"life" and "light"—to which I shall return shortly.

This emphasis on the preserving aspects of Luther's work as a reformer makes clear to us an element typical of Grundtvig's perception of Luther. Grundtvig saw Luther as closely linked with the other great inspirational sources of his own theology, namely, the church fathers, most notably Irenaeus. This is expressed in another wonderful passage from the article mentioned above:

> Anyone may mention it as they like, and may laugh at it as loud as they can, but in the church of Jesus, the Savior, I have made the words of Joshua my own: Choose you this day whom you will serve, but as for me and my house, we will serve *the Lord*. We will serve our Lord *Jesus Christ*, conceived of the Holy Spirit, born of the Virgin Mary, and we will serve him *as did* our Christian fathers, *Martin Luther* and *Ansgar*, *Augustine* and *Irenaeus*, *Paul* and *John*, in short, as did the old disciple, who shall not die but shall joyously sing: Come, Lord Jesus! When the sky will sparkle with the glory of his Father and He returns to judge the living and the dead.[7]

And yet, asked Grundtvig, did Luther not sweep the church clean? Yes, but in Grundtvig's opinion, he did not do so in the way the arch-Protestants understand cleansing—those who had made cleansing into the very issue itself. Rather, he did so in the way Baptism and the life of the baptized is a process of cleansing. Adam had to be driven from the garden, the Christian had to be cleansed of sin, just as faith and hope had to be cleansed of the obstructions that stood in their way. In this sense, Grundtvig could regard the cleansing of the church as a central element in Luther's Reformation and could continue to promote that cause.[8]

Grundtvig on Reason

With regard to Grundtvig's views on modernity, the fascinating thing—and the area in which I believe he can also help contemporary theologians—is

6. Ibid., 226.
7. Ibid., 227.
8. Cf. ibid., 228f.

that despite his conservative inclination, or perhaps precisely because of it, he was by no means an antimodernist. On the contrary, he was deeply committed to modernity. Grundtvig knew he was accused of hating reason.[9] He did not refute this accusation when speaking about a kind of reason that saw itself as an independent force and posed as a pope. When reason means the ability to judge, however, Grundtvig had nothing against reason, for by that definition reason cannot claim to find justification in itself but can only be founded in the circumstances over which it judges. In other words, it can only be founded in that which it has gained from experience. Reason must base its judgment upon experience. Grundtvig, then, defended a perceiving kind of reason.

The Danish term for the Enlightenment is *oplysningstiden*. In this context, the noun *oplysning* is "enlightenment," which implies "information, knowledge," but the verb *oplyse* can also mean "to shed light on, elucidate, explain" and "to make clearer, more obvious." These last two meanings played a particularly decisive role for Grundtvig. He loved to link *oplysning* to the word *liv*—"life"—forming the Danish compound *livsoplysning*—"life enlightenment." The connotations include "explaining life" and "bringing clarity to people's lives," which is not possible without life experience. Grundtvig built his entire groundbreaking approach to education around these concepts. And by emphasizing the importance of these elements of light, explanation, and clarity, Grundtvig consistently incorporated, as their contradiction, darkness—the darkness of evil, for evil loves darkness, and the grave is dark.

Grundtvig ultimately derived every true "life enlightenment" from John's prologue: "In him was life, and the life was the light of all people" (John 1:4). Grundtvig spoke repeatedly of Jesus as he who is *lyslevende*—the Danish equivalent of "in the flesh" or, idiomatically speaking, "alive and kicking," but with the literal meanings "alive and brightly shining" and "alive and aglow with light." It is obvious that here we are close to the theology of the ancient church.

Thus Grundtvig ultimately saw enlightenment (or more literally "shedding light" or "making clearer") as christologically justified and consequently Trinitarian. It would be too extensive an undertaking to explain this in detail here. But whenever a perceiving kind of reason, or judgment that relies on life experience, truly sheds light on reality, it finds known or unknown nourishment in the divine light that shines fully in Christ. This is true for every genuine and true recognition, whether it comes to a pagan or to a Christian. Grundtvig was quite fond of the expression "the pious pagan," for which I believe we can also find corresponding elements in Luther. In relation to modernity, this gave Grundtvig an open-minded but thoroughly critical freedom. His criticism was aimed at the kind of reason that claims to be free of its divine origin and consequently of its responsibility, since this

---

9. Cf. ibid., 230.

reason assumes for itself divine proportions as the judge of all of reality. This leads to a destructive freedom, and in the introduction to his article on continuing Lutheran Reformation, Grundtvig very accurately portrayed its destructive effects—a portrayal that remains relevant even today.[10]

Grundtvig on Human Nature

We have now reached a point where the similarities and differences between Luther and Grundtvig can be clarified. To do so we must enter the field of anthropology, and in this connection I call to mind what Gerhard Ebeling said about Luther's concept of nature: on the one hand, "nature" can mean unspoiled nature as represented in creation while, on the other hand, sin can be regarded as the nature of humankind. Grundtvig vehemently refuted the latter view, especially in orthodox Lutheran thinking. He called it the "demonization" of humankind, and his chief argument against it was the incarnation of the Son of God. How can anyone claim that God's Son became a true man himself if sin is the nature of humankind? Grundtvig considered it indisputable that in the Fall, human nature was seriously injured, sustaining wounds that could be healed only by the coming of Jesus Christ. But that does not mean that the nature of humankind, as God's creation, is corrupted. Humankind is a divine experiment, embodying spirit and dust, which is why God does not let go, even when faced with humankind after the Fall.

Grundtvig shared with Luther the perception of human existence as ecstatic existence. He admittedly did not formulate anywhere in his writings that human beings exists outside themselves (*homo subsistit extra se*), but Grundtvig the poet knew that human beings express themselves fully and truly only when praising the Lord.

> Humankind is created in the likeness of God,
> with living words on his tongue,
> and hence they can speak and sing with gods
> birds and animals among.[11]

Grundtvig found the human's likeness to God, the *imago Dei*, in human language—not only in our ability to speak, our capacity for being affected by language, and consequently his responsibility, but also in the actual language people use when they speak. Note here the unmistakable evidence of influence from Herder. Human language echoes God's creative Word, which is Christ (cf. John 1:1ff.). That is why human beings can do such great things with language. This relationship between the Word of God and the echo of human words is broken in the Fall but not irreparably destroyed.

10. Cf. ibid., 220ff.
11. Translation of stanza eleven of the poem "Menneske-Livet er Underligt," originally written in 1861. Cf. *N. S. F. Grundtvigs Poetiske Skrifter* (Copenhagen 1929), 8:494ff. Published by Georg Christensen.

Strictly speaking, humankind is only capable of sinning by virtue of their likeness to God, for only in being like God are they able to oppose him. This is how, although it is broken, language stores and keeps the original recognition that is in accordance with God himself. "No one has ever cried golden tears who has not also seen the gold sparkle," as Grundtvig wrote in his great poem *Kristenhedens Syvstjerne* (the seven-star of Christendom, in which the title's "lodestar" also refers to the seven congregations at the beginning of the Revelation of John in the New Testament). Therefore, here and in many other places, he advised all to uphold and cherish the mother tongue.[12] And as his most significant argument in favor of this, Grundtvig called to mind the penitent thief on the cross and the crucified Christ. These two have a human language in common, enabling Christ to offer the thief these comforting words: "Truly I tell you, today you will be with me in Paradise" (Luke 23:43)—words the thief understood.[13]

Wherever human beings rightly use their language, making reality become more enlightened, making life become clearer, and putting human existence into words, then their language, be it ever so broken, echoes the divine Word that is the light and life of humankind.

Here lies the reason for Grundtvig's open-mindedness to all aspects of human existence, to culture, to folk life, to education, to politics. Here is the reason for Grundtvig's insistence on the inherent value of all things related to human life and national culture. This is closely related to the ecstatic understanding of human existence mentioned earlier. Salvation does not transform the sinner into a different person, for instance, something that is half human and half Christian. Rather, the sinner reaches truth as human. This, however, necessitates the basic assumption that human beings, although sinners, have their own inherent value. This is the basis on which Grundtvig can claim: "First comes the human, the Christian next: life knows no other order."[14] In saying this, he was emphasizing both the distinction and the beneficial interaction between life as a human being and life as a Christian.

> If each man strive upon this earth
> First to be truly human
> To open the ear to the Word of Truth
> And give to God his Glory
> Then, grants Christian faith be true
> If Christian he be not today
> He shall be by the morrow.[15]

---

12. Cf. N. S. F. Grundtvig, *Kristenhedens Syvstjerne: Et kirkeligt Sagakvad samt Dansk Ravne-Galder* (Copenhagen: P. A. Rosenberger, n.d.), 169, stanza 71.

13. Cf. *Den kristelige Børnelærdom*, in *Udvalgte Skrifter* (Copenhagen, 1909), 9:429.

14. The famous first line of Grundtvig's instructional poem "Menneske først og kristen så"; cf. *Grundtvigs Sang-Værk*, 3:296ff. English metrical prose translation by S. A. J. Bradley, York, England.

15. Ibid., strophe 8.

"First comes the human, the Christian next." That is how Grundtvig interprets the doctrine of law and gospel. Is this in accordance with Luther or in opposition? That, indeed, is the question.

At the same time, one must not forget that the human being's own inherent value is justified in having been created by God in God's likeness, that is, having been created in Christ. Moving once again to the prologue of John, which played such an essential role for Grundtvig: "He came to what was his own." Precisely. Therein lies the dignity of humankind. "And his own people did not accept him." Therein lies the tragedy of human existence, the Fall of humankind, the fragmented nature of the human condition. Yet, even so, the latter does not cancel out the former.

This reasoning may contain a decisive divergence between Grundtvig and Luther. Humankind does not lose its likeness to God in the Fall. They are not remade in the image of the devil. This does not mean, however, that Grundtvig did not recognize the danger of being possessed by the devil. It is noteworthy that the Danish national church begins the Apostles' Creed each Sunday by renouncing the devil: "I renounce the devil and all his works and all his ways." This practice makes the Danish church unique in the ecumenical community, and it is due to Grundtvig. Living a life in Christ and in the faith, living the new life after Baptism, is an on-going struggle in which one must renounce evil continually—not just once during the Sacrament of Baptism. According to Grundtvig, a person can only do this through Christ. And therefore, in his view, the renunciation ought to begin as follows: "In the name of Jesus Christ, I renounce. . . ."

Grundtvig and *Sola Scriptura*

I now consider another complex of problems.

Like Luther, Grundtvig unconditionally maintained and strongly emphasized *solus Christus* and *sola fide* as the foundation of Christianity and of the church, whereas he rejected *sola scriptura* as the foundation of the church. Christ alone can serve as the foundation and the cornerstone of the church, not a dead book.[16]

To understand this, one must realize that, in the nineteenth century, Grundtvig was probably the single individual in Denmark who was best acquainted with the Bible. He lived within the linguistic universe of the Bible, and its words were ever present in his mind. Virtually every line of every hymn Grundtvig ever wrote contains three, four, or five references to the Scripture. The same is true of his sermons, which were also seasoned with allusions to proverbs and with imagery from Nordic mythology. He was a prolific writer of hymns and songs inspired by biblical history or based on

---

16. Cf. in this connection, for instance, *Kirkelige Oplysninger især for lutherske Christne*: *Værker i Udvalg*, 3:380ff. English translation by Heidi Flegal.

biblical texts and stories from the Bible. One of his aspirations was to write his way through the entire Bible, rendering its content so it could be sung in verse, for this was the best way to recount God's glorious deeds. In this undertaking, the psalms of the Old Testament served as an incomparable example to him.

What lay at the root of Grundtvig's rage—for rage he did—against the principle *sola scriptura?* Grundtvig saw what the Scripture principle became in Protestant theology—and what, in his opinion, it was destined to become. If the Scripture is to convey Jesus Christ to us, it must convey him through the interpretation of those versed in the Scriptures, in other words, through the theologians. The lay Christian is tossed out of the frying pan and into the fire, liberated from the papacy in Rome, just to fall under the papacy of the exegetes. In his essay *Kirkens Gienmæle* (the rejoinder of the church), an infuriated Grundtvig accused H. N. Clausen on two accounts: he first blamed him for having turned the Scripture principle and the doctrine of righteousness into the basic principles of the Protestant church. Next, he criticizes Clausen for having drawn attention to the flaws, ambiguities, and contradictions contained in the Bible. Grundtvig by no means denies the existence of these flaws, for he was a historian himself. Even so, he disliked the way Clausen used the authority of the Scripture as the foundation of the church, and in the same breath undermined this authority with reference to all of the exegetical problems. This made fools out of the ordinary Christians who did not know what to regard as the truth when one interpreter said one thing and another interpreter something different.[17]

I believe that here Grundtvig draws attention to a serious problem, to which we have not found an adequate answer even today, namely, why piety with respect to the Bible is still in danger of developing into biblicism or fundamentalism—unless we can make Grundtvig's response to this problem our own.

What is it that makes a Christian a Christian? Grundtvig asserted that Baptism does. That is the way it has always been in the church. Baptism reveals to us the foundation of the church, and this foundation is Jesus Christ. Christ meets us in Baptism as our living Lord, crucified and resurrected, alive and kicking—*lyslevende*, to use Grundtvig's term. Christ gives his life for us and lets himself be born in us—an aspect that Grundtvig underscored. From the Lord, spoken by his servant, we hear the Apostles' Creed as the covenant God makes with God's child. To Grundtvig, the creed was mainly a covenant, a promise from God, which in itself embodies the entire gospel. Here Grundtvig concurred on the most profound level with Luther, who also found the entire gospel in the Apostles' Creed. Grundtvig praised Luther for presenting and interpreting the entire Apostles' Creed in his Small Catechism on the basis of Christ being the

17. Cf. in this connection *Kirkens Gienmæle, Værker i Udvalg,* 4:420ff.

Lord, of forgiveness for our trespasses, and of eternal life. Grundtvig referred to the Apostles' Creed as coming directly from the lips of Jesus Christ. He traced the contents of this creed back to Christ, although not the actual words themselves (which, however, he had done for some time). Other quotations from the living Christ include the commandment of Baptism and the blessing of the children in Mark 10 as well as the Lord's Prayer as the prayer of God's children, which Grundtvig regarded as a miracle. In fact, Grundtvig calls it "the little Word of God." We pray to God in his own words, handed down to us through his Son, who is the Word, existing from the beginning, and who is God. Certainly that *is* a miracle. And we meet yet another quotation from Christ in the baptismal ritual—the words of peace with which the resurrected Christ greeted his disciples. "Peace be with you" (John 20:19)—a greeting that is repeated by the resurrected Christ at each Baptism. But we still have to look at one more quote from Christ, one that is not spoken during the ritual of Baptism. It contains the words of institution at the Lord's Supper, the meal that is to nourish the Christian life given to us in our Baptism.

According to Grundtvig, the church and the individual Christian need no more of a foundation than what is due to them through the presence of the living Lord Jesus and the words from his mouth that are spoken during the divine service. In Grundtvig's interpretation of Article VII of the *Confessio Augustana*, the pure preaching of the gospel based on the creed, and the correct administering of the sacraments—as originally in Baptism and the Eucharist—must take place as prescribed by Christ. *Solus Christus* and *sola fide* are retained but retained freely in relation to the Scripture. For so it was in the early church, Grundtvig said, before the New Testament had been written.

One could perhaps characterize Grundtvig's position in relation to Luther by saying that in his rejection of the Scripture principle under the influence of its degeneration in Protestantism, Grundtvig precisely took Luther's claim seriously that Christ is the Lord of the Scripture. Grundtvig developed this principle independently of the Scripture in his church view: Christ is the Lord.

Having deprived the Scripture of its authority as the foundation of the church, Grundtvig gave everything back to it, presenting it as the book of enlightenment for Christians.[18] In this capacity, the Bible is indispensable. The New Testament bears witness to the faith of the Apostles and the first Christians. It expresses the confessing *reply* that the Apostles and the early congregations gave when confronted with Jesus Christ as the living Word of God, and it therefore contains the diversity that is a part of life, and which also belongs to the new life in Christ. This diversity is actually an advantage, if the New Testament is meant to contribute to enlighten and explain the

---

18. Cf. *Kirkelige Oplysninger især for lutherske Christne, Værker i Udvalg* (Copenhagen: Gyldendal, 1942), 3:390f.

covenant of Baptism and the new life under this covenant—in other words, the life in Christ. For this diversity corresponds to the diversity of life. In its capacity as a book of enlightenment, the Scripture also fulfills a critical, authoritative function. It has come into being through the Holy Spirit, though of course not literally in the form of letters but in the content that is conveyed. It can therefore serve as a touchstone for the congregation when there is a need for distinguishing between being infused with the Spirit of Christ and being infused with other types of spirits. Grundtvig did, however, emphasize that the Holy Spirit has prepared the Scripture to serve as a touchstone for its own *free*, *independent* use, as a source in which the tools of the Holy Spirit (among which Grundtvig counted pastors and theologians) can find confirmation for the infusion of the Spirit—just as the Lord as he was growing up found confirmation in the Scriptures of the Fathers, that is, in the Old Testament. This comparison with the way Christ uses the Scripture is interesting. This freedom of the Holy Spirit in its use of the Scriptures is also the base for the freedom of theology, which is manifested in the diversity—and occasionally the adversity—of theological scriptural interpretations. This freedom has only one critical limitation: whether in its interpretation of the Scripture as a book of enlightenment it refers to Christ himself as the living Word of God or not. The Scripture is not allowed to turn itself into this living Word. Assuming that the theological interpretations of the Scripture respect this critical limitation, then, because the human condition is confined by history, these interpretations must be worded differently, also in relation to the interpretation of Christian life in the New Testament if they are to enlighten modern Christian living.

Here again I see a parallel to Luther's hermeneutics, as it is expressed in Luther's preface to the letter of James:

> All the genuine sacred books agree in this, that all of them preach and inculcate (treiben) Christ. And that is the true test by which to judge all books, when we see whether or not they inculcate Christ. For all the Scriptures show us Christ, Romans 3(: 21); and St. Paul will know nothing but Christ, I Corinthians 2(: 2). Whatever does not teach Christ is not yet apostolic, even though St. Peter or St. Paul does the teaching. Again, whatever preaches Christ would be apostolic, even if Judas, Annas, Pilate, and Herod were doing it.[19]

At the same time, this parallel makes the difference between the periods when Luther and Grundtvig lived more obvious.

If one were to briefly characterize the piety of Grundtvig, it would be as a sacramental, Christ-oriented piety that recognizes both the distinctiveness and the interrelatedness of *extra nos*, *pro nobis*, and *in nobis* (outside of us, for us, and in us). This is quite clearly expressed in the following poem:

19. Cf LW 35:396.

Despite pain of longing
Say not to your heart
"Ah, who shall descend to the deeps
To bring forth my Savior
So sweet from the dead
To bring him to joy and to peace?"

More lovely this rings:
"Who shall, as on wings
Ascend up to Heav'n kingdom's hall
And bring down to us
The Lord we await?"
Yet too this is false to God's Word

We exist, we abide
We are stirred we, we have life
In Christ who is God's living Word
Lay this Word on your lip
With heart and soul love it
In you he shall dwell, in his name.

Believe, yes: Confess
To the end of your days
Of blessedness this is the path
Let us sing as we tread it
With hearts and with voice
"We have him, we shall not let go!"

To the heart he speaks comfort
To the heart he brings solace
He answers, as God, to his name
When the heart in its warmth
Embraces the Word
Our Saviour we take to our breast.[20]

---

20. Cf. Grundtvigs *Sang-Værk*, 5:531f. Also for this metrical prose translation I am grateful to Prof. S. A. J. Bradley, York.

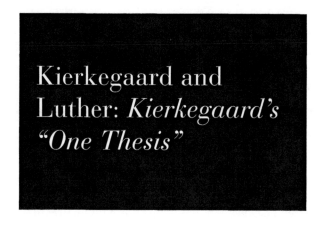

CHAPTER 16

Kierkegaard and Luther: *Kierkegaard's "One Thesis"*

Hermann Deuser

Perspectives

> "O Luther! And yet in one sense a fortunate situation—at that time there were ninety-five theses and a controversy over doctrine—now there is but one thesis: that Christianity does not exist at all."[1]

This polemic exclamation was uttered by Kierkegaard in 1853, two years before his death, when he was occupied with outlining a radical critique of established Christendom.[2] Kierkegaard published his critique, timed well and attacking church as well as culture, in various newspaper articles and treatises. Luther was cited by him for several reasons:

1. Denmark had been Lutheran for centuries, to an extent that to be born Danish meant to be born Lutheran. Especially in his later years,[3] Kierkegaard took offense at this quasi-causal connection, because in his eyes the individual's relationship to God, which is entirely subjective, is not to be made dependent on geopolitical circumstances, the latter being objective facts. So Luther's authority was invoked by Kierkegaard against the Lutheran state church (*Folkekirken*) and against the historical development of Danish Protestantism.

2. Although Kierkegaard never studied Luther in detail, he in later years showed a growing interest in Luther's theology. As late as December

1. *Søren Kierkegaard's Journals and Papers*, ed. Howard V. Hong and Edna H. Hong (Bloomington and London: Indiana Univ. Press, 1978), vol. 6, no. 6842, 481 (*Pap.* X 6, B 232, 377).
2. Cf. Søren Kierkegaard, *The Moment*, ed. Howard V. Hong and Edna H. Hong (Princeton: Princeton Univ. Press, 1998): "A Thesis: Just One Single One [January 26, 1855, S. Kierkegaard]. O Luther, you had 95 theses—terrible! And yet, in a deeper sense, the more theses, the less terrible. The matter is far more terrible—there is only one thesis."
3. Kierkegaard's late writings are dealt with at length in my *Dialektische Theologie: Studien zu Adornos Metaphysik und zum Spätwerk Kierkegaards* (Munich: Chr. Kaiser, 1980), esp. 129–231.

1847 he even started reading Luther's sermons continuously[4] and for the sake of theological controversy. For by then Kierkegaard sharply distinguished his own idea of a Christianity of religious and ethical seriousness, based on existential appropriation and on the imitation of Christ, from Luther's concept of grace, a concept he considered more and more a bourgeois deformity and even a means of deception in the hands of established Christendom. So Kierkegaard vehemently attacked the article of justification by faith alone as well as its subsequent interpretations under the conditions of modernity.

3. Kierkegaard's critique of culture did not lack a wistful undertone—as he was well aware that the huge theological battles of the sixteenth century had become obsolete. The dogmatic systems of Protestant tradition stood unquestioned then and were considered true and valid. However, Kierkegaard sensed that the real conflicts of his time were of an ethical or political nature, because what he observed was that a still predominately Christian society was making individual spirituality more and more dispensable. These tendencies of degeneration he kept emphasizing in order to support his "one thesis" (as opposed to Luther's ninety-five), saying that in the industrial era Christianity had ceased to exist, and what was left was a pure struggle for power. This was the religious and ethical problem Kierkegaard drew attention to in his writings and also by his conduct toward the end of his life.

4. If Kierkegaard's one thesis applied, we would have to assume that there was no truly Christian church in the nineteenth century or later on, and the then-existing forms of Christianity would have to be judged fallacies or, at best, mere museums of bygone artifacts. Kierkegaard's harsh criticism, though, must be viewed as a reaction to the deep crisis into which historical criticism had thrown contemporary theology. His concept of simultaneity (*samtidighed*), modeled after Luther's idea of faith in justification by God, includes the concepts of personal decision, of existential intensity, and of the demands of present situation without having built in any mediating elements. It thereby contrasts the quasi-objectiveness and self-distance to which modern theology is committed. So Kierkegaard leads us to the question of how to develop a concept of church that allows for the institutional character church in fact undoubtedly has but also admits the immediacy required by faith.

---

4. Kierkegaard's knowledge and reading of Luther's works (sermons, edifying discourses, editions) is explained in detail by Niels J. Cappelørn, Gert Posselt, and Bent Rohde, *Tekstspejle: Om Søren Kierkegaard som bogtilrettelægger, boggiver og bogsamler* (Copenhagen: Rosendahls Forlag, 2002), 133–38. See in addition Henning Schröer, "Kierkegaard and Luther," *Kerygma und Dogma* 30 (1984): 227–48; and for a systematic comparison, cf. Deuser, *Dialektische Theologie*, 145–195. Kierkegaard's criticism of Luther's theology is found almost entirely in his *Journals and Papers*; cf. Niels J. Cappelørn's index to the Danish edition of *Søren Kierkegaards Papirer* [*Pap.*] (Copenhagen: Gyldendal, 1976), 15:203–11.

These are the four perspectives on the relation between Kierkegaard and Luther I deal with here. Essentially, not only critical comments are to be found in Kierkegaard, but also respectful, approving, and even enthusiastic ones on the man Luther and his theology. The fact that in his later years Kierkegaard's negative remarks tend to prevail is not a sign of an anti-Lutheran position. Kierkegaard was seeking for his own point of view, and indeed this point of view presupposed Lutheran traditions of theology and spirituality, although Kierkegaard modified them heavily because the philosophical, political, and social conditions of modernity had shaken contemporary theology to the core. So Kierkegaard's one thesis may help to analyze the alterations fundamental theological problems have undergone from Reformation to modernity, but it itself must also be made subject to criticism.

Christendom versus Christianity, Culture versus Existential Relation to God

The distance of time between Luther and Kierkegaard is evident even when Kierkegaard directly made selections from Luther's theology. For example, Johannes Climacus (Kierkegaard's pseudonymous author of the *Concluding Unscientific Postscript*, 1846), to back up his argument against infant Baptism, fell back on Luther's concept of the sacraments in which Luther made faith the crucial element for the transmission of sacramental grace. In Kierkegaard's language, existential appropriation and inwardness stand against false objectivity. Here Kierkegaard added the term "objective" to the original quotation from *The Babylonian Captivity of the Church*, which only talks about *"virtutibus ipsis sacramentorum"* (the virtues of the sacraments).[5] Kierkegaard did so because he intended to take into account the distinction between an objective world of things that can be scientifically described and the subjective reflection upon that world, with faith belonging to the latter sphere. Analogically, and in a truly modern way, Kierkegaard distinguished between a relationship to God based on an externalization of God's grace—the outcome of which he calls "Christendom"—and a relationship to God consisting of a special relationship to one's very own self—"Christianity." So, according to Johannes Climacus, it is easier to become a Christian when one is not a Christian than it is when one is already born into Christendom. The latter case applies to sociohistorical developments especially in Europe, the former to the process of individual appropriation, which has to happen always anew, since nobody is born a Christian even if one is born a member of Christian society.[6] Kierkegaard's

5. Cf. Søren Kierkegaard, *Concluding Unscientific Postscript to Philosophical Fragments*, ed. Howard V. Hong and Edna H. Hong (Princeton: Princeton Univ. Press, 1992), 366; cf. Luther, "De captivitate Babylonica ecclesiae praeludium," WA 6:571.
6. See Kierkegaard, *Concluding Unscientific Postscript*, 367 (footnote), with explicit reference to *Philosophical Fragments*, ed. Howard V. Hong and Edna H. Hong (Princeton: Princeton Univ. Press, 1962), 95f.

accusation was that the automatic connection between birth and Baptism as practiced by the state church in Denmark prevented any real confrontation with the paradox of God-within-time. In attacking the church, Kierkegaard used the distinction between Christendom and Christianity for his "one thesis" that within Christendom Christianity has vanished, so that at that time the expansion of Christendom could no longer be wished for. Only by strengthening the category of the single individual could this unfortunate situation be corrected.[7]

Without a doubt, Kierkegaard's critique of an anonymous collective in favor of the single individual and his or her responsibility has kept its significance until today. Personality develops through individual learning processes and through the formation of sociality. This has to be remembered, especially as the categories of individuality and personality are more and more retreating as late modernity goes on. Kierkegaard not only anticipated these developments but also fought against them through his very own conduct of life. However, because the Christian culture he battled was a firm fact to him, he failed to reflect on the conditions of Christian culture's continuing existence. Whereas the Reformation intentionally transformed culture, Kierkegaard merely tried to utter warnings, regarding himself not as a Reformer but as a Christian Socrates undercover, a historical "detective talent."[8] Considering this, we need not construe an artificial contradiction between Protestant Christianity and Kierkegaard's critique of culture. On the contrary, unlike Kierkegaard we today have to emphasize the existential relationship to God as culturally significant, maybe even as a condition of culture.[9] Personal faith is not identical with the social functions of Christianity and cannot be reduced to them, just as the single individual is to be distinguished from the collective. Keeping up this difference is prerequisite for maintaining the idea of responsible individuality and for securing its social influence.

Justification, Faith, and Works

Like Lutheran tradition, Kierkegaard subscribed to the doctrines of sin, of justification, of scripture, and of Christ being man and God. If Kierkegaard criticized the person Luther as well as Luther's concept of *sola gratia*, he did so because he wanted to see the *process* of becoming a Christian more emphasized than the status of *being* one. His anthropological analysis of anxiety and his phenomenology of despair do not deal with sin and faith in terms of abstract dogmatics but in terms of existential conflicts that have to be lived through. Kierkegaard never proclaimed a break with Luther's thesis of

7. See Kierkegaard's newspaper article of March 30, 1855, *The Moment*, 42 (esp. footnote).
8. Kierkegaard, *The Moment*, 40.
9. Volker Gerhardt, "Die Religion der Individualität," *Philosophisches Jahrbuch* 109 (2002), 1–16.

the enslaved will;[10] on the contrary, his dialectic of a freedom that becomes concrete only through anxiety and despair presupposes the Protestant belief in the sinner's justification by God, which cannot be chosen but is given. Still, Kierkegaard transformed Luther's doctrine of grace by two arguments that were a reaction to nineteenth-century postidealism. First, he categorically distinguishes religious faith from the integration of faith into systematic reflection (against idealistic philosophy). Second, he locates the indissoluble connection between faith and works in the very core of human existence and its self-interpretation through conflict (against Schleiermacher's foundation of religion on feeling).

Turning to Luther and his famous preface[11] to the first volume of his Latin writings of 1545, in which he describes his discovery of God's justice through faith according to Romans 1:17, we find that what Luther calls *iustitia passiva* (passive justice)[12] has a twofold meaning: God does not define himself by actively implementing his justice against human beings. God thus becomes the gracious God. At the same time, human beings gain God's justice passively by faith alone and without performing acts in advance. Luther puts this kind of relationship between God and humankind in opposition to justification by works and thus deals with it in a soteriological context.

Due to the situation of modernity, however, Kierkegaard was not primarily interested in soteriological controversies. Rather, he suspected Christianity of having insidiously obtained, due to the romantic-aesthetic or the idealistic-philosophical *zeitgeist*, either a wrong immediacy or a quasi-objectivity, both being contradictory to the very essence of Christian faith. Faith, according to Kierkegaard, necessarily includes works. Only a faith separated from works can be made a problem of reflection or be reduced to a mere state of feeling. But Christian faith is a paradoxical faith, and as a relationship to God-within-time it is neither immediate feeling nor can it claim epistemological objectivity. Faith is never safe, always simultaneous with the paradoxical experience of God-within-time, always interwoven with conflict, always dependent on being released from wrong decisions. This is why Kierkegaard emphasizes the element of action, of existential situations, and this is why he comments that Luther's life was "better than his preaching."[13]

10. Cf. Deuser, *Dialektische Theologie*, 254ff.; Walter Dietz, "*Servum arbitrium*: Zur Konzeption der Willensfreiheit bei Luther, Schopenhauer und Kierkegaard," *Neue Zeitschrift für Systematische Theologie und Religionsphilosophie* 42 (2000): 181–94.

11. See Luther, WA 54:179–87; cf. Wilfried Härle, "Luthers reformatorische Entdeckung: damals und heute," *Zeitschrift für Theologie und Kirche* 99 (2002): 278–95.

12. See Härle, ibid., 284–87; cf. Hermann Deuser, *Kleine Einführung in die Systematische Theologie* (Stuttgart: Reclam, 1999), 127ff.

13. See *Søren Kierkegaard's Journals and Papers*, vol. 3, no. 2509, 78 (*Pap.* X 2, A 263, 194): "Luther acted rightly, but his preaching is not always clear or in agreement with his life—a

Despite his sarcastic criticisms of Luther and his demand for imitation of Christ and martyrdom, we will have to conclude that Kierkegaard's philosophy is a nineteenth-century descendant of Lutheran theology, interpreting the polarity of law and gospel in ethical terms. Kierkegaard's talk of "grace in the first place" and "grace in the second place" is no denial of justification solely by God, but an action-oriented reformulation of the Lutheran faith.[14] Whereas the concept of prevenient grace, "grace in the first place," can be misused as an excuse for idleness or quietism, "grace in the second place" encourages action, and this latter kind of grace has nothing to do with justification by works but means an "inward deepening" of true Christianity.[15]

Christianity and the Ethics of Modernity

Kierkegaard intended his dogmatic critique to contradict the traditional concept of grace, which had become anachronistic because at his time the priority of grace over works was no longer understood as what it had originally been—a polemic denial of justification by works. Indeed, Kierkegaard made ethical decision-forming the entrance to Christian life. His *Either-Or* resists romantic-aesthetic immediacy as well as speculative dialectics, both of which dissolved Christian faith rather than saving it. While speculative dialectics does not relate to concrete self-experience, aesthetic immediacy denies the ultimate seriousness of existential situations. Kierkegaard's ethics, on the other hand, summons to deal responsibly with conflict, whether successfully or not, for conflict situations ultimately reveal the human being's relationship to God.

The concept of modernity, which I introduced here to characterize Kierkegaard's position within history of philosophy, becomes clearer when brought within the scope of Kierkegaard's ethics. As soon as Kant replaced faith in God by the autonomous insight into moral law through practical reason, faith lost its philosophical dignity, because it could no longer claim ultimate theoretical justification. This became the mark of European modernity. Kierkegaard, however, presupposing modernity already, suspended faith from any such dependence on ultimate justifications altogether. This is the reason why Jürgen Habermas calls Kierkegaard "the first modern ethicist."[16] Kierkegaard, as an author of late modernity[17]—or,

---

rare occurrence—his life is better than his preaching!" Cf. ibid., 77 (*Pap.* X 2, A 263, 193): "Was it not of his own free will that he exposed himself to certain danger by opposing the Pope? It certainly was not the Pope who attacked Luther; it was Luther who attacked the Pope." See Deuser, *Dialektische Theologie*, 258–67, for more references in this respect.

14. Cf. *Journals and Papers*, vol. 3, no. 2559 (*Pap.* X 4, A 446); for further discussion of Kierkegaard's late treatment of the Lutheran doctrine of law and grace see Deuser, *Dialektische Theologie*, 267ff.

15. Cf. *Pap.* X 6, B 261, 433; Deuser, *Dialektische Theologie*, 208.

16. Jürgen Habermas, *Die Zukunft der menschlichen Natur: Auf dem Weg zu einer liberalen Eugenik?* (Frankfurt am Main: Suhrkamp, 2001), 107 (n. 65) and 17ff.

as Habermas puts it, as a postmetaphysical[18] author—elaborates on the unconditionedness of the ethical situation and on the pressure to form decisions without any ontological securities.[19] We should keep this concept of late modernity in mind when considering whether Kierkegaard's description of existential challenge seems plausible or not, and whether his theology establishes a metaphysical relation between thinking and existing. Indeed, Kierkegaard brings metaphysics in by his concept of repetition, which results from the transformation of the concept of recollection under the conditions of late modernity by existential philosophy.[20] He uses *Repetition* as well as the ethical concept of *Either-Or* to describe his own experience as an instrument for criticism of church and society.[21] Repetition makes continuities possible. They are essential for the process of becoming one's self, or becoming a Christian, even if situations and therefore concrete ethics vary.

In this sense, Christianity and modern ethics are mutually related. Kierkegaard transfers Luther's doctrine of justification by faith into this very context[22] by appealing to the human *can* as to an *ought*. Can and ought are realized through works of love;[23] they need processes of learning; they open up freedom though may also lead to enslavement; but always they are interpretations of the individual's relationship to God.[24] This is the basic fact the ethics of our late modernity today seems to rediscover. In human experience, success is joined to failure, hubris to self-accusation, autonomy to dependence; and ultimately these ambivalences are religious ones. So the ethics of our late modernity has transformed Reformation's great insight into ethics, and for this process Kierkegaard was instrumental.

17. For a more detailed exploration of this concept, see Robert C. Neville, *Religion in Late Modernity* (Albany: State University of New York Press, 2002), 144–50.

18. Cf. Habermas, 17f.

19. Cf. ibid., 26.

20. See Kierkegaard's early unpublished fragment "Johannes Climacus or De omnibus dubitandum est," *Philosophical Fragments/Johannes Climacus*, ed. Howard V. Hong and Edna H. Hong (Princeton: Princeton Univ. Press, 1962), 171, and *Repetition*, ed. Howard V. Hong and Edna H. Hong (Princeton: Princeton Univ. Press, 1983), 149; cf. on both texts Dorothea Glöckner, *Kierkegaards Begriff der Wiederholung: Eine Studie zu seinem Freiheitsverständnis* (Berlin and New York: W. de Gruyter, 1998), chap. 3.

21. Cf. *Pap.* X 6, B 236.

22. This is of main importance for Luther's understanding of the First Commandment; see Hermann Deuser, *Die Zehn Gebote: Kleine Einführung in die theologische Ethik* (Stuttgart: Reclam, 2002).

23. See Kierkegaard's *Works of Love*, ed. Howard V. Hong and Edna H. Hong (Princeton: Princeton Univ. Press, 1995); and cf. for recent interpretations Ulrich Lincoln, *Äußerung: Studien zum Handlungsbegriff in Søren Kierkegaards* Die Taten der Liebe (Berlin and New York: W. de Gruyter, 2000); Ingolf U. Dalferth ed., *Ethik der Liebe: Studien zu Kierkegaards "Taten der Liebe"* (Tübingen: Mohr Siebeck, 2002).

24. Cf. Dalferth, ibid., 43f.; Lincoln, ibid., 118f. Luther's theology of the cross might be the key to understanding human experience and suffering even in modernity; cf. Ingolf U. Dalferth, *Gedeutete Gegenwart: Zur Wahrnehmung Gottes in den Erfahrungen der Zeit* (Tübingen: Mohr Siebeck, 1997), 60 (n. 7).

Church, Christian Sociality, and Institution

Kierkegaard's view of the church as an institution is paralleled by his views of public and state. This means that his criticism of the growing influence of economy and politics on all areas of life also affected his position on church.[25] However, despite his undeniable detachment from church, he remained a Christian—and a Protestant Christian—even though he, by proclaiming society's loss of Christianity, had to stick to his Socratic role and therefore could not even claim to be a Christian himself. His model for the true representative of Christianity is the socially despised individual bearing witness to truth to his contemporaries. This is why he accused Luther of seeking the world as an ally and even of being negligent of the paradoxical relationship of Jesus to God, due to Luther's overemphasis on the letters of the apostle Paul. Kierkegaard meant that Paul, to find personal acknowledgment as well as to help the young church grow, lessened the importance of temptation, which Kierkegaard thought was not compatible with radical simultaneity with the crucified Christ. And while Kierkegaard told us so, he at the same time added a footnote saying that he himself is not a Christian.[26] The ambivalence of this position leaps to the eye: the alleged non-Christian set out to show Christians what true Christianity is.

Toward the end of his life, Kierkegaard's "one thesis," intended as a corrective, became more and more dominant in his writings as well as biographically—and unfortunately so. It wiped away his richness of thought, his poetic language, his philanthropic attitude, his Socratic empathy. It wiped them away but did not destroy them for good. This is why we today are still allowed to turn to Kierkegaard for a better and critical understanding of the cultural conditions of the Christian church. Of course, his concepts of ethics and religion need mediation, as church and state have undergone multiple changes. But in his work, Kierkegaard outlines true Christian sociality in opposition to the politically well-established Christendom of his day; and while he attacked the institutionalized church, he at the same time pictured the community of Christians. Indeed, the church so badly missed by him in the real world was reconstituted by him through his literary activity as a deliberately chosen form of existence as a religious author. The church is and always will be dependent on the individual Christian's appropriation of the article of justification, and this appropriation is just what the Christian writer Kierkegaard exercised. Unlike Kierkegaard, however, we today will have to take into account the churches' growing loss of political, social, and cultural influence and the various problems caused by these developments. If our task is to connect church and Christianity, Christendom and religions, theology and science anew, then Luther's emphasis on individual faith and Kierkegaard's existential dialectics will prove to be two all-important guidelines—and this is more than just one thesis.

Translated by Gesche Linde

---

25. Cf. Deuser, *Dialektische Theologie*, 195ff.
26. Kierkegaard, *The Moment*, 341 (footnote) in connection with 181f.

ECUMENICS

Part

VI

With respect to the reformation of the entire church, the Protestant Reformation was a failure. This historical fact should not be overlooked in present-day discussions of the catholicity of Lutheran theology. For obvious reasons, the understanding of tradition has been a part of the Lutheran critique from the very beginning. However, the present situation of globalization seems to raise new questions and to point toward new directions for a Lutheran theology in an ecumenical context.

Part VI does not intend to present a picture of the various ecumenical discussions in which Lutheran churches are currently involved. Rather, the essays deal with ecumenical stances found in Lutheranism, concentrating on issues such as missiology, scripture, tradition, and the exclusive particles: grace alone, faith alone, scripture alone, Christ alone.

For Richard H. Bliese, the ecumenical deficit of the Lutheran legacy displays itself in its muteness concerning mission. The malaise of current Lutheranism shows itself in occluding present-day missiological challenges in favor of remembering victories of past debates. If traditional Lutheranism was marked by its focus on reactive reform, future Lutheranism has to learn the discipline of innovation. Evangelism is required for a church, which seems to be stagnating or even declining.

According to Mickey Mattox, Lutheran ecumenical engagement needs to clarify its own understanding of the relationship between scripture and tradition. This relation is no longer obvious, as it was in the Reformation age. In the present situation, this question is just as important for the Lutheran–Reformed dialogue as for the Lutheran–Catholic interface. The Lutheran way of doing theology historically, grammatically, and critically may be said to make up an anti-tradition. While scripture is never actually alone, Lutheran theology should reach a more positive evaluation of tradition, also according to its own standards of faith.

Peter Widmann investigates not-yet-exhausted potentialities in the Reformation's emphasis on the sufficiency of the common Christian faith. The content of Luther's position was catholic in the sense that it was an actualization of the *fides catholica* (catholic faith) without any specific addition, subtraction, or qualification. The stress on the sufficiency of the common faith may be the most important Lutheran contribution to the *oikumene.* According to Widmann, the inclusiveness of various forms of catholicity is made possible only by using the aforementioned exclusive particles.

Developing a catholic voice of Lutheran theology may be a major task for a future Lutheran theology in an era becoming more and more postconfessional. Future Lutheran theologians will have to deal with the problem of being simultaneously innovative, critical, and sensitive to the common concerns of catholic faith without losing the sharpness of its own bite.

—Bo Holm

Lutheran Missiology: *Struggling to Move from Reactive Reform to Innovative Initiative*

Richard H. Bliese

M ission and evangelism—understood within a Lutheran framework and crafted for the North American context—suffers today from a lack of clarity and purpose. Few North American Lutherans would contest this basic *affirmatio*, which must also serve the dual purpose at the turn of the twenty-first century as a *confessio*. Other Lutheran churches, especially in the West, might also share in the American plight of a mission-challenged theological tradition. So, what does this mean? And what challenges might this *affirmatio* present to the future of Lutheran theology? Not so long ago (in the 1950s and 1960s) American Lutherans prided themselves in having a German theological inheritance from the sixteenth century whose unparalleled emphasis on God's grace in Christ needed only a contextually relevant ministerial practice. "Our theology is the best in Christendom," we proudly confessed. The question concerning *how* to put our theology of grace into practice did need constant attention by—it should be noted—practical theologians, not systematicians. Technique and commitment were the only missing ingredients for a missionally effective and faithful church.

Today, in contrast, the need for a fundamental evaluation of our European theological foundation for doing mission in a changing North American context seems long overdue. This evaluation needs to be conducted by practical *and* systematic theologians. If a body of theology does not or cannot clarify the church's witness within a particular context, fundamental questions must be ventured. Furthermore, if any theological tradition consistently avoids or sidesteps certain mission agendas, as Lutheran theology does in the United States, the "why" question must be asked. Why are Lutheran theologians mute on mission when others in the ecumenical community are consumed by its agenda?

A typical example of the Lutheran theological malaise for mission is contained in past bilateral dialogues between Roman Catholics and Lutherans.

---

1. Carl Braaten, *The Apostolic Imperative: Nature and Aim of the Church's Mission and Ministry* (Minneapolis: Augsburg, 1985), 66.

As Carl Braaten pointed out already in 1985,[1] all of these bilateral dialogues with Catholics dealt with traditional intra-ecclesial topics and had little or no bearing on the burning issues of mission and evangelism in the world. Here the evangelicals got more quickly to the point in their dialogues with Catholics. It is clear that evangelicals found powerful reinforcement for their convictions about mission and evangelism from the official documents of the Roman Catholic church. Lutherans were more obsessed with a past-oriented hermeneutic of inquiry. This same lack of clarity concerning mission, I would contend, has likewise marked recent Lutheran ecumenical dialogues with various Reformed and Episcopalian communities in the United States. The irony, of course, is that the chief motivation behind the ecumenical drive toward unity is for the sake of mission. But this mission note "that the world might believe" has been virtually absent from our many rounds of dialogue. Braaten thus laments, "It is more than irony; it is tragedy."[2]

Yet Braaten, one of American Lutherans' chief missiologists in the 1980s and 1990s himself almost completely overlooked mission as a loci of theology within his monumental work with Robert Jenson, *Christian Dogmatics*.[3] Mission never seems to guide or frame the Lutheran theological agenda, even from some of its best proponents. Summarizing the present system, Kenneth Inskeep remarks that concerning mission, North American Lutherans are "retrospectively vital."[4] We seem passionate when rehashing past debates where we have certainty, while succumbing to a certain intellectual malaise when addressing present missiological challenges.

The questions this chapter raises are: Are Lutherans' mission problems in North America ultimately more theological than practical in nature? Do Lutherans need better theology rather than better ministry techniques in the new millennium? If mission is the mother of theology, what does this insight say about the difficulties in forming a Lutheran missiology for North America today?

An initial contention of this paper is that the Lutheran posture toward missiology in North America can be characterized as "reactive reform." We let other theological traditions innovate missiological programs, ideas, and theologies. Lutherans then respond with critique. We adopt, adjust, and *reform* these missiologies as needed. We react. While others innovate, in other words, we constantly reform their work by making them "more Lutheran."

Now, reforming other missiologies by forcing them through the sieve of Lutheran hermeneutics isn't always a bad theological program. It is

2. Ibid., 67.

3. Carl E. Braaten and Robert W. Jenson, eds., *Christian Dogmatics* (Philadelphia: Fortress Press, 1984).

4. Ken Inskeep and Jeffrey Drake, "Worship Attendance in the Evangelical Lutheran Church in America Faith Communities Today" (Chicago: Department for Research and Evaluation, ELCA, 2001), 10.

ecumenical and open, not parochial or sectarian in nature. But "reform" as a permanent theological posture is insufficient for mission vitality. Every church must discover, finally, some basis for its own tradition's missiological genius. The key for Lutheran missiology in the future is to move from "reactive reform" to some kind of "innovative initiative." Does Lutheran theology lend itself to the creativity and innovation needed to think missiologically in our changing environment?

Clarifying the Issue

Although statistics cannot tell the whole story about the Lutheran praxis of mission in North America over the past thirty years, they do point to some disturbing tendencies. Membership in the Evangelical Lutheran Church in America (ELCA) has been in slow decline since the mid-to-late 1960s. In 1991, baptized membership in the ELCA stood at 5,245,177.[5] In 2003, membership hovers at approximately 5,100,000 members—a loss of some 150,000 people. The trend among Missouri Synod Lutherans is no different. Since 1991, forty of the sixty-five synods in the ELCA experienced membership losses. The good news is that the overall drop in membership for Lutheran congregations has been slower than in the other mainline denominations, for example, the United Methodists, Presbyterians, and Episcopalians. Nevertheless, losses have been so characteristic of Lutheran churches for so long that an ethos of decline has permeated the pews. Not only has baptized membership in the ELCA declined, but so too has worship attendance, stewardship numbers, and outreach programs. ELCA bishop Mark Hanson points to the revealing fact that only 1.5 of 5.1 million North American Lutherans are in church on any given Sunday. Most of the mainstream religious groups in the United States, including the ELCA, are now *annually* losing approximately 1 percent of their members. Experts predict that anywhere from 20 to 40 percent of all 11,000 ELCA congregations are labeled "at risk"; that is, these congregations have fewer than one hundred persons worshiping on any Sunday and are therefore at risk of closing within the next ten years. With these grave statistics on the rise, the question must be asked: Is there nothing in our theological tradition that might aid Lutherans in reversing these trends or that can distinguish Lutherans from the rest of mainline denominations suffering mainstream religious decline?

Statistics witness to a declining church since the mid-1960s. This is clear. What is not so clear is what these statistics mean. Statistical trends do not clarify by themselves whether Lutherans suffer from theological and/or

5. Ken Inskeep, "The 1991–2002 Decade Report on ELCA Evangelism Strategy: Telling Witness to God's Good News" (Chicago: ELCA Department for Research and Evaluation, 2001). See the introduction.

practical issues. Opinions differ widely on this question. Sociological data concerning Lutheran clergy, however, is beginning to shed additional light on the problem. Lutheran pastors within surveys concerning clergy effectiveness, for example, consistently rate evangelism and community outreach as spiritual gifts they do not possess or areas of ministry where they are weak. This is particularly fascinating when seen in the light of the Lutheran doctrine of ministry. From one of a growing number of studies, the "Effective Ministry and Membership Growth Study" in 1996, it was learned that both the clergy and council members of ELCA congregations ranked "proclaiming the gospel to the unchurched" as one of the twenty-four congregational activities in which they were least effective.[6] In a recent study of ministry conducted by the Missouri Synod, only 5 percent of all Lutheran pastors ranked evangelism as one of their five best gifts. At the top of their list, these same pastors rated preaching, teaching, counseling, and administration all as high.

This same negative or selective "ethos" toward mission is also reflected in our seminaries. Of the Lutheran seminarians that I have interviewed over the last seven years at my former school (the Lutheran School of Theology at Chicago), 75 percent characterize evangelism and outreach as negative concepts and/or ministerial gifts they do not possess. It is ironic to note that despite the decline in Lutheran numbers over the past thirty years, no ELCA Lutheran seminary today has reacted by requiring a course in evangelism within their curriculum. Preaching, counseling, education, and liturgy are the "classic" pastoral disciples, not evangelism.

It is true that evangelism doesn't encompass all mission theology. Mission is seen as much broader than evangelism. This is progress. But there is consensus among most Lutherans that evangelism lies at the heart of all the church's mission efforts. So if a church is confused about the theology and practice of evangelism, where does this leave their holistic approach to mission?

One reason for this theological fuzziness is that Lutheran theologians aren't publishing many books in the area of missiology. This is true despite the explosion of missiological literature that is flooding the rest of the church market today. (One recent search showed a book-publishing ratio of twenty-five to one for Baptists and Lutherans, respectively, on mission.) As we survey the growing missiological literature in North America in areas of evangelism, interreligious dialogue, mission theology, church growth, cross-cultural witness, community organizing, social outreach, and so on, we are shocked that the Lutheran voice is weak, if not almost entirely absent within the ecumenical discussions. Evangelical, Pentecostal, Reformed, and Roman Catholic literature abounds in many mission areas. Lutherans are the glaring exception to this trend. This paucity of literature is likewise reflected in the "real absence" within the missiological academy. Lutherans

---

6. Ibid.,10.

have virtually no identity of their own in these circles and are usually lumped together with the general camps of conciliar, ecumenical, or mainline Protestants.

To summarize: Given the present statistical trends of the Lutheran Church in America, the needs of the North American church for mission, the negative "ethos" surrounding mission among many clergy, and the lack of resources for Lutherans trying to understand mission today, the future of Lutheran theology must direct its attention to Lutheran theology and mission as one of its primarily tasks. Lutherans simply need to better understand how their theological inheritance applies to mission.

Why Are We at This Point?

Whereas before the 1960s Lutheran identity was forged primarily over against Roman Catholic and Reformed churches, today's Lutherans usually distinguish themselves theologically over against Evangelicals, Pentecostals, and/or growing independent churches. That means that Lutheran identity is often forged in contrast to growing "mission driven" congregations. Where did this trend start? A broad reading of recent mission history points to two formative periods for Lutherans in response to mission.

Historians point to significant polarizations among North American Lutherans at two critical points during the twentieth century. First, an initial polarization emerged during the first several decades of the twentieth century between three Lutheran groups: pietists, social gospel advocates, and confessionalists. For pietistic Lutherans, harking back to the nineteenth century, evangelistic activity was chiefly associated with the salvation of souls and the building of churches. This concept of mission was an import to America from pietistic circles in Europe and fit well into the wide open North American mission field. This evangelistic-expansionist emphasis began to be evaluated as insufficient at the turn of the twentieth century, however, when the stark alternative of the social gospel was strongly endorsed by Lutheran leaders in response to growing social needs. Mission among these groups was linked with the kingdom of God. This kingdom, representing God's entire reign on earth, necessitated that Christians work for justice, social concerns, and the poor. A third wing among Lutherans emerged in the middle of the nineteenth century as well. This confessional wing of mission critiqued both pietists and social gospel advocates from the standpoint of the Confessions. Whatever mission was, it had to correspond to the Reformation principles for understanding the gospel. Confessionalists were constantly committed to maintaining Lutheran identity over against Roman Catholic and Reformed Christians. This was most certainly true. But their crusade was also directed against Lutheran pietists who were using new evangelism methods like revivalism to further mission on the American frontier,

and social gospel Lutherans who were watering down the gospel message
into "mere" social programs.

Among Lutherans before World War II, however, there existed a fragile
unity among all three wings of Lutheran missiological thought. Why?
Lutherans, by and large, did not reflect the larger divisions among North
American Christians along the lines of the evangelical (and fundamentalist)
and modernist (liberal) approaches to mission. The reason for this tenuous
unity lay in the common roots of all branches of American Lutheranism.
North American Lutherans came from various European pietistic traditions,
Lutherans identified with social needs within society, and all Lutherans,
finally, embraced to some degree confessional conscription. Consequently, a
large tent existed under which Lutherans, although diverse in their
approaches to mission, could live, talk, and cooperate with one another. The
rifts within missiological thought among Lutherans, therefore, was not as
great as among other mainline churches at this time.

This fragile unity in Lutheran circles on the meaning of mission and
evangelism, however, completely disappeared in the 1960s. By the 1960s, it
became obvious that mainline Protestantism's enthusiasm for mission and
evangelism had significantly dissipated. Mission was being fundamentally
questioned and seemed to be hopelessly mired in "crisis."[7] Vatican II forever
changed the perception of Roman Catholics and started to reshape the
Lutheran concept of mission. Other Lutherans sought more clarity about
mission praxis by following Billy Graham into the evangelical movement.
Growing opposition to American military involvement in Southeast Asia
generated a corresponding suspicion of any forms of imperialism—national
or religious. And secularism, once considered antithetical to the Christian
cause, was now being praised by Harvey Cox, Paul Tillich, and other advocates of "the secular city."

The 1960s brought a fundamental shaking of the foundations.
Alongside the questioning and reshaping of mission came a shift from confidence to malaise in the church's attitude toward outreach.[8] Wax Warren,
for many years General Secretary of the Church Missionary Society in Great
Britain, referred to this shift as "a terrible failure of nerve about the missionary enterprise."[9] Whereas Lutherans had enjoyed a fragile unity of mission praxis before World War II, the 60s destroyed that unity and created a
missiological vacuum. In the absence of any dominant Lutheran approach
to mission that could adequately fill the vacuum, Lutherans borrowed heavily from outside sources, which led to various "schools" of mission praxis.

The 60s not only questioned mission but also inaugurated new, alternative approaches to mission. The concept of the *missio Dei*, for example,

---

7. David Bosch, *Transforming Mission: Paradigm Shifts in Theology of Mission* (Maryknoll,
N.Y.: Orbis, 1991).
8. Ibid. Note how Bosch describes this mission malaise in the introduction.
9. Ibid., 7.

rediscovered at the Willingen Conference in 1952, now came to refer to God's total activity in the world aimed at shalom and humanization. While in the 1950s, *missio Dei* was "classically" used to refer to God's mission of salvation through Christ carried out through the church, now God was seen as active in the secular political and social events of the world as well. J. C. Hoekendijk's Dutch school of mission started to dramatically shape ecumenical thought on mission. His thought took many American churches by storm, including Lutherans. The role of the church's mission now was to discern what God was doing in the world and then participate in it. The world was to set the agenda for mission.[10] This is one among many examples of how Lutherans borrowed from other traditions in order to react to the growing mission needs within North America.

To summarize: with the breakdown of convergence in the 1960s, Lutheran missiology did not simply return to the kind of unified-divergence that had prevailed in the pre-war period. Many Lutheran leaders were no longer enthusiastic about "traditional" mission theologies and programs. Nevertheless, they wanted to hold on to the concepts of mission and evangelism. For most Lutherans, as a result, "evangelism" became transformed into "witness" and "mission" into "service" of the world. In this sense, everything the church did bore witness to Jesus Christ, so everything was understood as mission and evangelism. Stephen Neil reacted to such tendencies with his famous quote, "When everything is mission, nothing is mission." Lutherans, in any case, didn't know how to define mission more concretely.

By the 1990s, therefore, even when there appeared to be growing agreement on the necessity of a renewed commitment to mission among Lutherans, it could not be assumed that Lutherans could agree about the "what" and "why" of that mission. Questions about mission technique ("how to" questions) were happily being replaced with fundamental questions about the "why" and "what" of mission. But what was mission for a Lutheran?

At the beginning of the twenty-first century, Lutheran theology has been mostly silent on mission and evangelism and has thus created a vacuum of missiological thought. Another way to describe the situation is that there has been a divorce between Lutheran theology and Lutheran missiology. This vacuum or divorce has been filled by borrowing mission theology from other traditions, thus creating numerous schools of mission. Because these schools were not born on Lutheran soil, they have often had difficulties relating to one another.

---

10. J. C. Hoekendijk, *The Church Inside Out* (London: SCM, 1967), 32f.

Missiological Questions for Lutheran Theology

Thus, given the present fuzzy state of Lutheran missiology in North America, three questions will guide the rest of this chapter in trying to determine how to move forward. To move ahead in mission, we must determine

- whether Lutherans need a common theology of mission
- whether Lutherans should embrace the *missio Dei* as a basis for their mission thought
- whether Luther and/or Reformation theology form an adequate foundation for a mission theology in the twenty-first century

Do Lutherans in North America Need a Common Theology of Mission?

One reason why a theology of mission among Lutherans has been slow to develop since the nineteenth century is that Americans have a penchant for pragmatism. Strategy and technique have usually taken priority over theology. Furthermore, mission efforts from America during the nineteenth and twentieth centuries were not centralized, emerging from countless churches and mission agencies. Likewise, many of those who occupied formal chairs of mission in seminaries and divinity schools were typically church historians by training, not theologians, and so focused their attention more on history than contemporary theological reflection.

The situation in the 1960s, as mentioned above, challenged the pragmatic approach to mission. New theological streams of mission exploded onto the scene. After meetings in New Delhi, Uppsala, Lusanne, and Rome (Vatican II), ecumenical, evangelical, and Roman Catholic streams of mission theology solidified. Each of these streams influenced Lutheran concepts of mission. The first trend in modern American Lutheran mission, therefore, is the movement toward a common missiological dialogue. Convergence in dialogue must not, however, mask trends toward divergence in theology. North America has proved to be a too fertile environment for experimentation to be reduced to one or two simple categories. The vacuum of a Lutheran missiology has allowed Lutherans to liberally borrow their mission theology from other churches. This has created numerous schools of mission thought among Lutherans, which I have tried to outline below. What makes these "schools" or "models" listed below interesting is that (1) Lutheran missiologists usually claim to belong to more than one school of thought; (2) each school (except confessionalism) runs across congregational, denominational and agency lines (among other traditions this "school" might be better labeled "orthodoxy"); and (3) each school brings out a particular strength of Lutheran theology. The schools will be referred to as evangelicalism, liberalism, confessionalism, the new diversity, pragmatism, and Pentecostalism.

1. *Evangelicalism,* broadly defined, is a distinct school for Lutherans with historical roots in European pietism. This stream of mission elevates proclamation and witness to all those who do not claim loyalty to Jesus Christ as Savior as central to mission. Conversion, church planting, and "making disciples" are dominant themes that don't disregard social activism, but usually place it in a secondary position. Evangelism is viewed as the one unique churchly task within the *missio Dei.*

2. *Liberalism*'s roots lie in modernity, the positive evaluation of human culture (*missio Dei* and the work of the Spirit), and a this-worldly comprehension of the kingdom of God (social gospel). The church is not only to "bring God" through proclamation and witness but to recognize where God is already active in the world and actively participate in this activity. Mission can also move mutually across many cultures and religions. Liberalism's roots for Lutherans lie in their recognition that God's revelation cannot be limited to the church. Thus the church must be open to revelation and truth wherever it is found.

3. *The new diversity*, like liberalism, takes an anthropological approach to mission. It does so, however, in reference to marginal over against dominant cultures. The "new diversity" among Lutherans includes voices (e.g., African Americans, women, Latinos/Hispanics, Native Americans, etc.) that have not always been included at the center of American society or theology. Liberation themes are common. The key feature is that mission is "caught" through communal praxis on the margins of society as a specific community seeks its own identity, its liberation, and its mission from within a particular context. The theology of the cross undergirds its thought.

4. *Confessionalism*: Lutherans are usually not content with a generic, ecumenical missiology. Mission is, as Martin Kähler suggested, the mother of theology. Mission demands a constant posture of "attending" to new voices. New mission trends have always forced Lutherans into periodic reappraisals of their theological heritage in light of these trends. Orthodoxy and mission trends must be brought into harmony. Thus, confessionalism asks how the *missio Dei* corresponds to principles such as grace alone, faith alone, word alone, Word and sacraments, law and gospel, justification by grace through faith, priesthood of all believers, two kingdoms, and so on.

5. *Pragmatism*, the marriage of theology and sociology, has always played a strong role within American religious life. The American church has often been characterized as entrepreneurial. Lutherans are no different. The "church growth movement" is built upon this foundation of pragmatism. Whereas the study of history changed biblical studies, the linking of sociology and theology has particularly changed how churches do local mission in America today. No church is unaffected by all the new techniques of how to do church effectively in the American context.

6. *Pentecostalism* is the newest force in American mission. The Pentecostal experience of God in worship, "signs and wonders" as pointers to God's activities, a "second" experience with the Holy Spirit, millennial expectations, and the dynamic power of prayer have influenced almost every community in America. This movement is no longer restricted to certain "lower classes" in U.S. culture. The size of this movement is growing as well as its ability to articulate its theological legacy. Lutheran charismatics bring much of this dynamic with them into mission praxis.

The 1960s for Lutherans represented an explosion in schools of thought. Lutherans began to think about mission in theological terms. This was positive. The negative result was that Lutherans found it more difficult to discover a common theological platform and vocabulary from which to discuss and to do mission. Since adherents to "the schools" don't agree on most mission issues, there appears to be no unifying theology today that can serve as a common basis for Lutheran mission reflection. Do we need such a common foundation for mission? My contention is yes. Without some common approach to mission theology, Lutherans will be left defenseless as they try to respond to the demands of mission within our present context. This is the present state of affairs.

The first challenge of Lutheran theology today, therefore, is to create a working theology of mission for the church, a Lutheran Vatican II for missiology.

Could Missio Dei *Serve as a Unifying Force for Lutheran Missiology?*

With all these schools of North American Lutheran missiology, is there any theological consensus among Lutherans on how to approach mission? The short answer is no. There does seem to be a consensus developing in wider church circles, however, to the effect that the theme of *missio Dei* should serve as such a missiological center for all Christian traditions—Catholic, Evangelical, Pentecostal, Reformed, and, yes, Lutheran. When a consensus is established among people of otherwise quite contrary views, however, it may indicate that the content of the consensus is understood quite differently and that the consensus therefore is more one of appearance than substance. This appears to be the case for Lutherans.

When North American Lutherans use the term *missio Dei* (see, e.g., the Lutheran World Federation Document on Mission to which the North American Lutherans contributed), two interpretations of the term come into play—sometimes both in the same document. Each interpretation leads to completely different views on mission. Georg Vicedom, in 1960, initially set the tone for Lutherans when he addressed the topic of *missio Dei* in what some have labeled the classical approach to mission. In his book *Mission of God*,[11] written in response to the Willingen Conference (1952), Vicedom emphasized that mission is God's work from the beginning to the end. God is the acting subject in mission. Mission is not initiated by the church nor is

---

11. Georg Vicedom, *Mission of God* (St. Louis: Concordia, 1964).

it to serve the church. The church is a community in response to the *missio Dei*, bearing witness to God's activity in the world by its communication of the good news of Jesus Christ in word and deed. Vicedom does not exclude the church from the mission of God, as later Dutch theologians were tempted to do. In the mission of God, God is both the sender and the one being sent. This accounts for the Trinitarian structure of the *missio Dei*. From this content of mission, Vicedom argues that the purpose of mission is salvation. God's revelation is God's mission, and God's mission is always for the sake of salvation. Mission is a continuation of the redemptive act of God.

But, as Norwegian missiologist Tormod Engelsviken has remarked, Vicedom's book not only outlines a classical approach to the *missio Dei* but also opens the *missio Dei* for larger conceptualizations of mission.[12] This "larger conceptualization" will be referred to as the "ecumenical" approach. Mission here begins to refer to all of God's activities, not just those restricted to the combination of Trinitarian perspectives and redemption. This reveals a basic problem that appears when the concept of *missio Dei* is combined with an understanding of the kingdom of God as the "rule of God." The differences in the understanding of *missio Dei*, consequently, correspond with differences in understanding the kingdom of God. Here is the key: the kingdom of God is either understood as the reign of God over the whole of creation, including redemption, or the present and eternal salvation that God offers only in Christ through the ministries of the church and received by faith. If "*missio*" is understood in the former ecumenical sense, the kingdom may be seen as universal and thus not restricted to the ministry of the church. If it is understood in the latter classical sense, the kingdom is restricted to salvation history; it is the realm where salvation is found through faith in Christ and participation in his church.

These two views of the kingdom of God, classical and ecumenical (also referred to as "narrow and special" *missio Dei* versus "broad or general" *missio Dei*), are both used widely in Lutheran circles with no clear consensus emerging. This may indicate that the time has come for a new paradigm, a fresh challenge of established ecumenical opinion by Lutheran missiologists. The *missio Dei*, consequently, as it has been developed in ecumenical and missiological circles and, without further clarity and development, is not helpful for Lutherans *at present* in providing a common starting point for their mission theology.

Is the Reformation a Basis for Mission Theology?

If the *missio Dei* is an insufficient common basis for a Lutheran theology of mission in the future, should one then go back to the Reformation to discover

12. Tormod Engelsviken, "Missio Dei: Understanding and Misunderstanding of the Theological Concept in European Churches and Missiology" (unpublished paper presented at Mission Congress, August 19, 2002, in Willingen, Germany).

such a foundation? Bosch cuts to the heart of the argument in his classic book on mission, *Transforming Mission* (1985), when he writes about Lutherans, "The church of pure doctrine was, however, a church without mission, and its theology more scholastic than apostolic."[13] In the end, Bosch sees in the Reformation only a fledgling foundation for the future ecumenical mission paradigm and, at that, he sees benefits mostly in Calvinism.

> Orthodoxy made deep inroads not only into Lutheranism, but also into Calvinism. Even so, Dutch and Anglo-Saxon Calvinism appears to have succeeded in keeping alive a missionary spirit more successfully than did Lutheranism. Dutch and English missionary endeavors, says Gensichen, pushed Lutheran attempts into the background. In Lutheranism, the church's missionary calling remained a theme for theological discussion; Reformed churches embarked on missionary action. The decisive factors were theological as well as socio-political.[14]

Bosch's assessment is only building upon what many Lutherans have already concluded about their own theological heritage. A heated debate still rages about whether or not Luther had a mission theology. Gustav Warneck, the father of missiology as a theological discipline, was one of the first Protestant scholars who promoted the idea that Luther and the Reformation didn't provide the theological rationale or motivation for mission. "We miss in the Reformation not only missionary action," he said, "but even the idea of missions, in the sense in which we understand them today."[15] This is so "because fundamental theological views hindered them from giving their activity, and even their thoughts, a missionary direction."[16] Other Lutherans have fought back and at least won some recognition that Luther—but not Lutheranism—laid out many of the modern insights into mission thought. Scherer contends that "Luther is a rich but untested potential for missiology."[17]

Still, in spite of positive voices for Luther's missiology—what Karl Holl, Carl Holsten, Walter Gensichen, Werner Elert, Scherer, and others have identified as "the missionary thrust of the Reformers' theology"—very little happened by way of a missionary outreach during the first two centuries after the Reformation. Protestants saw their mission as reformation, not outreach. One of the chief rationales for pietism, in fact, lies in the missionless state of Lutheran orthodoxy. One hundred and fifty years of missing mission had to be corrected.

13. Bosch, *Transforming Mission*, 249.
14. Ibid., 255–56.
15. Ibid., 244.
16. Ibid.
17. James Scherer, *Gospel, Church and Kingdom* (Minneapolis: Augsburg, 1987), 54.

For John Calvin, in contrast, the Christ who was exalted to God's right hand was preeminently the active Christ. He used the term *regnum Christi* (the reign of Christ) in this respect, viewing the church as an intermediary between the exalted Christ and the secular order. Such a theological point of departure could not but give rise to the idea of mission as "extending the reign of Christ," both by the inward spiritual renewal of individuals and by transforming the face of the earth through filling it with "the knowledge of the Lord." The relationship between these two dimensions, the vertical and the horizontal, was to characterize much of Calvinism during all subsequent centuries and exercise a profound influence on the theory and practice of mission. Most of the renewal in mission thought today in the United States among Reformed churches can be traced back to this idea of the reign of God in Calvinism. It can be argued, however, that it is the other non-Reformation churches (e.g., Pentecostal, Methodists, and Baptists) that show more innovation in mission theology in North America today than Reformation churches.

In summary, among Reformation churches, Lutherans have not yet shown that their Reformation heritage is adequate to the task of constructing an innovative theology for mission within the wider North American discussion. Lutherans usually use their hermeneutics in critiquing other traditions, what I have labeled above "reactive reform." The genius and potential of Lutheran theology for innovative initiates in mission within the North American context has yet to be tested.

Conclusion

Before 1950 the study of the "theology of mission" in today's sense hardly existed in Lutheran churches in North America. Much "mission work" was carried on without the benefit of serious theological reflection. "Mission principles and practices" dominated the agenda, creating both innovation and confusion. Missiology today, in contrast, is once again becoming a growing field in America, even if it is still a theological stepchild in the academy. Theological issues are becoming of overriding importance and claim as much attention as mere questions of methods and strategy. Issues concerning the reign of God, the *missio Dei*, gospel and culture, missional ecclesiology, mission at the margins, inter-religious dialogue, eschatology and mission, and so on dominate the conversation. The literature is vast and growing. But whereas many of these questions are raised throughout the theological community, rarely are they asked within the context of a Lutheran theology of mission. Mission issues are often addressed in a piecemeal fashion (e.g., Lutheranism and interreligious dialogue) but never within an entire theological system. Lutheran missiology needs to assist congregations and mission agencies on how to frame their work theologically within such a comprehensive missiological system.

I suggest that the future of Lutheran theology needs to directly address the issue of missiology. A vacuum in missiological thought has left Lutherans open to every wave of programmatic caprice. "Schools" are developing without common foundational threads between them. Ecumenical attempts at mission theology (e.g., with the *missio Dei*) have failed to serve in uniting Lutherans, and our own attempts at updating Reformation theology for the twenty-first century have failed as well. Finally, defining Lutheran hermeneutics consistently isn't the same thing as working out a consistent Lutheran missiology. In summary, Lutheran theology really must be judged as inadequate to the mission task thus far. Or, as Ed Schroeder has suggested:

> If Lutheran theology has a future at all, a deserved future, that future is linked to the gospel's own future. . . . Nothing else in creation has a guaranteed future, Jesus says. It will all pass away. So Lutheran theology too will pass away if/when it disconnects from the gospel, even if people called Lutherans continue to theologize. Fixation on the gospel is the genius of the Lutheran reformation, and the fixation of Luther's "mission theology."[18]

The history of Lutheran mission theology, meager as it is, has reflected more aptitude at reforming other missiologies than innovating its own. Reformation rather than innovation has been our mission motto. Even in the age of Christendom, such an attitude was deficient. In the post-Christendom environment of North America today, such an attitude simply can't survive. Nor should it. The question remains how Lutherans can move from a posture "reactive reform" to "innovative initiatives" in mission theology.

Robert Schreiter notes in his 1997 article "North American Mission Theology"[19] that "inasmuch as North American contributions to mission theology have been relatively recent, it is difficult to assess their long-term effect." The contributions have been most notable in the areas of contextual and ethnic studies, the theology of religions and inter-religious dialogue, Pentecostal theology, and church growth. But one of the most significant overarching developments is the recognition of a regional approach to mission called "North American missiology." My hope is that Lutheran theology will move beyond our present mission malaise and take up the challenge of doing theology with a vision for God's mission within the context of North American—and the world.

---

18. Edvard H. Schroeder, "Some Thoughts on Mission Drawn from Luther and the Lutheran Confessions," in *The Role of Mission in The Future of Lutheran Theology*, ed. Viggo Mortensen (Aarhus: Center for Multireligious Studies, University of Aarhus, 2003), 31.
19. Robert Schreiter, "North American Mission Theology," in Dictionary of Mission: Theology, History, Perspectives, ed. K. Muller, Th. Sundermeier, S. B. Bevans, R. H. Bliese (Maryknoll, N.Y.: Orbis, 1997), 333.

CHAPTER 18

Holy Scripture, Holy Tradition? *Ecumenical Prospects for the Lutheran Churches*

Mickey
L.
Mattox

I n his science-fiction novel *Out of the Silent Planet*, C. S. Lewis tells the story of a professor of philology, Ransom by name, a Cambridge don who is kidnapped and taken against his will on a journey to the planet Mars. Unbeknownst to Ransom, his captors intend to hand him over to the Martians, presumably so they can sacrifice him to their gods. In an insightful narrative, Lewis describes the reaction of his unlikely protagonist as he takes a first bewildered look at the fictionalized planet Mars. Forced out of the spaceship and onto the planet's surface, Dr. Ransom is not merely unprepared for *what* he sees; instead, he is unprepared to see *at all*: "The air was cold," Lewis writes, "but not bitterly so, and it seemed a little rough at the back of his throat. He gazed about him, and the very intensity of his desire to take in the new world at a glance defeated itself. He saw nothing but colors—colors that refused to form themselves into things. Moreover, he knew nothing well enough to see it: you cannot see things till you know roughly what they are."[1]

The interpretation of the Scriptures lands the Christian churches squarely in the middle of just such an interpretive circle as the one Lewis recognized in Professor Ransom's initial attempts to make sense of the Martian landscape. Recognizing the paradoxical wisdom compactly embedded in Lewis's "You cannot see things till you know roughly what they are," the world's Christians have come today to enjoy a large measure of scholarly and ecclesial consensus regarding the constructive role of church and tradition in the interpretation of Holy Scripture. Surveying the confusing landscape of the Bible, Christians are enabled to see only when they learn from the community of faith what to expect there.

The broad agreement in this matter is reflected in the statements Lutherans have issued with their ecumenical partners, statements that frequently draw attention to a shared conviction that faith in the Triune God and therefore life in Christ's church with its rich traditions of liturgy,

1. C. S. Lewis, *Out of the Silent Planet* (New York: Macmillan, 1965), 41-42.

worship, and spirituality forms the crucial hermeneutical context within which the Holy Spirit enables Christians to understand the Holy Scriptures.[2] However, this widely shared consensus has long been strictly limited among Lutherans, notably where it seems to stand in tension with the understanding of the normative function of tradition alongside Scripture, and in the role of an authoritative teaching office (*magisterium*) in interpreting the Bible.

Of course, a whole host of other contextual questions can be raised in relation to biblical interpretation, many of which have to do with readers' "social location," including issues of race, gender, and social class.[3] In addition, there is a crucially important discussion of the scope and content of the canonical Christian writings themselves.[4] In this chapter, I focus on neither of these important questions but on the classical problem of the relationship between church, tradition, and Scripture. In what follows, I sketch out this problem, examine the current ecumenical consensus and its limits, and then ask under what conditions Lutherans might in the future find sufficient grounds for reinterpreting their understanding of Scripture and tradition in a more ecumenically productive direction. Church authority, and therefore the church itself, are the underlying and deeply problematic issues toward which a consideration of the Scripture and tradition problem still lead.[5] Future ecumenical engagement on this issue will therefore increasingly challenge the Lutheran churches in their self-understanding *as churches*.

This problem has bedeviled Lutherans primarily in their relations with Roman Catholics. Quite naturally, this debate was defined in the terminology and conceptual structures characteristic of Western, Latin Christian thought. Thus, while questions of Scripture and tradition have also been addressed in Lutheran–Orthodox relations, differences between Orthodox

---

2. In the Lutheran–Roman Catholic dialogues, see the "Malta Report," paragraphs 14–30, in *Growth in Agreement: Reports and Agreed Statements of Ecumenical Conversations on a World Level*, ed. Harding Meyer and Lukas Vischer (New York: Paulist Press and Geneva: WCC, 1984), 172–75. This consensus is also clearly reflected in the American regional dialogues; see *Scripture and Tradition: Lutherans and Catholics in Dialogue 9*, ed. Harold C. Skillrud, J. Francis Stafford, and Daniel F. Martensen (Minneapolis: Augsburg, 1995). Cf. the 1985 statement on "Scripture and Tradition" in *Lutheran-Orthodox Dialogue: Agreed Statements 1985–89* (Geneva: Lutheran World Federation, 1992), 14–17.

3. These issues have been addressed ecumenically, e.g., in the 1998 Faith and Order study, *A Treasure in Earthen Vessels: An Instrument for an Ecumenical Reflection on Hermeneutics*, Faith and Order Paper 182 (Geneva: WCC). A further Faith and Order study entitled "Ecumenical Hermeneutics," is ongoing.

4. On the issue of the biblical canon, see, e.g., *Verbindliches Zeugnis*, 3 vols., ed. Pannenberg and Schneider (Freiburg im Breisgau: Herder and Göttingen: Vandenhoeck & Ruprecht, 1992–98).

5. Ecclesiological problems took center stage in the Lutheran–Roman Catholic dialogue with the publication of "Church and Justification" in 1995. For the full report, see *Growth in Agreement II: Reports and Agreed Statements of Ecumenical Conversations on a World Level, 1982–1998*, ed. Jeffrey Gros FSC, Harding Meyer, and William G. Rusch (Grand Rapids: Eerdmans and Geneva: WCC, 2000), 485–565.

and Roman Catholic ecclesiology and the understanding of tradition mean that the Lutheran-Orthodox conversation takes on a somewhat different shape and content, although from the Lutheran side many of the issues seem quite similar. Therefore, at crucial points, the following discussion draws from documents produced by Lutherans and their Roman Catholic partners and, where it helps illuminate the issues, their Orthodox conversation partners. Filling out the ecumenical circumference of the discussion somewhat, it should be noted that agreements between Lutherans and Roman Catholics and/or Orthodox would not extend automatically to Reformed Protestants. Lutherans and the Reformed have long differed over questions of the value and authority of tradition, and this difference is worthy of ecumenical exploration. However, there has not been a long history of dialogue over this problem as a crucial one in restoring unity between Lutherans and Reformed.

A Brief History of the Problem

Luther and Lutheranism

The question of the authority of Scripture in relation to the authority of church tradition(s) was at issue from early on in the Reformation. Following Luther, Lutherans leaned heavily on scriptural authority in their critique of the theology and practice of the Western church in the later Middle Ages. *Scriptura sola* eventually became one of the rallying cries for the Lutheran reform.[6] Holy Scripture, Luther had argued, was itself its own interpreter (*scriptura sacra sui ipsius interpres*), which meant most importantly that the Scriptures could bring a word of God from without or from above, so to speak, in criticism of God's church or of God's people. As a "creature of the Word" (*creatura verbi divini*), the church and its leadership, its doctors and teachers, indeed all its members, stand ever and again under the authority of the Word of God: "*ecclesia*," as others often later said, "*semper reformanda*" (the church always being reformed).

Of course, this phrase is more often and more properly associated with the Reformed tradition than with the Lutheran. Nevertheless, at least in this respect it accurately reflects the views of countless influential Lutherans.[7] Moreover, the vigorous assertion of the ongoing critical function of the Word of God did not amount to mere rhetorical posturing on the Lutheran part. Instead, in claiming for the Word authority over the church (even under the guidance of the Holy Spirit), Lutherans emphatically asserted that also in

6. The best English-language introduction to Luther as an exegete is probably still Jaroslav Pelikan's *Luther the Expositor: Introduction to the Reformer's Exegetical Writings* (St. Louis: Concordia, 1959). But see now also David C. Steinmetz, *Luther in Context*, 2nd ed. (Grand Rapids: Baker, 2002).

7. See, e.g., Krister Stendahl's "What Does It Mean to Be a Reforming Church? available at http://web.mit.edu/afs/athena.mit.edu/activity/l/lem/www/stendahl.html.

ecclesiology we must let God be God. Christ, the Word of God, is the present and effective Lord of the church and reigns over it in the power of the Holy Spirit to the glory of God the Father. Holy Scripture witnesses authoritatively to the Word who reigns, and this Word therefore retains—and not merely in principle—a critical function over against every merely human custom, even customary usages within the church itself.

There was, however, another side to Luther's approach to this problem. As a professor of Bible, he could also say, and he clearly taught his students so, that the interpretation of the Scriptures could never be reduced to a humanistic task for which one could be fitted solely by historical and grammatical training. Authentic scriptural interpretation cannot be separated from the authentic traditions of Christian faith. To the contrary, the understanding of the Scriptures as the Holy Spirit intends it depends vitally upon what we today might call the proper readerly disposition, that is, living faith in God, the Triune God whose grace and life are mediated through the proclamation of the gospel and the administration of the sacraments in the church. In more traditional Lutheran terms, faith comes by hearing (*fides ex auditu*), and this hearing happens in the proclamation of the Word of God in the worship of the congregation. One's grasp of the words of God (*verba*) therefore depends on one's prior knowledge of their substance (*notitia rerum*), that is, the reality of the faith they are intended to teach and impart.[8] This faith, moreover, is faith in Christ, so the guiding hermeneutical principle for scriptural interpretation is "whatever promotes Christ" (*was Christum treibet*).

Thus, the Scriptures as a whole can and must be read as the book of the church, one whose interpretation is summarized in authoritative creeds, catechisms, and confessions. Moreover, because there have always been Christian readers of the Bible, and because these faithful readers knew God (both cognitively and experientially), there is a tradition of faithful interpretation summarized in the church's rule of faith. The Christian interpreter enters into the company of these faithful readers, not only relying on their guidance and experience, but also building upon it. Both the rule of faith and the exegetical traditions of the faithful contribute to the task of faithful scriptural interpretation in the here and now. The critical voice of Scripture to which Lutherans wished to appeal was therefore not at all a voice from outside the church as the community of saints. To the contrary, the reforming Word of Holy Scripture makes itself heard, even in its critical function, precisely within and for the church.

---

8. On the distinction between *res* and *verba*, see Friedrich Beisser, *Claritas Scripturae bei Martin Luther* (Göttingen: Vandenhoeck & Ruprecht, 1966), 54–62. See now also my "Defender of the Most Holy Matriarchs": Martin Luther's Interpretation of the Women of Genesis in the *Enarrationes in Genesin*, 1535–1545, *Studies in Medieval and Reformation Thought 92* (Leiden: Brill, 2003), chap. 4.

Of these two trajectories in Luther's thought—a critical one pointing ahead toward modern methods of interpretation, another pointing back toward the patristic and medieval exegetical traditions—the former has probably played the greater role in Lutheran circles in the modern period among both more conservative and more liberal Lutherans. Indeed, one hears from both sides the claim that grammatical, historical and, thus, *critical* methods of exegesis are requisite to the would-be Lutheran interpreter, essential to our self-understanding, embedded in the very structure of Lutheran thought such that to think as a Lutheran about the Bible means ever and again to think historically, grammatically, and critically.

While one might take this as a plausible and perhaps even laudable construal of the Lutheran tradition—or in this case, an *anti*-tradition!—it is more historically accurate and certainly more ecumenically desirable to say with the Formula of Concord (1577) that Lutheran biblical study and reflection, critical as ever it may be, assumes as its context the authentic faith tradition of the church catholic. Thus, the Formula can assert that the Holy Scriptures are the "only rule and guiding principle according to which all teachings are to be evaluated and judged," the court of last resort for resolving conflicts within the church. In this very specific sense, the Scriptures *alone* are the *norma normans* (the normative rule) of Christian faith. However, the formulators recognized that the Scriptures are in fact never alone, never isolated from or set over against the authentic traditions of the catholic faith. Thus, while the Lutheran confessional writings speak often and critically of "human traditions" (*Menschensatzungen*), the Formula nevertheless accepts and encourages the use of the authentic extra-biblical traditions embodied in the creeds of the ancient church and the catechisms and confessional writings of the sixteenth century.

This extrabiblical tradition of faith and faithfulness in no way contradicts the Lutheran commitment to the sole final authority and sufficiency of Holy Scripture. But it does suggest that there is a long and living tradition of the faithful reading of Scripture and that Christians are at the very least well advised to familiarize themselves with it. Luther's catechisms, for example, are described as the "layman's Bible," texts that contain everything necessary and useful to know for salvation, *norma normata* (the norm, which itself is ruled) on which the Christian may safely rely. Of course the confessions also encourage reading "other writings" of other doctors and teachers, those of Martin Luther and the great church fathers, for example, particularly their exegesis. In this way, the theological and exegetical traditions of premodern catholic Christianity, broadly construed, conditioned and informed the theology and exegesis of Lutheran Christianity, that is, not as infallible extrabiblical sources of authoritative revelation but as the living testimony of the faithful dead. Although these extrascriptural written traditions are, at least in theory, fallible, the tradition of faith and faithfulness to which they bear witness is itself nothing less than the history of the work of the Holy Spirit in time—and this work never fails.

Roman Catholicism

Classically, the opposite position, that is, the position of the opposition, could be stated with equal clarity. From early on, defenders of the Roman church in the "Luther affair" insisted that an authoritative Holy Scripture required an authoritative interpreter. Left alone, in short, the Scriptures are insufficient. After the Council of Trent (1545–63), Roman Catholic theologians typically set Scripture alongside tradition as two equally authoritative sources of divine revelation. In a phrase itself amenable to quite different interpretations, the council had pronounced that the truth and discipline of the Christian faith were to be found both in the sacred books and in the unwritten traditions (*sine scripto traditionibus*) of the church. Thus, the faithful were to receive Scripture and tradition "with equal reverence" (*pari pietatis affectu ac reverentia suscipit et veneratur*).[9] Opposite the Lutheran insistence on the clarity and self-sufficiency of Holy Writ as the Word of God, the Roman church consistently insisted that Scripture alone is insufficient without the church and her magisterium to act as its authoritative interpreter and without the authoritative traditions that had been handed on orally. Importantly, however, Trent did not make clear the scope of authoritative tradition. Does this refer only to apostolic traditions that have been handed down since apostolic times? Or are new traditions developed by the church's hierarchy also included?

Tradition in Vatican II and in the Montreal Documents. While the majority of Roman Catholic theologians in the modern era seem to have understood Trent to intend a so-called two-source theory of revelation, that is, in Scripture and in tradition, Vatican II's Dogmatic Constitution on Divine Revelation, *Dei Verbum*, made clear that both Scripture and tradition "flow from the same divine wellspring." Both have their source, in other words, in the gospel of Christ, the very Word of God. As Anton Houtepen points out, *Dei Verbum* should not be understood simply as an attempt to overcome the dichotomy between either a *Scriptura sola* or a Scripture supplemented by separate written traditions.[10] Yes, Vatican II pointed toward the one tradition of the gospel, in which Scripture and the traditions of the church have their common origin. But perhaps even more important, the council fathers clearly conceived Scripture and tradition not as discrete deposits of rational truths to be believed, but as distinct aspects

9. *Enchiridion Symbolorum: Definitionum et declarationum de rebus fidei et morum*, 36th ed., ed. Henricus Denzinger and Adolfus Schönmetzer S.J. (Barcelona: Herder, 1976), no. 1501.
10. See his "Hermeneutics and Ecumenism: The Art of Understanding a Communicative God," in *Interpreting Together: Essays in Hermeneutics*, ed. Peter Bouteneff and Dagmar Heller (Geneva: WCC, 2001), 1–18; here 10.

of the one continuous tradition of the gospel, revealed in salvation history from Israel to the present day.

In the early 1960s, a similar route was taken in study papers of the World Council of Churches on the issue, most importantly in the reports and papers issued from Montreal in 1963.[11] In "Scripture, Tradition and Traditions," the WCC emphasized that both Holy Scripture and the authentic traditions of faith have their source in the Gospel, Christ himself. Attempting to articulate an appropriate vocabulary for communicating their position, they also leaned rather heavily on the distinction between capitalized and uncapitalized English language nouns:[12]

> We speak of the *Tradition* (with a capital T), *tradition* (with a small t) and *traditions* [also with a small t]. By *the Tradition* is meant the Gospel itself, transmitted from generation to generation in and by the Church, Christ himself present in the life of the Church. By *tradition* is meant the traditionary process. The term *traditions* is used in two senses, to indicate both the diversity of forms of expression and also what we call confessional traditions, for instance the Lutheran tradition or the Reformed tradition.[13]

To paraphrase somewhat, *Tradition* and *tradition* denote the Christian gospel in its *content* and in the *means and acts* by which the gospel is transmitted through time. Both these terms appeal to a common point of reference representing the gospel in its objective and actuary senses. On the other hand, *traditions* refer to something else, namely, the diverse ecclesial forms in which the gospel has found expression.

As was and still is common elsewhere in ecumenical theology, a distinction was here being made between the foundation of the Christian faith and its diverse forms (German, *Grund und Gestalt*). *Tradition* understood as the "gospel itself" or the *Grund* of the Christian faith is one: the *traditions* (*Gestalten*) in which the gospel (*Grund*) has been embodied are many. Ecumenical theology generally has relied heavily on this distinction as a crucial conceptual tool in the struggle to reunite the estranged

---

11. Apart from the Montreal documents themselves, perhaps the most important studies of the problem of tradition are Yves M.-J. Congar's magisterial essays *La Tradition et les Traditions: Essai Historique* (1960) and *Essai Théologique* (1963), published together in English translation under the title *Tradition and Traditions: The Biblical, Historical, and Theological Evidence for Catholic Teaching on Tradition* (Tunbridge Wells, England: Burns & Oates, 1966).

12. Martin Cressey points out that even in the English-language version of the Montreal reports, the writers were unable consistently to observe their own capitalization conventions, particularly when the word appears at the beginning of a sentence! See his "'Scripture, Tradition and Traditions': A Reflection on the Studies of This Issue in the 1960s," in *Interpreting Together*, 92–97.

13. P. C. Rodgers and L. Vischer eds., *The Fourth World Conference on Faith and Order, Montreal 1963*, Faith and Order Paper 42 (London: SCM, 1964), para. 39.

Christian *traditions*. In short, the distinction between the gospel and the churches is a stock element in broadly Protestant ecumenical thought, and the distinction applies not only in ecclesiology but in the understanding of Scripture in relation to tradition as well.

Even in the Montreal documents, however, this distinction had proved problematic for the Orthodox churches. For the Orthodox, the *Tradition* could not be reduced to an abstract gospel or Christ, nor could the church be reduced to a series of historically contingent, sociologically identifiable "expressions" of the gospel. Instead, the *Tradition* as such includes already "the Christian faith itself, transmitted in wholeness and purity, and made explicit in unbroken continuity through definite events in the life of the catholic and apostolic Church from generation to generation."[14] This church, the Orthodox insisted, cannot be and has never been divided. Moreover, their critique also made clear that in sharply distinguishing *Tradition* from *tradition*, that is, the gospel from the process of its transmission, Montreal ran the risk of separating, for example, the means of grace from the gospel in a manner that the Orthodox seem to have found alarming—and which probably ought to be so for Lutherans as well.

Orthodox resistance to the ecclesiology(ies) implicit in the Montreal documents also pointed toward an incoherence—a more sympathetic observer might label it a paradox—at their center, one of which participants in the study process were well aware but unable to resolve. On the one hand, none of the *traditions* is to be identified with the *Tradition*. On the other hand, the *Tradition* as such is known only by means of these *traditions*. The Christian gospel, in short, is made known in tangible historical forms—the person of the incarnate God, the Holy Sacraments, the proclamation of the Word, and so on—or it is not made known at all. The "gospel" cannot be reduced to the mere proclamation of a disembodied *kerygma* but must instead refer to concrete historical realities. The width of the gap between Orthodox and Protestant Christians on this point can perhaps most clearly be shown simply by contrasting Montreal's somewhat ethereal definition of *Tradition* with the thoroughly incarnate one of the late Orthodox theologian John Meyendorff: Tradition is the sacramental continuity in history of the communion of the saints; in a way, it is the church itself.[15] As Meyendorff's words suggest, the study of the problem of "tradition" pointed away from itself toward what remains arguably the central problem in ecumenical theology today: ecclesiology.

Interestingly, Meyendorff's compact definition approximates rather closely to the more expansive definition of tradition adopted by the international Lutheran–Orthodox Joint Commission in its 1987 statement "Scripture and Tradition." According to this agreed statement,

---

14. Ibid., 57.
15. See his *Living Tradition* (New York: St. Vladimir's, 1978). Cited in Cressey, "A Reflection," 96.

The Holy Tradition is the authentic expression of divine revelation in the living experience of the Church, the Body of the Word incarnate. The Church in its sacraments and spiritual life transmits this "euangelion" of our salvation through the operation of the Holy Spirit. Therefore, apostolic faith is not only a matter of proclamation but an incarnate faith (Heb 11:1; cf. *"enhypostatos pistis,"* Maximus Confessor, Quaestiones 25, PG 90, 336 D) in the Church.[16]

Without waxing overly enthusiastic in the matter, one might simply point out that this bilateral agreement shows that, when given the opportunity, Lutherans have willingly developed their understanding of tradition in a decidedly incarnate direction, thus solidly connecting the gospel, "Christ himself," with the process of its transmission in the means of grace in the ongoing life and faith of the church.

In addition to ecclesiological questions, the framework adopted by Montreal also suffered from what might be called a "criteriological deficit." It was inadequate to explain how one could distinguish between those *traditions* that authentically embody *Tradition* and those that express "human traditions," that is, "traditions" in which the one *Tradition* has been substantially obscured or falsified. In short, the hermeneutical function of *Tradition* in adjudicating competing claims to authentic readings of Scripture had been lost. After all, apart from a widely shared understanding of the gospel and its continuing historical embodiment in this-worldly forms, how could the *Tradition* condition or inform the Christian reading of Scripture?

Scripture and Tradition in the Recent Lutheran Dialogues

As noted above, the problem of Scripture and tradition has been addressed at varying lengths in numerous of the regional and international dialogues conducted by the Lutheran churches.[17] Perhaps the most promising result of these dialogues is that there is now general agreement regarding the primacy of Holy Scripture. In the American dialogue, for example, participants were able to conclude together that the Scriptures have a "preeminent status as

---

16. *Lutheran–Orthodox Dialogue*, 14.
17. The discussion here draws on some of the better known results of the ecumenical dialogues, including the joint declaration entitled "Kanon—Heilige Schrift—Tradition," produced by the Ökumenischer Arbeitskreis evangelischer und katholischer Theologen in Germany (1992; hereafter KHST); "Scripture and Tradition," from the American Lutheran–Roman Catholic dialogue (1995; hereafter, STe); "Communio Sanctorum," from the bilateral working group from the German Roman Catholic Bishop's Conference and the VELKD (2000; hereafter CS); and the statements from the international Lutheran-Orthodox dialogue found in *Lutheran-Orthodox Dialogue*, cited above, including "Divine Revelation" (1985; hereafter DR) and "Scripture and Tradition" (1987; hereafter ST).

the Word of God."[18] Similarly, in the German regional dialogue, Catholic representatives were able to affirm in unison with their Lutheran partners that Holy Scripture enjoys the highest honor as the final norm in matters of faith, and that as such it should be understood as *norma normans non normata* (the normative rule, which is not itself ruled).[19] Perhaps even more important, this dialogue distinguished apostolic tradition from human traditions in the church and insisted that Scripture is the criterion over against which all the churches' traditions must be tested and tried.

At the same time, Lutheran representatives have been increasingly willing to acknowledge the constructive role of church and tradition in the task of exegesis. As noted above, this reflects not only the encouraging ecumenical climate of the last few decades, but also developments in hermeneutics that emphasize the reader's side and the communitarian aspects of textual interpretation.[20] Thus, in "Divine Revelation" (1985), Lutherans and Orthodox were able to agree that

> in the Church's ongoing experience of its life in Christ, in the faith, love and obedience of God's people and their worship, the Holy Scriptures become a living book of revelation which the Church's kerygma, dogma and life may not contradict.[21]

Although the statement is rather compact, it is clear that for the writers, Scripture is open to interpretation as divine revelation within the church, and that it simultaneously exercises its critical function both within and over against the church. The necessity of an ecclesial context for biblical understanding and interpretation thus precludes neither the norming nor the reforming role of Holy Scripture.

Elsewhere, in answer to Protestant concerns, Roman Catholics have repeatedly recognized the sufficiency of Holy Scripture. The well-known German ecumenical working group of Roman Catholic and Lutheran theologians, for example, has published a joint declaration that insists that the Scriptures include the substance of the whole faith. The Bible contains all the truths of the faith necessary for salvation and makes them known as such.[22] Reaching back to the classical Catholic–Protestant impasse, participants point out that Trent itself did not deny the sufficiency of Scripture but instead insisted simply—and rightly—that the truths of Scripture can be

---

18. STe 64.
19. CS 48.
20. For an assertion of the positive relationship between interpretive community and the interpreted text written from a determinedly confessional Lutheran perspective, see James W. Voelz, "Reading Scripture as Lutherans in the Post-Modern Era," *Lutheran Quarterly* 14 (2000): 309–34.
21. DR 5.
22. KHST 3.1.1.

grasped in their completeness and fullness only in the light of tradition, a statement with which the Lutheran participants also agreed. As it was later also argued in the German regional dialogue, Scripture and tradition belong together and "can neither be isolated from one another nor placed in opposition."[23] Alternatively, as it was put already in the Malta Report of 1972, "The Scripture can no longer be exclusively contrasted with tradition, because the New Testament itself is the product of primitive tradition. Yet as the witness to the fundamental tradition, Scripture has a normative role for the entire later tradition of the church."[24]

Thus, as in the Montreal documents,[25] Lutherans and Roman Catholics have agreed that the Scriptures themselves developed historically out of the early Christian tradition. As the book of the church, the New Testament in particular proceeds from and is handed on within the church itself. Of course, the temporal sequence, church–Scripture, cannot be appealed to in order to set the church itself over Scripture, and Lutherans have attempted to be consistent about this in their dialogues. As Luther pointed out, the Word of God proclaimed by the apostles, that is, the gospel itself, precedes both church and Scripture. This Word in its proper form, moreover, is to be proclaimed and therefore belongs to the living and historically continuous reality of the church in its experience and in its ordered ministry. The *viva vox evangelii* (living voice of the Gospels) remains fundamental.

Still Divided?

Impressive as these agreements are, substantial difficulties remain. Not surprisingly, they are located just where the traditional Lutheran insistence on the self-authenticating character of the Holy Scriptures as the Word of God runs up against the Roman Catholic notion of an authoritative teaching office and, hence, an authoritative extrabiblical tradition. As noted in "Communio Sanctorum," Lutherans attempt to leave the final authority in matters of scriptural exegesis neither with the traditions of the church, nor with the church's teaching office or magisterium, but with the inherent power of the promises of God to make themselves understood. Roman Catholics, on the other hand, attempt to coordinate scriptural interpretation with authoritative tradition in such a way that the Scriptures and authentic tradition are never opposed.

---

23. CS 53
24. "The Gospel and the Church," para. 17.
25. Cf. *The Report of the Theological Commission on Tradition and Traditions*, Faith and Order Paper 40 (Geneva: WCC, 1963), 21: ". . . many theologians continue to insist on the anti-traditional formulae of early Protestantism, thus maintaining the tradition of *sola Scriptura* despite the historical actuality of *Scriptura numquam sola*! . . . The Scriptures in whose name the Reformers defied traditions as *Menschensatzungen* have their roots in tradition as *paradosis*."

Ecumenically, this problem will remain church dividing for Lutherans and Catholics only if the concept of the self-interpreting power of the Bible can be shown to be inconsistent, indeed irreconcilable, with the notion of an infallible teaching office in the church. Unlikely as it may seem that Lutherans could ever accept an *infallible* teaching office, this remains an area in which we may continue to hope for fruitful research and reflection. In this connection one must note and take seriously the oft-repeated Roman Catholic insistence that the church's tradition, understood as living and authentic interpretation of the Word of God, remains, like the church's teaching office and even the papacy itself, subordinate to the norm of Holy Scripture.[26] This means that from a Roman Catholic perspective, the church and its authoritative teaching office stand, as Luther insisted they must, ever under the authority of the Word, ready, when necessary, to be reformed. In the dialogues, however, Roman Catholics have had difficulty convincing their Lutheran interlocutors that their commitment to authoritative non-biblical tradition does not in fact set ecclesial traditions beyond the reach of potential reform. From the Lutheran perspective, this makes it seem as if Catholics improperly restrict the authority of the Word of God, subordinating it to authoritative church traditions.

Apart, therefore, from an agreement on the relationship between a self-authenticating Scripture and an infallible teaching office in the church, there can be no real agreement, no genuine consensus even of a "differentiated" kind, between Lutherans and Roman Catholics on the issue of Scripture and tradition. This reminds us that the question of authoritative teaching in relation to the church and its ministry has long bedeviled Lutheran–Roman Catholic ecumenism. These questions are in fact so deeply interrelated that the solution of one probably requires and presumes the simultaneous solution of the other. At a bare minimum, however, the dialogues to date have more thoroughly described the extent of our agreement and more carefully delimited the scope of our disagreement, and this holds out considerable promise for future Lutheran ecumenism not only with Rome, but with the Orthodox as well.

One way to begin to push forward in this area is simply to observe that important elements in the life and faith of the Lutheran churches have their origin more in customary piety and practice—*lex orandi*—than in straightforward biblical teaching. Perhaps the best example of such a practice is that of infant Baptism. Even in his Large Catechism, Luther offered only a proof from tradition for this practice. Luther's argument is that infant Baptism must be valid because, well, so many fine Christian saints were baptized as infants, including Bernard of Clairvaux, Jean Gerson, John Huss (*sic*), "and others." To deny the practice would seem to entail a denial of

---

26. See, e.g., CS, 72; KHST, 3.1.1: "Dabei bleibt das Lehramt der Kirche nach DV 10 der Autorität der Schrift als Gotteswort untergeordnet."

these saints' status as Christians, an idea Luther finds unthinkable, even blasphemous. "God has sanctified many who have been thus baptized and given them the Holy Spirit. . . . If God did not accept the Baptism of infants, he would not have given any of them the Holy Spirit."[27] The Scriptures make it clear that Baptism has been instituted by God, but the church's practice and experience make clear that the Baptism of infants is licit and pleasing to God. As a result, Lutherans have always baptized infants and have emphatically asserted the salvation of persons so baptized, in spite of the paucity of scriptural proof, *expressis verbis*, for the practice. Infant Baptism is a tradition we recognize as holy and right on account of its consistency with the gospel, its congruence with Scripture, and the generations of practice by which it has hallowed so many of the saints. Authoritative Lutheran teaching—imagine the fate of the pastor who refused to baptize infants on strict biblical grounds!—thus has its foundation in church tradition and practice that is not contradicted, even if not explicitly required, by Holy Scripture.

Perhaps the time has come for Lutherans to recognize in a binding theological decision such as this the working of their own version of an authoritative teaching office, one capable not only of commending a practice but of mandating it with a certitude sufficient for one to assume that the practice is regular, subject, to be sure, to further authentic development, but otherwise irreformable, a part of the theology and practice they believe, teach, and confess. Whether teaching infallibly could be equated with promulgating faith and practice in this way could then be discussed. The differences between such a Lutheran concept of the true church's unfailingly authentic witness and promotion of Christ and the Roman Catholic understanding of infallibility could then be examined. Perhaps the Lutheran understanding of how the church dogmatizes would end up substantially closer to the arguably more collegial Orthodox conception.[28] If so, this would make for yet another curious ecumenical alignment in which the Lutherans could join the Orthodox as a partner in the centuries-old conversation regarding the authority and ecumenical function of the Roman patriarch.

As the example of infant Baptism suggests, however, the question is not whether church traditions like infant Baptism can be confessed and taught to the people of God with confidence and authority, and therefore understood as irreversible[29] (one cannot change the decision to baptize Saint

---

27. *BC*, 462–63.

28 For a spirited argument that the Lutheran churches should chart a course toward Orthodoxy, see A. G. Roeber, "Justification, Christ and Grace: The Orthodox Future of Lutheranism," *Lutheran Forum* 34/2 (Pentecost, Summer 2000): 20–27.

29. For the notion of "irreversibility," see Robert W. Jenson, *Systematic Theology: Volume 2. The Works of God* (Oxford: Oxford Univ. Press, 1999), 238ff. To put it in Jenson's terms, infant Baptism seems to qualify as a practice on which the church stakes its "futurity."

Bernard as an infant!) and, at the very least, provisionally irreformable. Nor is the question whether such irreformable "traditions" are subject to the reforming authority of the Word of God. Instead, it simply involves which of the churches' traditions can rightly be so confessed, taught, and understood. Thus, when one questions the Roman Catholic approach to authoritative church teaching, one ought to have in mind not authoritative teaching as such but rather particular problematic teachings and the process—that is, magisterial or synodical—by which they are reached.

Clearly, the two most prominent cases of such problematic authoritative teachings are (1) the Marian dogmas of the Immaculate Conception and the Assumption and (2) papal infallibility. As has often been pointed out, the Marian dogmas seem to many Lutherans insufficiently grounded in the scriptural witness to be taught authoritatively. The notion of papal infallibility, on the other hand, seems closely connected to what seems an excessively hierarchical and potentially falsely authoritarian mode of ecclesial dogmatizing. Instead of rejecting the church's capacity for authoritative teaching, and instead of insisting on the production of biblical proof texts sufficient to establish these teachings, perhaps one ought simply to put to these traditions just the kinds of questions Martin Luther put to infant Baptism. Has Marian piety, as shaped by Roman Catholic understanding, enabled or inhibited the formation of Christian people and their witness and promotion of the gospel of Christ? Are there sufficient grounds for considering papal infallibility an authentic and therefore holy tradition, which likewise witnesses to and promotes Christ? However these questions may eventually be answered, the answers should not be allowed to obscure the fact that Lutherans, like Roman Catholics and Orthodox, have always enjoyed the benefits of an authentic, authoritative, and, yes, holy tradition.

CHAPTER 19

"Reformation" as an Assertion of the Common Christian Faith

Peter
Widmann

In this chapter, I wish to show that there are potentialities that have not yet been exhausted in the early Reformation's emphasis on the sufficiency of the commonly accepted Christian faith. Recognition hereof may be a helpful starting point for a Reformation-inspired contribution to a future ecumenical self-understanding of the church.

In Robert W. Jenson's initial statement in his chapter in this volume, he argues that Lutheran theology has a future only if it is no longer "Lutheran," if this label refers to a peculiar alteration of Christianity initiated by Luther and his followers. If Lutheranism is defined as a certain historical tradition, this tradition has no legitimacy by Luther's own standards. Rather, Lutheran theology should make an ecumenical effort toward Christian theology done by the heirs of the Reformation. This is an important point of view, which I want to stress and qualify in the following.

I recall that, in order to brand his teaching as heresy, it was Luther's adversaries who first used the label "Lutheran." Luther himself, as well as the other Reformers, always rejected this label. The whole meaning of their protestations and confessions (not least CA) was to show that their teaching and preaching was catholic (maintaining the church's unchanged faith) and orthodox (preserving the wholesome and pure doctrine).

In order to show their catholicity and orthodoxy, they certainly had to contradict important positions held by the leading authorities of the Roman church. They accused these authorities of having introduced a number of additions to the catholic teaching to the effect that people were no longer being given a clear understanding of the gospel. The Reformers' attack on the pope was directed against the implicit or explicit Roman Catholic claim that those additions, though human decrees, are nonetheless necessary for humanity's relation to God.

The critical edge in Luther's striving after true catholicity was the very fact that the Reformers disagreed with the ruling consensus expressed by the appointed hierarchy. "How can you make catholic claims when you break the all-encompassing unity of the church?" That was the question the

Reformers constantly had to answer. How is it at all possible to dissent from a consensual position without becoming arbitrary, peculiar, narrow, and in the end, heretical? According to the Lutherans, this is possible only if one can point to something implied by the accepted, common faith that is denied or blurred in the ruling interpretation of this faith.

This was Luther's criticism, which at the same time formulates the very standard by which Luther himself must be judged. Insofar as Luther, or any other Reformer, invented a peculiar understanding of the faith (maybe a "genuinely Reformation" understanding), this would have to be rejected by the magisterial Reformers' own standards. They stand and fall with their statement that their argument is based on the common Christian faith and that they were compelled to hold to it while criticizing the false teaching by the leading church authorities of their time.

Luther has sometimes described his own stance as drawing a "conclusion."[1] His insistence on "assertions" as well as his stress on "certainty" (faith as the conscience's certainty of salvation) rests on conclusions drawn from the premises of the Christian faith as witnessed in Scripture. Obviously, "to conclude" means something more here than deriving a new true statement from already accepted statements, although this ordinary meaning of conclusion, well-known from philosophy, is also covered by Luther's use of the concept.[2] The crucial conclusions in Luther, however, are not merely statements founded on other statements but rather judgements reached on the basis of the Christian faith, as clearly expressed in Scripture.[3] The Bible (always understood as the accepted expression of the Christian faith) is to be heard as speaking authoritatively and as communicating decisive judgments about humanity and world. The hearer of those judgments is now able to apply them to his or her own situation, to use them as the basis for personal conviction, and to use them as the criterion for preaching and teaching. Thus, speaking to an actual situation, Scripture reveals itself as expressing an "oral word" reaching people's hearts and minds right now.

The Reformers used the Bible—universally recognized as the foundation of catholic teaching—to identify the true, untainted meaning of this

---

1. See esp. the preface to his Latin works 1545, WA 54:183ff. It can also be noted that Luther called his 95 Theses "conclusiones" in his Resolutiones disputationum (1518), WA 1: 530ff.

2. This ordinary meaning is very important to Luther and his followers. It is essential to their practice of disputations, which heavily influenced theological reasoning, especially in polemical and exegetical works. It can be said in general that this "conclusive" trait is manifest in the doctrinal and theological character of the teaching and preaching inspired by Luther's theology.

3. This is the point of Luther's reference to the Bible; see esp. the introduction to Assertio omnium articulorum (1521), WA 7:96–99. The Bible has to be interpreted according to its own Spirit, and this means that the Scripture has to be heard as the judge over and principle for all Christian utterances. The hearer of the Word must not be content with understanding what is written but go further to the conclusion that just this Word is Christ concerning him or her now.

very teaching. By using the oldest versions of the biblical texts available to them, they simply stressed the accepted view of the Bible as the authentic witness of the prophetic and apostolic faith. They took "Scripture alone" as their slogan because they wanted to exclude alien intrusions into the body of the doctrine. Luther's challenging claim was that large parts of the tradition that the Roman church held to be expressions of catholicity were in fact not catholic. But also here the Reformers stressed the ruling view that no tradition can contradict Scripture.

If I am right in my description of Luther's decisive step, I can conclude that the whole content of his position was the common Christian faith without any specifically "Reformation" addition, subtraction, or qualification. The thesis that made it inevitable that he became a reformer of the church was precisely that this common Christian faith was sufficient: enough is enough. This meant particularly that the faith witnessed to in the Bible was a sufficiently clear basis on which to make decisions with regard to personal conscience, public preaching, and the official teaching of the church.

I therefore concur with Jenson's view quoted in the beginning with regard to the ecumenical character of a legitimate "Lutheran" theology. At the same time, I want to highlight this point in a way that does not necessarily fit with Jenson's position. If the "Lutheran" thesis is valid only insofar as it maintains the common Christian faith, then it must also be claimed that a catholic position is valid only insofar as it agrees with Luther that the common faith is enough and that it therefore functions as a critical principle over against all other developments within the church. As long as Luther's emphasis on the sufficiency of the Word is not fully recognized in the whole church, a task for a theology informed by the Reformers remains, which has relevance for ecumenical fellowship.

The ways in which the Reformers continued to insist on the common faith reflect, of course, certain limitations due to their time and environment, and not least of all the responses of their opponents. To understand these historical limitations and conditions ever more clearly is an ongoing task. The task, moreover, is to understand them so that other possibilities, which transcend these historical limitations and conditions, might be applied in other contexts.

Some of those potentialities can be summarized as follows.

Concentration on the Ultimate Meaning of Faith

If one wishes to understand the Christian message, one has to find its most far-reaching implications. Only the ultimate aspect of the Christian message reveals the liberating and unifying force of the gospel.

For the Reformers, this ultimate meaning was to be found in the gospel's ability to bring the suffering Christ to sinners in order to include them in his resurrection. This stress on the gospel can be understood only as a consequence of the definitions conceived of by the church fathers, namely, the definition of the biblical God as the Triune God, who in the Son's unity with Christ's humanity confers grace on humankind. The search for scriptural witness was never meant to undo such definitions but rather to renew them. The Bible does not speak to human beings until it tells them *one* story, the story of Christ, which can be summarized by its most far-reaching point, the resurrection of the Crucified.

This *summa* can still be formulated as "the gospel of grace," which at once defines God and human beings and serves as the focal point of the church's message. This point is ecumenically significant, because it names a maximum rather than a minimum as the unifying power of the church.

Liberating Force

The appeal to the Word of God speaking through the Bible stood against the hierarchy's claim of having the right to determine valid interpretation. It was not contested, however, that it is Christ who stands for the common Christian faith. From this common point of departure, the Reformers drew the conclusion that by hearing and believing this word wholeheartedly the hearer is qualified as "Christian" in the sense of being a person constituted by Christ's being in his or her place. The Christian has received all that Christ can give, that is, himself, and is thereby liberated from all other powers, set free to give himself/herself away in *agape*. Christ's living presence constitutes human freedom both as the individual's sovereignty over all powers and as the unselfish and voluntary commitment to the community of mutual love.

This twofold freedom is not something people can possess or take as their property. A person has to be liberated by the act of receiving Christ, the Word, so that the human person no longer belongs to herself or himself. This understanding of freedom is still the basic model for interconnecting individuality and sociality and is the church's most important contribution to human society.

Disclosing Distinctions

Luther's contribution to theology is often seen as consisting of a series of distinctions, especially between law and gospel.[4] I share this view, but only in the understanding that the distinctions serve the precise understanding

---

4. Gerhard Ebeling's article "Das rechte Unterscheiden." *Zeitschrift für Theologie und Kirche* 85 (1988): 219–58, is still worthy of study, together with the bulk of this scholar's Luther-studies. The main point of view is also elaborated in an impressive way by Eberhard Jüngel, not least of all in his main work *Gott als Geheimnis der Welt*, esp. part E (Tübingen: J. C. B. Mohr), 1977; Eng. translation: *God as the Mystery of the World* (Grand Rapids: Eerdmans, 1983).

of the common Christian faith, rather than function as additional "Lutheran" items.

In Luther's view, it is faith alone that can maintain the difference between God and human beings. Sin consists of the human attempt to undo or blur this difference in order to gain divine properties and conversely to degrade God. This vain attempt cannot be avoided by stressing the human condition bound to matter, body, and worldly circumstances, on the one hand, and the divine highness, transcendence, and supremacy, on the other. A human "interest in God" can very well entertain human self-elevation. The only way of acknowledging the difference between God and human beings is to find God in Christ. This means that God in Godself is not merely a self-assertive absoluteness; rather, God is the unity of the Father and the Son living as the Holy Spirit. The difference between God and humanity is manifest only in the Son of God becoming a human being. If we try to speak of God in abstraction and of humanity in abstraction, we distort both God's and humankind's being. We should rather speak "of the God incarnate and of humans made godly."[5]

The dogma's irrevocable union of God and man in Christ is the power to realize the salvific distinction between divine and human. In the Scholastic distinction between grace and nature, which makes the whole harmonious system of reconciling faith with reason possible, Luther found a dangerous inclination of identifying the divine with a realm far away from our own condition and finding salvation in becoming something else than human being. Against those misplaced distinctions, Luther insisted on the gospel of grace, which is not content with defining the human person as the one who has to live up to God's standard (the law); God's word takes us further in the gospel and identifies us with Christ as the person in our place. In Christ, God is the one who justifies, and the human being the one who, though a sinner, is justified.

An obvious reason why this and other distinctions have to be made is the unconditional character of the gospel, which can be summarized in a sentence such as "Grace is all." The living Christ stands for the unconditional and all-embracing grace of God, for God's love, which seeks those who are lost.

This expression of the Christian faith is threatened by deviations. If "grace" is a general principle stated indiscriminately about everybody under all circumstances, thus eliminating all concepts of demand and judgement, then grace is empty. If, on the other hand, grace is taken as discriminating between those who are fitted for grace over against others who are not, then grace is empty, too. The middle way, represented by the leading doctrines of the medieval church, was, in Luther's eyes, itself another deviation, namely, the conferring of grace through a balanced system of

5. See the whole passage in the Anti-Latomus WA 8:126.

guarantees and conditions securing the way to final salvation. Such a middle way can only create uncertainty because one never knows when one has done enough for being worthy of grace.

The distinction between law and gospel is necessary to maintain the gospel of grace without emptying it. The grace of God meets a person as grace only if it means forgiveness of nothing less than the person's guilt in the face of God. Only such grace is all-embracing and unconditional. This grace can only be spoken of as bridging a gap between God and humanity, between God's gracious will and the human resistance of this will. In this it is implied that God's grace faces a situation in which God already has chosen humankind. God's law means the constitution of humanity as God's partner, and as people who should live in accordance with God's purpose. Grace is responding to the dialogue with God, which is interrupted by sin, and grace is overcoming the division between God and humankind.

The distinction between law and gospel is important also in regard to the church's task of preaching and teaching. The gospel of grace has its time when people are aware of the disgrace that they are not acting in accordance with God's will and therefore seek God's forgiveness and are ready to forgive others. As long as people do not feel this need, the proclamation of God's law has its time. This is especially true in the situation of social injustice, when one group lives at the expense of another. The call of the church is here to make God's demands clear: to call for justice and at the same time to prepare the conditions in which the gospel of forgiveness can be heard again.

Other important distinctions, such as the twofold "use" of the law, the two realms, and so on, have a similar clarifying and disclosing function with regard to the common Christian faith.

Inclusiveness Made Possible by Exclusions

These distinctions are the background of the marked exclusions in Reformation theology: Christ alone, grace alone, faith alone. They have often been contrasted with the acceptance of more inclusive terms so characteristic of the Catholic tradition: Christ *and* humanity, grace *and* human freedom, faith *and* love. Admittedly the Protestant exclusions often functioned as a divisive principle that violated the unity of the common Christian faith.

Nevertheless, a specific use of exclusions is necessary to maintain the common faith and especially its all-embracing character revealing itself in *agape*. In this respect, the exclusions of the Reformation set a task for the future.

Christ alone: this excludes every possibility to define God and human beings apart from each other. By this exclusion all true inclusions are made possible, founded on the acceptance of the unacceptable in Christ.

Grace alone: this excludes every possibility of coming to God without the recognition that God has overcome the division between God and humanity through the life and death of Christ. All other possibilities must vanish in order to open up for the only saving possibility.

Faith alone: this excludes the possibility, through human activity, of receiving grace prior to grace. Otherwise, one cannot receive the gift of Christ taking one's place on the cross. This does not at all mean that human activity is without worth; on the contrary, the one who receives grace is freed to use all his or her possibilities in the service of *agape*.

We cannot speak of God unless we eliminate elements contrary to God's own Word; those corrupting contradictions have to be excluded. This exclusiveness is not necessarily a rejection of other religions. The point is not: "Our God, not yours; our Savior, not yours; our faith, not yours." The point is rather: "Our God, who *is* God, the Creator and Savior of all." When we encounter another religion, we expect it to make similar claims to our own. We can then ask each other whether we are really speaking of the same God.

These potentialities in Reformation theology have a future if they are used to actualize the common Christian faith. At the same time, they can serve as critical principles to analyze and correct the historical developments both in Protestantism and in other traditions.

WORLD

Part VII

THE REFORMATION MOVEMENT rearranged the relationship between God and world. According to the Small Catechism, even the world's most daily things are to be considered as gifts of the creative God, to be received and to be used in ongoing communication. On the one hand, nothing is left outside of the manifold relationship between God and human beings. On the other hand, nothing should blur the fundamental difference between worldly gifts and the divine giver, creation and Creator.

Construing creation as communion, Oswald Bayer takes his point of departure in the process of a divine action that meets human beings in an effective address. Transcending a theistic-personalist theology beginning with the "creator-subject," Bayer focuses on the "creator verb," making God's *promissio* the common category of both God's creative and salvific work. In a discussion with process philosophy and theology, the process aspect is reformulated as a necessary narrative dimension of creation, overcoming the dualism between nature and history, and securing the distinction between Creator and creation.

The much disputed question about a third use of the law, directing the Christian's involvement with the world while opposing evil, is the pivotal point in Eric W. Gritsch's proposal of a new catechism built up around Matt 10:16. Following the *Book of Concord* rather than Luther, he sketches out in the form of a catechism how "justification by faith" through Word and Sacraments becomes both a liturgy on Sunday and a discipline on Monday morning for Lutheran congregations.

The doctrine of the two kingdoms has been the major Lutheran model for handling the differentiation between God as giver and God's earthly gifts. From a Nordic perspective, Jan-Olav Henriksen discusses several possible functions of this doctrine, including the secularization and privatization of religious belief in an increasingly pluralistic world. In a differentiated society, where strategic or functional approaches have made content less important, the Lutheran churches have to recognize their new role and deal with the negative consequences of aspects of its own heritage, such as individualism and skepticism toward institutions.

Paul Chung brings the discussion back to the issue of earthly justice. Chung argues that Luther's teaching on justification cannot be understood without reference to his socioeconomic considerations regarding social justice. Neither can Luther's doctrine of justification be understood apart from his explanation of the church as fellowship. When interpreted as the recognition of "the other" as "otherness," the doctrine can be seen as reflecting a theology of solidarity and recognition. It is further demonstrated how a cosmic interpretation of Luther's theology of the cross could be the place where Asian theology and spirituality meet the very heart of Luther's theology.

These chapters show ways for handling and understanding the intimate relationship between creation and Creator. They also demonstrate how the doctrine of the two kingdoms is both a challenge to the church, with regard to the historic consequences of this very doctrine, and also how it contains the potential for a fruitful reconstruction of Lutheran theology, allowing the world its manifold character.

—Bo Holm

CHAPTER 20

Creation as History

Oswald Bayer

The Verb

Creation means the establishing and preservation of communion. This thesis[1] relates critically to the usual view that follows the scheme of causality and, simultaneously, of Indo-Germanic grammar. It suggests that we first inquire into the subject of creation (*poietes*), the Triune God, and afterward into the predicate, that is, creation as act (*poiein*), and finally into the object, the outcome, the finished work (*poiema*). In contrast to this way of proceeding, the following reflections focus on the verb "to create": on the process (or event; in German, *Geschehen*) of *poiein*, which—to a certain extent still open to further specification—is marked by its communicative character.

This character is situated within the linguistic form of the dialogue between Creator and creature as well as between the creatures themselves; "Day to day pours forth speech, and night to night declares knowledge" (Ps 19:2). Creation as communion takes place as address to the creature by the Creator, so that the creature may answer and pass on to the fellow creatures through word and deed what he or she has heard and received. This takes place within hearing and speaking, reading and writing in their temporal and local constitution, within times and spaces permeating each other—themselves, too, being creatures, by which the Creator addresses us.

What does it mean not to set out from a creator-subject—to be pinned down beforehand in a theistic-personalistic manner—but from the *process* of divine action in the form of an effective address? This can be learned from Luther's explanation of the creation article of the Creed in the Small Catechism. First, Luther speaks of the process of divine granting; then the ground of this giving, the Giver himself, is spoken of: "and all this out of mere paternal, divine goodness and mercy."

---

1. For further reference cf. Oswald Bayer, "Schöpfer/Schöpfung VIII: Systematisch-theologisch," *Theologische Realenzyklopädie* (*TRE*) vol. 30 (Berlin and New York: De Gruyter, 1999), 326–48.

Setting out from the process of giving, through which God gives himself wholly and fully, Luther then speaks of God's "attributes," of his goodness and mercy. This way of proceeding is remarkable, for the doctrine of creation is usually fixated on nouns, inquiring into the subject of creation and its attributes, which are then, in a secondary step, added as accidentals to the subject (supposed to be existing in itself beforehand). The trouble is that, along these lines, theological thinking and speaking become stiff and petrified. Therefore, nouns have time and again to be liquefied, transformed back into verbs. If God's attributes cannot be *narrated* vividly and dramatically anymore, then they are nothing but timelessly stiff and pale conceptual fetishes.

Creation is paradigmatically narrated as history—as a (hi)story (*Geschichte*) of wondrous salvation—in Paul Gerhardt's morning hymn "Awake, My Heart, and Sing."[2] This hymn praises creation by praising the morning of creation that overcomes the night of chaos. It does so in telling, through prayer, a (hi)story that has happened:

> 2. Tonight, when enshrouded
> by shadows, dark and clouded,
> the devil tried to seize me,
> God kept him far and set me free.

> 3. You said, "My child, now lie down,
> despite cheating Satan's frown,
> sleep well, and be not terrified,
> you'll see the sun after the night."

> 4. Your word, it has become true,
> now I can see the light anew;
> of anguish I've been set free,
> your loving care renewed me.

At the beginning and at the end of this creation (hi)story, told in the mode of a prayer of praise, two situations are recounted that do not just differ relatively from each other, but are opposed in the extreme—as shade and sun, darkness and light, cheating and truth, constriction and redemption, old and new. The "mediation" of these extremes takes place through a turn. Through this turn recounted in the center, actually *as* the center of the story, this (hi)story receives its unity. It is characteristic of this turn that it is not caused by the "me" of the narrator but happens to him in the course of his

---

2. *Evangelisches Gesangbuch* no. 446 ("Wach auf, mein Herz, und singe"). For a more elaborate interpretation, cf. Oswald Bayer, *Schöpfung als Anrede: Zu einer Hermeneutik der Schöpfung* (Tübingen: Mohr Siebeck, 1990), 109–27.

being addressed. Thus, the address recounted in the third stanza—forming a downright promise, a *promissio* ("My child, now lie down / despite cheating Satan's frown . . .")—is the pivotal point of the whole (hi)story. It displays paradigmatically that and how creation *happens* as address and therefore seeks to be *recounted* through the narration of praise.[3]

Where Process Philosophy Is Right

The one who conceives of creation as history, as Paul Gerhardt does, will take a critical stance over against the strict distinction, even diastasis, that broke up in the second half of the nineteenth century between creation or nature, on the one side, and history, on the other. By the end of that century, it lead to drawing boundaries between the methods of "humanities" and those of "sciences," a boundary, according to which sciences were to "explain" and humanities to "interpret": "We explain nature, but the life of the soul we interpret."[4] The recent discourse of the philosophy of nature tries to bridge this chasm; thus, Carl Friedrich von Weizsäcker speaks of the "history" of nature.[5] And vice versa, one tries to overcome the isolation of humanities from natural sciences by restoring, in principle, the nexus between the sciences' theories of evolution and the humanities' theories of history.[6] This nexus had already been advocated by J. G. Herder, but radically rejected by I. Kant, who insisted on this dualism.[7]

Herder's intention, in substance, has in recent times been picked up and carried on by process philosophy and theology. When striving to understand creation as history in the way outlined above, we may well in the first instance welcome process philosophy as an ally. Alfred North Whitehead,

3. Cf. the difference between "narrating" and "describing" praise suggested by Claus Westermann, *Das Loben Gottes in den Psalmen* (Göttingen: Vandenhoeck und Ruprecht, 1951); Claus Westermann, *Praise and Lament in the Psalms* (Atlanta: John Knox, 1977). The task of elaborating the systematic-theological significance of this distinction has not yet been accomplished. The issue at stake is the one hinted at above when distinguishing verbs, on the one hand, from nouns and adjectives, on the other.

4. Wilhelm Dilthey, "Ideen über eine beschreibende und zergliedernde Psychologie," in *Gesammelte Schriften*, vol. 5: *Die geistige Welt. 1. Abhandlungen zur Grundlegung der Geisteswissenschaften* (Leipzig: Teubner, 1990 [1924]), (138–240) 144. In his introduction to his book on Jesus (1926; English trans., *Jesus and the Word*), Rudolf Bultmann substantially adopts this distinction, which in fact is a separation.

5. Carl Friedrich von Weizsäcker, *Die Geschichte der Natur: Zwölf Vorlesungen* (Stuttgart: Hirzel, 1948).

6. However, there is today also a "tendency of raising the model of evolution to the level of a paradigm for the whole understanding of reality, of a basis for a merger of sciences and humanities" (Reinhold Bernhardt, "Die Soziobiologie als Anfrage an die Theologie," *Theologische Zeitschrift* 58 (2002), (172–88), 173.

7. This rejection can be seen at best in Kant's 1785 review of Johann Gottfried Herder, "Ideen zur Philosophie der Geschichte der Menschheit." Immanuel Kant, *Werke in 10 Bänden*, ed. Wilhelm Weischedel (Darmstadt: Wissenschaftliche Buchgesellschaft, 1970), 10:781–94.

for instance, insists in *Process and Reality* (1927) on a liquefaction of the thinking of substance and noun, comparable with the philosophy of Hegel[8] and opposed to the Aristotelian monarchic principle of the world. Thus, so to say, Whitehead in his way brings to bear the prevalence of the verb before the noun.

In doing so, he deals with the problem of the relationship between singularity and plurality—a problem already reflected upon in Plato's *Parmenides* and which can be avoided neither by philosophy nor by theology—in an instructive and stimulating way. While theological as well as philosophical tradition have usually been pledged to the concept of unity and have striven, in a Parmenidean fashion, to conceive of God as *ens simplex* (unified entity), Whitehead's process philosophy insists on an antideterministic interplay of God's "primordial nature" with his "subsequent nature." Thus, he can do justice to the contingencies of the single "events" in their plurality. The chaos theories of our time are further enforcing the antideterministic element when focusing on instability and on nonpredictability of single events.

From process philosophy, one may learn to perceive complexity and not to precipitately dissolve the plurality of (hi)stories into the singular "history."[9] However, the sense in which it is necessary to employ the singular when speaking of "creation as history" will be elaborated below. For now I stress that we do not possess "God's (hi)story as (a) meta-story." "Rather, the talk of God's history is an abbreviated way of talking of the plurality of concrete stories by which humans experience being addressed by God."[10]

A further reason why process philosophy may be called an ally of a theological doctrine of creation is its antideistic attitude. Process philosophy does not reduce the creator to a "prima causa (efficiens)" (primary [efficient] cause), conceived as an initial ignition. Instead, in its own way, it brings to bear what Luther—in a fashion very similar to Spinoza[11]—designated as the persistent and intense presence and this-worldliness of the

---

8. Cf. Friedrich Kambartel, "The universe is more various, more Hegelian"; "Zum Weltverständnis bei Hegel und Whitehead," in *Collegium Philosophicum*; Festschrift for Joachim Ritter, ed. Ernst-Wolfgang Böckenförde et al. (Basel and Stuttgart: Schwabe, 1965), 72–98.

9. The collective singular *"Geschichte"* emerged between 1750 and 1770. Cf. Reinhart Koselleck, "Geschichte V.: Die Herausbildung des modernen Geschichtsbegriffs," in *Geschichtliche Grundbegriffe: Historisches Lexikon zur politisch-sozialen Sprache in Deutschland*, vol. 3, ed. Otto Brunner, Werner Conze, and Reinhart Koselleck (Stuttgart: Klett, 1975), 647–91.

10. Gunda Schneider-Flume, *Leben ist kostbar: Wider die Tyrannei des gelingenden Lebens* (Göttingen: Vandenhoeck & Ruprecht, 2002), 67. Cf. ibid., 114 ("overall perspective").

11. "I claim, namely, that God is the immanent, as one says, but not the externally effective cause of all things. Everything, I say, is in God and is moved within God, as I claim together with Paul [Acts 17:28]" (Baruch Spinoza to Heinrich Oldenburg, November or December 1675, in Franz Kobler, *Juden und Judentum in deutschen Briefen aus drei Jahrhunderten*, 1935 (repr. Königstein: Athenaeum, 1984), 33. Cf. Bayer, *Schöpfung VIII* (see above, n. 1), 331, 6–28.

"Deus actuosissimus":[12] God is incessantly at work in the world. He remains immanent to his work, which is to be conceived verbally as a "working," and does not cease to work new things. In the sense of this "working," Whitehead even, in drawing on Plato's *Timaios* 28c, can call God the "poet of the world": "He is the poet of the world, with tender patience leading it by his vision of truth, beauty and goodness."[13]

Theology of Creation and Process Philosophy in Dispute

The dispute between a theology of creation and process philosophy arises where the understanding of "poet" is further inquired into. In what sense is God the "poet of the world"? And what does his salvific working consist of, which for Whitehead constitutes, yes, is even identified with the very essence of God's being the Creator?[14]

God as Poet

Though the title of "poet" has a kinship to linguistic phenomena, this linguistic element is not really attended to by Whitehead. Rather, he says that God creates and saves the world "by patiently exercising the overwhelming rationality of his conceptual [!] harmonizing"[15]—but not by sensibly addressing the creature through the creature.[16] Process philosophy, together with the theologies that follow it, underestimates the principally linguistic and, linked to this, forensic basic feature of those processes forming created life. Paradigmatic utterances of these processes can be found in Psalms 96 and 98, as well as in the saying of Anaximander.[17]

For Luther, God's trustworthy, faith-creating address, his *promissio*, is not only the fundamental category when speaking of the sacraments and the sermon, but also in view of the realm of creation—which has only recently

---

12. WA 18:747, 25; cf. 711, 1; LW 33:233, 7 (*On the Bondage of the Will*, 1525).

13. Alfred North Whitehead, *Process and Reality: An Essay in Cosmology Corrected Edition* (New York: Free Press, 1929), 346 [526].

14. God "does not [only] create the world, he saves it; or rather: He is the poet of the world. . ." (ibid.).

15. Ibid. However, the broad semantics of "conceptual" are to be taken into account.

16. Johann Georg Hamann, "Aesthetica in nuce" (1762), in *Sämtliche Werke: Historisch-kritische Ausgabe*, ed. Josef Nadler; 6 vols. (Vienna: Herder, 1949–1957), henceforth cited as "N." Here: N vol. 2 (1950), 198, 29: "Schöpfung" as "Rede an die Kreatur durch die Kreatur." On the interpretation of this formula cf. Bayer, *Schöpfung als Anrede* (see above, n. 2), 9–32.

17. "The source from which existing things derive their existence is also that to which they return at their destruction, according to necessity [or obligation]; for they give justice [or punishment] and make reparation to one another for their injustice, according to the arrangement of time" (Anaximander of Milet, in *Fragmente der Vorsokratiker*, vol. 1, ed. Hermann Diels and Walther Kranz, 5th ed. [Berlin: Weidmann, 1951], 80 [no. B1]). Kathleen Freeman, trans. and ed., *Ancilla to the Pre-Socratic Philosophers: A Complete Translation of the Fragments in Diels*, Fragmente der Vorsokratiker (Oxford: Blackwell, 1948), 19. Cf. Oswald Bayer, *Living by Faith: On Justification and Sanctification* (Grand Rapids: Eerdmans, 2003), 6.

been rediscovered in Luther research. However, transferring the category of *promissio* to the realm of creation gives rise to some problems: Is it really possible to use one and the same category to designate God's cosmic work and his salvific work?

The thesis that Luther conceives of creation as a linguistic and salvific phenomenon is more than just an interpreter's invention. It can be proved, for instance, by giving heed to his translation of verse 4b in the psalm of creation Psalm 33: "For the word of the LORD is truthful, and what he promises, he certainly keeps." This translation provides a key to Luther's understanding of creation, for the Hebrew text, in a noun clause, merely speaks of God's "work" taking place "in truth." With his bold rendering, Luther witnesses that God's work of creation is not just a work but a speaking work. God's work speaks itself—it is *sui ipsius interpres*, making itself understandable. It is the effective word of address—a work through which God's truthfulness can be heard; it is a pledge and promise.

Through his trustworthy, reliable, and loving word, God rules the world. The one who responds to the word and lives by it has faith. The one who closes oneself to the word will experience that heart, mouth, and hand close themselves as well. The whole world becomes too narrow for such a person. Such a person experiences fear and suffers God's wrath. For then, the world is no more the medium of a promise to me, by which I am—addressed by God—placed within a granted space of life, a granted rhythm of day and night, summer and winter, youth and old age, a grant I may enjoy and savor. If the world is not believed as promised, then it is experienced as "horrible naturality,"[18] as an inexorably pressing, forcing law that demands: "You have to make sense of this chaos, of this horrible naturality in all its vagueness! You must first give a sense to this world which is chaotic in and of itself! It is you who first has to establish order." If the world is not believed as promised, then it turns into "a thousand deserts, mute and cold,"[19] as Friedrich Nietzsche aptly says. In such falling silent and such coldness of the world, God's wrath is experienced—albeit in such an anonymous way that it may not be identified as *God's* wrath. All creatures around me—be it just a rustling leaf terrifying me[20]—announce and speak of this wrath, above all my own heart in its defiance and its desperation. Luther does not know of a neutral sphere "beyond" wrath and grace. This is the reason for the fundamental ambivalence of his feeling of world, of his language and his understanding

18. Arnold Gehlen, *Anthropologische Forschung: Zur Selbstbegegnung und Selbstentdeckung des Menschen* (Reinbek: Rowohlt, 1961), 68.

19. Friedrich Nietzsche, *Der Freigeist*, Part 1: "Abschied," stanza 3 (autumn 1884) in *Werke: Krit. Gesamtausgabe*, ed. Giorgio Colli and Mazzino Montinari (Berlin and New York: de Gruyter, 1974), 7/3:37

20. Luther frequently quotes Lev 26:36, e.g., LW 45:58 ("A Sincere Admonition"); WA 8:677, 3f. ("Eine treue Vermahnung"; 1522).

of history. This is where the struggle is rooted that has to be fought and was fought by Luther throughout his lifetime.

Luther did not give in to the temptation to search for a clarity other than that of the reliable word of promise. Therefore, the world is not perspicuous to him, not through and through calculable and disposable; his theology is unyielding to any historical-philosophical speculation of unity. To the extent to which his theology contradicts such speculations—for instance, the illusion of a constant progress of world history—it is sober, realistic, and full of concrete experience of the world.

Thus, the much-invoked but frequently misunderstood "worldliness" of Luther is something thoroughly theological. For with this worldliness the world is perceived as created by God's reliable word and preserved throughout constant threats. This perception is a forensic one—a perception of judgment and grace.

As opposed to Luther's view, the Calvinist-Reformed tradition tends to conceive of God as a transcendental authority, acting, so to say, vertically from above, almost a mute causality. The realm of the creatures, correspondingly, is here "related to God primarily in the mode of dependence";[21] Schleiermacher's "feeling of absolute dependence" is to be seen within this Reformed tradition. No matter how much "the world of creatures is constantly exposed to the acting of the creator and mirrors his omnipotence," still the Reformed view "cannot think of the Creator's might as something that could itself become a creature. Lutheran theology, on the other hand, without confining God's freedom, interprets the reality of creation mainly as a communicative connection."[22] It is not only in the redemption of the world, but already in its creation that God humbles himself, pours himself out, fully and wholly gives himself away. His omnipotence is humble. Creation is God's fully giving himself, as pledge and promise—as establishment and preservation of communion, and in this sense as an event of word and language!

The trace of such an understanding of creation as communicative connection can still be seen today in concepts that conceive of the world as readable text.[23] This is the case, however, in differing grades of intensity and metaphorical discourse—right down to the talk of the "genetic code" or to the use of the term "information," which cannot be totally abstracted from the linguistic realm.

When facing the two extremes dominating today's theologies of creation—abstract personalism here, immanentist Spinozism there—we may gain decisive insights from the Old Testament scholar Luther. On the one hand, he firmly clings to the verbal, addressing character of creation when

---

21. Johannes von Lüpke, "Schöpfer/Schöpfung VII. Reformation bis Neuzeit," *TRE* 30:305–26, here 312.
22. Ibid.
23. Cf. Hans Blumenberg, *Die Lesbarkeit der Welt* (Frankfurt: Suhrkamp, 1981).

rooting his position in God's primordial promise, "I am the LORD, your God."[24] Simultaneously, on the other hand, he points out that the Creator is present in his creation in freely chosen immanence and thoroughgoing this-worldliness: God is no less present "in the hole of a beetle or even in a sewer than in Heaven."[25] Both instances, that of immanence and that of address, inseparably belong together.

If now creation is to be conceived in the way a theology of the word does it, and accordingly to be reflected on by means of a philosophy of language, then it ipso facto can be perceived and thought as "history." "History" then interprets what happens (*geschehen*) or the events (*Geschehnisse, Geschichten*), not in a causal-mechanical way as a mere sequence of effects, but as an interplay of "challenge and response," to use the apt phrase by Arnold Toynbee. To be sure, "(hi)stories" do not merely take place in the human realm but wherever conditions of granting and granted freedom prevail. Though humans in a special way are granted with the "critical and archontic dignity of a political animal,"[26] i.e., humans especially are historic beings, yet in a graduate way also animals and plants, even the seemingly inanimate creatures participate in that freedom granted to them by God—at least they display analogies with human freedom.[27] In this sense, together with the biblical primordial narrative and the psalms of creation, through a theology of the word the whole creation can be perceived and conceived as history.

Categorical Distinction

If we interpret creation by means of a theology of the word, we presuppose, to be sure, a fundamental and categorical distinction: the distinction between Creator and creature. Process philosophy and process theology tend to blur, even to de facto evaporate this distinction—and this is, after the underestimation of linguistic phenomena, my second objection—by speaking of gradual transitions. In opposition to this view, in all process and temporal-spatial extension of creation histories happening ever anew, the distinction between original being and imparted being is still to be acknowledged. This means to acknowledge and to bear in mind when thinking a distinct sequence and difference: "Original being is truth, imparted being is

---

24. Exod 20:2; *BSLK* 647, 36–38 (Large Catechism).

25. LW 33:45 (*On the Bondage of the Will*, 1525); WA 18:621, 16–18. Luther adopts a provocative sentence of Erasmus ("On Free Will," I a9) and intensifies it.

26. Hamann, *Philologische Einfälle und Zweifel* (1772), N 3 (1951), 39, 17f. (italics removed); cf. 37, 24f. Hamann, in this formula, poignantly links Aristotelian tradition with an exposition of the biblical primordial narrative. Cf. Oswald Bayer, *Zeitgenosse im Widerspruch: Johann Georg Hamann als radikaler Aufklärer* (Munich and Zurich: Piper, 1988), 108–37.

27. Cf. Hans Jonas, *Philosophische Untersuchungen und metaphysische Vermutungen* (Frankfurt and Leipzig: Insel-Verlag, 1992), esp. 13–25.

grace."[28] An understanding of creation informed by a theology of the word thus leads us to give a justification-theological account of the difference between Creator and creature and of the irreversibility of their relation. As all other creatures, the human is that being which is in need of justification but unable to justify himself or herself. God, on the other hand, the Creator, is the one who justifies by categorically giving—*ex mera bonitate*.[29]

It is only from this fundamental stance, from this distinction between Creator and creature perceived by a theology of justification, that Christian theology can then tell in what way Creator and creature are closely and totally together, yes even—through a communication of idioms—intertwined and folded into each other: *Creator et creatura unus et idem est* (Creator and creature are one and the same)[30] does not hold true as a general definition of creation as history but only on the horizon of the specific story of Jesus Christ. This specific story, which turns out to be the center and criterion of all other stories—yet without becoming a "metanarrative" that would force all others to submit[31]—is not perceived by process theology. The same applies to the sacrament. In process theology, either the whole world is declared to be sacramental[32] or the specific sacrament can only be one "event" among others.

Surely, we live in a plurality of (hi)stories; indeed, we ourselves are woven into them. Life does not happen monotonously in a single perspective but discloses ever anew a wealth of possibilities and chances. This is the optimistic perspective postmodern philosophy prefers to adopt. But from this perspective, one does not see "how everything is not of sugar," as Döblin says in "Berlin Alexanderplatz," "but of sugar and dirt and all mixed up."[33] He works "life and death and all in all"; that is what Luther says of the *deus absconditus* (hidden God).[34] The one happens to me as well as the other; many stories occur in my story—often simultaneously. They overlap, collide, and come into conflict with each other. When facing such plurality and diversity of stories, the question arises, Who or what keeps me from getting lost in their ambivalence and uncertainty in the face of my own failure or of the death of whole peoples?

28. Johann Georg Hamann, *Briefwechsel*, ed. Walther Ziesemer and Arthur Henkel [ZH], vol. 5 (Wiesbaden: Insel-Verlag, 1965), 271, 28f.; to Friedrich Heinrich Jacobi, Dec. 1, 1784.

29. *BSLK* 511, 4 (Latin translation of Luther's exposition of the First Article of the Creed in the Small Catechism).

30. WA 39/2:105, 6f. (*Disputatio de divinitate et humanitate Christi*, 1540).

31. On this problem, cf. Joachim von Soosten, "Arbeit am Dogma: Eine theologische Antwort auf Hans Blumenbergs 'Arbeit am Mythos,'" in Oswald Bayer, ed., *Mythos und Religion* (Stuttgart: Calwer Verlag, 1990), 80–100.

32. On this problem, cf. Bayer, *Schöpfung als Anrede* (see above, n. 2), 30–32.

33. Alfred Döblin, *Berlin Alexanderplatz: Die Geschichte vom Franz Biberkopf* (Munich: Deutscher Taschenbuchverlag, 1972 [1929]), 392.

34. LW 33:40. (*On the Bondage of the Will*, 1525); WA 18:685, 22f.

It is the criteriological power of the Creator's word folded into the creature's word and element that, in the midst of a plurality of (hi)stories, creates assurance of salvation[35] and only thus gives meaning, even necessity, to
the use of the singular "history." This criteriological power is brought to
bear solely at that one contingent point, one that is of universal importance,
called "Jesus Christ." It is brought to bear solely here, but here wholly and
fully. In Whitehead the talk of God's truth, beauty, and goodness has no certain place, no unequivocal, assuring identity, locality, and personality, but is
extended to the whole world process. But Jesus Christ, precisely as an "accidental truth of history"[36] (from the external perspective) is the "concretum
universale" (the concrete universal).

The Center

We can evade the compulsion of a unity concept, of a metanarrative subdu-
ing other narratives only if we do not set out in thinking from an absolute
origin nor toward an ultimate goal but out of a given center. We have to take
our start from a key event that encompasses the meaning of the preceding
and the following events, simultaneously prefiguring their final perfection.

It is all too easy to turn the talk of being seized by such a perfection of
(creation) history into an arbitrary and illusionary anticipation of the end.
To avoid this danger, I have to be presently transferred and relocated (cf. Col
1:13) into the center of the whole (creation) history. With J. G. Hamann
(1730–88), we can see in Homer's poetic strategy a parable of God's speaking and acting as history. "Our lives," even the history of the whole creation,
"become similar to the *Iliad*," beginning with Homer immediately transferring his reader into the center of the whole story, "if a higher Muse rules over
their threads from the spindle of the first goddess of destiny right through to
the scissors of the last—and inscribes them into the fabric of her drafts."[37]

So, in no way do we talk of placing ourselves at the center of (hi)stories
that would thus become history (in the singular!), such as to self-referentially
produce the origin and the goal and to become creators of ourselves. Nor do
we talk of always already finding such a center within the self, as, for
instance, the "immediate presence of the whole, undivided . . . being
(*Dasein*)."[38] Nor, third, we do not strive to perceive this center as an isolated

---

35. On the following, cf. Oswald Bayer, "Systematische Theologie als Wissenschaft der
Geschichte," in *Autorität und Kritik: Zu Hermeneutik und Wissenschaftstheorie* (Tübingen:
Mohr Siebeck, 1991), 181–200, here 194f.
36. Gotthold Ephraim Lessing, "Über den Beweis des Geistes und der Kraft" (1777), in *Werke*,
ed. Herbert Göpfert; 8 vols. (Munich: Hanser, 1970–1979), 8:12.
37. ZH 1 (1955), 360, 36—361, 2 (in the context of 360, 21ff.); to his brother, July 5, 1759.
38. Heinrich Steffens, *Von der falschen Theologie und dem wahren Glauben: Eine Stimme aus
der Gemeinde* (Breslau: Max, 1823), 99f. Cf. F. D. E. Schleiermacher, *Der christliche Glaube
nach den Grundsätzen der evangelischen Kirche im Zusammenhange dargestellt*, ed. Martin
Redeker (Berlin and New York: de Gruyter, 1960), 1:17 (§3.2); Friedrich

"instant" (*Augenblick*),[39] thus mistaking the wealth of creation's communicative coherence; an isolated instant would be "nothing but a dead torso deprived of head and feet."[40] The center into which we are transferred is a wholly specific key event: it is the word that became flesh, imparting itself to us. "Every philosophical contradiction and the whole historic riddle of our existence, the impenetrable night of its termini a quo and termini ad quem, are solved by the primordial announcement or charter (*Urkunde*) of the word become flesh."[41]

The German word "*Urkunde*" by a fortunate coincidence draws our attention to both the literally definitive character and oral vividness of the bodily linguistic event of Jesus Christ imparting himself to us. As the "primordial charter" (*Urkunde*), he vouchsafes the truth. "Truth" is thus not any longer understood, as an old and powerful tradition has it, in the sense of a priori evidence. It is removed from the sphere of spell surrounding that type of apodictic, purely anamnetic certainty of which mathematics is the prototype.[42] Now, truth is the truth of that historic "record of the word become flesh." Thus we can speak "of no [other] eternal truths but of those interminably temporal,"[43] for the primordial record of those truths as "history" and "narrative" "bears within itself" the end and "the origin of all things. Thus a historical plan of a science is always better than a [purely] logical one,"[44] which would just explain things. Hamann says this precisely in view of those sciences dealing with nature. If we want to perceive nature as creation—explaining through narrating and through the address that occurs within this narrating—and understand creation as history, then we need to specify that an explanation without narrative would be blind as well as that a narrative without explanation would be empty.[45]

Translated by Martin Abraham

Schleiermacher, *The Christian Faith*, trans. H. R. MacIntosh and J. S. Stewart (Edinburgh: T & T Clark, 1989), 6–7.

39. Thus, following Søren Kierkegaard: Rudolf Bultmann, *Geschichte und Eschatologie* (Tübingen: Mohr Siebeck, 1958), 184; Rudolf Bultmann, *History and Eschatology, The Gifford Lectures 1955* (Edinburgh: The University Press, 1957), 154–55.

40. Johann Georg Hamann, "Biblische Betrachtungen eines Christen, on 1st Chronicles 12:32," in *Londoner Schriften*; new ed. by Oswald Bayer und Bernd Weißenborn (Munich: Beck, 1993), 186, 31f. Cf. Bayer, *Zeitgenosse* (see above, n. 26), 220, in the context of the whole chapter.

41. Hamann, "Zweifel und Einfälle" (1776), N 3 (171–96), 192, 22–26.

42. Cf. Hamann, "Metakritik über den Purismum der Vernunft" [1784], ZH 5:212, 31—213, 17. Cf. Oswald Bayer, *Vernunft ist Sprache: Hamanns Metakritik Kants* (Stuttgart: Frommann-Holzboog, 2002), 296–312.

43. Hamann, "Golgotha und Scheblimini", N 3, 303, 36f.

44. Hamann to Kant, 1759, ZH 1:446, 33f.

45. Cf. Oswald Bayer, "Erzählung und Erklärung: Das Verhältnis von Theologie und Naturwissenschaften," in *Gott als Autor: Zu einer poietologischen Theologie* (Tübingen: Mohr Siebeck, 1999), 240–54.

CHAPTER 21

Lutheran Theology
and Everyday Life

Eric
W.
Gritsch

A Neuralgic Problem?

Lutheran confessional theology is clearly linked to everyday life. All of Christian life is thus to be governed by the distinction between law and gospel as a life between the first and second advent of Christ—a life in the meantime, a meantime, according to Luther, because of the continual temptation to succumb to evil and commit idolatry ("to be like God," Gen 3:5).[1] That is why Christians, in order to survive life in the two kingdoms, must be on guard against evil through worship and education. Luther viewed law and gospel as part of the Augustinian distinction between "two realms" or "kingdoms," one ruled by God and the other by evil. The rule of God is most visible in the authority of the gospel in the church, and the rule of evil is curbed by a political government of law and order. Christians, Luther contended, live in both realms as well as in three "stations of life" (*Stände* or hierarchies): family, government, and church.[2]

But Lutheran theology has had different views of life in two kingdoms. The specific issue was the meaning of the law. Luther taught two functions of the law: first, civic law provides justice and, second, the accusing, spiritual law leads to repentance. Philip Melanchthon developed a doctrine of three uses of the law, the third being rules for faithful living, known also as "spiritual formation" in the face of sin.[3] The difference between him and

---

1. Luther's interpretation of the First Commandment of the Decalogue stressed this idolatry: "To wrest heaven from God." Large Catechism 22; *BSLK* 565; *BC* 388.
2. Luther, at times, varies these "estates," speaking also of economics as one of three, sometimes of more than three. See Eric W. Gritsch, *Martin—God's Court Jester: Luther in Retrospect* (Philadelphia: Fortress Press, 1983), 111–29.
3. Usually a Roman Catholic designation. Luther viewed all "formation" in the context of Baptism, not linked to a "third use of the law." See Bernhard Lohse, *Martin Luther's Theology: Its Historical and Systematic Development*, trans. and ed. Roy A. Harrisville (Minneapolis: Fortress Press, 1999), 275–76.

Luther spawned the first quarrels among Lutherans, which the Lutheran Confessions tried to settle.[4]

This chapter focuses on the "third use of the law" as the confessional Lutheran basis for a contemporary way of shaping everyday life, using biblical paradigms as stepping stones for catechetical instruction. The link of "justification by faith" to rules for everyday living is a neuralgic problem. Lutheran orthodoxy (1580–1675), with its "religion of the mind," and pietism (1675–1817), with its "religion of the heart," tried to separate doctrine and life, resulting in neuralgic pain along the nerves of Lutheran church bodies. The rediscovery of Luther and the Lutheran Confessions in the nineteenth century did little, if anything, to overcome the problem. Even the massive attempt on the part of the Lutheran World Federation to reach a consensus in 1963 failed.[5] A statement by the Ecumenical Institute in Strasbourg in 1977 on "Lutheran Identity" was virtually ignored.[6] In 1991, Lutheran essayists from around the world presented various "perspectives" without disclosing a consensus.[7] "Justification by faith" may become an empty slogan if it is not related to everyday life; and "spiritual formation" may remain a Roman Catholic stepchild of Lutheranism.

The Third Use of the Law

Shortly after Luther's death in 1546, the conservative theologians of his reform movement, led by Matthias Flacius (1520–1575) and labeled "Gnesio-Lutherans" (from the Greek *gnesio*, "authentic"), taught that the reborn do not need any law to live the "new obedience." Accordingly, they do "spontaneously what God demands of them through the prompting and impulse of the Holy Spirit." The liberal opponents, led by Melanchthon (1497–1560) and labeled "Philippists," taught that "the Holy Spirit uses the written law on them, to teach them, so that through it believers in Christ learn to serve God not according to their own ideas. . . ."[8] FC affirms the Philippist position in a definition of "law" in general.

> The law has been given to people for three reasons: First, that through it external discipline may be maintained against the unruly and the disobedient; second, that people may be led through it to a recognition of their

---

4. FC VI, Solid Declaration. "Concerning the Third Use of the Law," *BSLK* 962–69. *BC* 587–91. On the controversies, see Eric W. Gritsch, *A History of Lutheranism* (Minneapolis: Fortress Press, 2002), 86–91.

5. *Proceedings of the Fourth Assembly of the Lutheran World Federation, Helsinki, July 30—August 1, 1963* (Berlin and Hamburg: Evangelisches Verlagshaus, 1965). Text of the Study Document "On Justification" in *Lutheran World* 12/1 (1965): 1–11.

6. *Lutheran Identity*. Final report on "The Identity of the Lutheran Churches in the Context of the Challenges of Our Time" (Strasbourg: Institute for Ecumenical Research, 1977).

7. "Whither Lutheranism . . .?" *Word and World* 11 (Summer 1991).

8. FC VI, 3. *BSLK* 963; *BC* 587.

sins; third, after they have been reborn—since nevertheless the flesh still clings to them—that precisely because of the flesh they may have a sure guide, according to which they can orient and conduct their entire life.[9]

Melanchthon linked law to reason. "God requires the righteousness of reason." In the first use of the law, "civil discipline," the law is to be a "disciplinarian" (Gal 3:24) that restrains evil.[10] Evil is manifested in chaos and confusion (from the Greek *diaballein*, "to confuse," "diabolical"), and God instituted government, be it Christian or non-Christian, to restrain evil. The first use of the law is to create a balance between good and evil, equity and justice.

The second use of the law is to create "change of mind" or penance (from the Greek *metanoia*). It is summarized as a mandate for the interim: "The time is fulfilled, and the kingdom of God has come near; repent, and believe in the good news" (Mark 1:15). The law creates a conflict between good (yet still sinful) intentions and the overwhelming reality of an evil world. "For I cannot do the good I want, but the evil I do not want is what I do" (as Paul describes it dramatically in Rom 7:19). Human reason detects the inability to fulfill the law.

Thus reason reveals sin (Rom 3:20). This is the right function of reason. The wrong function of reason is to think that it can achieve salvation by doing good—or by trying to explain the mystery of Christ's presence in the Lord's Supper, as Ulrich Zwingli did. Here reason becomes "the old witch" who tricks people to believe in salvation through human merit rather than through faith in Christ alone.[11] The Lutheran Confessions regard this second function of the law as its chief function, the theological or pedagogical use. "For the law always accuses and terrifies conscience. Therefore it does not justify since the conscience that is terrified by the law flees the judgment of God."[12] *Christian* reason is, at its best, diagnostic; it functions to detect what is truly real before God, to overcome illusions, and to yearn for faith in Christ who liberates from sin.

The third use of the law is to shape Christian life for ministry, ordained or nonordained. Luther viewed worship and education as the twin pillars of the church, equipping members for ministry in the world. Lutherans are not "fideists" who prohibit good works, as their Catholic opponents contended.[13] Realistic Lutherans accept spiritual discipline, indeed care for spiritual formation. Luther called it a "return to Baptism," the task of penance by drowning "the old creature in us" every day so "that daily a new person is to come forth and rise up before God in righteousness and purity

---

9. FC VI, 1, emphasis added. *BSLK* 962; *BC* 502.
10. AP IV, 22. *BSLK* 164; *BC* 124.
11. FC VIII, 49. *BSLK* 1029; *BC* 623.
12. AP IV, 38. *BSLK* 167; *BC* 126.
13. CA XX, 1. *BSLK* 75; *BC* 53.

forever."[14] Lutheranism relocates good works from their medieval purpose to cooperate with divine grace for salvation to their proper function as part of a ministry and witness in the world. Good works must be done, but there are never enough good works to guarantee the forgiveness of sins.

Melanchthon clearly states the case for a third use of the law as distinguished from the gospel:

> Therefore we call godly minds back to a consideration of the promises, and we teach them about the free forgiveness of sins and reconciliation that comes through faith in Christ. Later *we also add the law*, not because we merit forgiveness of sins by the law . . . but because God requires good works. For the law and the promises need to be "rightly distinguished" [2 Tim. 2:15] with care."[15]

Melanchthon rediscovered the Hebrew meaning of "law" (*Torah*) as a way of life of the people of God. FC tried to preserve this meaning during the controversy about the uses of the law. The third use of the law is a discipline or spiritual formation for preventing believers to succumb to the everlasting temptation to violate the first commandment of the Decalogue ("You are to have no other gods") and become idolatrous (or "backsliders," as American revivalist preachers like to call them). "For this reason, *believers require the teaching of the law: so that they do not fall back on their own holiness and piety and under the appearance of God's Spirit establish their own service to God on the basis of their own choice without God's Word or command.*"[16]

Such discipline is necessary so that believers can remain anchored in the double commandment of love: to love God and neighbor (Matt 22:37-39). This commandment removes self-love from the center of life. Using the paradigm of the cross, one can say that the human mind must bend sideways, as it were, from the center cross, from faith, to the sidebar into the direction of love and service in the world. For without such a disciplined move reason always tries to move upward, trying to storm heaven and use good works to merit salvation. The Good Samaritan (Luke 10:25-37) uses his mind to help the victim without asking, "What's in it for me?" The bad Samaritan just looks at the victim and says, "Whoever did this to you needs a lot of help."

The third use of the law reveals the church as a pilgrim people journeying between birth (Pentecost) and death (end-time) as "strangers and foreigners on earth" toward a new, transformed life. Like Abraham, Isaac, and Jacob, Christians live by the promise of a new homeland, "the city of

---

14. Small Catechism, "Baptism," 12. *BSLK* 516; *BC* 360. Large Catechism, "Baptism," 79. *BSLK* 706; *BC* 466.

15. AP IV, 187–88. *BSLK* 197; *BC* 150.

16. FC, Solid Declaration, VI, 20, emphasis added. BS 968; *BC* 590.

God" (Heb 11:13-16). Once baptized, they must stay on guard against evil, the first pledge in the liturgy of Baptism ("Do you renounce all the forces of evil . . . ?").[17] The Lutheran catechetical tradition assumes that there is a life-long struggle with evil. Baptism "signifies that the old creature in us with all sins and evil desires is to be drowned and die through daily contrition and repentance, and on the other hand that daily a new person is to come forth and rise up before God in righteousness and purity forever."[18] Post-baptismal sins are part of the Christian life. Penitential catechesis is needed to deal with such sins. "Those who have fallen after Baptism can receive forgiveness of sins *whenever they are brought to repentance*; the church should impart absolution to those who return to repentance."[19] There is, then, education for the struggle with evil and worship as the celebration of the new life that is already here in part but will be complete at the end time; the Lord's Supper offers "a foretaste of the feast to come."[20]

Servant-Dove and Serpenthood

Never before has there been a greater awareness of global problems. Evil, in particular, has been rediscovered as the irrefutable omnipresent reality in the world, masked by many disguises or just brutal in its terror. That is why spiritual formation for survival in an evil world has become an indispensable mandate. Luther's radical spiritual turmoil (*Anfechtung*) was caused by evil in his own church, and Lutheranism developed a strong awareness of sin on all levels of life, but especially within the rank and file of Christians. Today all spiritual formation must begin with a realistic recognition of evil with its power of illusion, seduction, and terror.

The encounter with evil was already part of the first mandate for mission by Jesus in the Gospel of Matthew, and it was accompanied by a description of his disciples as humble servants because they must never be exalted and honored like the leaders in the world. "The greatest among you will be your servant. All who exalt themselves will be humbled, and all who humble themselves will be exalted" (Matt 23:11-12). Servanthood, as embodied obedience to Christ, is the foundation for faithful living in the interim between his first and second advent. Servanthood is neither a cowardly humility nor a triumphalist dignity; it is alert eschatological existence. But servanthood is linked to a discernment of earthly reality, especially evil whose name is "legion" (Mark 5:9).

---

17. *Lutheran Book of Worship* (Minneapolis: Augsburg, and Philadelphia: Fortress Press, 1978), 123. The pledge may have various other versions but always asks for the life-long promise to exorcise evil in the name of Christ.
18. Small Catechism. "Baptism," 12. *BSLK* 516; *BC* 360.
19. CA XII, 1–2. *BSLK* 66; *BC* 45.
20. Offertory in the liturgy of the Lord's Supper. *Lutheran Book of Worship*, 66.

I am sending you out like sheep into the midst of wolves; *so be wise as serpents and innocent as doves.* . . . Brother will betray brother to death, and
a father his child, and children will rise against parents and have them put
to death; and you will be hated by all because of my name (Matt 10:16,
21-22).

The four types of animals describe the experience of the mission
entrusted to the disciples. If they behave just like "sheep," belonging to an
unguarded and naïve flock, they will be devoured by "wolves," symbolizing
ganglike violence. If they behave like "doves," cooing with love and joy on
rooftops, they represent a childlike faith often manifested in the public use
of spiritual gifts, such as speaking in tongues. But in a hostile environment,
they will quickly die, because they are easy targets for hunters (who know
that most fowl can be shot at close range when they make love). Jesus called
for disciples who combine the gift of the Holy Spirit (symbolized by the
dove) with cool-blooded wisdom (symbolized by the serpent).

The image of the serpent has an interesting history in the Bible. First,
the serpent is the instrument of temptation in the garden, promising Adam
and Eve that they "will never die" and that they "will be like God" (Gen
3:6) when they follow their own desires. Then the serpent becomes a symbol of salvation from death during the exodus of the people of Israel from
Egypt. Moses was told by God to make a bronze serpent, and anyone who
was afraid of being bitten by a poisonous serpent was saved by looking at
the bronze serpent (Num 21:9). Finally, when Jesus met the Jewish leader
Nicodemus at night for a discussion on how to be born again, he was told
by Jesus: "Just as Moses lifted up the serpent in the wilderness, so must the
Son of Man be lifted up, that whoever believes in him may have eternal life"
(John 3:14). So the serpent becomes a symbol of healing and salvation, an
image also shared by ancient Greek as well as modern medicine. The serpent appears on the logo for medicine, curled around a staff.

But healing and salvation do not occur without a precise, correct and
cold-blooded diagnosis of an illness. To be wise as a serpent means to use
the mind for a proper diagnosis in order to move to a realistic prognosis.
Serpenthood is the sharp discernment of evil and disease, a form of tough
love for the neighbor in need. Luther practiced humble servanthood, cheer-
ful dovehood and especially effective serpenthood. He became a monk to
serve; he sang the gospel as "the Wittenberg nightingale";[21] and when he
discovered the abuse of hierarchical authority in the church, he moved from
innocent dovehood, to a sagacious serpenthood. Luther offered the world a
shocking diagnosis of the medieval church, contending that it had transformed the gift of salvation in Christ into a credit/debit system of human
merit as the way to appease an angry God. The biblical slogan "justification

---

21. See Hans Sachs, *Die Wittenbergisch Nachtigall* (Wittenberg, 1523).

by faith" (Hab 2:4; Rom 1:16-17) summed up Luther's rediscovery of the gospel as the "good news" of God's unconditional love for the people of God.

Critical hindsight has shown that Luther was only partially successful in his attempt to reform the church.[22] The Lutheran reform movement in the sixteenth century lost Luther's serpentine sagacity and dovelike joy. Luther himself was naïve in his assessment of the plight of the peasants who viewed Lutheranism as a force against the evil of feudalistic slavery. He also supported fanatic medieval anti-Semitism.[23] On the other hand, Lutheranism initiated reforms in education and social welfare through pioneers like August Hermann Francke (1663–1727), Nikolai F. S. Grundtvig (1783–1872), and Friedrich von Bodelschwingh (1831–1910). Their servanthood improved everyday life. Johann Sebastian Bach (1685–1750) was an excellent example of musical dovehood. Dietrich Bonhoeffer (1906–1945) in Germany, Eivind Berggrav (1884–1959) in Norway, and Lajos Ordass (1901–1978) in Hungary are models of serpenthood in their resistance against the evils of Fascist and Communist tyranny.

Lutheran confessional theology views everyday life as an opportunity to receive and to offer strength in the struggle against evil. Clever serpenthood is needed to use language, ritual, polity, doctrine, ethics, and other human ways to do a faithful ministry in a world ruled by "Murphy's law."[24] Serpentine distinctions are to be made between "word" and "spirit," "law" and "gospel," "essentials" and "nonessentials" or *adiaphora* (from the Greek, "things in the middle," neither commanded nor forbidden). For without sharp discernment—indeed debate—evil is neither diagnosed nor contained. In this sense, the church can appreciate the slogan of democratic government, "The price of liberty is eternal vigilance."[25]

The serpenthood of law—civil, penitential, and formational—needs to shape everyday life. But the "third use of the law" as spiritual formation to detect evil is what is most needed today. Christians have too often succumbed to the lure of the world and become confused in their ministry. The result was a gospel romanticism combined with the enduring temptation to package the gospel into a Puritan ideology without dovelike joy, or into entertainment, marketing devices, or other "childish ways" (1 Cor 13:11). Recent research has shown that the Lutheran Reformation cherished the tradition of canon law after it had been distinguished from the gospel.

---

22. See the formal public disputation on "Luther's Success and Failure as a Reformer of the Church" between Albert Brandenburg and Eric W. Gritsch at the Fifth International Congress for Luther Research in Lund, 1977, in *Luther und die Theologie der Gegenwart*, ed. Leif Grane and Bernhard Lohse (Göttingen: Vandenhoeck & Ruprecht, 1980), 97–111.

23. On the peasants, see Eric W. Gritsch, *Martin Luther—God's Court Jester: Luther in Retrospect* (Philadelphia: Fortress, 1983), 118. On anti-Semitism, see 137–45.

24. The law or principle that if anything can go wrong, it will. Named after the American engineer Edward A. Murphy (1917–).

25. Commonly attributed to Thomas Jefferson (1743–1826).

Medieval canon law fused the two and created an ecclesiastical trauma for those who sought help from the grip of evil in their everyday lives. Lutheranism converted canon law into a process of catechetical and juridical education for survival in the world.[26]

The enduring challenge of spiritual formation is the unmasking of evil through reality checks and the sharing of the analyzed results with those who are unable or unwilling to face evil, even though they need to know what is real in order to survive in everyday life.[27]

Lutheranism was born in the conflict with evil in the church. Everyday life was a mixture of fear and idolatry. Luther made a correct diagnosis or reality check through serpentine wisdom and theological skills. Lutheran theology should continue in his steps by strengthening the faithful through effective spiritual formation in the face of an unprecedented expansion of the power of evil in the world.

The Need for a New Cathechism

Effective spiritual formation needs to become the center of Christian education for everyday life, which is traditionally known as catechesis before or after Baptism (depending on adult or infant Baptism). A "catechism" is a handbook, indeed a survival kit, as it were, for lifelong spiritual formation. Luther's catechisms of 1529 were based on a careful, rational examination of contemporary life. Together with Melanchthon he arranged "visitations" of the Saxon countryside to determine what was needed for catechetical instruction. The results of the visitations were a real eye opener: neither the pastors nor the people knew much, if anything, about their faith or what was happening around them. Pastors lacked the most rudimentary theological and catechetical knowledge. Luther diagnosed the situation with great consternation:

> Dear God, what misery I beheld! The ordinary person, especially in the villages, knows absolutely nothing about the Christian faith, and unfortunately many pastors are completely unskilled and incompetent teachers. Yet supposedly they all bear the name Christian, are baptized and receive the holy sacrament, even though they do not know the Lord's Prayer, the

---

26. See the ground-breaking study of John Witte, Jr., *Law and Protestantism: The Legal Teachings of the Lutheran Reformation* (Cambridge: Cambridge Univ. Press, 2002), esp. chap. 2.

27. Example: A teacher was unable to teach because of fear. He consulted a psychiatrist who, after a lengthy analysis, offered the diagnosis: "You have an inferiority complex that paralyzes you in the classroom. Find another occupation." The teacher was advised by a good friend to get another expert opinion. So he went to another psychiatrist who, after a lengthy analysis, offered the diagnosis: "You do not have an inferiority complex. *You are inferior.*" Now the teacher could teach, though not as well as many others, but well enough to make a living. He was weak but not paralyzed. One could say with Paul that whenever one suffers for the sake of Christ, one is strong in weakness (2 Cor 12:10).

Creed, or the Ten Commandments! As a result they live like simple cattle or irrational pigs and, despite the fact that the gospel has returned, have mastered the fine art of misusing all their freedom.[28]

Lutheranism today surely appears to have a better reputation than it had in sixteenth-century Saxony. But only a detailed investigation and analysis of each historical situation will provide evidence for a judgment about the state of Lutherans. But there should always be a periodic examination of the Lutheran state of affairs, especially the level of dealing with evil and with the gift of the gospel. Luther assumed that Christians must always do battle with evil (the devil). For in the battle it becomes evident how Christ fights evil through his disciples. "Therefore whoever desires to see the Christian church existing in quiet peace, entirely without crosses, without heresy, and without factions, will never see it . . . or must view the false church of the devil as the real church."[29] Comfort and security always seem to be more popular in the church than struggle and freedom. Lutheran theology in Europe and North America tends to assume that liberation from evil is a problem in the "developing countries" (also know as the Third World). But evil may be as strong in one location as it is in another, and theology must detect, diagnose and fight its particular power wherever it dominates. Some Lutherans no longer use what the missionaries brought them. The Batak Lutherans in Indonesia, for example, substituted their own doctrinal confession for CA in a confession of their own, also accepted by other Protestants, the *Confession of Faith of the Huria Kristen Batak Protestant Church*, drafted in1951. They no longer wanted to subscribe to a German confession that was strange to them and did not succeed to prevent Lutherans from becoming followers of Adolf Hitler.[30]

Today, global communication has made it possible for evil to become organized as a global terror, be it in the guise of international terrorism or under the mask of a rampant religious fanaticism. In addition, poverty, disease, war, and apathy seem to have become the contemporary four horsemen of the apocalypse (Revelation 6). Such a new world needs a new catechism, which takes into account the drastic changes during the last century. Lutheran confessional theology is bound to encounter evil in all its faces and phases, to diagnose its power, and to engage in battle with it.

What follows is an attempt to sketch the foundation for a new catechism as the way in which Lutheran theology ought to be linked to everyday life.

---

28. Preface, Small Catechism 2, 4. *BSLK* 501–2; *BC* 347–48.
29. "Commentary on the Creeds," 1538. WA 50:272–73.
30. English text in John H. Leith, ed., *Creeds of the Churches*, 3rd ed. (Atlanta: John Knox, 1982), 556–66. See also Theodore E. Bachmann and Mercia Brenne Bachmann, eds., *Lutheran Churches around the World: A Handbook* (Minneapolis: Fortress, 1989), 232–34.

Preface

We Christians are a pilgrim people, living between Christ's ascension and his return at the end-time. "Remember," he said, "I am with you always, to the end of the age" (Matt 28:20). We are people of "the Way" (Acts 24:14) to a future with "new heavens and a new earth, where righteousness is at home" (2 Pet 3:13). We, like Abraham, are "strangers and foreigners on the earth" (Heb 11:13), "ambassadors for Christ" (2 Cor 5:20) in a strange land. Being a pilgrim people, we must travel with few comforts, face unforeseen obstacles, and remain alert in order to stay on track. As the people of God, we know that human life is filled with evil that cannot be fully measured or explained. We need to be moving targets, as it were, constantly trying to contain evil enough to move on. Otherwise we become like "sheep in the midst of wolves" and perish (Matt 10:16). In this mean meantime, there are scheduled occasions to gather for worship and education as the sources for new strength. In worship, we are like "innocent doves" (Matt 10:16) who praise God in childlike faith and give thanks for our salvation from evil through Christ. In education, we become "wise as serpents" (Matt 10:16), trained for rational, cold-blooded battle with evil. Serpenthood is the key to our effective Christian education or spiritual formation for survival. The catechism is our survival kit, a handbook for Christian living and dying in the world. We should use it with great diligence and passion, being certain that "we have taught the devil to death."[31]

1. Evil

God-talk or theology must begin by directing the mind to expose evil. Evil works with illusion, deception, fear, and terror. The human mind cannot detect or destroy its power. Like a clever motion picture made for escapists, evil creates artificial realities, thus lulling its audience into illusions of comfort, or instilling fear through threatening illusions. Escapists love the veiling of reality on a screen through optical illusions. But they, like the realists, also have to face the reality of the outside world. In a similar way, we must continually redirect our mind to face evil.

The domination of evil means idolatry. Its religious form is the rejection of the first commandment of the Decalogue, "You are to have no other gods." Playing God is the dangerous pastime of tyrants who terrorize any opponent. But Christians are empowered to diagnose evil, just as physicians are authorized to detect disease through skillful examination leading to a diagnosis as the basis for a prognosis, which issues a verdict of healing or death. This is done through the use of reason. The diagnosis of evil in everyday life is the first step of spiritual formation.

---

31. Luther's Preface to *the Large Catechism* 19. *BSLK* 553; *BC* 383.

2. Justice

Once evil is diagnosed as the most powerful reality in the world, we can cooperate with non-Christians in creating laws for the restraint of evil. There must be law and order through the power of government, ranging from rules of family living to complicated yet necessary juridical configurations. Thus the first aim of spiritual formation, justice, is symbolized by the scale with equal weight on each side. The quest and work for justice, through laws and their enforcement, is the basis for human cooperation on all levels of society.

3. Baptism

Baptism is the initiation into the Christian community, the church, at any state of life, be it right after birth (infant Baptism) or later (adult Baptism). It is called "sacrament," a consecratory act consisting of words and actions, based on the mandate of Jesus.[32] The ritual of Baptism includes a pledge to fight evil, to adhere to the apostolic faith (summarized in the Apostles' Creed) and to be alert to the gift of the Holy Spirit. Thus the liturgy begins with attention to serpenthood and ends with a reminder of dovehood. Our baptismal certificate is the most important document for survival, the passport, as it were, for safe travel through earthly life to the city of God. The water bath is a symbol of the daily drowning of what is evil in us and the emergence of what is pure in the sight of God. Thus Baptism becomes the focus of our life, which must be continually formed by the daily reminder that God is in charge. Otherwise, spiritual formation will just be a generic discipline, similar, if not identical, with self-centered exercises of minds and bodies.

4. Church

The church is the gathering of those who are baptized. Members support and help each other in their daily struggle to remain faithful. If one member becomes weak, indeed is in danger of loosing his or her faith, that person lives on another member's faith, just as is the case in financial survival when money is borrowed on credit and is paid back later. For faith is a shared commodity rather than the exclusive possession of an individual. The church is like a human body in which all members are to function for the good of the whole. But the head of the body is the resurrected Christ. As a visible institution, the church is always tempted by evil to become idolatrous, to be like God. That is why the church needs elected leaders, such as pastors and bishops (from the Greek *episcope*, "oversight"), who pledge to serve and preserve the gospel. But other designations may be used to

---

32. The indispensable words are "I baptize you in the name of the Father, the Son and the Holy Spirit," based on the traditional mandate "Go and make disciples of all nations, baptizing them . . ." (Matt 28:20); and the action is a water bath (*Lutheran Book of Worship*, 123).

describe such leadership. Thus juridical, serpentine wisdom is needed in the church to keep it faithful.

5. The Lord's Supper

The Lord's Supper is the center of public worship because of Christ's special presence in the meal. It sustains and strengthens us in our lives in the midst of evil in the world. That is why its celebration ought to be frequent, at least every Sunday when Christians gather to recall the day of Christ's resurrection. In this sense, the Lord's Supper is also a celebration signaling a future life without evil.

6. Prayer

Prayer is our direct communication with God through the mediation of Christ and the Holy Spirit. That is why prayer should end with the phrase "in the name of Christ." Prayer encompasses all aspects of life and consists of petitions mirroring many situations. Good prayer begins with gratitude for the gifts of God and ends with intercessions for others in need of help. We may sometimes be unrealistic and pray for something God wisely never grants; and we may receive something we never prayed for. But prayer is the direct lifeline to God.

7. Music

Music transcends the problem of language through words; it expresses the whole scale of human emotions and, if played for the glory of God, often relieves from the evils of anxiety, depression, and fear. We are significantly poorer without musical communication. It is the kind of dovehood we need in our trek through time to the "promised land." We need to be cheered on by songs and hymns while journeying through the maze of good and evil.

Summary

We must do the cool-blooded, serpentine diagnosis of evil in everyday life to remain faithful agents of reconciliation in Christ's name. Such diagnosis is done best by more than one member of the church, be it a local congregation or another gathering.

A three-step program is recommended as an effective way to implement the seven-part catechism. The program should be carried out by a carefully chosen cadre of one-tenth of the active members of a local congregation—a living "tithe," as it were. These members should represent men and women with sound minds, representing various standards of living. Led by their pastor, the cadre should meet for at least one year in weekly sessions, dealing with the issues of everyday life as they emerge in their particular world. Their work should be based on a pragmatic use of resources, active listening, and informed discussion. Each session should begin with prayer and conclude with the Lord's Supper. The cadre should become an attractive model for others.

First, there should be fact-finding sessions to determine the health of the congregation. The cadre should diagnose the state of affairs. If a specific problem or a basic issue is dominating the life of the congregation, a realistic prognosis should be attempted, based on careful reviews of the history and impact of the ecclesial disease.

Second, the cadre should stage catechetical events, such as adult forums or similar gatherings, to inform, convince, and activate the congregation to face, contain, indeed eliminate, the problem(s). A final decision should be made by the governing body of the congregation (e.g., a church council) with assistance from the church at large, represented by other congregations in town and by regional and/or national church authorities. The range of assistance would be determined by the weight of the problem. Such action would be the move from a diagnosis of evil to justice.

Third, the trained cadre of serpenthood should become and remain a watchdog for the congregation and should be a resource for assistance, renewal, and witness. Fully aware of the power of the church as a baptized community nourished by word, sacrament, prayer, and, at times, by music, the cadre should share its collective wisdom with others who need to face the power of evil.

Conclusion

In its best and brightest moments, Lutheran theology has focused on the biblical image of the church as a pilgrim people during the interim between the first and second advent of Christ. Consequently, everyday life is marked by a peculiar freedom and a doxological joy in the face of a future promised by the gospel. Too often Lutherans have made bad distinctions between justification and sanctification or between doctrinal fundamentalism and moral pietism, losing sight of the natural interaction of faith and life. At times, Lutherans have been like German shepherd dogs, hunting the enemy of the herd rather than enjoying being with the shepherd. Yet "justification by faith" through word and sacraments is also a liturgy on Sunday and a discipline for Monday, reflecting eschatological freedom and joy. Solid confessional Lutheran theology ought to convey to its adherents the powerful reality of evil and its exorcism in everyday life. In this sense, Lutheranism should invite people to be a gathering of those who embody the ancient, apostolic sense of the church as a community with a future when "Christ is all and in all" (Col 3:11).

CHAPTER 22

Pluralism and Identity: The Two-Kingdoms Doctrine Challenged by Secularization and Privatization

Jan-Olav
Henriksen

In the Lutheran tradition, one important element is the so-called doctrine of the two kingdoms. Though sometimes controversial, often discussed, and differently interpreted, this doctrine should be seen as an attempt to differentiate between the various realms in the work of God for, in, and with the world. In this chapter, I discuss the potential of this doctrine for gaining perspective in interpreting the present cultural scene and recent phenomena in Western societies. My basic thesis is that this doctrine is consonant with both the establishment of a specific, religiously based identity as well as the growing cultural plurality in those societies. Paradoxically, then, it seems to establish a specific confessionally based position that in some sense contributes to important features in Western societies, namely, the secularization and privatization of religious belief generally and the Christian faith more specifically. To develop a supportive argument, I first briefly outline some of the main points of the doctrine and then present and discuss some elements related to current sociological features.

The Two-Kingdoms Doctrine: A Brief Sketch

When God acts in the worldly realm, God acts in a way that involves all people, irrespective of faith. Here, God acts as Creator to make sure that creation is working according to his will and plan. God carries out this task through people of all faiths as they fulfill their calling as parents, craftsmen, professors, peasants, and so on. By and through them, God manifests his law in the world as a means for governing the Creation. Sometimes God also has to ordain the use of force (by legitimate authorities) to make people do what they are obliged to do: pay tax, avoid stealing, and so on.[1] Such enforcement is legitimate as long as it is related to the "outward human," that is, to the

1. Cf. Martin Luther, *Von Weltlicher Obrigkeit*, WA 11:376.

beings who through their bodily constituted[2] relationship with others share in one another's world and influence one another's lives and resources.

In these brief comments, there is already implicit a hint that the Lutheran doctrine of the two kingdoms should be seen as based on the distinction between the "inner human" and the "outward human."[3] The inner human is ruled by faith, and in the inner realm of human life—in which that which we call subjectivity is constituted—no one is allowed to enter with force. This is a "privatized space," the space of personality. The only means of legitimate entry here is the proclamation of the gospel, whose entrance is not one of intrusion but of a calling to freedom. By entering here and creating a specific configuration of inner human subjectivity based on faith, the gospel liberates the human being from reliance on the works of the outward human for merits. Consequently that person lives in faith and trust toward God and God's gospel.

The distinctions between the worldly realm and the realm of faith, between the outward human and the inward human, have importance for the way religious faith is seen and perceived by the *Lutheran* Christian believer. Faith is not based on or configured by a certain practice nor by belonging to a specific institution. Such elements are not constitutive but rather consecutive elements in the shaping of a life of faith. This allows—sociologically—for the possibility of privatizing one's faith, as faith can exist withdrawn from a common life in institutions or practices.[4] This is not a privatization in the sense of a totally idiosyncratic faith in shape, practice, and substance. Nevertheless, it is a faith based on how one personally appropriates the elements of tradition in one's own way—and in a way not necessarily shaped by common rituals, practices, or institutionalized practices or community bonds.

The possibility of this development was not easy to anticipate as a problem in the time of Luther. He could assume that, in a society where a large part of the people in some way or another related to the same institutions and shared a common faith, they would also relate to a common framework of faith and practice. However, in the present, far more pluralistic world, and given the institutional influence on human beings, this element cannot be ignored as a significant factor in the shaping of people's faith and life. In this sense, the location of faith in the inward human can be seen as contributing to the privatization process in which faith itself is part.

---

2. This mode of speech is an attempt to phrase more positively what Luther says when he calls this a "Bauchsreich."

3. For how this distinction is used, cf. Martin Luther, *Von der Freiheit eines Christenmenschen,* WA 7:59–60.

4. I draw attention here to the phrasing "allows for" as different from "causes"—which I take to need an alternative way of dealing with the topic than the one I attempt here. Hence I do not present an argument saying that the two-kingdoms doctrine has caused the development here dealt with.

However, even more important for the following is the fact that the differentiation made here opens up for the recognition of the worldly realm as a realm in which God acts. This recognition, consequently, also implies the recognition of people of other faiths as legitimate participants in pluralistic society, in which one—according to the two-kingdoms doctrine—must assume God governs. In an increasingly pluralistic culture, this can be seen as a gain; that is, it allows for different institutions in society to become—legitimately—secularized. State, law, jurisprudence, education, and politics need not be stamped "Christian" in order to appear as legitimate and valid from a theological point of view. The differentiation thus also allows for a wide spectrum of people to participate in various realms of society, thereby securing and contributing to the democratization process as well.

Accordingly, the two-kingdoms doctrine can be seen as consonant with the development of a more pluralistic society, insofar as it expresses a positive interpretation of the conditions for what takes place within the secular realm. Concomitantly, it can still contribute to the development of a specific and religiously based identity in the realm where the gospel is preached and faith exists. Given these considerations, I will in the following argue that the two-kingdoms doctrine

- contributes to the development of a "soft" approach toward religious and moral pluralism
- contributes to the secularization of institutions in modern, Western society. In order to develop an understanding of this, I will refer to results from the Nordic group of research that based their work on the RAMP investigation.[5]
- contributes to and gives an impetus toward a more noninstitutional approach to religion. To substantiate this, I will refer to a dialectic theory of secularization and resacralization that differentiates between religion in the societal and the cultural sphere.

The two-kingdoms doctrine can accordingly also be seen as attuned to the process of democratization, secularization, and privatization of religious belief that have taken place in Western societies. This also provides a backdrop for understanding the present scene, in which religious interests seem to be awakening—but not on the same terms as those given at the time of Luther. To this I now turn.

Ways of Shaping Pluralism and of Relating to the Churches

The above suggests that the two-kingdoms doctrine can be seen as providing an ideology for a more liberal and pluralistic society in which people's

5. *Religious and Moral Pluralism*, a survey study made in most European countries in 1999.

faith is not a qualification for legitimate participation. At the same time, it allows for the development of a distinct faith-identity that can stand in a critical and reflective relationship to society in general. However, within the Scandinavian context, the pluralism that this doctrine allows for can to a certain extent also be seen as having entered the sphere of the churches as faith-based communities. This makes the picture far more complex. I discuss this complexity in the present section of this chapter.

There are different ways of shaping and understanding pluralism in a society. One of the more interesting elements in a Nordic context, however, is that the assumed increase of religious pluralism does not seem to have a strong impact on the formal church membership of most of the members of society. They remain in the Lutheran "folk" churches. The pluralism of worldviews seems, in other words, to get along well with being a member of the national church. A different way of phrasing this is to say that the existence of large national churches, which have more or less the status of a monopoly, does not seem to forestall the increase of pluralism in worldviews. It might even be suggested that these churches to a certain extent contribute to the accommodation of new worldviews, since they allow for a rather privatized approach to religious viewpoints. As indicated above, the two-kingdoms doctrine could have contributed—although not intentionally—to this development.

I take a point of departure in a rather general understanding of pluralism: "Societies are sometimes called pluralistic, meaning that they incorporate a variety of ways of life, moral standards and religions."[6] A pluralist society thus gives rise to a plurality of identities. Given that the Lutheran national churches understand themselves as, or are understood by the public as, churches for most (but not all) members of Nordic society, it then follows that also the churches must incorporate differences in the membership's morality and lifestyle. Consequently, the churches also allow people to relate to them in different ways. As long as this is made possible by an approach that first and foremost—and rightly so—locates faith in human subjectivity and personality more than in practice, this remains rather unproblematic.

With regard to the issue of identity, then, this indicates that people can use the resources provided by the churches in different ways. As long as one remains within the framework of the churches, the moral issues in question can in general be described as rather liberal. Also, in terms of doctrine, you may hold almost whatever opinions you like, as long as you are simply a lay member of the church and not part of the clergy. The churches do not interfere with that in any way or excommunicate people on the basis of faith or lack of such. Hence, the national churches can be seen as liberal institutions,

6. E. Craig, "Pluralism," in *The Encyclopaedia of Philosophy* (London: Routledge, 1986), 463–64.

meaning that they reflect a liberal society where people have their right to think and do what they like as long as it does not constitute a threat to anyone else. To some extent, this could be seen as the churches allowing for the plurality of the differentiation process that is shaping the secular realm, also within themselves as churches.

On this basis, it is fruitful to address some of the patterns expressed in the material from the RAMP investigation.[7] We can there identify two different ways of relating to pluralism. The first way of understanding pluralism is this liberal, open mode that is oriented toward integration between different identities. The way churches can exemplify this is especially on occasions of national importance, where the teaching and substantial content of the church's message is framed in a way that encompasses all members of society, including those with other religious affiliations, and seeks to integrate them into a larger, tolerant community. Here, in this "soft mode" of expressing pluralism, conflicts are tuned down and emphasis is laid upon the common values of society. Given an increasingly pluralistic society, the only way that national churches can continue to function in a way that enables them to maintain the strong status they now have is if they are able to support this liberal mode of addressing a pluralistic society.[8]

The alternative to this liberal approach to pluralism is a more boundary-oriented mode, where other identities are understood as something potentially in conflict with one's own. This is present when a religious community is defined as opposed to another or where one perceives existing differences as threats to one's own identity. This mode of understanding and relating to pluralism can be found within the constituency of the national churches also. However, it is not at all clear that this is the only attitude that is present among the more active members of these churches.

We can distinguish between these two forms of relating to pluralism at a macro level, a meso level, and an individual level. The levels, of course, cannot be separated completely, but it is interesting to see how this offers us a rather nuanced picture of how the national churches can function—given the built-in ambiguity that I addressed initially.

At the macro level, the churches officially and generally function and address pluralism in a rather soft mode. Conflicts with other parts of society

---

7. For a more extensive presentation and discussion of the results of RAMP, cf. G. Gustafsson and T. Pettersson, eds., *Folkkyrkor och religiös pluralism: Den nordiska religiösa modellen* (Stockholm: Verbum, 2000), and J. O. Henriksen and O. Krogseth, eds., *Pluralisme og identitet: Nordiske nasjonalkirker i møte med moralsk og religiøs pluralisme* (Oslo: Gyldendal Akademisk, 2001).

8. It is noteworthy, however, that this is a role that the churches would not exercise if it had not been for the historical circumstances that had allowed for it. Hence, it is also hard to imagine how any other church or religious community could take over this role, given the present circumstances. Consequently, it is still possible to recognize the privileged role that the Lutheran national churches have compared to any other religious community in the Nordic countries.

are toned down. "The official church" is tolerant and expresses itself as the "common voice," and issues that involve conflicts are generally voiced in ways that do not harm this openness. At this level, then, the churches seem to support and underpin a rather privatized mode of practicing religiosity without there being much emphasis on the preaching of the gospel, about the atoning death of Jesus Christ, for example.[9]

At a more local level, however, that is, in a local community, the picture is probably more mixed. Here, it is fruitful to distinguish between those who relate to the church as an institution that is of importance to the formation of their identity and those who have a more accidental and instrumental (but in no way nonreligious) relation to it. Especially for those who see the church as an important part of their identity, the pluralist society can be addressed in more ambiguous terms. This is due not only to the "competitive" element between different religious groups but also to the fact that, to maintain a strong identity in the long run, the identity of the group one belongs to cannot be too open or vague. The same is the case on the individual level. The level of privatization of religious commitment varies here, and consequently, also the way one is able to relate to pluralism. The stronger the commitment, the larger is the chance of having less tolerance for (or need for!) pluralism.

To get a deeper understanding of the mode in which religion is privatized and secularized, I suggest using Habermas's distinction between communicative and strategic action.[10] Strategic action is instrumental and is not based on mutual recognition between involved parties but focuses on the achievement of aims external to the given situation. Communicative action, on the other hand, is based on mutual recognition between all involved parties and aims at mutual understanding and common goals. If we look at Nordic citizens and their relation to the national churches in the light of this distinction, we get an interesting picture.

Those who relate to the churches as an important element in the formation of their identity express their relationship to the church more in terms of communicative action. The supposition here is that basic elements in the relationship to the churches also exist in their life-world. Here we can talk of relating to the church in a "we" relationship, where one identifies with the church in a way that involves commitment and the sharing of basic elements in doctrine and faith.

On the other hand, there are patterns of communication in which the church becomes part of a strategic mode of action and in which it functions more as a service agency. Then there is no need for a full recognition of its more substantial content and doctrine of faith, as the identities and faith

---

9. There are here also some features that can be associated with the content and the function of so-called civil religion, although it is not possible to develop that further in this context.

10. Jürgen Habermas, *Theorie des Kommunikativen Handelns I–II* (Frankfurt: Suhrkamp, 1981).

of those relating to the church are also not made an issue. Here the church is not understood as the community of those holding the same beliefs as oneself, but is perceived as part of a service-offering system. It can contribute to the maintenance of my identity but not in such a manner that I find myself situated within a symmetrically shaped community where I belong and want to contribute actively. Here it is not the church as the place where the gospel is preached that stands in the center but the church as an institution that provides for some of my needs, given by the very fact that I live in the world. Here the church is perceived in a way that we could, more crudely, designate as part of the worldly realm, providing services for anyone interested, on his or her own terms. Consequently, the basis on which people act is their own and is private, and is not that which constitutes the church as an institution.

In the last instance, we see how the relationship to the church makes the relationship to other people who participate there secondary. This can shed light over all the different ways of saying "believing without belonging" and "belonging without believing" that we find in recent literature by sociologists of religion. In general, the relationships between people here are shaped more according to their functional roles and according to the rationality given by one's goals. Here agents need not have identical purposes for interacting with one another: The pastor (as part of the religious system) and the mother who wants to have her child baptized might "live in different worlds" religiously and in terms of how they understand what takes place in the service on Sunday. Each can be religiously meaningful for each of them, but on quite different terms.[11]

On the other hand, when you take part in the church as a member of the community, you make far more use of the resources of a common lifeworld. Here mutual recognition and understanding, confidence and symmetry are of larger importance, as the structuring of the common world is here not as strongly defined in terms of external goals as in how to develop and maintain a certain and distinctive religious identity.

The systemic or strategic attitude toward religion and ethics makes the way one handles the worldviews of other people increasingly more ambiguous. Such a strategic approach is typical for governmental relation to these realms in most Scandinavian countries and probably reflects an understanding of the two-kingdoms doctrine in which the importance of the realm of the gospel is given little or no importance in comparison with the common, worldly realm. It is first and foremost a question of how to handle or administer the functional and not the substantial sides that are related to religious convictions. I think this sheds light over how the national churches function as the religious institutions of the state in the Nordic countries. On the other hand, this also indicates that there is a tendency toward ignoring the sub-

11. G. Gustafsson, *Tro, samfund och samhälle* (Lund: Liber, 1997), 167.

stantial convictions of other people and the impact that these have on the actual shaping of people's lives. Strategic or functional approaches make content less important, and it should be critically asked whether the two-kingdoms doctrine contributes to that as well.

This discloses an ambiguity in the sociological status and the cultural function of the large majority churches. On the one hand, what these churches offer is something that can support more utilitarian and more expressive modes of religiosity and church membership. Both of these modes contain different opinions of what counts as legitimate religiosity, and neither of them can be understood on the basis of a merely functional approach. However, both of them have importance for the shaping of personal identity.

The expressive mode of religious practice can be developed within a life-world that the church organizes through rites and social life. Alternatively, a utilitarian and more functional approach to what the church offers will be something that individuals can partake in without having a strong, primarily church-based life-world. Such an approach will, nevertheless, still take care of the need for expressing or maintaining a religious identity. This points toward the fact that a utilitarian mode of religiosity—which doubtless contributes to religious pluralism—can still support the churches' functional role as a part of the national service system. In contrast, a more expressive relationship toward religion, based on stronger impact of communicative action, will imply that one has a more internal religious basis for one's relation to this institution. This is one side of the issue.

However, when the churches are part of the institutional apparatus within society as a whole, they also become part of the system side of society, where the institutional agents have distinctive and clearly defined roles. Here the church offers services like weddings or funerals to others, who in order to receive them have to engage in other functional roles. Nevertheless, it is at the same time an important task for the churches to try to overcome this systemic way of functioning, because the life-world on which basis the church lives is dependent upon symmetric relations between people. If this is not overcome, it contributes to a consumerist, asymmetrical experience.

Given the problems related to pluralism and identity, this is complicated, because the church as institution is at the same time an important factor in their public—and publicly regulated—appearance. It is generally acknowledged that the church shall include all those who seek its services. Hence the church functions to integrate the different groups in society, including groups that have different attitudes toward the church itself. However, as previously said, it is a basic presupposition for the shaping and maintenance of a church-based community that those who participate in the community can develop their identity in a contrasting relationship to other groups in society. This expresses the very ambiguous character of the national churches, which are forced to exist in the tension between pluralism and identity. This character can be seen to be sustained by the very way the relation between church and society is framed in the two-kingdoms doctrine.

Retraditionalization against the Background of Secularization

In the preceding section I have presented a picture of the church at a rather institutional or societal level. However, I think that it is also possible to interpret the functions of the two-kingdoms doctrine against the backdrop of the cultural or symbolic level of society. Especially important here is the relationship to the tradition that constitutes the framework in which people develop and frame their own identity.

One of the well-known traits of modernity as secularization is its weakening of the relationship between the individual and the traditions that offer resources for the subject's self-understanding (as well as the self-understanding of groups and societies). The differentiation process leads to the detraditionalization of social phenomena. One of the striking features in this context is that the churches, as tradition-based communities and institutions, seem to offer some kind of alternative (be it compensatory or not) to this detraditionalization. In a culture without definitive and strong traditions, life can seem meaningless and without purpose, and one way of overcoming this is to turn to tradition. The detraditionalization process is also linked to pluralization; pluralization may weaken the commitment for one tradition, one form of faith, but it may also contribute to the strengthening of it.[12] But the churches maintain the longest and perhaps largest tradition we have in Europe, and this also applies to the national churches in the Nordic countries. It offers narratives and patterns of meaning that go beyond the present situation: the church represents the roots that the individual has lost in the process of modernization and detraditionalization.

However, the picture is complicated, because along with the detraditionalization process goes also the process of individualization. The result of this process is that the individual relates to processes of tradition in a manner that is more eclectic and also more autonomous than one would expect at first glance. When we talk about a retraditionalization process, it is in the context of this individualization and secularization. Hence, retraditionalization is not about some (re-)emergence of a premodern mode of relating to tradition. And secularization must, in the light of this, also be understood as something that takes place on the individual level; it has to do not only with the social structuring of religion in the church institutions but also with the conditions for the development of personal identity.

---

12. I know this is discussed more thoroughly in schools of sociology of religion working with American material. However, it is not possible to go further into this in the present context.

Thus, the pluralism that the churches face in a postmodern context does not immediately lead to the disappearance of religion, but religion now takes over new functions, for example, to be the cement of society. Religiously based traditions can contribute to the need people have for experiencing and making manifest their belonging to a larger framework of meaning. But this relation between individual identity and the traditions that exist in the churches must be seen as contingent, that is, shaped by personal choices and nonnecessary conditions. Against this background, religion gains more personal-expressive features, a development that also implies that any "given" connection between religion and social identity is made weaker.[13]

Technological development and cultural aesthetization of religion must be seen as important factors that generate a more comprehensive access to cultural resources (which increases pluralism) and that offer the opportunity to relate more experimentally and exploratively to these cultural resources. This underlines the importance of not taking for granted that religion only has decreasing influence in the Nordic societies. At least parts of the processes of detraditionalization can be read as an indication of the opposite, although the conditions for the influence and contribution of religion are different from what they might have been previously. Although the following quotation comes from an American study, it can also accurately describe the Nordic situation:

> Participation in more traditional forms of religion may have declined, but . . . the majority have not rejected religion. Instead, they appear to be reshaping religion, providing alternative definitions of religious reality and forms of involvement. Such reshaping of religion into a variety of alternative and often competing definitions is a correlate to the weakening (if not collapse) of the regulatory power of religious establishment. The diversity makes description and analysis difficult.[14]

This perspective also makes it possible to see how institutionally based religion is no longer the decisive point of departure for religious life and religious expression. The decisive point of departure is the secularized individual and his or her need for finding a more comprehensive pattern of meaning and understanding in life. However, this perspective also offers us an understanding of retraditionalization as a consequence of pluralism and globalization. Because globalization and pluralization make worldviews more relative, recognize the equality of different forms of sociocultural

---

13. Cf. on this also B. Wilson: "Toleration, Pluralism and Privatization," in *Religion in Modernity*, ed. P. Repstad (Oslo: Scandinavian Univ. Press, 1996), 29.

14. W. C. Roof, J. W. Carroll, and D. A. Roozen: "Conclusion: The Post-War Generation: Carriers of a New Spirituality," in *The Post-War Generation and Establishment Religion. Cross-Cultural Perspectives*, ed. W. C. Roof, J. W. Carroll, and D. A. Roozen (Boulder: Westview, 1995), 247.

formation, and simultaneously celebrate heterogeneity and variation, questions related to "identity, tradition and the demand for indigenization" become more important.[15]

The concept of retraditionalization is thus meant to identify elements of a postmodern culture that counter the effects of secularization and differentiation, be it in forms of morality, community shaping, narratives, aesthetic expressions, and/or sacred symbols. It is important to underline that it also involves processes that we would not normally count as religious in a strict sense. Its moral aspect is related to the purpose of establishing a framework for understanding and an identity in which certain values are to be legitimized and made accessible.

That retraditionalization is a postmodern phenomenon can be argued along the following lines: it is selective and/or eclectic, it is based on and made possible by a pluralistic culture, and it reflects quite strongly the active and constructive element in the *individual's* relation to the "tradition." On the other hand, it is not possible to see it as something that leads to the ongoing promotion of a nonreflexive and unchallenged authority. As previously said, authority in a retraditionalization process lies not with the tradition in question but with the individual. Thus, when the national churches offer resources for the shaping of personal identity in a culture of pluralism, they are in no way justified in assuming that their authority is something they can take for granted. This perspective is supported in the more recent work of Ronald Inglehart, who writes,

> This has not only opened for tradition to regain status, but created a need for a new legitimating myth. In the Post-modern worldview [*sic*] tradition once again has positive value—especially non-western traditions. But the revalorization of tradition is sharply selective.[16]

In a society with far more information than earlier, we also have access to far more materials from traditions that we are able to relate to and make active use of. The two-kingdoms doctrine also allows for the Christian to take part in the worldly realm as a place and space for a plurality of resources for identity-formation.

To speak of a tradition in this context thus presupposes that we make a choice from a wide spectrum of resources that can be called tradition because they are handed over from former times, and from another cultural location than the one in which we find ourselves at the present. As indicated, this choice is an important element in the reflexive construction of retraditionalization.

15. L. Voyé, "Secularization in a Context of Advanced Modernity," paper presented at Aarhus University in 1998, 10.
16. R. Inglehart, *Modernization and Postmodernization: Cultural, Political and Economic Change in 43 Countries* (Princeton: Princeton Univ. Press, 1997), 25.

> Even more generally, tradition is always a matter of human attribution:
> nothing about the materials themselves requires that designation. Even
> ongoing customary forms of action and belief do not constitute a tradition
> until they are marked as such and thereby assigned a normative status.[17]

Retraditionalization takes place where one is challenged to reinterpret
one's own tradition in the light of the presence of other religions and faiths.
That is what happens when the national churches get involved in processes
of retraditionalization that have relevance for the shaping of their own identity in a pluralist society. On the other hand, the individuals that live in the
society through the churches are allowed access to cultural resources that
are instruments for the shaping of their own identity, although this is something that is also dependent upon participating in structures of community
(as we know, traditions are never individual). Hence, the individual's appropriation of the traditional resources for identity formation that are found in
the churches indicates that the churches are perceived as relevant for the
contribution of resources to this process. This might be one of the reasons
for the still rather large membership in the national churches.

Given the large membership of the Nordic folk churches, I am now
able to suggest a perspective with which to understand the fact that many
people maintain their membership in these churches without actively practicing religion or sharing the "official faith" or confession of these
churches. We can understand this in the context of people finding themselves able to make use of the aesthetical, moral, identity-shaping, and/or
identity-defining elements offered in these churches (a relationship that
also presupposes a differentiation between different elements contained in
the churches). The Nordic paradox of the national churches is then perhaps
possible to describe in the following way: the national churches offer
resources for living and believing in a variety of different ways because
they have been able to maintain their own identity in a way that does not
make themselves agents of only a specific confession or specific confessional group. That is, they also provide or represent resources of morality,
history, cultural identity, and so on, that are recognized by most members
of society as relevant for their own shaping of identity, irrespective of their
personal faith. The two-kingdoms doctrine supports and provides an internal theological legitimization for this pattern.

The paradox, then, is that in a pluralist society we seem to become more
dependent upon traditions, viewed as resources or instruments for coping
with pluralism. It can be argued that there is a decrease in the way traditions function as legitimizing and normative, but traditions seem to have an
increasing impact on the development of a meaningful framework for the

---

17. K. Tanner, *Theories of Culture: A New Agenda for Theology* (Minneapolis: Fortress Press,
1997),133.

interpretation of personal life and the changes that take place in a culture more shaped by pluralism. Traditions also seem to contribute to the experience of belonging—a need that has not disappeared in modernity.

This means that traditions do not themselves rule but are used by human subjects (often subjects with some authority) to organize collective understandings of thought and action.[18] Thus, in reflexive modernity or postmodernity, traditions are to be recognized as having an instrumental function and as constructions that fulfill some important purposes. One important task is to reflect on how our traditions, as we now see and reconstruct them, also reflect to some extent how we perceive the future. By doing so, it is my hope that we can make more transparent how the postmodern way, or reconstructing and relating to tradition, mirrors some important aspects of our present situation and not only our past. This supports the suggestion that even the church as a tradition today is mostly providing its services due to the more functional approach established by a more or less privatized believer.

So, the church is present in the recent events and processes of retraditionalization. This shows clearly that the Christian churches in the Nordic countries not only have a cultural context but also that they themselves have an active part in this context and in the attempt to shape it—with more or less success. The church tries to meet the longing and the spiritual quest of people. Although our countries are counted among the most secularized in the world, this does not mean that the interest in religion is declining. It probably means that the interest in the traditional forms of church services is weakened, but it by no means indicates that the churches no longer function as a kind of uniting framework for peoples with different religious attitudes or perspectives.

Conclusion

The challenge to the churches is to recognize their new role in a diversified society without losing sight of the fact that the resources they provide in the cultural context are only possible to maintain if they are able to maintain a clear and distinct tradition and identity, so that people know that they can find in the church what cannot be found elsewhere. After all, the churches have something to say about living a life that God takes part in and helps to shape that is not said elsewhere. Hence I can sum up the challenge to the churches in this cultural context as openness to a diversity of approaches to religion and responsibility for maintaining a unifying tradition based on preaching the one Word of God for all people at the same time.

18. T. W. Luke, "Identity, Meaning and Globalisation," in *Detraditionalisation. Critical Reflections on Authority and Identity*, ed. P. Heelas, S. Lash, and P. Morris (Cambridge: Blackwell, 1996), 116.

The two-kingdoms doctrine should be reviewed critically as contributing to a more differentiated religious "market" in which religion is privatized and individualized. It also in some instances serves to commodify religion. The present "escape" of religion from the institutional framework, which I have indicated the doctrine "unwittingly" supports, also leads to new expressive and differentiated forms of religion that need to be addressed and sometimes also supported by the churches themselves.

A challenge for the use of the two-kingdoms doctrine is to develop and express it in such a way that it still provides the possibility of linking religion to the institutional sphere and contributes to the strengthening rather than the weakening of social bonds. At the same time, it must be interpreted in such a way that it still allows for a certain amount of pluralist and personal appropriation of the content of faith when it comes to how one is to live as a believer. Although this is a "postmodern" reading of the interest, it is important to underline, in order to secure that the human being is basing his or her faith on the Word of God and not on his or her own works or demands. However, it is hard to see how this can be done in the present pluralist situation, given a mode of faith liberalism that—paradoxically—should be affirmed as one of the important outcomes of the Lutheran heritage itself.

CHAPTER 23

An Ecumenical Legacy of Martin Luther and Asian Spirituality

Paul S. Chung

Martin Luther is of profound interest in the ecumenical context. In parallel, there has also been growing interest in Martin Luther from the perspective of liberation theology in Latin America. Leonardo Boff characterizes him as the one standing in favor of the movement of liberation in the age to come. Bringing about a grand process of liberation, he calls Luther "a necessary point of reference for all who seek liberation."[1]

However, Luther is not well explored from an Asian perspective. It is not easy to see Luther as the one recognizing and affirming otherness in a postmodern, religious pluralistic context. Therefore, an attempt to actualize Luther for the future in Asian context calls for a spirit of audacity. Luther was a man of his time, with limitations, weakness, and mistakes. Notwithstanding, Luther's insight into the discovery of the Bible, and his teaching of grace in particular, serve as an inspiration for setting Western theology free from its bondage to Greek formulations regarding Christian beliefs, system, and doctrine. Therefore, Luther may encourage Christianity to undertake an encounter with otherness by listening to the word of God openly and honestly in our pluralistic context.[2]

Unlike liberation theology in Latin America, most Asian theologians are concerned more about the issue of inter-religious dialogue. Aloysius Pieris, a representative of Asian religious liberation theology from Sri Lanka, is an experienced theologian in contact with Buddhism and in touch with many multireligious groups in the struggle for the liberation of the poor. According to Pieris, theological reflection in Asia must take both these elements—poverty and religiosity—together. As far as poverty and religiosity come together in this way, both become liberative. Pieris points to this as the specific difference of Asian liberation theology from liberation theology in Latin America.[3]

---

1. Richard Shaull, *The Reformation and Liberation Theology: Insights for Challenges of Today* (Louisville: Westminster John Knox, 1991), 25.
2. John B. Cobb, Jr., *Transforming Christianity and the World: A Way beyond Absolutism and Relativism* (Maryknoll, N.Y.: Orbis, 1999), 139.
3. Aloysius Pieris, S. J., *An Asian Theology of Liberation* (Maryknoll, N.Y.: Orbis, 1988), 69.

My concern in this chapter is about the Martin Luther of tomorrow
rather than the transplanting of his theology into Asian soil without further
ado. This would call for a daring task of understanding and transforming
Luther's thoughts from an Asian hermeneutics of experience. For this task,
I try to shed light on some issues in Luther's thought in regard to complex
realities of Asia: its overwhelming poverty and multifaceted religiosity.

God or Mammon

Luther's theology of the cross is reflected and echoed in Asian context by
Kazoh Kitamori, a Japanese Lutheran theologian, in his theological program of the pain of God. According to him, the pain of God is at the heart
of the gospel. Luther's metaphor "God fighting with God" (*da strydet Gott
mit Gott*) at Golgotha is utilized to combine God's wrath with his love from
the perspective of divine suffering. Therefore, "the essence of God can be
comprehended only from the 'word of the cross.'"[4]

However, Kitamori's *Theology of the Pain of God* is frequently criticized
by *minjung* theologians in South Korea (the so-called Korean liberation theology; *min* means "people" and *jung* "mass suffering") because he ignored
the suffering of the victimized. Bonhoeffer's keen sensitivity to the poor
gives a basis for minjung theology to reflect on a relationship between God
and the poor. "We have for once learnt to see the great events of world history from below, from the perspective of the outcast, the suspect, the mal-
treated, the powerless, the oppressed, the reviled—in short, from the
perspective of those who suffer."[5] Following in the footsteps of Bonhoeffer,
minjung theology agrees to include "both the question of human guilt and
man's liberation from it, and also the question of human suffering and
man's redemption from it."[6]

Developed from this minjung theology is the concept of *han*, which is
more profound than the concept of pain. *Han* is a particularly difficult
Korean term to articulate but is used to delineate the depths of human sufferings rooted in the anguish of a victim on the emotional, social, and even
ecological levels. Minjung theologians generally accept *Han* as important
indigenous theological terminology to understand divine suffering/human
suffering, or the forgiveness/sin relation. Therefore, minjung theology radi-
calizes the concept of sin from the perspective of the *Han* of the victimized.
It would underpin the doctrine of justification with the doctrine of justice

4. Kazoh Kitamori, *Theology of the Pain of God* (Richmond: John Knox, 1965), 41.
5. Dietrich Bonhoeffer, *Letters and Papers from Prison*, 17; cited in Gutiérrez, *The Power of
the Poor in History* (Maryknoll, N.Y.: Orbis, 1984), 231 (in a different translation).
6. Jürgen Moltmann, *The Crucified God: The Cross of Christ as the Foundation and Criticism
of Christian Theology*, trans. R. A. Wilson and J. Bowden (New York: Harper & Row, 1974),
134. Cf. Andrew Sung Park, *The Wounded Heart of God: The Asian Concept of Han and the
Christian Doctrine of Sin* (Nashville: Abingdon, 1993), 114–20.

for the oppressed. In this regard, Luther's teaching of justification is heavily attacked for its forensic way of ignoring liberating praxis on the one hand and for its neglect of social relations on the other.

From the Roman Catholic side, Pieris develops his Christology in two ways: (1) Jesus' struggle to be poor in terms of renunciation of the world and (2) Jesus' struggle for the poor in terms of renunciation of mammon as it appears in power and principalities. In his view, "religion and poverty in their coalescence offer the cultural context and the liberationist breakthrough for Asian Christology."[7] Complementarity plays an important role in inter-religious dialogue, especially concerning each religious core-experience. What is of significance to Pieris, it seems to me, is that the theology of forming *caritas* and *via negativa* are revitalized in option for the poor and go beyond justifying faith.

Given this fact, Luther's theology of justification and the impulse of theology of the cross need to be rediscovered as the counterpart of an Asian theology and spirituality. Sin was the language of the hierarchical-sacerdotal structure of the church in Luther's time. Luther's radical understanding of justification is expressed in a socioeconomic context by including the victims of the sin of the oppressor. In the socioeconomic context, the medieval phrase "fides caritate formata" (faith formed by love) motivates human beings to get merit for salvation through good deeds and charitable activity in an achievement–oriented piety and account book mentality. The scholastic phrase "facere quod in se est" (do what lies within you) secured a relationship between economic charitable works and mathematics of salvation in which the rich of innumerable cloisters and thousands of priests lived primarily by support of stipends and money given for masses to aid souls in purgatory.[8]

In contrast to "fides caritate formata," Luther's "fides Christo formata" (faith formed by Christ) put the emphasis on human vocation in secular works. Here Luther turned upside down medieval economic teaching and its understanding of salvation. For Luther, human labor is to be understood as a divine commission in terms of faith. Human works are the masks of God, behind which he continues creation and opposes evil in order to give every person the necessities of life.[9]

Luther took human work to be significant for the economic justice for the poor—against medieval economic teaching in which manual labor is devalued and vocation is limited only to spiritual and ecclesial professions. What is at the heart of Luther is not self-sanctification or almsgiving, but prophetic *diakonia* (service) for the poor and the weak in creating a just social economic order and system—that is to say, a form of worship within

7. Pieris, *An Asian Theology of Liberation*, 62.
8. Cf. The Smalcald Articles, in *BC* 303f., 316.
9. LW 14:114–15.

the world ("Weltlicher Gottesdienst"). In contrast to medieval *Zweiten-Stufen Ethik* (two-level ethic), Luther's discovery of the significance of the world from the perspective of the gospel led him to challenge the begging of mendicant monks and denounce the issue of usury and the economic practices of early capitalism.[10] Luther opposed the expanding money system and credit economy. Anyone who manipulates prices in his own interest "springs from sheer wantonness and greed" contrary to God's Word, reason, and every sense of justice. "All such fellows are manifest thieves, robbers, and usurers."[11] Luther's criticism of the socioeconomic system led the parish assembly of all the baptized to "efficacious social welfare policies."[12]

Luther's theological reflection on God (the First Commandment) in relevance to the economic realm showed explicitly that mammon was regarded as the chief example of opposition to God. Luther's critique of mammon in his time led to his economic ethics based on the commandment "You shall not steal."[13] This commandment became the vehicle of Luther's struggle with early capitalism. Therefore, economic issue became an integral part in theological reflection on God. In other words, a theological and dogmatic problematic for Luther included and integrated socioeconomic issues. God, who is in contrast to capital, motivated Luther to fight for the sake of the poor and the needy against the devouring capital process and system. A usurer is idolatrous because he serves mammon. The greedy are servant and captive to their mammon. In point of fact, Luther understood mammon as a totality and a system of reality conditioning and dominating the socioeconomic life in every respect. The problem of capital expansion was even described by a metaphor of "devouring capital."[14]

In light of his profound understanding of God, Luther exercised his critique on the reality of early capitalism. If I am not mistaken, Luther's teaching of justification cannot be adequately understood without reference to his reflection on the relevance of the theology and economy. In his debate with Eck, Luther states: "O non Theologi, sed Plutologi" (O, not theology but plutology [viz., wealth])![15] In the Smalcald Articles (1537), Luther articulated his critique of alliance between mammon and the medieval church on

---

10. Cf. "Brief Sermon on Usury" (1519), "Trade and Usury" (1524), "Admonition to the Clergy to Preach against Usury" (1540).

11. LW 45:261–62; on Luther's socioeconomic ethics, cf. Carter Lindberg, *Beyond Charity: Reformation Initiatives for the Poor* (Minneapolis: Fortress Press, 1993), 91–127.

12. Carter Lindberg, *Beyond Charity*, 127; cf. "Preface to an Ordinance of a Common Chest," LW 45:172–73

13. The Large Catechism (1529), in *BC* 386–92, 416–20.

14. Cf. Martin Luther, *An die Pfarrherren, wider den Wucher zu predigen*, WA 53, 331–424; cf. F.-W. Marquardt, "Gott oder Mammon: über Theologie und Oekonomie bei Martin Luther," in *Einwürfe* 1 (Munich: Chr. Kaiser, 1983), 189.

15. WA 1:304, 22—305, 4 ("Asterisci Lutheri adversus obeliscos Eckii," 1518). On Luther's critique of mammon and capital, see WA 10:2, 125 ("Wider den falsch genannten gesitlichen Stand des Papstes und der Bischöfe," 1522).

the basis of early capitalism. Psalm 127 provided a basis for Luther to understand that human beings are not "causa efficiens" (the efficient cause) in the area of "politia" and "oeconomia," but "instrumentalis causa" (the instrumental cause), through which God acts ("per quam Deus operatur"). Therefore, they are servants and coworkers with God.[16]

Luther's struggle for economic justice may give an impetus for church and initiative groups to stand on behalf of resistance against violence and injustice and carrying out a new constructive way for the rights of the poor.[17] What Luther criticized concerning the economic development of his time was based on his radical understanding of God, Christ, and gospel from the perspective of the poor. Luther's theology in face of early capitalism can remain a valid lesson for Asian Christians who struggle with the inequality of world trade in recent global capitalism. We may see that justice for the oppressed was an integral part of Luther's teaching of justification.

Theologia Crucis and God in Creation

The theology of the cross becomes a necessary context for the participation in divine nature. God became human in order to divinize human nature and the whole cosmos. This doctrine of patristic theology, which still is deeply echoed in Luther's statement that Christ is present in faith itself (*in ipsa fide Christus adest*), has been denigrated from the perspective of the anthropological Christology of Lutheranism. Moreover, in view of the ecological crisis, the cosmological breath of patristic Christology is to be rediscovered in the new paradigm for Asian theology from the Lutheran perspective.

For Luther, God the Father gives himself not only to us but also to all his creatures. God makes all creation, however small or unimportant, to help and provide the comforts and necessities of life.[18] For the reformer, faith in God implied that the Creator gives himself to all his creatures, by looking after human beings as well as all creatures generously in this earthly life. Luther explicitly stated the eschatological implication of justification. Luther's idea of justification was oriented toward the new creation on a cosmic dimension through the work of the Holy Spirit. For Luther, God was immanent powerfully in nature, in which we see God's dynamic presence and compassionate care "in, with, and under" all living sentient creatures. The whole creation was envisioned as "the mask of God."[19]

God the Creator is present with all creatures, flowing and pouring into them, filling all things. However, the beauty of God's goodness and glory—in other words, the aesthetics of God's glory in nature—is more deeply

16. *Enarrationes in Psalmos* 1533–1534. Cf. Marquardt, "Gott oder Mammon," 196.
17. Ulrich Duchrow, *Weltwirtschaft—heute—Ein Feld für Bekennende Kirche?* (Munich: Chr. Kaiser, 1986), 82. Cf. F.-W. Marquardt, "Gott oder Mammon," 176–216.
18. *BC* 432f., 449.
19. WA 40:1, 94; LW 14:115.

grounded in his teaching of justification. "Now if I believe in God's Son and bear in mind that He became man, all creatures will appear a hundred times more beautiful to me than before. Then I will properly appreciate the sun, the moon, the stars, trees, apples, and pears, as I reflect that He is Lord over all and the Center of all things."[20] In Luther's view, a lively faith goes hand in hand with a praise of God's beauty and glory in the cosmos. We Christians are encouraged to listen attentively to the beautiful music coming from others. Luther's marvelous sense of nature appears in his usage of a metaphysical metaphor from an ancient Greek sage. He bemoaned his time, saying that "we have become deaf to what Pythagoras aptly terms this wonderful and most lovely music coming from the harmony of the motions that are in the celestial spheres."[21]

This is a beautiful text, especially for Asian theology and for the Asian church, which strives to relate faith and justification to ecological fellowship, in other words, to improve the Asian sense of an inspiration to harmony and the interconnection of human being in nature. "The lovely music of nature," which is at the heart of Luther's aesthetics of creation, signifies wonderment of nature that gradually strengthens our faith. We are encouraged to regard God's wonderful and lovely music more attentively outside the walls of the Christian church, because Christian faith without wonderment would be reduced to a deaf faith. For Luther, the Spirit of justification is the Spirit of creation—and the Spirit of resurrection and a final transformation of all things, a new heaven and a joyful earth. "Then there will also be a new heaven and earth, the light of the moon will be as the light of the sun, and the light of the sun will be sevenfold, that is, immeasurably brighter than now."[22] The true Christian foundation of the theology of divine aesthetics, i.e., doxology comes from the theology of the cross, and the realistic direction of the aesthetics of divine suffering will arrive at aesthetics of cosmic eschatology.

In speaking of a justification/theosis relationship in Luther from the ecumenical perspective, Luther's spirituality of *humilitas* (humility) left the *via moderna* of the *absolute potentia Dei* (absolute power of God) as well as the *via negativa* of Platonizing mysticism. The question, "What does it mean to have a God?" or "What is God?" was decisive for Luther to drive the theology-economy connection.[23] Social justice and ecological stewardship grow out of participation in the divine nature. Liberating praxis can remove a sinful social and political system of victimization in Asia. This needs to be stressed and reinterpreted in terms of participating in the divine nature (including the ecological area). It would mobilize liberating praxis to

20. LW 22:496.
21. LW 1:126.
22. LW 12:121.
23. Cf. G. Ebeling, *Luther: Einführung in sein Denken* (Tübingen: J. C. B Mohr, 1964), 280–309.

renounce and to remove a sinful social and political system always producing victimization in Asian context.

In addition, Luther's *theologia crucis* needs to be extended and actualized in the direction of the resurrection of the crucified, in which God's active justification leads to a justice-creating kingdom of God, speaking out against human passive quietism and violent social structures. God's justification refers to creating justice on the side of the victims and, at the same time, to bringing the sinner to righteousness. That being the case, the suffering and death of Jesus Christ in the context of forgiveness of sin *pro me* (for me) and *pro nobis* (for us) should be grounded in and understood from the resurrection of the crucified *pro me* and *pro nobis*, especially with respect to God's justice for human life and God's ecological concern for all living sentient creatures. The new beginning of life seen in light of the resurrection of the Crucified leads to the life of forgiveness, reconciliation, and *metanoia* (repentance, or transformation of mind) by establishing the justification and compassion of God's grace socially, politically, ecologically, and culturally. We remain always as sinners in the past. However, we are always created righteous from the Future of God. *"Simul justus et peccator"* (at the same time justified and sinful) points to a Christian as an eschatological existence in light of the resurrection of the crucified.

Justification and Compassion in Christianity and Buddhism

When Luther comes to Asia, a Buddhist teaching of *dukkha* (suffering) is one issue in dialogue. A Buddhist starts with the realization that everybody and everything is in cosmic *dukkha*. The Buddhist solution to it becomes explicit in the great compassion of Amitabha for all sentient beings. We make note of a universal grace of the absolute Other Power in Amitabha Buddha.

According to a Buddhist tradition, Amitabha Buddha, after enlightenment, refused to reside in nirvana. Instead, he made forty-eight vows to active people by bringing them to the West Pure Land. He declared that if his vow was not fulfilled and realized, then he would not become a fully enlightened Buddha. Those who believe in Amitabha and wish to be reborn in earnest and with sincerity must repeat the name of Amitabha. Amitabha, infinite light, immeasurable, illuminating and radiant in every direction, refers to his infinite wisdom, his all-illuminating and infinite omniscience. In terms of his infinite light as wisdom, he exists for the sake of all sentient beings, helping them in many different ways. This compassion is the driving force for Bodhisattva's path. Resulting from deep compassion for the suffering of others, one experiences life-transforming reality and becomes "a son or daughter of the Buddhas."[24]

---

24. Paul Williams, *Mahayana Buddhism: The Doctrinal Foundation* (London and New York: Routledge, 1989), 199.

For Luther, faith is grounded only by the power of the Spirit, not by human strength or reason. If faith is interrelated to sacraments as God's promise for forgiveness of sins and eternal life, faith is not merely anthropocentric, but centers on Jesus Christ in the promise of sacrament. The Jesus Christ whom faith venerates is the crucified and risen Lord who rules the universe. The great compassion (*mahakaruna*) of Amitabha can be taken up to God's unselfish cosmic *agape* (love) in Jesus Christ by becoming an integral part of deepening the aspect of great compassion in Christianity. Therefore, when justification comes to Asian spirituality, it does not restrict itself to a forensic moment imputed *extra nos* (outside of us) but also refers to God's *mahakaruna* for all sentient beings, which finds its climax in the death of Jesus Christ on the cross. The Father's *mahakaruna* for the Son as well as for all living creatures in *dukkha* reveals Godself as God with the motherly mercy of coparticipation in the Son's death and cosuffering love in cosmo-theandric unity with everybody and everything. This understanding of God leads to an understanding of the *theologia crucis* that includes and integrates the *Han* of Asian minjung and the universal compassion of the Buddha within the framework of an Asian Christology of divine suffering in affirmation of the lowest of the low outside the walls of Christianity (Matt 25:45).

A Theology of Two Kingdoms: Toward Solidarity and Recognition of the Others

Luther stressed that God was at work in the secular domains manifest in *oeconomia* (the economy) and *politia* (the political structures). Following Augustinian tradition, Luther divided human beings into two parts, one under the reign of God, the other under the reign of Satan (*civitas dei/civitas diaboli*). Luther understood human history as a battlefield between God and Satan in an apocalyptic-eschatological perspective. However, for Luther—in spite of this distinction—the two kingdoms or two governments should be seen under the divine sovereignty.

Luther's view in this regard was distanced from Augustine or the medieval view of the *corpus christianum* (body of Christendom). In addition, Luther's distinction between the three estates (the priestly estate, the estate of marriage, and the temporal authority) serves to the protection and preservation of the creation. In all three estates of *ecclesia, oeconomia,* and *politia*, which God established, the Christian is called to act responsibly for others.[25] Christians and churches fight for their own rights when the official institution threatens to dominate their spiritual mandate. Christians also should be in solidarity with those who work in the official institution to pro-

---

25. LW 1:104; cf. Bernhard Lohse, *Martin Luther's Theology: Its Historical and Systematic Development*, trans. and ed. Roy A. Harrisville (Minneapolis: Fortress Press, 1999), 323–25.

mote the common good and well-being for the people. Therefore, Luther stood apart from the fanatics, who retreated from social life or transformed the secular areas of life totally into the kingdom of God by force and violence. The church is called and encouraged to become a coworker of God on behalf of protecting creatures from injustice and oppression, and promoting human life with mutual love and equity.

This is what Luther would express in terms of two kingdoms in relation to three estates. Luther's doctrine of the two kingdoms has been frequently criticized, because he is regarded as limiting the claim of Jesus Christ only to the spiritual area of life, leaving secular areas to the kingdom of the world. However, Luther's thought on these matters has been reinterpreted and rediscovered by some scholars. Here Luther's political idea is contextually to be understood from the threefold perspective: (1) a critical-constructive participation, (2) a critical-passive resistance, and (3) a critical-active transformation.[26] Luther's primary concern lay in closely relating the spiritual kingdom to the worldly kingdom and admonishing both of them to stand in line with God's struggle against the world of the devil.

1. Given this fact, the theory of two kingdoms can be extended not only as a way of understanding Christian political responsibility and solidarity for the sake of God's kingdom but also as a theological model of understanding people outside the walls of Christianity as integral parts of God's kingdom. What is at stake for Luther is not to guarantee *Eigengesetzlichkeit*, an independent order of creation (*Schöpfungsordnung*) in static coexistence with Christ's kingdom, but to highlight God's twofold way of governing each world.

2. A Christian is not free to avoid life in religious-cultural context. Luther regarded common life in culture as the realms in which God and the neighbor could be served. At this point, Luther's remark on Ishmael is remarkably striking: "For the expulsion does not mean that Ishmael should be utterly excluded from the kingdom of God. . . . The descendants of Ishmael also joined the church of Abraham and became heirs of the promise, not by reason of a right but because of irregular grace."[27]

3. This may refer to Luther's irregular way of reflecting on God's strange, even ominous voices outside the walls of Christian church. The world of wisdom in the area of creation should be included under the domain of the secular kingdom in which we are encouraged to listen to God's strange and strident voice with humble attitude and openness. Luther's language of the two kingdoms seen in this light of irregular grace does not remain in peril of a dualism or exclusivism, but should be open for and integrative of the world

26. Walter Altmann, *Luther and Liberation*; trans. Mary M. Solberg (Minneapolis: Fortress Press, 1991), 82–83. Cf. U. Duchrow, *Christenheit und Weltverantwortung: Traditionsgeschichte und Systematische Struktur der Zweireichelehre* (Stuttgart: E. Klett, 1970).

27. LW 4:42–44.

of wisdom in other religions. The world of wisdom in creation is not in contrast to the *regnum dei* (reign of God) but belongs to it as the sign and guidepost in light of the resurrection of the crucified. Luther's language of two kingdoms can be reappropriated and reread as the language of solidarity with and recognition of the different as different.

This is an important mission aspect of Luther's theology toward witnessing the gospel in the prophetic *diakonia* (service) and engaging in earnest dialogue with other religions and cultures in light of God's kingdom. Hermeneutical interaction or fusion of horizon (H.-G. Gadamer) does not allow us to go about syncretizing the gospel with other ungodly elements, but can help us to go into a deeper understanding of the gospel from an Asian perspective. Given this fact, the significance of Luther's idea of two kingdoms can be reinterpreted and reclaimed to promote the need for cooperation with different religions for bringing justice, peace, and perseverance to the creation.

Luther's Ecclesiology in the Face of the Others

Justifying faith expressed in the proclamation of the Word and celebration of the sacraments is at the heart of Lutheran spirituality. However, the spirituality of liturgy based on the priesthood of all believers goes hand in hand with the liturgy of life active in the social, political realm through love seeking justice, peace, and coexistence for all living creatures. For Luther, the true church is the *communio sanctorum* (fellowship of saints).[28]

The life together of Christians under the body and blood of Jesus Christ involves forgiveness, new life, and salvation. For Luther the liturgical-sacramental worship entailed the renewal of social life. The real participation in the sacrament of the Lord's Supper is identical with real participation in the fellowship with Christ and his poor brothers and sisters in the sense of Christ's universal presence with them. Luther emphatically emphasized this point:

> Here your heart must go out in love and learn that this is a sacrament of love. As love and support are given you, you in turn must render love and support to Christ in his needy ones. You must feel with sorrow all the dishonor done to Christ in his holy word, all the misery of Christendom, *all the unjust suffering of the innocent, with which the world is everywhere filled to overflowing. You must fight* (Widerstand leisten), *work, pray—if you cannot do more—have heartfelt sympathy.*[29]

28. The Large Catechism (1529) in *BC*, 417: "I believe that there is on earth a little holy flock or community of pure saints under one head, Christ. It is called together by the Holy Spirit in one faith, mind, and understanding. It possesses a variety of gifts, yet is united in love without sect or schism. Of this community I also am a part and member, a participant and co-partner in all the blessings it possesses"

29. Timothy Lull, ed., *Martin Luther's Basic Theological Writings* (Minneapolis: Fortress Press, 1989), 247–48; emphasis added.

Anyone who is incorporated into the body of Christ is called to "fight, work, pray" with heartfelt sympathy in the world where "all the misery of Christendom, all the unjust suffering of the innocent are filled to overflowing." The universal cosmic body of Christ is present in the poor and the oppressed in the world. This is an aspect of Luther's universal Christology in the midst of world suffering.

In his late text *Of the Councils and the Church* (1539), Luther identified seven marks of the church.[30] The true church as holy and catholic, i.e., the communion of the holy, can be found in these *notae ecclesiae* (marks of the church), in which the Holy Spirit is the guide and Christ the Lord. The gospel is preached purely and the sacraments are offered according to the gospel. In Luther we make note of a spirit-formed communion. According to Luther, *communio* has a twofold meaning: the gathering of the people of God and the dynamic participation in the sacraments of Jesus Christ. In other words, *communio* is horizontal as well as vertical. The sacrament is in this regard related to love of transformation with one another. The church as *communio* is the serving community in the discipleship of the world with which God is reconciled in Jesus Christ. In an ecumenical project of "Communion, Community, Society," a spirit-formed communion is proposed, especially with respect to a postmodern challenge.[31]

God comes ahead of time in the sacrament, partially but proleptically. An Asian approach to the Lord's Supper is concerned about both the spatial dimension of the real presence and the time dimension of it. Unlike Newtonian physics, the discourse of modern science (especially with respect to the complementarity of quantum physics) takes space not to be separated from time, and vice versa.[32] God's eternity is the supra-temporal source of the temporality of the world and its eschatological future. If the divine eternity is authentically temporality, the source of all time, we may experience with the encountering dynamic between past event and future hope in the present reality of the Eucharist. A limitation of language concerning Christ's real presence in the Eucharist needs to be extended and broadened to the point where Jesus Christ as the slain lamb of God comes to us in the Eucharist from the perspective of space-time coordination.

The real presence of Christ is realized and fulfilled in the relation of space and time. If I see the Lord's Supper as related to the time of Jesus'

---

30. (1) The Word of God, (2) Baptism, (3) the Lord's Supper, (4) the keys, i.e., public and private confession, (5) the ministry to serve according to Christ's institution and on behalf of the church and in the name of the church, (6) prayer, service, and catechesis; and (7) the cross.

31. Cf. LWF Studies, Wolfgang Greive, ed., *Communion, Community, Society: The Relevance of the Church* (The Lutheran World Federation Department for Theology and Studies: Geneva, 1998).

32. Cf. Robert John Russell, "Quantum Physics in Philosophical and Theological Perspective," in *Physics, Philosophy, and Theology: A Common Quest for Understanding*, ed. Robert J. Russell, William R. Stoeger, S.J., and George V. Coyne, S.J. (Vatican City: Vatican Observatory Publications, 1988), 359.

descent to hell, the Asian spirituality of ancestor rites comes into dialogue with Luther. Ancestral worship is regarded by many scholars to be the root of all world religions. The family holds a central place especially in Confucian culture, in which reverence for and glorification of one's ancestors belong to the greatest duty as well as the honor of the living family of descendants. Confucius approved the cult of the ancestor within the framework of filial piety and social moral stability. With good reason, however, Confucius banned any speculations about the state of the departed. In response to the question of a disciple about life after death, Confucius said, "While you do not understand life, how can you know about death?" The Fourth Commandment is deeply relevant to Asian people's mind-set, one in which there is no reverence for God without a reverence for parents. This ritual for ancestors is regarded in the Asian cultural context as a way of life that strengthens their understanding of human beings culturally and spiritually in a most profound way and prevents them from destroying their indigenous culture and spirituality under the influence of Western civilization.

In the Christian tradition, the communion of saints shows a proper relationship of living and departed in the eternal life of Jesus Christ. The duty and privilege of prayer for the departed has certainly been recognized from an earliest Christian tradition. For example, St. Augustine prays for the soul of his saintly mother, Monica, and encourages all readers of the book to "remember her at the altar."[33] However, the veneration of departed saints becomes questionable when a certain soteriological function is added to the communion of saints. After the Reformation rediscovery of *solus Christus*, the interpretation of the communion of saints does not mean the veneration of but fellowship with saints. The idea that the church is a fellowship not only in space but also in time challenges spiritually and eschatologically any historical provincialism and parochialism and further affirms emphatically the departed within the communion of saints in light of the cross and resurrection of Christ.

For example, the Great Prayer of Thanksgiving in the *Lutheran Book of Worship*[34] begins with creation, highlights redemption, and moves in expectation of the consummation of all things that are not yet but are to come. The salvation drama includes the witness of creation (Genesis 1; Psalm 104), the christological completion (Col 1:15ff.), and vision of eschatological consummation in Revelation 21. The God of the holy meal is the God who is "in, with, under" all things, not merely with human beings, and finally recapitulates all things in the vision of the new heaven and the new earth. The Son, when he comes again to make all things new "as victorious Lord of all," is eschatologically identified as the one who will come in power

---

33. St. Augustine, *Confessions*, 9.37.
34. Cf. *Lutheran Book of Worship* (Philadelphia: Fortress Press, and Minneapolis: Augsburg 1978), 69.

"to share with us the great and promised feast." The Lord who is host at this cosmic banquet is the Lord of all, the *Pantokrator* (almighty) in whom all things, things in heaven and on earth, are gathered up (Eph 4:6). The great cosmic banquet that is yet to come is itself experienced and realized *hic et nunc* (here and now) in eschatological openness. This is the cosmic aspect of the "cloud of witnesses" in the communion of the Lord's Supper.

If the ancestral rite is not meant to be the veneration of the departed but the fellowship and communion with our beloved parents, filial piety is the cornerstone of Confucian culture, and thus beyond a tradition or custom, it becomes a constituent element of Asian spirituality. Confucius, in fact, is thought not to have cared about any belief in personal immortality or in the power of spirits exercising influence upon the life of their descendants. What is more at stake for Confucius himself lies in his emphasis on the solidarity and continuity of the family, which can be strengthened and preserved by the memorial acts of ancestral rites.

Luther, following the patristic tradition, viewed the descent to hell as Christ's victory over the power of sin and death, which means a breakthrough of his triumphal procession. Luther took Jesus' descent to hell to be the subjugation of Satan, with all powers and the domain of death turned over to Christ. What was at stake for Luther was a cosmic soteriology of total liberation embracing not only the sociohistorical dimension, but also the cosmic universalistic dimension. In this regard, I would like to actualize Luther's reflection on Jesus' descent into hell in light of the total liberation of soteriology in anticipation of the participation of the Gentiles in the coming eschatological salvation (Luke 11:31f., Matt 8:11f.).

The God of justification is the God of justice for innocent victims. Jesus Christ on the cross, experiencing the present wrath of God against the world without God, embraces the future of God's wrath and the hell of the future, too. The cosmic understanding of Christ in terms of his descent to hell is, I think, the most radical, most valuable, and costliest grace of the gospel for the Asian people, which can be bestowed only by God in terms of divine suffering as victim and his wounded heart. If we understand the church as the assembly of saints with the proclamation of the gospel and the celebration of the sacraments, we come to talk about the unity of the church in the midst of pluralism.

This can be a different ecclesiology of solidarity with and affirmation of the others in light of the in-breaking reign of God in Jesus Christ's death and resurrection. Lutheran spirituality expressed in the real presence of Jesus Christ in the Eucharist needs to be actualized and reappropriated up to the point where the "otherness" of Christianity is no longer alien and is recognized anew in terms of the reconciliation taking place in Jesus' descent to hell.

Fides Christo formata, which is at the heart of Luther's justification and his spirituality, is the basis for the coming of Christ in the Eucharist, including the cosmic universalist salvation of our ancestors in the past. This is what the Eucharist means as the time-related event from an Asian context. The crucified God as the cosmic one is the Lord for Asian people in encouraging them to be in recognition of and in solidarity with the otherness, in anticipation of the coming kingdom of God. The cosmic Christ as "the crucified God" dies in solidarity with victimized humanity as well as victimized nature, and rises in anticipation of the Gentile's participation in eschatological salvation and the new creation of all creatures. This is where a conversation with Luther can be centered, and this is how Asian theology and spirituality can appropriate Luther's "*fides Christo formata*" in the future.

SCIENCE

Part

VIII

LUTHER'S THEOLOGY CAME INTO BEING in opposition to natural theology, that is, the attempt to gain knowledge of God through rational inferences from the world. Yet at the same time, Luther developed a rich theology of nature from the perspective of faith. "Our house, home, field, garden, and everything is full of the Bible, because God through his wonderful work knocks on our eyes, touches our senses, and shines right into our hearts." Luther's interest in nature, however, did not focus on nature in itself, but centered on the manner in which nature and culture interweave to make up a multifaceted life-world. It was into this world already filled with nature and culture that God became incarnate. Discarding the inherited distinction between the natural and the supernatural, Luther claimed that Jesus Christ was omnipresent in the material world. Therefore, Christ could also reveal Godself "in, with, and under" bread and wine, common products of nature and culture. Hence the famous Lutheran principle *finitum capax infiniti* (the finite is capable of the infinite), and the infinite God yearns to be found within the finite world.

This view has paved the way for an aesthetic-meditative attitude toward nature, an attitude that we later find in the Romantic Movement. But have Lutherans been sufficiently open to scientific and technological approaches to nature? Certainly, Philipp Melanchthon strongly supported natural philosophy (as the sciences were called), and Copernicus's *On the Revolution of the Heavenly Spheres* was published and prefaced by the Lutheran theologian Andreas Osiander in 1543. On the other hand, the principle of *sola scriptura* was also used to question the revolutionary implications of the nascent science of astronomy.

Today Lutheran theologians are fully engaged in the cross-cultural dialogue with the sciences. Ted Peters is known for defending the position that there is growing consonance between the sciences and theology. In "Grace, Doubt, and Evil," however, he also points to the particular barriers to grace that appear when science is aggrandized into scientism. In a culture of doubt, it does not suffice to say with Paul Tillich, "Serious doubt is a confirmation of faith." Theologians must also address the objective question of

1. WA 49:434.

how divine grace is compatible with the amount of evil that is generated by the mechanisms of natural selection. Even though the theology of the cross reminds us about the hiddenness of God in nature, theology should, according to Peters, be engaged in developing a theodicy.

In his response, Choong Chee Pang appreciates Peters's analysis, but he also questions the project of theodicy as part of theology's vocation. In "Science and Scriptural Interpretation," Dirk Evers reviews the old idea of nature as a book of God. By contrast, modern science no longer sees nature as promoting a message apart from itself. Nature just *is*. Thus, the question of meaning is a meta-scientific one. Yet the question of interpreting nature unavoidably confronts us, since the mathematical descriptions of science have to be translated into a wider worldview. Here, at the hermeneutical level, the dialogue between science and theology starts. Antje Jackelén shows, however, that a scientific understanding of nature is practically marginalized in present-day liturgies. The sciences, and technology in particular, are often presented as dangerous, if not contagious. As a remedy, Jackelén proposes various ways in which "the power of genes and molecules" may radiate into the worship of God, without conflating God and nature, but also without forgetting the distinction between the prosaic language of science and the poetic language of worship.

After all, the sciences are concerned with uncovering the structure of created reality, not with revealing the mind of God, the Creator.

—NIELS HENRIK GREGERSEN

CHAPTER 24

Grace, Doubt, and Evil: *The Constructive Task of Reformation Theology*

Ted
Peters

onstructive theology for heirs of the Lutheran Reformation is built on a foundation of grace. Commitment to grace is vocational; it is the Lutheran charism. Lutheranism has been conscripted, so to speak, to construct a theology of grace in every context.[1]

The conscription took place during the sixteenth-century Reformation, during which termites were weakening the structures of grace: "merit," "works righteousness," "faith formed by love," and Tridentine statements such as, "If anyone shall say that by faith alone the sinner is justified, so as to understand that nothing else is required to cooperate in the attainment of the grace of justification, and that it is in no way necessary that he be prepared and disposed by the action of his own will: let him be anathema."[2] Christian theology needed a reconstruction, the pouring of a new foundation in bedrock. By the end of the twentieth century, what was being built was much sturdier. "Together we confess," said Lutheran and Roman Catholic theologians together, "by grace alone, in faith in Christ's saving work, and not because of any merit on our part, we are accepted by God and receive the Holy Spirit, who renews our hearts while equipping and calling us to do good works."[3]

It appears that the underpinnings of grace have been reestablished. We are now free to rebuild the house of systematic theology on a firm foundation. What this means is that explication of remaining theological loci should cohere as complementary articulations of the graciousness of the God in whom we put our faith. Everything we say should be grace imbued.

This will not be easy. Nearly invisible barriers obstruct easy construction. Of course, we are familiar with perennial barriers in anthropology,

1. A previous version of this article appeared in *Dialog* 41(2002): 273–94.
2. The Council of Trent, Decree on Justification, canon 9. See Karl Lehmann and Wolfhart Pannenberg, eds., *The Condemnations of the Reformation Era* (Minneapolis: Fortress Press, 1990), 34.
3. *Joint Declaration on the Doctrine of Justification*, par. 15, The Lutheran World Federation and the Roman Catholic Church (Grand Rapids: Eerdmans, 2000), 15.

such as the human propensities for self-justification and hypocrisy. Here I would like to look at two other impediments to an easy construction of a grace-based theology: doubt and evil. The form that reflection on doubt and reflection on evil takes in contemporary culture does not appear automatically on the theological agenda as questions for which grace is the answer. The form in which these theological questions is ordinarily posed presupposes an understanding of God that disregards the question as to whether God is gracious or not. If doubt and evil are to be given room in theological construction as Lutherans envision it, we need reformulations so as to make the foundation in divine grace visible.

Doubt and evil have been with us since biblical consciousness helped form the Western mind, but they have become increasingly virulent over the last century and a half due to the cultural impact of modern science, especially evolution-based ideologies. When science becomes tied to naturalism as it did in the late nineteenth century, aggression against faith's foundations shakes us into re-wrestling with classic doubts. What we will see in the first decades of the twenty-first century will be attempts in some quarters, especially socio-biology and evolutionary psychology, to provide an allegedly scientific explanation for the foundations of religion. Theologians will be compelled to return to their own roots to see whether the roots are still there.

When science tries to provide a comprehensive picture of reality—such as the picture of the evolution of life over deep time as drawn by biology—the problem of evil returns with expanded scope. This picture of biological evolution includes 3.8 billion years of development from simple to complex life forms, a development in which life feeds upon life and in which 98 percent of earth's species have gone extinct. More than merely violence caused by human sinning in history, the problem of evil now incorporates millions of years of suffering on the part of sentient beings who are the victims of evolution. With this picture of the natural world being devoured by violence in the predator-prey fight for survival, theologians find it difficult to place within this picture a gracious God or a good creation. In the twenty-first century, theologians will be compelled to give an account of creation that finds grace in a world constituted by violence at every level of life.

In what follows, I would like to remind Lutheran theologians of their original and enduring vocation to cultivate our understanding of divine grace in the work of redemption, but also in creation. My point here will be that the concept of grace refers us first and foremost to a quality of God, namely, that God is loving, and this love is unilateral and unconditional. With this in mind, I would like to see if we can jump these two barriers to a healthy understanding of grace: doubt and evil. On the one hand, both doubt and evil are perennial opponents to God's gracious activity. On the other hand, contemporary intellectual life provides them with recognizable uniforms on the cultural battlefield. Doubt wears the uniform of a scientifically based agnosticism and even atheism; and evil wears the uniform of a scientifically based purposelessness as it raises the theodicy problem. Since the sixteenth century, the cultural context has changed, but the Lutheran charism—the call to construct an understanding of the whole of reality based upon the grace of God—remains intact.

Sola Gratia, Sola Fide

By "grace" we refer to the "unmerited assistance from God, especially as it pertains to salvation," in the words of David Yeago.[4] The final phrase here, "as it pertains to salvation," recognizes the original context in which Lutherans received their charism. As we shift from the sixteenth to the twenty-first century, the terrain has shifted somewhat away from salvation and back to creation. Not that salvation has been forgotten, to be sure; yet the challenge is to extend our boot-camp preparation in salvation to loci such as God and creation.

As it pertains to salvation, Martin Luther found himself analyzing the dynamic interaction between grace and faith as a Swiss watchmaker analyzes each gear in a an elegant timepiece. Among other things, the spring for faith is an "alien righteousness." Faith receives justification and salvation from beyond, from God. "This alien righteousness, instilled in us without our works by grace alone—while the Father, to be sure, forwardly draws us to Christ—is set opposite original sin, likewise alien, which we acquire without our works by birth alone. Christ daily drives out the old Adam more and more in accordance with the extent to which faith and knowledge of Christ grow."[5]

What makes this alien righteousness effect salvation in us is the presence of Christ placed in our faith by the Holy Spirit. By God's grace, Christ is present in our faith. His presence is that alien righteousness. True faith "takes hold of Christ in such a way that Christ is the object of faith, or

---

4. David S. Yeago, "Grace," *The Oxford Encyclopedia of the Reformation*, ed. Hans J. Hillerbrand, 4 vols. (New York and Oxford: Oxford Univ. Press, 1996), 2:184.

5. Martin Luther, "Two Kinds of Righteousness," in LW 31:299. Here in 1519 Luther saw the dynamic of grace's effect on faith in terms of growth or even progress. "For alien righteousness is not instilled all at once, but it begins, makes progress, and is finally perfected at the end through death" (ibid.). As Gerhard Forde develops the theology of justification by faith, he decries the notion of growth or progress. Grace at the beginning must be final, he emphasizes. "In its simplest form the problem may be stated thus: If justification conceived as forgiveness comes at the beginning of the process, the process is superfluous . . . if, on the other hand, justification comes at the end of the process, justification is superfluous. . . . Both the divine act of justification and the human process of becoming just according to the law cannot simultaneously be real" (Gerhard Forde, "The Christian Life," in *Christian Dogmatics*, ed. Carl E. Braaten and Robert W. Jenson, 2 vols. [Philadelphia: Fortress Press, 1984], 2:404). The instillation of salvific alien righteousness, according to Forde, is then immediate and total; righteousness or justification is not distributed bit by bit over time. Despite what Luther says, is this what Luther actually means?

rather not the object but, so to speak, the One who is present in the faith itself."[6] Faith justifies and hence saves, according to Luther's theology, because Christ is himself present in our faith.

The presence of Christ and the accompanying alien righteousness effect salvation through what has come to be known as "the happy exchange" (*frölicher Wechsel*), the Lutheran answer to atonement theology. "Christ is full of grace, life, and salvation. The soul is full of sin, death, and damnation. Now let faith come between them and sins, death, and damnation will be Christ's while grace, life, and salvation will be the soul's."[7] We are deemed just and hence justified because Christ is just and we have received his justness through this exchange of properties.

At stake here is something more important than death. It is ultimate. In fact, justification by faith incorporates death and life, death to a sinful state of existence and resurrection to eternal life with God. The promise of resurrection is the future hope of the Christian gospel; yet there is more. That future resurrection can be present in faith now because the Easter Christ is present in faith. The gospel means "death and new life in the crucified and risen Christ," writes Gerhard Forde.[8] The Christ present to faith has already died, so his death becomes our death. The Christ present to faith has already risen from the dead, so his resurrection becomes our resurrection. This makes the pronouncement of grace unconditional. "To the age-old question, 'What shall I do to be saved?' the confessional answer is shocking: 'Nothing! Just be still, shut up and listen for once in your life to what God the Almighty, creator and redeemer, is saying to his world and to you in the death and resurrection of his Son! Listen and believe!'"[9] Because God has acted toward us in an unconditioned way, we speak of salvation as *sola gratia*, by grace alone. Because faith here refers less to a human activity and more to the dynamic of Christ's presence in the life of the believer, we speak of salvation as *sola fide* and *solus Christus*, by faith alone and by Christ alone.[10]

6. Luther, *Lectures on Galatians* of 1535, LW 26:129. Tuomo Mannermaa recognizes that the role of the indwelling Christ in faith is central to Luther but not necessarily to Lutherans. "According to Luther, Christ (in both his person and his work) is present in faith and is through this presence identical with the righteousness of faith. Thus, the notion that Christ is present in the Christian occupies a much more central place in the theology of Luther than in the Lutheranism subsequent to him. The idea of a divine life in Christ who is really present in faith lies at the very center of the theology of the Reformer." "Why Is Luther So Fascinating? Modern Finnish Luther Research," in *Union with Christ*, ed. Carl E. Braaten and Robert W. Jenson (Grand Rapids: Eerdmans, 1998), 2.

7. Luther, "The Freedom of a Christian," LW 31:351.

8. Gerhard O. Forde, *Justification by Faith: A Matter of Death and Life* (Philadelphia: Fortress Press, 1982), 3.

9. Ibid., 22.

10. If the phrase "justification by faith" implies salvation achieved as the result of human faith as a human work, complains Paul Tillich, then we risk a misleading interpretation. "The cause is God alone (by grace), but the faith that one is accepted is the channel through which grace is mediated to man (through faith)" (*Systematic Theology*, 3 vols. [Chicago: Univ. of Chicago

Grace as God's Favor toward the World

Worthy of note here is the locus of the activities of grace. It is historically assumed by Lutherans that grace, "as it pertains to salvation," acts primarily in the human soul and in the life of the church. The interaction of grace and faith takes place in human subjectivity, in the faith of the individual and in the church, the *communio sanctorum*. Lutherans affirm an objective component, namely, the real presence of the body and blood of Christ in the elements of the Eucharist, to be sure; yet the arena of action is the subjective domain within persons of faith. Does this exhaust the scope of grace?

What about other domains, such as the attributes of God or the created order of nature? Certainly we consider the loving disposition within the divine life to be the fountain of all God's gracious activity; and the physical world God has created is a sign of God's glory and a means of divine grace. Grace is God's favor, and God favors the world.

Grace is a quality that belongs first and foremost to God. "I take grace in the proper sense of the favor of God," remarks Luther, contrasting it with a quality of the human soul.[11] Joseph Sittler reiterates that grace is rooted in God's love, and it is expressed toward creation: "The fundamental meaning of grace is the goodness and loving-kindness of God and the activity of this goodness in and toward his creation."[12] What we know as the temporal creation is a gracious act deriving from God's eternal love. "Love is the only real answer we have to the startling question, Why should there be anything at all rather than nothing? Love grants existence and grants it contingently," writes Wolfhart Pannenberg.[13]

Thinking of grace in terms of God and creation expands our frame of reference. We, today's people of faith, are but a brief paragraph within the chapter on the church, which in turn is but an episode in the epic narrative of God's creation stretching back to a Big Bang beginning and forward to a transformative new creation. The Christian gospel is the message that all of this is graced. "The gospel reaches backward and forward all along the line from creation to consummation because Christ is the eschatological revelation of God already at the beginning of things," writes Carl Braaten. "The world was created through Christ, and all things will ultimately reach their end in him as the Judge and Lord. This is the biblical meaning of calling Christ the *alpha* and the *omega*."[14]

Press, 1951–1963], 2:279). He suggests using the phrase "justification by grace through faith" to emphasize that salvation is a divine, not a human work. When properly understood as involving the presence of Christ, the biblical phrase "justification by faith" sufficiently implies *sola gratia*.

11. LW 32:227.

12. Joseph Sittler, *Essays on Nature and Grace* (Philadelphia: Fortress Press, 1972), 24.

13. Wolfhart Pannenberg, *Theology and the Kingdom of God* (Louisville: Westminster John Knox, 1969), 65.

14. Carl E. Braaten, *Principles of Lutheran Theology* (Philadelphia: Fortress Press, 1983), 111.

The divine grace of which we speak, in summary, has certain charac-teristics. First, the word "grace" is a descriptor for a divine disposition, namely, the disposition for love that leads to both creation and redemption. Second, grace is unconditional; it originates solely in divine aseity and at God's initiative. Third, in our faith, grace is experienced as a gift, not as a reward for works accomplished or merits earned. Fourth, the content of this gift is the presence of Jesus Christ, the uninvited but very welcome guest from heaven dwelling with us on earth.

The sixteenth-century Reformation was rocked by controversies over the role of grace in justification and salvation, and Lutheran theology was born with a special vocation to champion the cause of *sola gratia* within Christendom. The former controversies have not entirely disappeared, to be sure; yet both the church and the world of the twenty-first century provide a significant shift in context. If to be a friend of grace is the distinctive Lutheran charism, then this new context extends the call to penetrate more deeply into understanding that grace by discerning spirits—by discerning the supports and barriers to grace—in the *Geist* of the new millennium.

Barriers to Grace

It is a most curious exercise to entertain the idea that barriers would stand in the way of grace, that grace would fail to prompt a fully paved road to welcome it. It seems so unlikely. If grace refers to a gift freely given, how could this possibly elicit a negative response? Gifts are almost universally welcome, and gratitude is the normal response. Yet the drama of biblical history and subsequent history demonstrates that divine love stirs up human anxiety, divine giving stirs up human pride, divine care stirs up human self-assertion, and divine presence leads to crucifixion and death. One of the challenges to God in this drama is for divine grace to turn human enemies into friends.

This biblical drama reminds us that existing friends of grace have two overlapping tasks. First, theologically, we need to penetrate surface images to an underlying understanding of human nature. We need to assess theo-logically just why we human beings have a predisposition to resist grace, a propensity to repudiate the God who unconditionally loves us. Second, we need to survey the contemporary cultural landscape to identify the topog-raphy of intellectual, spiritual, and political landmarks where grace has no safe haven. We need to mount a theological apologetic, speaking directly to contemporary discontent within the church and within the world. This chapter will deal primarily with the latter task.

Yet, before we turn to our contemporary context, a word about human nature is in order. In the New Testament the word for "sin" (*hamartia*) connotes missing the mark, as an archer may miss the targeted bull's-eye. What is positive about this metaphorical image is that we human beings are aiming at something, perhaps at a target God has placed before our eyes. Note in the quotation from Luther above that original sin is a form of alien unrighteousness just as what grace imparts is an alien righteousness. This could imply that our deepest human inclination is to aim for what is holy and divine, but our trajectory misses the mark and strikes a substitute for the true God. With Augustine's helpful insights, we understand this substitute for the true God to be ourselves. We are, said the Bishop of Hippo, turned in upon ourselves, "homo incurvatus in se." By missing God, we hit ourselves. God's grace can straighten out the arrow so that the bull's-eye gets hit, according to Augustine.[15]

If we draw anthropological corollaries from the controversies over justification by faith, we can posit that we human beings have a built-in propensity for self-justification. The medieval derailing of Christian spirituality by the merit system should not have been unexpected; whether within Christendom or without, the pressure will always be with us to build our own ladder to heaven, our own Tower of Babel, and then climb up. Deep within the human soul is a sense of justice—more, an inchoate sense that justice represents what is eternal. As temporal beings pursuing eternal life, consciously or unconsciously, we seek to appropriate justice to ourselves, because we presume that in justice is power, and in power is life. "Self-justification" becomes the term for describing the fruit of our passion for ourselves, for establishing our security and our stature in our public image and before God.[16] Here, then, is the unavoidable conflict. If justification is given us by God, then self-justification is unnecessary. If justification is a gift, then our earning it is unnecessary. If justification is the result of an alien righteousness, then possessing it as an attribute of our own is unnecessary. If justice is something we wish to own for ourselves rather than borrow from Christ, then we have located a point of conflict. We must conclude that a potential for resistance to God's grace inheres in universal human nature; so we should not be surprised to find such resistance occasionally actualized in human spirituality, religion, and culture.

In what follows, I would like to name and review two barriers resisting grace: doubt and evil.[17] Like a natural geyser, resistance to grace lies under pressure well beneath earth's surface and then gushes forth when an opening appears. Resistance can spurt up without warning within the privacy of

15. "The fault in man is contrary to nature, and is just that which grace heals . . . not that nature is a denial of grace, but that grace is the mending of nature" (Augustine, *The Spirit and the Letter*, 47 [xxvii]).

16. Such an analysis of self-justification is taken up in chapter 6 of *Sin: Radical Evil in Soul and Society* by Ted Peters (Grand Rapids: Eerdmans, 1994).

17. I first introduced discussion of these four as "hurdles" to be jumped in an editorial, "Barriers to God's Grace," *Dialog* 37/2 (Spring 1998): 82–83. In this editorial I listed four enemies: doubt, evil, legalism, and hypocrisy. Legalism and hypocrisy are still with us, and they also cry out for an updated analysis.

our individual psyches, within the spiritual customs of our religion, or within secular realms of self-understanding.

Doubt

Doubt in our era is sometimes formulated as a question: Does God exist? Those who find it difficult to affirm a positive answer may attach a bumper sticker to their car that says, "Dog is my co-pilot" ("dog" is "God" spelled backwards). Beyond bumper stickers we find a range of tacit assumptions and articulate ideologies about the nonexistence of God voiced in various forms of naturalism, materialism, scientific humanism, and overt atheism. Short of atheism, most prevalent in modern intellectual culture is agnosticism, the position of considered doubt. The term "agnosticism" comes from Thomas Huxley in 1869 and reflects the image modern science has of itself; namely, as being modern, it replaces the religion of the past. Using the metaphor of maturity, Huxley says:

> When I reached intellectual maturity and began to ask myself whether I was an atheist, a theist, or a pantheist . . . I found that the more I learned and reflected, the less ready was the answer. They [believers] were quite sure they had attained a certain 'gnosis'—had, more or less successfully, solved the problem of existence; while I was quite sure I had not, and had a pretty strong conviction that the problem was insoluble.[18]

Maturity, it is assumed here, refers to an open-minded agnosticism that has outgrown the narrow-minded dogmatism of premodern religion.

Agnosticism both depends on and yet fosters naturalism. According to modern naturalism, nature is the only reality there is. The natural realm is self-sustaining, self-regulatory, and even self-explanatory to those who know how to understand it, namely, the scientists among us. The world of nature has no windows that open toward another world; no such thing as transcendence can be relied upon to ferry us beyond the material shore of existence. We simply cannot know anything about a noumenal reality that allegedly transcends the phenomenal world, which we can study through science.

Even though religious people among us speak of heavenly realities, skeptics doubt that such speech refers to anything heavenly. What appears clear since Feuerbach and Freud, Marx and Lenin, is that religious symbols express human wishes, that religious visions are unconscious projections onto heaven of wishes for fulfillment that are unattainable on earth. What exists is human subjective desire, to be sure; what is doubted is the divine object of that desire. What needs explanation, contend the skeptics, is not God but rather religion.

Evolutionary theory has in recent decades become the materialist explanation of choice. Fields such as sociobiology and evolutionary psychology

18. Cited by Michael Shermer, *How We Believe* (New York: W. H. Freeman, 2000), 7.

are trying to develop a comprehensive naturalism that will explain theological claims about God exhaustively in terms of evolutionary principles such as adaptive advantage. Religion, some claim, increases procreative advantage for some human groups over others; therefore, the religions that have survived to the present day must be the most reproductively successful. According to this theory, religion provides ethics as a cultural justification and inspiration that enhances our biological drive to produce children, an epigenetic tool in the construction of a preferred gene pool. Robert Wright speaks for the field of socio-biology here: "The reason they want children is because their genes 'want' children . . . why fight it?"[19] Because of this, says Harvard entomologist E. O. Wilson, "Ethical and religious beliefs are created from the bottom up, from people to their culture. They do not come from the top down, from God or other nonmaterial source to the people by way of culture."[20]

What we find here is an alternative explanation for religious beliefs about God and about human values. It is a purported *scientific* explanation. The scientist says that we should abandon asking the theologian to explain religion; rather, we should ask the scientist to provide a more accurate understanding of why people believe in God or adhere to ethical principles. The underlying agnosticism with regard to matters divine justifies drawing a strictly mundane or this-worldly picture of religious believing.

Agnosticism supports religious pluralism. The impetus derives primarily from the opposition to perceived dogmatism on the part of traditional religion, an opposition thought to be supportive of open-minded science. "I believe that gods exist to the extent that people believe in them. I believe that we created gods, not the other way around," writes the director of the Skeptics Society, Michael Shermer; "whether God *really* exists or not is, on one level, not as important as the diverse answers offered from the thousands of religions and billions of people around the world. . . . My only gripe with religion is when it becomes intolerant of other peoples' beliefs . . . or the cultural suppression of diversity."[21] The impetus for religious pluralism among such skeptics and agnostics does not derive from a desire to pursue theological knowledge. They are not traveling many roads up a single mountain—that is, no motive exists here to study a large number of religious claims in order to accumulate increased knowledge of transcendent reality. Rather, pluralism protects the right of each religious tradition to create its own projection of gods.

In some instances, agnosticism can make way for full-fledged atheism. Atheism is the positive assertion that no transcendent reality answers to the name of God. Paul Kurtz, avowed secular humanist and editor of *Free Inquiry*, makes this point by asserting that no God is listening to our

19. Robert Wright, *The Moral Animal* (New York: Pantheon, 1994), 148.
20. Edward O. Wilson, *Consilience: The Unity of Knowledge* (New York: Alfred A. Knopf, 1998), 247.
21. Shermer, *How We Believe*, 11, xiii.

prayers and supplications. "Prayers to an absent deity . . . merely express one's longings. They are private or communal soliloquies. There is no one hearing our prayers who can help us. Expressions of religious piety thus are catharses of the soul, confessing one's fears and symbolizing one's hopes. They are one-sided transactions. There is no one on the other side to hear our pleas and supplications."[22] There is no grace for atheism, because there is no God who could be gracious.

What appears on the surface here is that the question looks like this: Does God exist? The emergence of the scientific method with its antipathy toward religious dogmatism and the emergence of a naturalistic worldview with windows closed to the transcendent make this a question of wide cultural significance. Yet it is not the Lutheran question per se. The Lutheran question is this: Is God gracious? It would matter little if we could find a way through empirical science or philosophical reason to demonstrate beyond a doubt that God exists in the sense that nature would have a creator and sustainer. As dramatic as such a proof might be, merely establishing a designer for nature falls short of establishing what is most vital to us existentially. The question of the existence or nonexistence of God takes second place to the question of God's graciousness. What makes the difference in our lives and in our destinies is the presence or absence of divine grace.

Paul Tillich positively incorporates doubt into his concept of faith. An honest agnosticism, thinks Tillich, derives from a commitment to truth. When evidence is insufficient to be convincing, a person committed to truth must withhold judgment. Because knowledge of God differs radically from knowledge of things of this world, convincing evidence comes in insufficient supply to provide apodictic knowledge of God. Some measure of doubt is unavoidable, even healthy, especially when it is serious doubt accompanied by a sense of ultimacy. It is healthy because it exhibits faith in the truth, and true faith is trust in the God of truth. Indirectly, doubt is a form of faith; it is trust in the same truth that faith knows as God. "Serious doubt is confirmation of faith."[23]

Yet this is insufficient as an apologetic because it deals only with the subjective side of the ledger, with a person's disposition toward pursuing what might or might not be true. What remains to be addressed is the objective question, If there is a God, is this God gracious? One resource Lutheran theologians can bring to the question is the theology of the cross (*theologia crucis*). "The manifest and visible things of God are placed in opposition to the invisible, namely, his human nature, weakness, foolishness. . . . It does him no good to recognize God in his glory and majesty, unless he recognizes

---

22. Paul Kurtz, *Transcendental Temptation* (Buffalo: Prometheus Books, 1988), 22. "The presupposition of contemporary Western atheism lies in the development of modern natural science and its mechanistic picture of the world . . . " (Wolfhart Pannenberg, "Types of Atheism and Their Theological Significance," *Basic Questions in Theology*, 2 vols. [Philadelphia: Fortress Press, 1970–1971], 2:184).
23. Paul Tillich, *Dynamics of Faith* (New York: Harper, 1957), 22.

him in the humility and shame of the cross. . . . God can be found only in suffering and the cross," says Luther.[24] According to this theology of the cross, the glory and majesty of the invisible Creator is hidden behind the visible phenomena of suffering and death. In addition, this suffering and death belong to the reality of God proper; they are manifestations of the invisible God's gracious presence within a visible world.

Among the many things the theology of the cross tells us is this: pursuing knowledge of God by speculating on the origins and design of the natural world is a diversion, whether successful or frustrating. The best it could yield would be knowledge—more than likely projected speculation accompanied by doubt—about a divine architect or celestial engineer. Only by looking at the cross—the finite, historical, this-worldly cross—does God's grace become visible. Only in the cross can we see God present as the one who shares our suffering, who becomes the victim of our sin, who by this very acceptance of victimage bestows forgiveness, and who by promising resurrection bestows eternal life. Only in the cross can we see an eternal love coming to temporal expression.

We may be dealing with three types of hiddenness here. The first is the philosophical concern for apprehending an infinite God from a finite perspective, a noumenal reality from the world of phenomena. This appears to be the way the problem as a metaphysical problem is formulated by modern agnosticism and atheism. The second is the hiddenness of God's grace, God's care for us in our human plight. This is where Luther felt the tyranny of *"deus absconditus"* (the hidden God), the God of majesty who foreordains our creation and our destiny in sheer mystery. Is this high God indifferent to our concerns? Why doesn't this God answer prayer the way we ask? Then, as Lois Malcolm argues, there is a third kind of hiddenness: the hiddenness of Christ in faith. Malcolm turns to an "apocalyptic epistemology" to refer to the light shed by a promised future transformation, a future reversal of darkness and light. God now "sees" in the depth of creation what we can only hope for by faith, a new reality.

> The full redemption we await lies in the future. Evil and suffering have not ceased. . . . Christians believe that the very redemption of the world (the primary sense of hiddenness) takes place in creaturely flesh. This, then, is the challenge of hiddenness language: to confess to the goodness of reality and God's redemptive purposes for it even when it is hidden by the brokenness and horrors of life.[25]

Looking at the cross will not provide the empirical evidence or philosophical proof sought by agnostics of the modern scientific era. But then the cross does not purport to deliver what agnosticism is searching for. Rather

24. Luther, LW, 31:52–53.
25. Lois Malcolm, "A Hidden God Revisited: Desecularization, The Depths, and God's Sort of Seeing," *Dialog* 40/3 (Fall 2001): 189.

than prove the existence of God metaphysically, the cross provides an oblique peek into the realm of transcendence and then turns our attention around so as to see the presence of the transcendent God in the most mundane of the mundane, the physical world replete with finitude, suffering, and death.

Evil

Suffering and death bring us to the problem of evil. According to philosophers of religion, the problem of evil combines doubt about God's existence with doubt about God's grace understood as God's goodness. Skeptical philosopher David Hume lays down the gauntlet: "Is he [God] willing to prevent evil, but not able? Then is he impotent. Is he able, but not willing? Then is he malevolent. Is he both able and willing? Whence then is evil?"[26] Raised as a problem of logic, philosophers of religion frequently point out the incompatibility of three propositions:

> God is omnipotent (all-powerful).
> God is omnibenevolent (all-loving).
> Evil and suffering exist.

As Hume points out, the affirmation of any two of these negates the third. Contemporary atheistic philosophers find the irresolvability of the problem of evil to be support for the denial of God's existence. Theologians who wish to defend the existence and the righteousness of God find themselves in the position of proffering a theodicy, an argument that justifies God in the face of the presence of evil and suffering.

What the logical problem alludes to without capturing the depth of existential concern is the anguish we undergo when faced with the ugliness of evil and the horror of suffering. Whether natural evil in the form of suffering from disease or disaster or historical evil in the form of human violence, we find ourselves victims of suffering we did not invite nor wish to endure. Agonizing questions are flung heavenward. Why do so many children who desperately need caring families and loving nurture find themselves trapped in cycles of abuse leading to torture and scarring for life? Why would European civilization with all its industrial advances and democratic achievements fall into wanton self-immolation by mustard gas and saturation bombing over two World Wars? Why would a nation with a millennium of Christian influence devise a secret police force, death camps, and gas chambers? Why would the Japanese army massacre a quarter million Chinese in Nanjing, or al-Qaeda incinerate three thousand of our globe's citizens in New York's World Trade Center? Why would the twentieth century chronicle genocide after genocide: the Ottoman Turk genocide of

26. David Hume, *Dialogues concerning Natural Religion*, ed. Richard H. Popkin (Indianapolis and Cambridge: Hackett, 1980), 63.

Armenians; Nazi eradication of people with disabilities, Jews, gypsies, and enemies of the state; Bosnian Serb massacres of non-Serbs; Hutu extermination of Tutsis?

Genocides are the result of human sin; we refer to them as *human* evil. But, in our own era, *natural* evil also challenges religious commitments to a loving God. The controversies over evolutionary biology, beginning already with Charles Darwin himself, include the observation that, given the overwhelming amount of suffering by sentient beings in the predator-prey struggle and the extinction suffered by the vast majority of species due to the cold law of natural selection, no God could be considered responsible for creating such a brutal and bloody world of nature. And, if God is in fact responsible for creating the world ruled by natural selection, such a God would be morally unworthy. Niels Henrik Gregersen poses the challenge:

> In two ways has the problem of theodicy been sharpened since Darwin, first because the existence of pain and suffering can no longer be explained by human sin, and secondly because the existence of what we (as ethical primates) cannot but term as brutal, can no longer be seen as accidental to evolution. The struggle for life is pre-human in origin and is built into the very way in which the world is wired for complexification. Wired by God?[27]

Marilyn McCord Adams would refer to such genocides and such suffering in nature as "horrendous evils." With this term she refers to victimage so destructive that, it would seem, no future redemption could reinvest the victim's life with meaning. "*Horrendous evils* . . . I define . . . as evils the participation in which . . . constitutes prima facie reason to doubt whether the participant's life could . . . be a great good to him/her on the whole."[28] In the middle of anguish over evil, it appears that the depth of suffering is so overwhelming that no incorporation into a more meaningful whole could provide healing.

Some theologians have dared to try to address the existential anguish by resolving the logical conundrum. One solution is to deny being to evil, to render evil something that has no being in itself. Augustine tried taking this route. Evil is the privation of what is good (*privatio boni*), he said.[29] It may work philosophically to say that evil is a parasite off the good and deny to it any independent being, but the way we experience evil is as a structure of destruction, as the force of nonbeing destroying what is.[30] Whether it has being or not, evil is real and we reel from the suffering it causes.

---

27. Niels Henrik Gregersen, "The Cross of Christ in an Evolutionary World," *Dialog* 40/3 (Fall 2001): 200.
28. Marilyn McCord Adams, *Horrendous Evils and the Goodness of God* (Ithaca and London: Cornell Univ. Press, 1999), 26.
29. Augustine, *City of God*, XI:22; XII.3; XIV:11; *Enchiridion*, XIV.
30. Tillich, *Systematic Theology*, 2:60.

Another of Augustine's tactics has become known as the free-will defense. In principle Augustine affirms all three propositions, but by adding free will he transmutes evil into an expression of divine omnibenevolence. The creation of free creatures is a higher achievement than the creation of mere things such as robots or automatons, the argument goes; but when God bestows freedom upon us, the risk arises that we might engage in evil and cause suffering. This is just what happened historically, says Augustine. Our primordial parents, Adam and Eve, voluntarily (*voluntas*) chose to turn away from God; they turned away from the eternal and immutable goodness of God toward the temporal and mutable goods of this world. From then on their choices and hence our choices (*arbitrium*) are made in behalf of ourselves, not God, because we are now "*homo incurvatus in se.*" We began with a free will and lost it to sin; later, God will restore us at a higher level of freedom where we will be freed from the inclination to sin.

> God's foreknowledge had anticipated both—that is to say, both how evil the man whom he had created good should become, and what good he himself should even thus derive from him . . . evils are so thoroughly overcome by good that, though they are permitted to exist for the sake of demonstrating how the most righteous foresight of God can make a good use even of them. . . . And evil is removed, not by removing any nature, or part of a nature, which had been introduced by the evil, but by healing and correcting that which had been vitiated and depraved. The will, therefore, is then truly free, when it is not the slave of vices and sins.[31]

Two notions are attached to evil for Augustine: first, evil is the privation of what is good and has no eternal being in itself and, second, it is a temporary concession God has made to human history to allow the story of human freedom with its loss and redemption to go forward. Evil and its concomitant suffering are the price paid for a redeemed creation of freely loving citizens in the City of God. Evil is a negation that is negated by grace; it becomes a means for a higher redemption.

Augustine's theodicy is lumped with others who make the free-will defense because, according to this account, evil is the product of the creature's free decision. Even though God could foresee the human fall, God did not create evil. Evil is not a created entity, so it is the creation of no one. Yet one can still assert that the responsibility for the fall into evil lies on human shoulders. God is responsible for providing us with the first freedom and the redeemed freedom by grace. God is justified by this theodicy because God is not responsible for the origination of evil and yet is responsible for our redemption from evil.

Free-will defenders contend that it is better for God to bring into being a creation that is capable of being corrupted, capable of having evil and

---

31. Augustine, *City of God*, XIV, 11.

suffering as a by-product of free will, than it is to bring into being creatures without free will. With this axiom, evil becomes a tolerable risk. "In
freely willing the other's freedom, God does come to be affected by the contingent reality of that which is not God," writes Paul Sponheim. "Evil
deeds carry such efficacy as to weave a web of brokenness in which every
human life is caught—that also speaks of the degree of risk and cost
involved in God's will for the freedom of the other."[32] God here is further
justified because freedom is such an overwhelming good that God rightly
risked evil in order to make freedom possible.

In addition to the free-will defense, other theodicies are available
among contemporary theologians, most prominently the developmental
view of John Hick, following Irenaeus, which sees evil and suffering as necessary to the growth process of soul-making.[33] Whiteheadian process theologians   offer   an   alternative   theodicy   that   denies   the   first
proposition—they deny that God is omnipotent—while strongly affirming
divine love and assigning God the role of luring actual entities beyond evil
toward God's subjective aim.[34] All three of these positions—free will
defense, soul-making teleology, and limiting God's power—affirm theism
and do not yield to the conclusion that our experience of evil is sufficient
to persuade us that no God exists. In addition, all three are not willing to
give up on affirming God as gracious. God's love is not a negotiable item.
If there is a God, then this God is loving, even all-loving. God is justified
because the world's evil either lies beyond God's power to control or is
taken up into a more inclusive good.

Is proffering a theodicy the vocation of a Lutheran theologian? Is it the
task of Lutheran theology to justify God in the face of complaints about evil
and suffering within the creation? Is theodicy the way to pose the
Fragestellung, to pose the question to be pursued? A summons to "justify
God" ought to ring dissonantly in Lutheran ears. For a theological tradition
struggling to understand how God justifies us whose sins lead to evil and
suffering, this reversal of the agenda ought to seem odd.

Just what is the barrier to grace here? It may seem that the evil we experience is the obstruction; yet, the cross, which takes sin and suffering unto
itself, is the fundamental symbol for the presence of grace. So this cannot be
the barrier. Perhaps then the barrier is found in those philosophical reflections
upon evil that nominate God as the one guilty for evil and, with a curious turn
in logic, count this as evidence that God does not exist. The argument against
God's existence includes the side corollary that if there were a God who would
permit such horrendous evils, this God would not be worthy of existence. In
short, this is a moral argument, not an ontological argument, against God's

---

32. Paul Sponheim, *Faith and the Other* (Minneapolis: Fortress Press, 1993), 91–92.
33. John Hick, *Evil and the God of Love* (New York: Harper, 1978).
34. Charles Hartshorne, *Omnipotence and Other Theological Mistakes* (New York: SUNY
Press, 1984); Marjorie Hewitt Suchocki, *The End of Evil* (New York: SUNY Press, 1988).

existence. Defenders of God unanimously affirm in their theodicies that God is moral; God is all-loving despite the way the world looks.

Is this the kind of argument Lutheran theologians ought to take on? Lutherans should be acutely aware of the dynamic of self-justification operative everywhere in human self-promotion, and we should look to see if it is operative even in theological discourse. Turning our attention in this direction uncovers a subtle assumption at work in both atheistic and theistic theodicies, namely, that our human perspective on evil and suffering is placed in the judgment seat. The theodicist has claimed the role of judge and placed God on trial. As Job found out, the mysterious and magnificent God who established the foundations of the world does not subject divinity to trial by humanity, even on moral charges (Job 38–42). Timothy Lull reminds us, "One thing we know about God, or ought to know about God, is that God is God and we are not."[35]

Perhaps this is what prompts Robert W. Jenson to side-step the task of providing a theodicy within the scope of his systematic theology. "No theodicy is proposed. It is in any case not possible within the system here presented to 'justify the ways of God to men.'"[36]

Yet an appeal to the privilege of divine mystery is but one resource Lutheran theology brings to the problem of evil. Again, the theology of the cross places itself front and center. Our concern in this instance is first an epistemological one, to be sure—the concern over knowing the hidden God within or behind the God revealed in the cross. The epistemological concern has to do with revelation. "Thus the characteristic of God as the *Deus theologicus* is that he is *Deus crucifixus* and *absconditus*," comments Gerhard Ebeling, indicating that to know God truly is to know God in the crucifixion.[37] This also has to do with avoiding a theology of glory (*theologia gloriae*), wherein we construct an image of God based upon the strengths and perfections we can imagine by looking at the works of creation. Such imaginings that seem to glorify God but in fact glorify our human imagination are just what get doused when turning our attention to the revelation of God in the cross. "No matter what the issue or the problem in life," writes Eric Gritsch, "the theologian must see it within the shadow of the cross. Thus theology must ultimately concentrate on Christ and not on the believer. True theology, therefore, always crucifies the theological ego."[38]

In addition to the epistemological problem with divine hiddenness, second, the theology of the cross also points to what is revealed, namely, that God is present in the suffering and death that comes with the cross. The

---

35. Timothy Lull, "God and Suffering: A Fragment," *Dialog* 25/2 (Spring 1986): 94.

36. Robert W. Jenson, *Systematic Theology*, 2 vols. (Oxford: Oxford Univ. Press, 1997–1999), 2:21.

37. Gerhard Ebeling, *Luther: An Introduction to His Thought* (Philadelphia: Fortress Press, 1970), 227.

38. Eric W. Gritsch, *Martin Luther: God's Court Jester* (Philadelphia: Fortress Press, 1983), 168.

crucifixion of Christ is God incarnate with us, taking evil and evil's guilt into the divine life. God is the victim of human evil, not its perpetrator; and God freely absorbs this victimage as an expression of a divine love that does not fight evil with evil but rather with the grace of forgiveness and reconciliation. Luther emphasizes "how much it cost Christ and what he paid and risked . . . he suffered, died, and was buried so that he might make satisfaction for me and pay what I owed, not with silver and gold but with his own precious blood."[39] One clear message relevant to the problem of evil is this: God is present with the world as it undergoes evil and present with us as we undergo suffering. God is not divorced from evil but rather has become one with those of us who suffer evil. God is not immune to the suffering of the world but rather shares in that very suffering.

The problem of evil is not reducible to a logical dilemma. Evil belongs to the drama of the world, a drama in which God struggles with and for the world. The resolution to the theodicy dilemma will not be found in clever redefinitions of the propositions or new insights into logical connections. Rather, we will find the meaning of evil and redemption from suffering in God's promise. By raising Christ from the dead on Easter, God has shown that the cross is not the last word. By promising an eschatological new creation, God has shown that the sins and sufferings of this present aeon are not eternal. Death will bring an end to suffering; and resurrection will inaugurate an aeon of healing. God's omnibenevolence is demonstrated by his empathic love in the cross; and God's omnipotence is demonstrated by his power over death, the power of creation and new creation. This is the drama in which we find ourselves, a drama with both evil and the promise of redemption from evil. Friends of God's grace share the anguish of those who suffer; they also share the promise of redemption.

Ethics

Friends of God's grace also share the ethical commitment to combat sin and serve those who suffer. "For Luther, concern for the true knowledge of God and concern for the right ethical attitude are not separate and distinct but ultimately one and the same," says Paul Althaus, making the move from the theology of the cross to ethics.[40] Tuomo Mannermaa makes the same move but departs from the indwelling of Christ in faith: "Faith means participation in the being and thus in the properties of God. And one of the properties of which the Christian in his faith partakes is love. Christ, who is present in faith as *donum*, brings love with him, because Christ is in his divine nature God, and God is love."[41] Via either route, the destination is neighbor love.

Neighbor love—a love that requires definition according to the needs of

39. Luther, Large Catechism, in *BC*, 434–35.
40. Paul Althaus, *The Theology of Martin Luther* (Philadelphia: Fortress Press, 1966), 27.
41. Mannermaa, "Why Is Luther So Fascinating?," 16.

the neighbor plus devotion to serve the neighbor as one's lord—has become a hallmark of evangelical ethics in Lutheran circles.[42] The attention of faith is turned from our relationship to God toward the world. "God does not need our works," says Marc Kolden, "our neighbors do."[43] Freed from the tyranny of judgment and death, the person of faith is freed to become voluntarily enslaved to the needs of neighbors who suffer. "The intimate connection in which Jesus places our relation to God and our relation to the neighbor presupposes that we are, as Luther expressed it, "daily bread" in the life of one another."[44]

Sin, evil, suffering: these matters alert us to our ethical responsibility. Yet Lutheran theologians have less to offer that is distinctive here; in fact, common cause with like-minded Christians and non-Christians of goodwill is readily available. What Lutherans lack in distinctiveness could be made up in passion or zeal. This remains an ever-present challenge and opportunity.

Conclusion

The original Lutheran vocation to build upon a foundation of grace was issued in the context of a struggle with works righteousness on the terrain of salvation. Conscientious Lutherans have been building a grace-oriented piety ever since. Many of the perennial impediments to enjoying grace, such as pride, legalism, and hypocrisy still obstruct development, to be sure; and these obstructions will require continued attention.

In our own era, doubt and evil appear as additional barriers to further construction. Each denies the existence of God, doubt making a metaphysical argument and evil making a moral argument. Without God, Lutherans cannot make the claim that God is gracious. Yet building a theological interpretation of reality is salutary only if it stands on a foundation of belief in a God who is gracious.

In addition, we must testify to a certain ambiguity. Both doubt and evil have some admirable qualities. Doubt, in the form of scientific agnosticism, retains an implicit commitment to truth. Evil, as reflected upon in theodicy, reminds us of our implicit commitment to a world that should be governed by love rather than suffering. What these barriers place before us requires respect. What Lutheran theology seeks is something short of total elimination of these barriers; instead, theological construction should incorporate them.

It is not the distinctive vocation of Lutheran theology to provide proofs for the existence of God, whether they are metaphysical or moral. What is a distinctive Lutheran charism is the theology of the cross. By appealing to

42. LW 31:329-377, "The Freedom of a Christian."

43. Marc Kolden, "Ministry and Vocation for Clergy and Laity," in *Called and Ordained*, ed. Todd Nichol and Marc Kolden (Minneapolis: Fortress Press, 1990), 196.

44. Knud E. Løgstrup, *The Ethical Demand* (Notre Dame: Univ. of Notre Dame, 1997), 5.

the theology of the cross, Lutheran theologians can point to Jesus Christ and say, "Here is grace." Grace comes in the form of suffering with us; and if by faith we can perceive the presence of the invisible God, then we can affirm that it is God who shares in our suffering. This is also the God who redeems, who heals the broken, who lifts up the unworthy, who reconciles enemies, who invites the stranger into his eternal home. This is the only foundation worthy of further theological construction.

CHAPTER 25

Grace, Doubt, and Evil: *A Response to Ted Peters*

Choong
Chee
Pang

Ted Peters's Argument

Professor Peters believes that Lutheranism is built on a foundation of grace. Following the signing of the *Joint Declaration on the Doctrine of Justification* by the Lutheran and Roman Catholic churches, Peters thinks that "the underpinnings of grace have been reestablished," so that "we are now free to rebuild the house of systematic theology on a firm foundation." However, this does not mean that the constructive task of Reformation theology is going to be easy, because perennial barriers still exist. Peters singles out two such barriers, namely, doubt and evil. And since contemporary culture disregards the question as to whether God is gracious or not, the Lutheran theology of grace alone is not adequate to deal with the questions of doubt and evil posed by agnostics and atheists. As such, "reformulations" are necessary in our theological construction.

Peters goes on to reaffirm the Lutheran principles of *sola gratia* and *sola fide*. He observes that there has been a very significant shift in our understanding of grace, that is, from the emphasis on human salvation in the sixteenth century to creation in the twenty-first century. Peters quotes Joseph Sittler approvingly: "The fundamental meaning of grace is the goodness and loving-kindness of God and the activity of this goodness in and toward his creation." Peters welcomes such a "shift," because "thinking of God and creation expands our frame of reference. We, today's people of faith, are but a brief paragraph within the chapter of the church, which in turn is but an episode in the epic narrative of God's creation stretching back to a Big Bang beginning and forward to a formative new creation." In the words of Carl Braaten, "The gospel reaches backward and forward all along the line from creation to consummation because Christ is the eschatological revelation of God already at the beginning of things." Peters believes that this shift from the sixteenth century's preoccupation with human salvation to the twenty-first century's concern with creation provides us with an expanded frame of reference to discern both the supports and barriers to grace "in the *Geist* of the new millennium."

Having accepted basic human nature and contemporary human culture, which have a "predisposition to resist grace," Peters thinks "we need to mount a theological apologetic, speaking directly to contemporary discontent within the church and within the world." And his chapter aims at dealing primarily with contemporary discontent within the world on the issues of doubt and evil. The main bulk of his essay is consequently devoted to the perennial problems of doubt and evil.

Expressed in various forms of naturalism, materialism, and scientific humanism, and from mild agnosticism to overt atheism, whether it was Feuerbach or Freud, Marx or Lenin—all these voices cause a serious thinker to doubt the very existence of a gracious God. Peters thinks that not even Paul Tillich's paradoxical assertion that "serious doubt is a confirmation of faith" is sufficient to respond to it apologetically. In the end, only the "theology of the cross," which Peters regards as a particular Lutheran source, may be adequate for the task: "Only by looking at the cross—the finite, historical, this-worldly cross—does God's grace become visible. Only in the cross can we see God present as the one who shares our suffering, who becomes the victim of our sin. . .and by promising resurrection bestows eternal life. Only in the cross can we see an eternal love coming to temporal expression." Yet, even in the cross we are still confronted with the hiddenness of God, so that Peters has to concede that "the cross will not provide the empirical evidence or philosophical proof sought by agnostics of the modern scientific era. . . . Rather than prove the existence of God metaphysically, the cross provides an oblique peek into the realm of transcendence and then turns our attention around so as to see the presence of the transcendent God in the most mundane of the mundane, the physical world replete with finitude, suffering, and death."

Suffering and death confront us with the problem of evil. But, unlike doubt, which provides a metaphysical argument against God's existence, the presence of evil in the forms of suffering and death provides a moral argument against God's existence. In the words of the skeptical philosopher David Hume, "Is he [God] willing to prevent evil, but not able? Then is he impotent. Is he able, but not willing? Then is he malevolent. If he is both able and willing, whence then is evil?" In response to such a formidable challenge, theologians throughout the ages have offered various types of theodicies to try to justify God to humankind. Peters cites Augustine's understanding of evil as the privation of what is good and his so-called "free will" defense. He also refers to John Hick's explanation of evil and suffering as being necessary to the growth process in soul-making. It is in the context of theodicy that Peters raises a couple of fundamental questions: "Is proffering a theodicy the vocation of a Lutheran theologian? Is it the task of Lutheran theology to justify God in the face of complaints about evil and suffering within the creation?" Instead of giving a simple yes or no answer to the questions, Peters solemnly reminds us that in any form of theodicy "the theodicist has claimed the role of judge and placed God on trial." And this should not be the case if we understood the book of Job rightly, because "the mysterious and magnificent God who established the foundations of the world does not subject divinity to trial by humanity, even on moral charges (Job 38–42)." On this crucial point Peters, agrees with Timothy Lull when the latter says, "One thing we know about God, or ought to know about God, is that God is God and we are not." Peters thinks that this is perhaps what has prompted Robert W. Jenson "to side-step the task of providing a theodicy within the scope of his systematic theology." "No theodicy is proposed. It is in any case not possible within the system here presented to 'justify the ways of God to men.'" But Peters believes that such "an appeal to the privilege of divine mystery is but one resource Lutheran theology brings to the problem of evil." Again, just as in the case of doubt, Peters puts the theology of the cross front and center in dealing with the problem of evil.

Peters also has a brief section on ethics in which he calls upon Lutheran theologians to make an ethical commitment to combat sin and serve those who suffer "with like-minded Christians and non-Christians of goodwill" for common cause, which he believes is "readily available."

While recognizing doubt and evil as barriers to further theological construction, Peters also acknowledges that "both doubt and evil have some admirable qualities," because "doubt, in the form of scientific agnosticism, retains an implicit commitment to truth. Evil, as reflected upon in theodicy, reminds us of our implicit commitment to a world that should be governed by love rather than suffering." As such, these "admirable qualities" should be incorporated in the Lutheran theological construction rather than being totally eliminated.

In conclusion, Peters declares, "It is not the distinctive vocation of Lutheran theology to provide proofs for the existence of God, whether they are metaphysical or moral." What is a distinctive Lutheran charism, Peters insists, "is the theology of the cross." It is in the cross that we witness the suffering of the gracious as well as the redeeming God together with us. "This is the only foundation worthy of further theological construction."

Response

I agree fully with Peters that the Lutheran vocation is to be a friend of grace. He is also right in singling out doubt and evil as perennial barriers to any grace-based theology, and he manages to cover the main issues regarding the problems of doubt and evil with remarkable clarity and fairness. In responding to the perennial barriers of doubt and evil, Peters is also right in making his final appeal to the "theology of the cross." As a fellow Lutheran, I can also fully affirm his conviction that in the end, this theology of the cross "is the only foundation worthy of further theological construction."

My main problem with Peters's paper is not his theology, which I could almost whole-heartedly endorse, but rather its targeted readers or audience. Let me quote him again: "We need to mount a theological apologetic, speaking directly to contemporary discontent within the church and within the world. This chapter will deal *primarily* with the latter task." Moreover, "the world" is understood by Peters as the place where there is "a predisposition to resist grace . . . and . . . where grace has no safe haven" (emphasis added). Peters's essay must be judged apologetically in this context. From this perspective, I must confess that even the "theology of the cross" is far from being satisfying and convincing. Because, as satisfying and comforting as it is to the Christian believer, the theology of the cross still leaves a host of questions unanswered, if not actually unanswerable, for agnostics, skeptics, and atheists. For one thing, unless you are a universalist, you will have to admit that the benefit of the cross of Christ is ultimately for the believers only. But evil is universal. So are suffering and death. The theology of the cross becomes even more problematic and offensive to the agnostics, skeptics, and atheists when it is expounded in relation to the Christian ideas of election and predestination. As such, we are still haunted by the disturbing questions posed by David Hume and the rest.

While I also recognize doubt and evil as the perennial barriers to any grace-based theology, I think it may just be a little too neat to treat them separately, with the suggestion that "doubt in the form of agnosticism and atheism provides a *metaphysical* argument against God's existence. . . . Evil and suffering provide a *moral* argument against God's existence"(emphasis added). This is because there is clearly a *causal* relation between doubt and evil so as to make separate treatment of the two very difficult if not actually impossible. From the time of Epicurus, through Irenaeus, Augustine, and Thomas Aquinas to Immanuel Kant, David Hume, Jean-Paul Sartre, Albert Camus and until our present century, problems of doubt and evil have always been *causally* related. It is the harsh reality of evil, which is empirically observed or personally experienced, that causes people, sometimes even Christian believers, to doubt the existence of God, especially the God who is supposed to be omnipotent, omnipresent, and omniscient, as well as gracious. Conversely, serious doubt leads not only to the denial of God's existence metaphysically but could also cause the dismantling of the very moral foundation on which ethics are built, resulting eventually in an amoral approach to life. Friedrich Nietzche's "beyond good and evil" and moral relativism, Sartre's cynicism, and Albert Camus's concept of the absurd and the meaninglessness of human existence all have their origin in the doubt or denial of God's existence. In fact, Peters himself is aware of this when he introduces the three propositions of David Hume.

As to the perceived "shift" from human salvation to creation, I can see why Peters thinks that it expands our frame of reference to discern both the supports and barriers to grace. However, I do not think that the Scripture and Lutheran theology quite see the relation between human salvation and creation in that way. The apostle Paul clearly understands human salvation in and through the risen Christ as "a new creation" (*kaine ktisis*, 2 Cor 5:17; Eph 2:10). Even more significantly, in Rom 8:18-25 Paul envisions the ultimate salvation or liberation of human believers in solidarity with the whole of creation (*ktisis*). Confronted with unprecedented ecological and environmental crises, it is important for human beings to be solemnly reminded that it is not only humanity that is suffering but the whole of creation as well (Rom 8:19-22). Evil must therefore be understood from this perspective.

Peters is right in pointing out that "it is not the distinctive vocation of Lutheran theology to provide proofs for the existence of God, whether they are metaphysical or moral." "What is distinctive Lutheran charism," he concludes, "is the theology of the cross." And this is "the only foundation worthy of further theological construction." And I would like to add that this should be the case not just for the Lutherans but also for all fellow Christians.

As for theodicy itself, not only is it not the distinctive vocation of Lutheran theology, but I venture to suggest that it may not even be appropriate as a serious theological exercise, and I certainly doubt its apologetic value, whether it is "within the church" or "within the world." I am glad that Peters refers to Job: "As Job found out, the mysterious and magnificent God who established the foundations of the world does not subject divinity to trial by humanity, even on moral charges (Job 38–42)." While God acknowledges the righteousness and integrity of his servant Job throughout the entire story, he evidently refuses to subject himself to trial whether by Job or by his friends who appoint themselves as God's apologists. Instead of answering Job, God assumes the role of a stern questioner when he appears "out of the whirlwind" and challenges the helpless Job: "Who is this that darkens counsel by words without knowledge? Dress for action like a man; I will question you, and you make it known to me. Where were you when I laid the foundations of the earth? Tell me, if you have understanding" (Job 38:1-3, English Standard Version). I honestly do not quite like God's manner of speaking with his servant Job, because it sounds more like intimidation than dialogue! But I welcome the message, a powerful and much needed message for arrogant skeptics and atheists as well as for well-meaning Christian apologists, even with the noblest intentions. Job was certainly not slow in getting the message when he responded in utter humility: "I know that you can do all things, and that no purpose of yours can be thwarted. . . . Therefore I have uttered what I did not understand, things too wonderful for me, which I did not know . . . ; therefore I despise myself, and repent in dust and ashes" (Job 42:2-6). But the penitent Job had now been greatly enlightened: "I had heard of you by the hearing of the ear, but now my eye sees you" (Job 42:5). Timothy Lull has clearly gotten the same message when he says, "One thing we know about

God, or ought to know about God, is that God is God and we are not"
(quoted by Peters). Robert W. Jenson is therefore wise for deliberately pro-
posing no theodicy in his systematic theology: "No theodicy is proposed. It
is in any case not possible within the system here presented to 'justify the
ways of God to men.'" God obviously does not appreciate the efforts of the
three friends of Job who have offered themselves as God's apologists (Job
42:7-9). Does this mean that we are committing "intellectual suicide"? Not
at all. For we are asked to love the Lord our God even with our mind (Mark
12:30) and that our mind should be constantly renewed (Rom 12:2). We are
here simply questioning the values of theodicy in relation to the problems
posed by doubt and evil. Our faith is not "blind" nor is it anti-intellectual.
The faculty of mind and its exercise are already assumed in the Lutheran
understanding of faith. In this sense we can concur with Anselm of
Canterbury (ca. 1033–1109) that it is "faith seeking understanding" (*fides
quaerens intellectum*). This is also the way of the cross and the journey of
the Christian pilgrim.

CHAPTER 26

Science and
Scriptural
Interpretation

Dirk
Evers

Sola scriptura was one of the fundamental principles of Reformation. One could even argue that the other great principles of the Reformation, such as *sola gratia, sola fide,* and *solus Christus* are dependent upon *sola scriptura,* as it is only through the biblical witnesses that we know about God's gracious will, which he realized in Jesus Christ and in which we participate through faith. The time of the Reformation also saw the rise of modern science with Copernicus, Kepler, and Galileo. Especially the biblical creation narratives and their cosmological and anthropological concepts were affected by the knowledge science gained in its due course through methodologically controlled experiment and mathematical theory. Although theologians from Augustine's time onward spent more effort in interpreting Genesis than almost any other biblical book, there is hardly anything substantially left of its creation narratives with regard to our scientific worldview. The biblical world of wonders, of demons, angels, and wicked beasts like the Leviathan is far away from the scientifically enlightened world in which we live. In matters of nature and the universe, science took the leading role.

And not only that, science now claims to extend its domain of competence into the areas of personal faith, religion, and social life. Neurobiologists intend to discover the neural basis for religious experience; some interpret the data of brain research such that God resides in our heads as an imaginary vision caused by special states of modules dissociating from the rest of the cortex.[1] Sociobiology and evolutionary anthropology try to identify the roots of religion and faith in a higher being in an evolutionary perspective, and they interpret ethical and moral principles in terms of the biological success of a social community.[2] Others see religious

1. Andrew B. Newberg et al., *Why God Won't Go Away: Brain Science and the Biology of Belief* (New York: Ballantine, 2001).
2. Cf., e.g., Volker Sommer, "Die Vergangenheit einer Illusion: Religion aus evolutionsbiologischer Sicht," in *Evolution und Anpassung: Warum die Vergangenheit die Gegenwart erklärt,* ed. Eckart Voland (Stuttgart: Hirzel, 1993), 229–48.

and theological implications in cosmology, elementary physics, and our theory of the universe. The physicist Paul Davies claims that "science has actually advanced to the point where what were formerly religious questions can be seriously tackled"; it now "offers a surer path to God than religion."[3] In his view, science not only has taken the leading role in everyday life and modern society but is also the much more effective and up-to-date tool for understanding the world and God. The "world's major religions, founded on received wisdom and dogma, are rooted in the past and do not cope easily with changing times . . .; the biblical perspective of the world now seems largely irrelevant."[4]

In this situation, what is the relevance of the *sola scriptura* principle? Is there any at all? Or is the existential interpretation of the Bible the proper means of avoiding conflict between science and Scripture—reducing the biblical narratives to the kerygmatic call into decision (*Entscheidung*), dissociated from any kind of ontology or cosmology? Or can we revise biblical hermeneutics so that scientific knowledge and scriptural interpretation can fruitfully interact?

In this chapter, I seek to deal with this challenge so as to develop a fresh look at both Scripture as well as at science. First, I review the predominant model, which related science and Scripture for traditional Christian theology, that is, the two-books model, and analyze its application to rising science and its final failure. I then take a fresh look at the *sola scriptura* principle as Luther developed it. The last section unfolds how understanding nature through science and scriptural interpretation are hermeneutical processes in their own right and how they can interact with regard to the quest of human self-understanding.

The Two-Books Model

It was Augustine who coined the term "book of Nature":[5] God is not only the author of the book of Scriptures (*liber scripturae*) but, even before that, the author of the book of Nature (*liber naturae*). Contra the gnostic contempt of this cosmos and its dirty matter in which our eternal souls are captured, as well as against neo-Platonist emanationism, Augustine insisted on the good creation, which the totally good Creator had brought forth out of nothing. In his contingent creation, the Creator actuates his sovereign will and discloses his nature and deeds to humankind to the extent he finds appropriate.

---

3. Paul C. Davies, *God and the New Physics* (Harmondsworth: Penguin, 1983), ix.
4. Ibid., 2.
5. Aurelius Augustinus, *De gen. ad litt.*, PL 32:219ff. Cf. Hans Blumenberg, *Die Lesbarkeit der Welt* (Frankfurt: Suhrkamp, 2000); Ingolf U. Dalferth, *Theology and Philosophy* (Oxford: Basil Blackwell, 1988), 67–70.

According to Augustine, however, the book of Nature is a cryptic one. Although it can be read even by the illiterate (*idiota*)[6]—and illiteracy was commonplace in those days, the Scripture being accessible only to the learned—its meaning is not easy to grasp. The book of nature is obscure because it is difficult for us human beings to decipher what it wants to say, and so it hides more than it reveals. It allows for many and varied interpretations and thus requires an interpretative key provided by revelation and the book of Scripture. Since the book of Nature and the book of Scripture have the same author, any contradiction between both books is excluded by principle. Philosophy of nature cannot contradict revelation. The clear and unambiguous Bible keeps the epistemic primacy. Augustine had always argued against the reliability and scope of cosmological speculations and was skeptical toward the possibilities of human accounts of nature. We have to know the Creator and what he reveals to us through Scripture in the first place if we want to make out something about the universe at all.

The Augustinian tradition was continued in the Middle Ages. Hugo of St. Victor, for example, one of the most widely read authors of the twelfth century, claimed that the universe as the sensible world is a book written by the finger of God,[7] while each and every creature is like a word or a letter designated by God's decree to proclaim the invisible. Not much later, it was Bonaventura who systematized the relation between the two books and thus founded what would gain the status of common opinion in creation theology. Originally, creation was designed to lead the creature to its Creator, and it was fully capable of doing so. It was human sin and fall that damaged this source of knowledge of the divine; the book of Scripture was seen as the means of recovering the original sense of creation. Through revelation, nature becomes readable again, and thus through revelation the meaningfulness of creation is restored.

This two-sources theory was also the model that Lutheran orthodoxy adopted: there are two paths that lead to the cognition of God, creature and Scripture.[8] Cognition via the book of Nature (*ex libro naturae*) is imperfect and ambiguous. The brute fact of God's existence and some of his properties and commandments might be inferred from it, but not in such a way that existential certitude or definite ethical guidance could rest on it. The reason for this imperfection is found in the moral deprivation of humanity after the fall, which is no longer capable of deriving appropriate knowledge of God through creation. For full and complete knowledge, we need the supernatural divine revelation.

6. Cf. Augustine, *Enarratio in psalmum XLV*, 7 (*Corpus Christianorum: Series Latina* 38:522): "*in toto mundo legat et idiota.*"

7. Hugo of St. Victor, *Eruditionis didascalicae libri septem*, 7:4; PL 176:814B: "Universus enim mundus iste sensibilis quasi quidam liber est scriptus digito Dei hoc est virtute divina creatus."

8. Johann Gerhard, *Loci theologici* (Tübingen: Cotta, 1763), vol. 2, chap. 4, with reference to Augustine: "Duo sunt, quae in cognitionem Dei ducunt, creatura et Scriptura."

But what was more important and soon became an obstacle in the relation to rising modern science was the Scripture principle of Lutheran orthodoxy. The written Bible was defined as the written Word of God, with no difference between the Word of God and Scripture, so that there is no Word of God that is not written.[9] The identification of the Word of God with Scripture, originally verified by its content, was now asserted on more and more formal grounds. The doctrine of the total and perfect inspiration of Scripture was established, in the end stating that even each dot of the Hebrew vocalization was directly inspired by the Holy Spirit. Scripture became infallible and the source of propositional theological axioms (*dicta probantia*). Linguistic or stylistic barbarism was a priori excluded, as well as any error or mistake in any detail.[10] The human authors of the biblical texts were reduced to amanuenses, to mechanical executors of divine inspirations. With this doctrine of the infallibility of Scripture, the *sola scriptura* principle seemed to be solidly affirmed against Roman theology, that is, the equivalence of Scripture and tradition as stated by the Council of Trent.

Ironically, the two-books model had been a driving force for the rising natural science when it was emancipated from traditional philosophical and theological constraints. Traditionally seen as obscure and hardly readable, empirical-mathematical science now seemed to have found the language and characters with which the book of Nature is written. In his famous *Il Saggiatore*, Galileo Galilei pointed out:

> Philosophy is written in this grand book that stands continually open to our gaze [i.e., the universe]. But the book cannot be understood unless one first learns to comprehend the language and read the characters in which it is written. It is written in the language of mathematics, and its characters are triangles, circles, and other geometric figures without which it is humanly impossible to understand a single word of it; without these one is wandering in a dark labyrinth.[11]

9. "Nullum . . . verbum Dei non scriptum" (ibid., vol. 2, chap. 16).

10. Cf., e.g., Johann A. Quenstedt, *Theologia didactico-polemica* (1685), pars 1., chap. 4, s. 2, q. V, Thesis: "S. Scriptura Canonica est infallibilis veritatis omnisque erroris expers, sive, quod idem est, in S. Scriptura Canonica nullum est mendacium, nulla falsitas, nullus vel minimus error, sive in rebus, sive in verbis, sed omnia et singula sunt verissima, quaecunque in illa traduntur, sive dogmatica illa sint, sive moralia, sive Historica, Chronologica, Topographica, Onomastica, nullaque ignorantia, incognitantia aut oblivio, nullus memoriae lapsus Spiritus S. amanuensibus, in consignandis S. Literis, tribui potest aut debet." (The Holy Canonical Scripture is infallible with regard to truth and completely untouched by all errors, or, what is the same, in the Holy Canonical Scripture there is no lie, no falsity, and not even the slightest error, be it with regard to things [rebus] or words [verbis]. But each and every thing is most true what is handed down in them, whether dogmatic, ethical, historical, chronological, topographical, or onomastical [regarding names]. And no ignorance, want of knowledge or oblivion, and no lapse of memory neither can nor must be designated to the amanuenses of the Holy Spirit when they wrote down the Holy Letters.)

11. Galileo Galilei, *Opere* (Firenze: Soc. Ed. Fiorentina, 1847), 6:232.

The Augustinian thesis that both books have the same author was now
used as justification for an independent study of the book of Nature through
experiment and calculation. A contemporary, the Dominican Tommaso
Campanella, defended Galileo by stating, "Both books of God conform."[12]
An open attack on the book of Scripture was not intended. On the contrary,
the book of Nature, which could now be studied with the methods of the
new science, seemed a welcomed means to glorify the Creator. Johannes
Kepler even regarded astronomy as a higher form of theology and saw himself as a "priest of God to the book of Nature";[13] in another letter he wrote:
"Once I wanted to become a theologian, I was long in doubt. But now see
how God is glorified through my effort even in astronomy."[14]

After the first obstacles were overcome, the success of the new method,
which opened more and more areas of precise scientific knowledge, led to
the reversal of the relation of the two books. The objective book of Nature
attained priority. Scientific knowledge could be proved by the eyes of every
human being and by careful calculation. William Harvey, for example, the
discoverer of the closed circulation of the blood, refuted competitive
hypotheses by remarking that one "shall also understand, how unsafe, and
degenerate a thing it is, to be tutored by other men's commentaries, without
making trial of the things themselves: especially, since Nature's Book is so
open, and legible."[15]

However, with the rise of humanities and historical sciences, the history
of science and reason itself became obvious. Existential and hermeneutical
philosophy established the difference between explaining (*erklären*, science)
and understanding (*Verstehen*, humanities). While science cannot provide
answers to human existential questions, written texts were seen as expressing their authors' understanding of existence. The book of Scripture was no
longer a provider of theological axioms but was dissolved into a multitude
of historic documents of past ages. Historical-critical exegesis concentrated
on small detachable textual units and tried to reconstruct the historical and,
as far as possible, the "original" intention of the authors and their redac-
tors. Anthropological and existential constants served as a bridge between
the past and the present. Modern science apparently contradicts all mythological worldviews, so that according to Bultmann, it "is impossible to use
electrical light and the wireless and to avail ourselves of modern medical
and surgical discoveries, and at the same time to believe in the New

12. Tommaso Campanella, *Apologia pro Galilaeo*, trans. Grant McColley; Smith College
Studies in History 22 (Northampton, Mass., 1937), 3.
13. Letter to Herwart, March 26, 1598, in Johannes Kepler, *Gesammelte Werke* 7; ed. Max
Caspar (Munich: C. H. Beck, 1991), 574.
14. Letter to Mästlin, October 3, 1595, in Johannes Kepler, *Gesammelte Werke* 13; ed. Max
Caspar (Munich: C. H. Beck, 1945), 33–46, lines 253–57.
15. William Harvey, *Anatomical Exercitations concerning the Generation of Living Creatures*
(London: Pulleyn, 1653), 23.

Testament world of spirits and miracles."[16] Consequently, the texts had to be deprived of their mythological and cosmological worldview in order to bring about the relevant kerygma calling modern man into a fundamental situation of decision (*Entscheidungssituation*).

But Bultmann considered this a helpful critique because it leads us away from the offensive contents of Scripture, which were in constant conflict with science, to the central question of human self-understanding. *Glauben und Verstehen*—faith and understanding—was the task, a task to be fulfilled without any positive reference to science. Thus, from the theological side, the two-books model was given farewell: there is only one book, and it is to be interpreted totally in existential terms of human self-understanding, while science explains the dead and mute world of things that do not speak anymore.

Sola Scriptura Revisited

This is a rough sketch of the historical roots of our question: the relation of science and Lutheran theology was bound to atrophy due to a sterile principle of Scripture. That is why in Lutheran tradition we must reshape the *sola scriptura* principle to fruitfully extend the process of scriptural interpretation to the relation between Scripture and nature and to make it relevant for exegesis. To do so, it is helpful to take a fresh look at Luther's original concept of *sola scriptura*.

Luther clearly distinguished between the Word of God and Scripture: "God and God's Scripture are two things, no less than Creator and God's creature are two things."[17] Scripture is a creature, the witness of God's eternal word; it is not in itself eternal.[18] God's one and only word is the promise of the gospel, so that Scripture is the Word of God insofar as it promotes Jesus Christ (*Christum treiben*).[19] Thus, the Word of God has a main theme, which is the effective communication of God's grace as it has become verified in Christ. The history of God's grace, as it prevails against human wickedness until it is unsurpassably established though the cross and resurrection of Jesus Christ, is the central subject of Scripture—just as God's effective communication of grace is the central intention of God's Word. In the light of these distinctions, the Psalms, for example, are more an expression of the Word of God than is the letter of James.

Luther's promotion of scriptural authority was inspired by the conviction rooted in authentic experience that only through a self-determined and

16. Rudolf Bultmann, "New Testament and Mythology," in *Kerygma and Myth: A Theological Debate*, ed. Hans W. Bartsch; trans. Reginald H. Fuller (New York: Harper & Row, 1961), 5.
17. "Dua res sunt Deus et Scriptura Dei, non minus quam duae res sunt Creator et creatura Dei" (WA 18:606, 11f.).
18. Cf. WA 39/1:203, 34f.
19. WA *Deutsche Bibel* (DB) 7:384, 27.

original interpretation of Scripture a sound faculty of theological judgment can be established. Only through the constant interpretation of Scripture can the freedom of a Christian be built and be preserved by executing and practicing it. Without a communal and careful reading of Scripture, there is no critical point of reference that guarantees that indeed God himself begins to speak into the human situation and context rather than that human beings start to invent surrogates for it. It is important to see that the subject of scriptural interpretation is the congregation in its original sense, that is, any local community of believers where the gospel is preached, where the gospel "goes around" as Luther writes,[20] where it circulates and penetrates life. Thus, the people of God have to make *use* of the Scripture: there is no acquisition of the Word of God without making use of it. There is no Word of God *extra usum* (apart from use), just as bread and wine are not body and blood of Jesus Christ to us apart from the sacramental use within the kerygmatic context of a Christian community.[21]

This concept of Scripture has important implications. First of all, it establishes a fundamental principle of critique at the center of all scriptural interpretation. *Sola scriptura* thus implies the critique of Scripture from within Scripture insofar as the texts have to be interpreted according to the central theme of Scripture. Scripture is self-explaining, *sui ipsius interpres*, because there is a difference of relevance within Scripture itself, with the clear and distinct passages explaining the more obscure. Luther himself did not hesitate to admit obvious mistakes and contradictions within the biblical Scriptures. Scripture is anything but perfect. Second, Luther saw Scripture mainly as oral speech. Gospel in the original sense of the word is proclamation. While the Old Testament is partly a written book of stories and histories and partly a documentation of proclaimed gospel, such as with the prophets, the New Testament, the good tidings, is originally not written but spoken with a living voice.[22] And thus the Word of God as witnessed through Scripture is "not words of reading . . . , but pure words of living."[23] Third, the Word of God, which imposes itself on us through human words, is never distant, but always God's present communication of grace. It is meant for us here and now. Fourth, the "Word of God" is as such a complex process that involves a community of readers and believers, asks for the original situation of the text, weighs text against text according to the promise of God's grace and liberation, and asks how we can accordingly keep up to God's grace confronted with our reality.

Fifth, large parts of the Bible tell stories about God's gracious, liberating deeds to Israel, to individuals, and to his people, and about how God

20. WA 11:408, 18.

21. Cf. Ingolf U. Dalferth, "Von der Vieldeutigkeit der Schrift und der Eindeutigkeit des Wortes Gottes," in *Die Zukunft des Schriftprinzips*, ed. Richard Ziegler (Stuttgart: Deutsche Bibelgesellschaft, 1994), 155–73, 163.

22. WA DB 6/2:23f.

23. WA 31/1:67, 10.

gave himself into the hands of us humans in Jesus Christ, thus establishing his kingdom. God's particular word of gospel comes to us through a multitude of stories, and only in and through its particularity does it point to a universal perspective. It is by no means coincidental that the Bible starts with Genesis and the story of creation and ends with the apocalypse and the consummation of the world. Scripture opens universal perspectives, perspectives of living, of self-understanding, of understanding all creation;[24] it is a source of "scientific" and political wisdom, so that we are able to realize what this world is like.[25] Instructed through Scripture, all of God's works and creatures can become a living sign and Word of God.[26]

The appropriate use of Scripture, therefore, is a hermeneutical process, which starts with careful reading, continues in proper understanding, and is applied in valuable teaching and authentic living.[27] Through the Christian community and its kerygmatic context, the reading becomes public teaching, and Christian public teaching has to be judged not just by professional theologians nor by the established church-leadership, but by the Christian congregation itself, which reads and uses the Bible itself. The congregation is not helpless without a teacher or leader; it is the other way around: if there is nobody to judge, then the preacher or teacher is lost.[28]

The Nature of a Book and the "Book of Nature"

Does this meaning of the *sola scriptura* principle as a critical-hermeneutical principle of a never-ending process of creative interpretation within an attentive community help us in any way to relate Bible and science? I think it does. Nature and Scripture are divided by fundamental differences, but they also share often overlooked structural analogies that allow for an integrated model of mutual enrichment. They can both be described as open heuristic and hermeneutical processes that contribute in specific ways to the questions human beings have for understanding themselves and their relation to creation and God.[29]

---

24. WA DB 10/1:105, 8f.: "Ja du wirst auch dich selbs drinnen, und das rechte Gnotiseauton finden, Da zu Gott selbst und alle Creaturn."
25. WA TR 1:380, 45f. (no. 799): "wie es gehet und stehet in mundo."
26. WA 7:650, 27–29: "Seyntemal alle gottis werck und creaturn eytel lebendig tzeychen und wort gottis, wie Augustinus sagt und alle lerer."
27. Cf. WA 53:218, 19–23: "Wache, studire, Attende lectioni, Furwar, du kanst nicht zu viel inn der Schrifft lesen, Und was du liesest, kanstu nicht zu wol lesen, Und was du wol liesest, kanstu nicht zu wol verstehen, Und was du wol verstehest, kanstu nicht zu wol leren, Und was du gut lerest, kanstu nicht zu wol leben."
28. Cf. WA 15:42: "Denn der prediger oder lerer mag wol die Biblia durch und durch lesen, wie er will, er treffe oder fehle [den Sinn], wenn niemand da ist, der da urteyle, ob ers recht mache odder nicht."
29. Cf. Dirk Evers, *Raum–Materie–Zeit: Schöpfungstheologie im Dialog mit naturwissenschaftlicher Kosmologie* (Tübingen: Mohr Siebeck, 2000), 381–98.

As we have seen in Luther's account of Scripture and the Word of God, there is a difference between the written book and the living word. Embedded into a complex hermeneutical process of interpretation Scripture becomes the living Word of God proclaiming God's grace, effective in and through this world. Science, on the other hand, with its empirical methods, cannot but reduce reality to silent objects that stand for nothing but themselves. Any process of measurement abstracts from individual properties and reduces objects to mathematical values. But it is as a whole a human endeavor and, as any human endeavor, it is embedded in humans' quest for themselves, for freedom and responsibility. In this paragraph, I explain this thesis.

Nature: Not a Book

Nature as investigated and presented by science is not a book. Books are *means* of communication, and we have to distinguish between the message and the medium. Books can be copied, handwritten or printed, or translated with an overall conservation of their content. Vehicle and information, medium and content can and must be categorically distinguished. In the case of nature, nature is the thing itself. Nature does not promote a content different from itself. Natural objects cannot be copied, they cannot be transferred to another medium, and they cannot be translated. They are whatever they are; they are no code of a message that does not meet the eye. The answer to our existential questions of meaning, of ethical and political values, is not encoded in the world of scientific objects and theories.

And nature is not *sui ipsius interpres* (its own interpreter). That seems to me a most certain result of modern science. Although science had started to interpret nature as analogous to a book, as a meaningful whole with its coherence traced back to its "author" and with its specific language, under the consequence and discipline of its own methodology, it came to realize that the calculable cosmos of things is silent. The unity and meaningfulness of the world is not obvious. It is coherent by virtue of mathematics, not by virtue of its content. The temporal spans of our existence and the time of cosmos; the realm of space at our disposal, our planetary ecological niche, and the infinite void of the universe—these show an appalling discrepancy. Who are we? Are we the telos for creational design as some claim referring to the anthropic principle or a kind of contingent and most transient rash on an offside planet, a strange quirk of nature? In which way ever we decide in this respect, we cannot decide on scientific grounds. Science cannot tell. Neither the view through a telescope nor through a microscope nor any formula can tell.

Science Seeking Understanding

On the other hand, science is embedded in a hermeneutical process as well. Scientific theories imply certain values of rationality resting on notions of unity, simplicity, and universality. Pretheoretic conjectures define what may count as an empirical fact, and all data, as data, are theory-laden. The scientific ethos itself as well as the prevalence of scientific law cannot be argued for on scientific grounds. Science can only state what is the case but, due to its own ethos of objectivity, is unable to state what should be the case. However, it must deal with this question when confronted with the potential of its technical applications and the questions of where and why society should invest money and effort for scientific research and progress.

And science intends to understand nature according to us; it reconstructs the world we live in and is for that purpose part of human culture in general. Or, as Erwin Schrödinger once wrote, "all science is bound up with human culture in general, and . . . scientific findings, even those which at the moment appear the most advanced and esoteric and difficult to grasp, are meaningless outside their cultural context."[30] Even the most theoretical science must be aware which of its constructs might be relevant and become part and parcel of the general world picture. Thus science itself is pushing us to ask for ourselves. Out of its authentic motives, it indeed strives toward understanding what is the endeavor of science itself, of the world we live in, and what it is that makes human beings themselves. However, it does not, through its empirical methods, supply objective answers to these questions.

Science, Scripture, and Worldview

So the first mutual interaction between science and scriptural interpretation must be that science puts constraints on the factual side of our worldviews. Conformity to those facts of scientific research, which cannot possibly be renounced, is the first and most obvious demand. However relative all scientific cosmology is, it cannot reasonably be doubted that we are born into an unimaginably immense universe that expands and is filled with myriad suns and galaxies, and in which we inhabit a tiny transient planet. And it is certainly no arbitrary hypothesis that biological evolution on this planet brought forth all forms of living beings we see or whose remains we still get hold of. Moreover, we ourselves are part of this, when a few million years ago the first forms of humanlike beings as the *homo habilis* arose, which led to *homo erectus* and, finally, something like 400,000 years ago, to *homo sapiens*, of whom we are descendants. And nobody can deny that our attributes as humans, both as species and as individuals, depend on our genes and that our mental abilities rest on and are originated by the neuronal activity of our cortex. At the same time, the estimated figures of 100,000 genes and 100 billion neurons for each individual show how complex a being we are and that our means of empirical methods and theoretical conjecture might be by far too simplistic to ever explain ourselves fully.

30. Erwin Schrödinger, "Are There Quantum Jumps? Part I (1952)," *Gesammelte Abhandlungen* 4 (Vienna: Verlag der Österr. Akad. d. Wiss., 1984), 478f.

When on this background we read the Genesis 1 account of creation, we must not see in it a kind of supernatural disclosure of information that otherwise could not be obtained. We see it as the historical witness of an affirmation of God bringing about space, time, and a manifold of possibilities for us and our cocreatures. And this is done with the concerns of its authors at their time and within the limited knowledge at their disposal. Whatever they have to tell us, they convey as a historical role model for an affirmation of the God of grace—the God of Israel being the creator of the heavens and earth—by adopting the natural history and science of their time (e.g., Babylonian wisdom). It calls us to try our own theology of creation with the means and knowledge of our time, thus bringing together in a hermeneutical process both aspects, the real progress of science and its methods as well as the never completed but ever-new affirmation of faith in the gracious God of Israel and Jesus Christ. Only if we get involved in such a process of interpretation do we stay faithful to the biblical witness.

Toward Mutual Enrichment

In this view, Scripture and faith refer to science and its progress by making the hermeneutical process explicit, linking it to the human quest for a significant understanding of ourselves and of nature and creation in relation to God. It does so, referring to the fundamental principle of critique at the center of all scriptural interpretation, the affirmation of God's effective grace in human life and history through Jesus Christ. Through this point of reference, this *punctus mathematicus sacrae scripturae* (the mathematical point of the Holy Scripture),[31] scriptural interpretation is established as an endeavor highly critical against all apparent self-evidence and a venture highly creative in discovering new insights while at the same being obliged to the authenticity of its sources.

Still, in this structure of a heuristic and hermeneutical process, theology has much in common with the process of scientific conjectures and refutations as such, referring to factual conformity and theoretical fertility. Lutheran orthodox theology missed a historical chance when it did not see this close parallel between a critical concept of *sola scriptura* and the critical process of empirical investigation. In this respect, parts of the Anglican Reformation tradition were much more alert.[32] Here—in these structural

---

31. WA TR 2:439, 25f. (no. 2383).

32. Cf. the astounding and still relevant statement of the later Bishop Thomas Sprat in his history of the Royal Society: Church and science "both may lay equal claim to the word *Reformation*; the one having compassed it in *Religion*, the other having purposed it in *Philosophy*. They both have taken a like course to bring this about; each of them passing by the *corrupt Copies*, and referring themselves to the *perfect Originals* for their instruction; the one to the *Scripture*, the other to the large Volume of the *Creatures*. They are both unjustly accused by their enemies of the same crimes, of having forsaken the *Ancient Traditions*, and ventured on *Novelties*. They both suppose alike that their *Ancestors* might err; and yet retain

and hermeneutical similarities between science and theology in the tradition of the Reformation's *sola scriptura* principle—lies the future potential for a dialogue between both realms of knowledge, rather than in futile apologies of biblical claims regarding natural history.

But it is also highly relevant to refute the claim that by referring to Scripture and religious or theological knowledge the otherwise silent book of Nature could be deciphered according to a key supplied by revelation or religion. Scripture or any kind of religious claim and the book of Nature cannot be compiled into one universal text of natural theology.

By linking the scientific endeavor and its discoveries to the ever new and open human quest for orientation, theology has to remind science not to give in to the temptation that because of the extremely successful connection of mathematical certitude with a positivistic theory of knowledge—referring to a correspondence between theory and reality science—has to be established as the monopoly of total explanatory competence. However, this task can be fulfilled only by a theology that for itself refers to a critical principle of interpretation and consequently leaves behind the pretension that based on Scripture, a logically sound system of the propositional truths of faith (*articuli fidei*) could be established as an unsurpassable representation of revelation. In dialogue with science, theology must consequently design and represent itself as theology on the way (*theologia viatorum*).

---

a sufficient reverence for them. They both follow the great Praecept of the *Apostle*, of *Trying All Things*. Such is the Harmony between their *Interests* and *Tempers*" (Thomas Sprat, *The History of the Royal Society of London* (London: Martyn, 1667, 363)..

CHAPTER 27

The Power of Genes and Molecules: *On the Relevance of Science for the Liturgical Language of the Church*

Antje Jackelén

> . . . I modernise the anachronism
> of my language, but he is no more here
> than before. Genes and molecules
> have no more power to call
> him up than the incense of the Hebrews
>
> at their altars. My equations fail
> as my words do. What resources have I
> other than the emptiness without him of my whole
> being, a vacuum he may not abhor?[1]

Thus wrote the Welsh priest and poet R. S. Thomas (1913–2000). In spite of the lack of inclusive language, which many readers may experience as a blatant anachronism, this piece of poetry conveys some precious insights. Every now and then we experience the anachronism of our language. Words, symbols, and metaphors fall out of the rhythm of successful communication. This happens in all sorts of talk, in God-talk as well as other kinds of conversation. It is a characteristic feature of living language that it is always busy with modernization.

Yet R. S. Thomas's "but" means a serious blow to the best of our ambitions: God "is no more here than before." The language of genes and molecules has no greater power to evoke the presence of God than any more obsolete words or practices. As definitions of God, equations are no more adequate than words. Our bravest and best attempts to find effective liturgical language cannot conceal the emptiness that resides at the core of being. And it shouldn't. Belief in a certain kind of language, as a mechanical system that fills the void of our being with content, is idolatry. The emptiness, without God, of my whole being needs to be acknowledged as

---

1. R. S. Thomas, "The Absence," in *Frequencies* (London: J. M. Dent, 1978); republished in *Collected Poems, 1945–1990* (London: J. M. Dent, 1993).

"the vacuum God may not abhor." Without this acknowledgment, faith is impossible. The emptiness without God of the whole being of the church is the corollary of the fullness *with* God of the whole being of the church. The promise that God will not abhor the vacuum provides the ground from which to probe the width, height, and depth of liturgical language.

Does that mean that we can leave things where they are, without bothering about the relevance of science for liturgical language? The answer is no!—and not just for rhetorical reasons. It is one thing to abandon the illusion that modernized liturgical language is a magic formula that will invoke the presence of God. It is a quite different thing to cherish the hope that overcoming the anachronisms of liturgical language will provide a formula for communication with those who today feel marginalized by the language of the church. This second aspect provides the motive for this chapter.

I argue that liturgical language suffers from a deficiency disease in regard to science. Building on a diagnosis of the problem, I offer some thoughts about a therapy.

The Symptoms: Desire and Marginalization

Some time ago, I had the privilege of serving as an observer at a consultation for scientists organized by the Evangelical Lutheran Church of America (ELCA). I was impressed by the seriousness and faithfulness with which the scientists approached the tasks of identifying issues, trends, and dilemmas and of listing "next steps" to be adopted by a church that wants to take science and technology seriously. Quite a number of the scientists present were dedicated Christians in spite of multiple experiences of how little the church, from Sunday school on, had done to nourish their growing interest in science and technology. Many of them had endured years of encounter with a language that alienated their experiences, thoughts, and worldview. They were longing for an affirmation of their vocation to work in science or technology, and they wished their church would strengthen them in their commitment to minister to fellow scientists. They hoped that the days when children, women, and men felt that they had to leave their brains at the church door would soon firmly belong to history. Encountering something of the power of genes and molecules in liturgical language should help them see that their hope is not in vain.

Yet, comprehensive standard works on liturgy, whether in German or English, give little hope. They do not even index the word "science."[2] Science is either neglected or associated with "scientism."[3] The theology of the cross is proposed as a remedy against the idea that the world is getting

---

2. E.g., Rainer Volp, *Liturgik*, 2 vols. (Gütersloh: Verlagshaus Gerd Mohn/Gütersloher Verlagshaus, 1992, 1994); Frank C. Senn, *Christian Liturgy* (Minneapolis: Fortress Press, 1997).

3. Frank Senn, *Christian Liturgy: Catholic and Evangelical* (Minneapolis: Fortress Press, 1997).

better through scientific and technological progress.[4] Statements like these
infallibly convey an image of science as a potential enemy.

Things look similar on the higher organizational levels of the Lutheran
churches. In July 2003, a "Message from the Tenth Assembly of the
Lutheran World Federation" in Winnipeg, Canada, was adopted.[5] It is an
eighteen-page document that summarizes the Federation's analyses and
commitments for the next six years. The theme of the assembly was "For
the Healing of the World." With this motto, one would expect that the positive contributions to healing made by science and technology would be
mentioned somewhere. But they are not. The message states that "healing
is not limited to curing in the scientific sense" (11). True as this statement
is, its rashness in ignoring the efforts and achievements of medical science
and technology is disturbing. Medical services are mentioned as included in
the ministry of service, *diakonia* (10). Technology surfaces only as biotechnology, and then with negative or skeptical connotations. The document
addresses the need for "reflecting on ethical and justice issues related to
modern biotechnology, whose social and medical consequences are yet to be
seen" (17). The assembly commits itself and calls on member churches to
"evaluate new biotechnological developments and advocate against those
that violate the dignity and integrity of human beings as created in the
image of God" (17). The need for critical reflection about biotechnology
cannot be disputed. The problem lies not in what the "Message" actually
says but in what it does not say. There is nothing about the potential of science and technology to alleviate suffering, poverty, and injustice, nothing
about the vocation of scientists to praise God by employing their minds in
the exploration of nature to the benefit of humanity and all creation. The
only image of science and technology that is urged upon the reader is the
image of biotechnology as a threat to humanity. It is then a small step to
look upon scientists who work in biotechnology as people who need to be
advocated against, because they tend to violate the dignity and integrity of
human beings.

Yet the biotechnologist advocated against might be the girl whose difficult questions were not appreciated in Sunday school. Nonetheless, she may
still sit in the pew next Sunday, wondering whether in her church spirituality means that there is a place for *all* difficult and important questions of
life and work. Or the scientist in question may do research on genetically
modified crops, hoping that his research will help to feed a hungry world,
yet simultaneously fearing that unjust structures might lead to the opposite,
and he may be troubled by the uncertainty about long-term consequences.
His struggles are worthy of being seen, reflected upon, and supported by the
church, not ignored or rejected by it. Rites of affirmation of the vocation of

4. Ibid., 697.
5. http://www.lwf-assembly.org/PDFs/LWF_Assembly_Message.pdf.

Christians in the world will not bring much improvement, as long as under-lying negative assumptions about science evade critical analysis.

Anamnesis: Recalling Resources

Before sketching some therapies for this deficiency, it will be useful to recall some resources for the therapy needed. I identify these as the Lutheran heritage, recent developments in the religion-and-science dialogue and liberation theologies—especially feminist theologies.

Lutheranism has a tradition of intellectual curiosity. It is not mere coincidence that increased literacy came to be a consequence of reformation theology. Not only were Wittenberg professors in the Reformation era open to discuss and live with diverging opinions about the Copernican theories. The Lutheran practice of learning the catechism and the catechetical meetings at which it was expounded entailed educational benefits in a broader population. Increased literacy contributed in the longer term to emancipatory and democratic movements. The critical engagement with texts and the high esteem of inquisitive minds inspired each other. A noteworthy detail is that, as late as the beginning of the twentieth century, there was a significant difference in literacy between traditionally Protestant and Roman Catholic European countries. It is time to reclaim that dimension of the Lutheran heritage by working for more scientific literacy in the church and by opposing anti-intellectualism. Such a deliberate effort will leave its marks also on the liturgical language of the church. At the very least, it will entail that science and scientists be met by their churches with positive curiosity rather than skepticism, indifference, or anxiety. If the church dares to undertake a few more steps, it will take the revelatory character of science seriously and realize that the relevance of science for liturgical language is not a luxury but an imperative.

Liturgical theology often refers to the famous statement by Prosper of Aquitaine (ca. 390–463), "ut legem credendi lex statuat supplicandi," that the rule for interceding should establish the rule for believing.[6] This statement suggests that theology grows out of liturgy; *lex orandi* (the rule for praying) precedes *lex credendi* (the rule for believing). Benedictine theologian Aiden Kavanagh sees *lex orandi* and *lex credendi* entering a subtle correlation, where *lex orandi* founds *lex credendi* and where *lex credendi* affects, but not founds, *lex orandi.*[7] He holds that the growth of liturgies "is a function of adjustment to deep change caused in the assembly by its being brought regularly to the brink of chaos in the presence of the living God. It is the adjustment that is theological in all this." This, he says, "is theology being born, theology in the first instance. It is what tradition has

---

6. PL 51:209.
7. Aidan Kavanagh, *On Liturgical Theology* (New York: Pueblo, 1984), 150.

called *theologia prima.*[8] Even though Lutheran theology by tradition seems predisposed to regard liturgy as a result of dogma, there is also evidence of a more Prosperian approach. Lutheran liturgist Frank Senn holds that "while [in *orthodoxia*, understood as right worship] the relationship between praying and believing . . . is a reciprocal one, the priority of right praise is such that the *lex orandi* establishes the *lex credendi.*"[9]

Although too strong an emphasis on this kind of first theology may conflict with the principle of *sola scriptura*, it seems that the concept of liturgy as *prima theologia* can very well be lodged within the confines of CA VII. It also harmonizes perfectly with what Vilmos Vajta has called the "Schmiegsamkeit der Ordnung" (pliancy of order) in his study "Luther on Worship."[10] Liturgy grows between the poles of freedom and love. Freedom is what comes with faith. Grounded in faith, love can bind itself to order for the sake of neighbor. Love is the freedom to constantly adjust to the need of neighbor. It is in this context that Vajta talks about the flexibility of liturgy in relation to different professions—in our case, this means that we need to work for the "Schmiegsamkeit" of liturgy according to the needs of people whose life and work are deeply influenced by science and technology.

The dialogue between theology and science offers a second resource. It is well known that this dialogue got some fresh starts during the second half of the last century and has since then passed through some very fruitful stages. However, more relevant here than to survey the history of this dialogue is to point to the tasks that are still ahead. Among the critical ones we are facing now is to transform the interaction from mere dialogue into *diapraxis*—dialogue in praxis, or learning dialogue by doing. As such, diapraxis can precede dialogue, a model occasionally adopted in ecumenical or interfaith relations. Diapraxis includes joint work and actions that facilitate the acquisition of new practical skills. The work on a liturgical language that reflects familiarity with the scientific and technological knowledge of our time is one significant aspect of such diapraxis.

Strategies that enhance equal participation and liberation represent a third resource for the tasks ahead. I have described the problem of deficiency as a problem of marginalization of scientists and people who are intentional about bringing their worldview of science to their church and their Christian faith into their science-based world. If this description is right, it is wise to seek advice from those who have experience dealing with problems of marginalization, and to learn from their strategies. Research on feminist liturgies qualifies very well for this purpose. The insight that as long as women are marginalized they cannot participate in ways that are

8. Ibid., 74.
9. Senn, *Christian Liturgy*, 46.
10. Vilmos Vajta, *Die Theologie des Gottesdienstes bei Luther* (Stockholm: Svenska Kyrkans Diakonistyrelses Bokförlag, 1952), 329ff. English trans.: *Luther on Worship*; trans. U. S. Leupold (Philadelphia: Fortress Press, 1958), 177ff.

truly reciprocal, accountable, and relational applies equally to people holding a worldview shaped by science.

In its attempts to counteract the marginalization of women, "feminist liturgy seeks to engage imagination, resist discrimination, summon wonder, receive blessing and strengthen hope. It intends to enact redeemed, free and empowered relationships."[11] The same goals can spur creativity when applied to science and scientists. Twentieth-century physics as well as biology and neuroscience provide ample opportunities for imagination and wonder. Where the problem of marginalization of a scientific mind-set in liturgy is taken seriously, the awareness will grow that discrimination against science and technology is discrimination against God. It is discrimination against God because it is gross neglect of a significant part of creation, both in terms of the natural world studied by the sciences and in terms of the intellectual capacities given to humans. Blessings received through science and technology need to be seen and celebrated. Science and technology need to be integrated into the hopes that the church wants to strengthen and manifest. Their present state and future developments need to be included in intercession. Their dark sides need to be lifted up in confession. Without that, our liturgy will not reach its goal of "enacting relationships that promote justice among us and beyond us."[12]

Though all those things could be said of both outlooks, a difference between the mission of feminism and the mission of science needs to be pointed out. The power structure is different. Women used to find themselves at the short end of power, yet often they are in the majority in the pew. Professional scientists and people who identify themselves with a scientific mind-set and a worldview shaped by science are usually held in high esteem; they often represent power and prestige in society while they experience themselves as a minority in the pew. The power issue adds an extra dimension to the position of these "science people." While the church needs to acknowledge that science people need to be made visible in liturgy, science people need to be confronted with the question, "How does what you represent and bring to the community promote justice among us and beyond us?"

Feminist work with liturgical language has resulted in special liturgies for special occasions and groups as well as in revisions of traditional standard liturgy. In her study of feminist liturgies in the Church of Sweden, Ninna Edgardh Beckman has identified some general features.[13] Often, the general structure of opening and sending was kept, although changes were made that reflect a different anthropological outlook and different image of God. Also the meal part was kept mainly intact. Most critique fell upon the

11. Janet R. Walton, *Feminist Liturgy* (Collegeville, Minn.: Liturgical Press, 2000), 31.
12. Ibid., 36.
13. Ninna Edgardh Beckman, *Feminism och liturgi: en ecklesiologisk studie* (Stockholm: Verbum, 2001).

Word part. Both its form and content became subject to change. Revisions strove for increased contextuality and a shift from justification toward justice.[14] The latter is to be seen as a result of an increasing immanentism, reflected in contemporary hymnody[15] as well as in official documents like the already quoted message from the LWF Assembly in Winnipeg.[16]

All liturgical revisions entail risks. Liturgical work from the perspective of science will profit from taking into account the risks identified by feminist analysis, such as reductions (one deficit being "cured" by creating another one), anthropocentrism, and immanentism.[17] While science has the potential to help the church overcome its anthropocentric constraints, the question of immanentism appears as the Achilles' heel of a worldview of science—especially when the transcendent is identified with the supernatural. In a world understood to be governed by natural laws, there is by definition no room for the supernatural. However, the identification of transcendent with supernatural is precipitate. The Lutheran motif of the "in, with and under" suggests a more sophisticated understanding of the relationship between immanence and transcendence.

Working with liturgy from the perspective of science, with an eye on the experiences of feminist analysis, will have the benefit of sharpening sensitivity to the diversity of languages. Not even scientific language—universal though it is, in its own way—must be raised to become normative, in the way white male language used to be the norm. Also the language of science is only one among all the dialects that try to join in worshiping God.

Therapy: Directions and Promises

Even though I here focus on language in a rather narrow sense, one needs to keep in mind that liturgy is much more than verbal language. It is also space, gestures, sounds, movements, and actions. Liturgy is not reflective language in the first place; above all, it is addressed language aimed at evoking and expressing encounter. Therefore, it needs to be multidimensional. There is no easy way of judging the success of liturgical language. Yet there are certain criteria that are helpful in determining its adequacy. Among these criteria are participation, inclusiveness, authenticity, and mutual challenge of the immanent and the transcendent. Liturgical language needs to be intellectually honest while also embracing feeling, will, and the sense of mystery. It needs to be at the same time hard-wearing and poetic, a condensed expression of experiences of faith and life, and open-ended.

14. Ibid., 371ff.
15. Antje Jackelén, *Zeit und Ewigkeit: Die Frage der Zeit in Kirche, Naturwissenschaft und Theologie* (Neukirchen-Vluyn: Neukirchener Verlag, 2002), 11–82 (English translation forthcoming).
16. Assembly Message, 3.
17. Edgardh Beckman, *Feminism och liturgi*, 382ff.

What I am suggesting is quite different from the adjustment of liturgy to rationalism that took place during and after the Enlightenment.[18] Neither escaping into moralism nor making way for sentimentality is a viable option now. More appealing is a method that Gordon Lathrop has called *juxtaposition*: things are brought in and put alongside the center of Christian liturgy to "enhance it, and serve it, not to obscure it."[19] This process should make a mutually critical correlation possible. It has the potential of breaking frozen forms open. According to this method, language that emerges out of a scientific understanding of the world can be juxtaposed to expressions for what is considered to be the center of the Christian tradition. However, for two reasons, the term "juxtaposition" may be misleading. First, it tends to imply a strong emphasis on the differences between what is juxtaposed. The juxtaposed elements appear as contraries rather than as partners. Second, when combined with the notion of a center, juxtaposition runs the risk of slipping into a supra-position of the Christian center and a sub-position of the other, which is then easily conceived as a potential enemy—a fate that, as we have seen above, easily befalls science. The second risk is overcome by the realization that the "real center" beyond its cultural and historical expression remains inaccessible unless mediated by language. The Word is heard in words. To me, it seems more adequate to speak of *juxtamotion* instead of juxtaposition in order to do justice to the dynamics implied in the process. What has been realized as critical in responding to the particularities of local cultures is relevant also to the "juxtamotive encounter" between liturgy and the world of science and technology. In both cases, we are well advised to look at four dimensions of worship: the transcultural (the acknowledgment of an underlying commonality that finds very different, culture-specific expressions), the contextual (sensitivity to a variety of factors that form a culture), the countercultural (challenging the prevailing cultural paradigm), and the crosscultural (leading to cultural exchange).[20]

Science can contribute new metaphors to liturgical language. Yet this does not mean that science can be used as a quarry where bits and pieces can be grabbed without discernment. Liturgical language is tessellation, not a heap of stones. Successful and responsible use of scientific imagery requires both scientific and theological knowledge as well as stylistic intuition. In other words, it is an ideal and urgent project for scientists, theologians, and poets in cooperation to create hymns and prayers that mirror the images of our age and to look at texts from the perspective of a scientific

18. Cf. Senn, *Christian Liturgy*, 538–67.
19. Gordon W. Lathrop, *Holy People* (Minneapolis: Fortress Press, 1999), 202.
20. For these four categories, see the "Nairobi Statement on Worship and Culture: Contemporary Challenges and Opportunities," in S. Anita Stauffer, ed., *Christian Worship: Unity in Cultural Diversity* (Geneva: LWF, 1996), 23–28. Excerpts of this statement quoted in Lathrop, 233–36.

worldview. New images need to grow out of inspiration, reflection, and practice. It is hard to invent them in a matter-of-fact frame of mind.

It may come as a surprise to many that dance offers itself as a metaphor to express and celebrate faith in a world of science. Yet, several authors in religion and science have used this metaphor.[21] Dance plays an important part in feminist liturgies as well.[22] Also in this respect, feminist experiences may be good sponsors for the work with science and liturgy.

The beauty of DNA and equations usually come quickly to mind when thinking about the use of science-inspired liturgical language. Both have their limits, however. The beauty of equations is not accessible to everyone. Furthermore, combining them with a version of the anthropic principle in defense of a deterministic creator God is deeply problematic from a theological point of view. The task of liturgy is not to verbalize defense; more adequately, it nurtures a sense of wonder. Elizabeth A. Johnson has used the double helix of DNA in this way. It has inspired her to speak of the Trinity as a spiraling triple helix.[23] While such free use of images can be innovative and ground-breaking, it can also be misleading; by itself it will not suffice as a therapy for the deficiency we have diagnosed.

Neither amateurish lectures about cosmology and DNA nor PowerPoint sermons will cure the problem. Even though there is no principle reason to ban technology from sacred spaces, its use in itself is not a sign of advanced learning in a congregation. We have probably all seen embarrassing examples of fascination with IT toys that turn gifted preachers and speakers into puppets of their medium. The user of IT in liturgy will benefit from weighing effectiveness and the feeling of being truly at the forefront of technological development against people's yearning for something that is different from what they meet "everywhere else." The flannelboard is still a great tool of communication with the computer game generation. Openness toward science and technology cannot be achieved at the expense of giving up the experience of otherness that is an important mark of the encounter with the sacred. A thoughtful and balanced user of technology will be wise enough to honor this need of otherness.

From this we may conclude that the lack of a worldview shaped by science in liturgy is not just a problem of information. While lectures about

21. Karl E. Peters, *Dancing with the Sacred* (Harrisburg: Trinity Press International, 2002) esp. 45–51. Jackelén, *Zeit und Ewigkeit*, 78f., 233ff., 311. Arthur R. Peacocke, *Creation and the World of Science*, 2d ed. (London: SCM, 1990), 173–77. Ann Pederson, *God, Creation, and All That Jazz* (St. Louis: Chalice Press, 2001).

22. It should be noted, however, that the metaphor itself does not guarantee a dance of life for the ecological well-being of God's creation. It may as well be a dance of death, a dance around the Golden Calf (Exodus 32) or a dance of self-glorification expressing utter contempt of weakness (Friedrich Nietzsche, "To the Mistral: A Dance Song," appendix of *The Gay Science*; trans. Josefine Nauckhoff; ed. Bernard Williams [Cambridge: Cambridge Univ. Press, 2001], 258–60).

23. Elizabeth A. Johnson, *She Who Is* (New York: Crossroad, 1994), 220ff.

curved space-time or the structure of DNA may well have a role to play in the life of a congregation, they will not touch the center of the problem. Knowledge is good, but reform of attitude is better. In that respect, a certain minimalism will be a more helpful strategy. In communicating essentials, it is often enough to present only the most characteristic strokes of the brush. This applies to the essentials of a person as well as to the essentials of a worldview. If the most important strokes are painted well, people will naturally get engaged and participate in filling in the rest. This is one of the secrets of living liturgy and preaching. The church does not need pastors who try to preach science and who sound as if they have read too many popular science magazines. The church needs pastors who know what pastorship entails because they reflect theologically. On the basis of that reflection, they will be able to give especial voice to the marginalized in their congregations.

In the past century, theology needed to spend much energy on the process of demythologization, but now a careful remythologization seems to be needed. In relation to cosmology, at least two examples by leading scientist-theologians are available. I am thinking of Arthur Peacocke's "Genesis for the Third Millennium"[24] and Willem B. Drees's creation story "From Nothing until Now."[25] Karl Peters's "Earth: A Child of God"[26] also provides material for such a project.

A thoughtful treatment of the mythological will also lead to a reinterpretation of the miraculous. Interpretations that are stuck with the question of how violations of the laws of nature can be possible will be left behind. Language that describes God's relation to the world in purely interventionist terms is not helpful. Better interpretations are available if one looks in the direction of creativity, serendipity, and complexity. Liturgical language needs to move from a rule-and-order framework toward expressions for relationality and emergence. Not single events but the whole network of natural events is in itself an expression of the creative and sustaining action of God. In that sense, God is indeed understood as more immanent than before. Yet this does not necessarily rule out what has been a strength in Lutheran theology: the radical distinction between Creator and creation. The difference between God's infinity and the contingency of finite creation is maintained.[27] Its reduction to monocausality is overcome and replaced by an understanding that takes into account the whole web of relations, essential parts of which have been revealed to us by science. As I have shown elsewhere, this shift toward relationality applies also to theological and liturgical language about time and eternity.[28] Concepts based on Newtonian

24. Arthur R. Peacocke, *Paths from Science towards God* (Oxford: Oneworld, 2001), 1–2.
25. Willem B. Drees, *Creation: From Nothing until Now* (London: New York: Routledge, 2002).
26. Peters, *Dancing with the Sacred*, 136–44.
27. For further models of understanding God's relation to created order that are compatible with a scientific worldview, see, e.g., Peacocke, *Paths from Science*, 39–64.
28. Jackelén, *Zeit und Ewigkeit*, 2002.

physics have often been mistaken for biblical understandings of time. Taking into account the theories of relativity, opens new perspectives for liturgical language about time and eternity.

A liturgical language that is wise enough to take care of insights from science and technology will overcome anthropocentric and spiritual reductions. It will make clear that anthropological language based on a dualism between body and soul is no longer tenable and that all language about the immortality of a substantive soul needs to be revised. It will take our human embeddedness in nature seriously, and it will recognize other species as our kin. It will also help to drain the furious stream of contempt of the body that has been flowing through the undergrowth of the church for centuries.

Moreover, the engagement of liturgical language with science and technology has the potential of enhancing care for our natural environment. The language of the church faces the double risk of either demonizing or divinizing nature. Nature is easily demonized when the interconnectedness of all life is overlooked, when matter is devalued in favor of mind and spirit, and when the immanent is swallowed up by preoccupation with the transcendent. Nature is equally easily divinized where romantic emotions prevail that build on the fact that most of us always encounter nature as already conquered and tamed. This makes it easy to ignore the life-threatening wildness of nature as well as the terrifying cruelty that happens in nature all the time. A liturgical language that incorporates scientific knowledge will be better able to avoid either demonizing or divinizing nature. Lutheran theology may profit from scientific knowledge in reflecting on what has been called the cruciform nature of nature[29]—indeed, it should feel a special interest in this reflection.

Language that acknowledges a scientific worldview will also be more careful with the use of words such as *earth, nature, world, space, stars, suns, planets, galaxies, universe, cosmos.* There are billions of light years in between some of those words, yet theologians and pastors sometimes use them as if they were almost interchangeable. Meditating on the differences is quite healthy. It sharpens our awareness about the unreflecting geocentrism prevalent in our world of ideas. Teilhard de Chardin has proved helpful in balancing anthropology with a universal outlook. His thought is one of the sources that has inspired George L. Murphy to develop the theme of "cosmic worship."[30]

Inspiration from science does not mean that only new images are worthwhile. In fact, taking science seriously can also result in fresh looks at imagery that seemed outdated. For example, the reinforced insight into our

29. Cf. George L. Murphy, *The Cosmos in the Light of the Cross* (Harrisburg: Trinity Press International, 2003); and, for a philosophical perspective, Holmes Rolston III, *Science and Religion* (Philadelphia: Temple Univ. Press, 1987), esp. 133–47, 286–93, 326–29.
30. George L. Murphy, "The Impact of Science on Christian Worship," *Seminary Ridge Review* 1/2 (Winter 1999): 63–74.

interconnectedness with the rest of the natural world gives a fresh voice to a song such as "the earth is full of your creatures [who] all look to you" (Ps 104:24, 27) and to the call to stars, fire, hail, mountains, trees, and animals to join in praise to God (Psalm 148). Likewise, themes out of the rich treasure of theological tradition may gain new actuality by deliberate interpretation within a scientific framework. The Eastern Orthodox way of speaking of "energies" is one example. Similarly, when one wants to think about creation, evolution, and ecology together, the Eastern Orthodox concept of "microcosm" may be better suited than the Western notion of "stewardship." Both "energies" and "microcosm" have the advantage of providing distinct theological meaning and open-ended poetic potential. Where these concepts and language are used in combination with a scientific worldview, we can expect an interesting shift of emphasis. Focus moves from a preoccupation with questions of origins, order, determination, and (mono)causality toward inquiries about the relationship between things, the emergence of something new out of and through the interplay of existing things, and the complexification of existing forms and processes. In the sciences, nonequilibrium thermodynamics represents a good example of such a shift in attention. It seems that theories from this field of research have had an inspiring impact on many other areas, from engineering to biology. This in itself does not surprise. Gravitation, relativity, and complementarity are examples of specific scientific theories that have influenced the agenda in many other areas—scientific and nonscientific. For theology, these developments concur with the renaissance of Trinitarian theology since the 1980s. The recent interest in this theme signifies increasing discontent with the monarchical and hierarchical concepts of God and the search for relational understandings in their place. As such concepts were developed, it became more and more obvious that pneumatology has long been theologically undernourished. In other words, the Third Article needs to receive a more distinctive profile. We may wish to reconsider the place of creation theology as an entry to Christian faith. Preoccupation with origins and causality is not necessarily the best way to introduce children of the twenty-first century to a religious sense. Teaching four-year-olds songs about a God who stretched the sky over the earth no longer seems very productive.

Using the best knowledge available in one's time to mold liturgy and theological reflection is nothing new. The church has always done so. Today it is "the power of genes and molecules" that needs to shine through our liturgical language if it is to celebrate God in creation as we understand this at its best. What we need to do is similar to what early theologians did when they developed a cosmic Logos-Christology. The church of the fourth and fifth centuries faced the task of communicating how to understand Jesus Christ as the center of Christian faith in a way that was consonant with the best science of their time. One of their major achievements was the concept of the cosmic Christ. In an ingenious move, they used the Greek concept of

Logos to express their understanding of Jesus Christ as the incarnate Logos. In his beautiful book *Jesus through the Centuries*, Jaroslav Pelikan states that "by the fourth century it had become evident that of all the various 'titles of majesty for Christ' adapted and adopted during the first generations after Jesus, none was to have more momentous consequences than the title Logos."[31] This identification of Jesus as Logos had enormous intellectual, philosophical, and scientific implications. For, by using the word *logos* with its multifold meanings as a christological title, Christians could interpret Jesus "as the divine clue to the structure of reality (metaphysics) and, within metaphysics, to the riddle of being (ontology)—in a word, as the Cosmic Christ."[32] In other words, the identification of Jesus and Logos provided the potential of yoking faith and science in theory and liturgical praxis. Logos came to be understood as the word of God that made the world possible, and also as the structure that makes the world intelligible. The history of science, like the history of theology, provides us with numerous examples of how this understanding of Christ the Logos worked as a stimulus to the exploration of both nature and ideas. The belief in a relation between divine revelation and human reason fostered an understanding of creation as nature and of nature as creation.

Pelikan praises the dialectic inherent in the concept of Christ as Logos. On the one hand, "the divine Reason disclosed in Christ had endowed human reason with a capacity for penetrating the workings of created nature,"[33] thus calling for an exploration of nature and for a scientific story of creation. On the other hand, the Logos is and remains the Logos *of God*, so that the very structure of the universe is not easily accessible for the human mind. In this sense, the concept of logos preserves an awareness of the limitations humans experience in their capacity of understanding ultimate reality. Due to this dialectic, "the cosmos was reliably knowable and at the same time it remained mysterious, both of these because the Logos was the Mind and Reason of God."[34] If the church is to live up to standards as high as those, which early medieval theologians set for themselves, an achievement at this level is needed today.

I conclude this essay as I started—with poetry. The following prayer by the Swedish writer Gunnar Edman (1915–1995) complements R. S. Thomas's experience of the Absence. Its celebration of the Presence is also an invitation to explore more of the linguistic possibilities of liturgy opened up by science.

---

31. Jaroslav Pelikan, *Jesus through the Centuries* (New Haven/London: Yale Univ. Press, 1999), 58.
32. Ibid., 58.
33. Ibid., 64.
34. Ibid., 65.

O God, through your word you created the world. Out of radiation you weaved it in one piece. From the tiniest particle to the immeasurable horizons of the galaxies it is filled with splendor. Your cosmos, O God, pulsates in every single breath I take. You let gravitation, although invisible, rule all matter: whether I walk or lie down, it is working in me. In that, it resembles, like a shadow, your wisdom's Spirit which, faster than light, goes into everything, creating and sustaining all.

And to me, a human being, you gave mind and senses, the ability to contemplate your wisdom and enjoy the poetry of your universe. Oh, give me the spirit of praise, so that with all my being, with all that is inside me, I may affirm your creation and extol your wonderful name![35]

---

35. Gunnar Edman, "Inför kosmos," in *Att bedja idag: En liten bönbok*, no. 123, *Den Svenska Psalmboken* (Stockholm: Verbum, 1986) (my translation).

Index

LaVergne, TN USA
07 November 2010
203846LV00004B/92/P